THE SEARCH
FOR AN
AMERICAN
INDIAN
IDENTITY

Modern Pan-Indian Movements

THE Iroquois AND THEIR NEIGHBORS

Laurence M. Hauptman, Series Editor

THE SEARCH
FOR AN
AMERICAN
INDIAN
IDENTITY

--------------- ❋ ---------------

Modern Pan-Indian Movements

HAZEL W. HERTZBERG

SYRACUSE UNIVERSITY PRESS

First Paperback Edition 1981
92 93 94 95 96 97 98 99   6 5 4 3 2

Library of Congress Catalog Card Number: 77-140889
ISBN: 0-8156-2245-7

Manufactured in the United States of America

HAZEL W. HERTZBERG (d. 1988) was associate professor of history and education at Teachers College, Columbia University. She also wrote *The Great Tree and the Longhouse: The Culture of the Iroquois* (1966) and its accompanying Teachers Manual; *Teaching a Pre-Columbian Culture: The Iroquois* (1966); *Teaching the Age of Homespun* (1965); and *Teaching Population Dynamics* (1965). She had been a Project Associate of the Anthropology Curriculum Study Project of the American Anthropological Association and was a member of the Social Science Education Consortium. She had conducted seminars at the New York State Historical Association and had lectured widely.

CONTENTS

III
RELIGIOUS PAN-INDIANISM

IV
SURVEY AND RETROSPECT

ILLUSTRATIONS
following p. 178

Arthur Bonnicastle / Thomas L. Sloan /
Charles A. Eastman / Quanah Parker /
Henry Roman Nose / Wovoka /
Carlos Montezuma / Francis LaFlesche /
Albert Hensley / Louis McDonald /
"Indian Printer Boys" / Sherman Coolidge /
Cleaver Warden / J. N. B. Hewitt /
Marie L. Baldwin / Navajos from New Mexico /
Navajos at Carlisle / Arthur C. Parker

PREFACE

All people with some common background who settled in the United States faced the problem of defining themselves as a part of American society. In the course of doing so, they also helped to define the nature of the total American society. It has been an adventuresome process, full of intellectual rigor and semantic imprecision, of sentimentality and prejudice, of idealism and venality. It gave rise to two dominating concepts about the relation of "minorities" to American nationality: First the "melting pot"—which came to be attacked as leading to the homogenization of Americans. Then "cultural pluralism"—which was in turn criticized as opening the way to cultural isolationism. The process continues and will not end so long as the United States of America remains an open society.

The Indians, of course, have faced the question of their relation to the wider society for a longer period of time than any other Americans. Their situation is in some ways singular. They were, after all, the aboriginal inhabitants of the land. Conquered, they were ruthlessly expropriated and became a special claim on the American conscience. From the beginning of the Republic they have had a unique relationship to the federal government.

Yet Indians have confronted the complete range of dilemmas familiar to other American minorities. They sought for ways to define themselves as Americans. They came to be regarded as a separate "race" and had to deal with the implications of that characterization. The reservation was their ghetto and they had mixed feelings about it. The education provided them was inadequate, often unrelated to their cultures, and frequently conducted in a language foreign to them. Their human rights were widely ignored. Their poverty was endemic.

vii

How the Indians dealt with these and similar problems can be enormously instructive in a time of intensifying concern with the position of minorities in American life. But we are in some danger of losing this rich experience because of widespread ignorance about contemporary Indians and their history even among otherwise knowledgeable Americans. While the general deepening of social consciousness has resulted in growing interest in Indian grievances, sympathy for the Indian is not the same as knowledge of him—and knowledge is not keeping pace. Those who are satisfied with simplistic answers to complex problems seem content to regard him as just another symbol of minority deprivation. Neither the Indian nor the wider society are well served by such a view. Indians must be seen not as symbols but as men and women and their history as the rich, complex, and tragic human experience which it is.

Historically, American Indians have reacted to alien penetration both in tribal terms and in the assertion of a wider Indian identity. Until the end of the nineteenth century, Indian response to white encroachment was largely tribal but included some loose, regional, intertribal groupings with a Pan-Indian flavor. Not until the Progressive Era, however, did a number of organized movements arise, national in scope, based firmly on a common Indian interest and identity as distinct from tribal interests and identities, and stressing Indian accommodation to the dominant society. This was the beginning of modern Pan-Indianism.

Pan-Indianism is deeply concerned with questions of race, ethnicity, and nationality. Modern Pan-Indianism is the crucible in which elements in the larger society combine with elements in Indian life to produce new definitions of identity within the American social order. Thus Pan-Indian movements afford us a double view. As Indian movements they constitute a major aspect of Indian history. As movements seeking an accommodation with the dominant society they tell us at least as much about ourselves as about Indians.

The present study is the first attempt to identify, analyze, and compare the basic varieties of Pan-Indianism and to trace their historical development. Its focus is on the formative period—the first third of this century—by the end of which the types of Pan-Indianism characteristic of contemporary society had clearly emerged. It covers their historical roots, their major ideas, their definitions of the Indian common ground, their leadership and constituency, their organizational forms, their connections with each other, and their relationship to basic trends in American life.

The study also considers the periods preceding and succeeding the formative years of modern Pan-Indianism. A background chapter recounts some of the tribal and early Pan-Indian responses to the encroaching white society and traces the major forces that produced modern Pan-Indianism. An outline of Pan-Indian movements since the New Deal shows their adaptation to new historical contexts and brings the narrative up to date. Finally, a summary chapter examines the significance of the total Pan-Indian experience in its relationship both to Indian life and to the wider society of which it was—and is—a part.

Autumn 1970

ACKNOWLEDGMENTS

In preparing this study I became indebted to many persons. For informative conversations on Pan-Indianism and some of its leaders I am indebted to the anthropologists Donald Collier, William N. Fenton, and Gordon MacGregor. Louis C. Jones and William A. Ritchie provided valuable impressions of Arthur C. Parker. Harold R. Isaacs suggested many useful lines of inquiry. For suggestions, advice, and interpretations from persons experienced in Pan-Indian affairs I am grateful to Henri Ben Ami, Robert Burnette, Mary Lou Payne Byler, Wesley Huss, Robert Reitz, Karen Rickard, and Elizabeth Slotkin, as well as others too numerous to mention. Charles E. Gillette was most helpful in making available the Arthur C. Parker Papers housed in the New York State Museum in Albany. Nancy Strowbridge, librarian of the Museum of the American Indian in New York, aided in innumerable ways. James Marshall kindly allowed me to read the papers of the Robert Marshall Fund relating to the National Congress of American Indians.

My special thanks go to Professor Frederick D. Kershner of Teachers College, Columbia University, who suggested and guided this study. To my husband, Sidney, and our two children, Hendrik Hertzberg and Katrina H. McClintock, I am everlastingly grateful for their interest, patience, and humor as well as for their editorial suggestions.

THE SEARCH
FOR AN
AMERICAN
INDIAN
IDENTITY

Modern Pan-Indian Movements

1

THE ROOTS OF MODERN PAN-INDIANISM

The men who rediscovered America in the fifteenth and sixteenth centuries had names for themselves which indicated some recognition of a
common identity. Whatever part of the Old World they came from and
however deep their divisions, they were also Europeans, sharing a sense
of place and differentiating themselves from men elsewhere. They fought
bitterly over religion, but they were Christians worshipping a common
god. They spoke different languages, but their educated men used Latin
as a common language. Their nationalist rivalries were intense, but
nevertheless they were conscious of a shared historical experience.

The men whom the Europeans discovered on these continents seemed
to have no such common ideas of themselves. Their sense of place was
localized, and their religions tribal. They shared neither a universal language nor a known historical experience. In fact, the indigenous societies
of the New World were in many important respects far more culturally
diverse than those of their discoverers. In what is today the continental
United States alone there lived hundreds of aboriginal groups speaking
some 250 distinct languages. Some were farmers with extensive fields
and permanent villages. Others were wanderers who lived by hunting
and by gathering wild plants. Some reckoned descent through the male
line, others through the female. The people of each culture had their
own relationships to the supernatural, their own heroes from the past,
their own conceptions of proper and improper behavior and their own
name for themselves—often meaning something like "the people" or
"original beings." Despite cultural similarities among peoples living in
the same regions and despite certain very broad characteristics shared

by most of the aboriginal societies—such as the dance as a central form of religious and social expression and the conception of the land as sacred with its control vested in some form of communal group—aboriginal loyalties rested with band, tribe, village, and locality.[1]

The pattern of relationships among aboriginal groups ranged from peaceful cooperation or coexistence to traditional enmities characterized by intermittent warfare carried on by small raiding parties. Only in the East did any tendency to political confederation exist before the coming of the Europeans, and this was confined to tribes similar in culture and language.

To these diverse peoples of the New World the Europeans gave a common name—"Indians." It should be noted that the name came from the European discoverers, not from the indigenous peoples themselves. Only slowly as contacts with the Europeans increased did the aboriginal peoples begin to think of themselves as Indians. On the whole it was a somewhat fragile identity, lacking the rich and deeply rooted associations of tribal identity. The tribe represented the way of life of the people; *Indian* was a way of differentiating aborigine from European.

The Indian response to European penetration was thus cast largely and almost inevitably in tribal terms. It was as tribesmen that Indians welcomed the Europeans, traded with them, negotiated treaties, raised the hatchet, were decimated by disease, whiskey, and war, fought for their homelands, and were driven farther and farther west.

As the Indians reacted to the Europeans in tribal terms, so the overwhelming effect of European penetration was to divide the tribes and further exacerbate tribal differences. Confrontation between Indian and white was gradual and piecemeal. The Indians were conquered tribe by tribe, locality by locality. Never was there a continental Indian war or a continental Indian peace. By the time the wave of white settlement had flowed over the Appalachians, for example, the seaboard Indians had been largely conquered, eliminated, removed, or had reached some accommodation with the whites. This process was repeated over and over as the whites pushed westward.

Rivalry among the European powers with whom the Indians came into contact promoted inter-tribal hostilities, for each state eagerly sought Indian allies. The alliances which resulted often dealt with such matters as trade, the acquisition of land, and military aid, thereby intensifying old intertribal conflicts and creating new ones.

Each of the European powers had its evolving perceptions of the Indian societies, and each operated somewhat differently. But all of them negotiated with the tribes as independent, sovereign "nations," a policy which further promoted tribal differences. In the early period Europeans treated with the Indians somewhat as if they were dealing with miniature European nations, while Indians treated with the Europeans somewhat as if they were dealing with other Indian tribes.

The process of treaty-making itself was fraught with innumerable possibilities of misunderstandings as peoples so diverse came into close contact with each other. Europeans believed that the treaties by which they acquired land from the Indians gave them permanent and exclusive possession of the real estate in question. The Indians, whose conception of land did not include buying and selling it, often believed that they had made some sort of temporary or partial arrangement which did not compromise their right to live, hunt, or fish on the land as they chose. As contacts between Indians and whites became more prolonged and extensive, sophistication grew on both sides. Yet tribe after tribe signed treaty after treaty only to find time after time that treaties were broken or that in the face of the pressure of white settlement, they were reopened for negotiation.

Treaty-making and war divided Indian societies internally as differences arose over whether or not to sign a treaty or whether or not to fight. The Europeans often worked diligently at fostering faction within the tribe. These bitter internal fissures were in part a result of the Indian custom of consensus which lacked mechanisms for the peaceful coexistence of majorities and minorities. They were deepened by the disillusionment which followed the breaking of treaties by the whites.

The treaty-making process continued until after the Civil War. In theory the tribes thus continued to be dealt with as independent nations. In practice, of course, the situation was quite different. Until the War of 1812 was concluded, the Indians could still play off one white power against another. But with the ending of any real possibility of European-Indian alliances, the fate of the Indian population became irrevocably a domestic American problem. In 1831, the Supreme Court called the Indians within United States borders "domestic, dependent nations" whose "relation to the United States resembles that of a ward to his guardian." In 1871 Congress clearly recognized the realities of the situation when it declared that "no Indian nation or tribe within the territory of the United States shall be acknowledged or recognized as an independent nation, tribe, or power with whom the United States may contract by treaty." By this time most of the tribes were on reservations.

But even when the Indians dealt with the single American nation, they faced a diversity of authorities, both official and unofficial. Until 1849, Indian affairs were in the hands of the War Department, within which a small Bureau of Indian Affairs had been established in 1824 and enlarged and upgraded in 1832 when wholesale removal of Eastern Indians to the West was in process. After responsibility for Indian affairs was transferred to the newly organized Department of the Interior in 1849, there was constant friction between civilian and military authorities. As new states entered the Union, the Indians within their boundaries were subjected to new demands.

The whites with whom the Indians came into contact in an unofficial capacity were also divided among themselves. The Christian missionaries represented a bewildering variety of religious persuasions, each contending for the Indian soul and for exclusive conversion rights. Remaining Indian lands were competed for and occasionally defended by different forces in the white community.

The friends of the Indian in the white world were themselves divided as to the best policies to be followed. At the same time, they frequently united with the Indian's foes in the support of specific policies for very different reasons, as in the case of two basic pieces of Indian legislation, the Removal Act and the Dawes Act. The Removal Act of 1830 provided for the exchange of Indian lands east of the Mississippi for lands to the west. Friends of the Indian hoped that removal would protect the tribes from further white encroachments and even envisioned an eventual Indian state. Enemies welcomed the opportunity to take over the lands which the Indians were leaving.

Similarly did friend and foe unite in support of the General Allotment or Dawes Act of 1887. This legislation, which was the foundation of Indian policy for the next half century, authorized the breakup of the reservations at the discretion of the president by alloting tribal lands in specific amounts to individual tribal members. Title to the individual properties thus created was to be retained by the United States for a trust period of twenty-five years, or longer if the president so decided. After the trust period had ended, the allottee was to receive full title and could dispose of the land as he wished. Meanwhile he could become a citizen upon receipt of a paper showing that he would eventually get full title. Citizenship was also granted to Indians who had voluntarily left the tribe, were living elsewhere in the United States, and had "adopted the habits of civilized life." Surplus tribal land left over from allotment was to be sold and the proceeds retained in the United States Treasury, together with annual interest. This money was to be used for the benefit of the tribe whose lands had been sold and could be appropriated by Congress for the education and "civilization" of the tribal members.

Friends of the Indian saw the Dawes Act as a means of liberating the Indians from the prison of the reservation, enabling them to become self-respecting farmers. They welcomed it as a way of opening the path to citizenship and integrating Indians fully into American society. Enemies again seized on the act as a way of separating Indians from their tribal lands.

The antipathy to the reservation felt by friends of the Indian was understandable, especially in view of the American commitment to a self-respecting individualism. One of the most pernicious effects of the reservation system was the reduction of formerly self-reliant and self-supporting people to wards of the government. For many Indians, the expected annuities assumed enormous symblic as well as practical importance. Resentment of—and reliance on—authority grew as Indians came to understand that they had little or nothing to say about their future. They became increasingly dependent on a capricious executive and a Congress that frequently neglected to vote the appropriations promised in treaties or agreements. Indian hunters were expected to become farmers overnight, frequently on land unfit for farming. In Indian societies where farming was the traditional occupation of women, men were expected to take to the plow easily if not joyfully.

Widespread corruption in the administration of Indian affairs aggravated these difficulties. The Indian Service was a classic example of a corrupt bureaucracy. Nowhere was the spoils system more destructive than in the Indian Service. The reservation agent, who held virtually dictatorial powers, was often a political appointee chosen for his services to the party in power rather than for his ability to deal with Indians. There were exceptions to the rule of venality and self-interest, of course; talented and able individuals, with the capacity to govern wisely and well, sometimes cropped up. But such men did not last long and usually departed with a change in administration.

Factionalism within tribes, which began to develop before confinement on reservations, was strengthened by the conditions of reservation life. Almost every reservation had its "progressive" and "conservative" factions, its "friendlies" and "hostiles." "Progressives" were those who attempted to cooperate with the government and to adapt themselves to the way of life of the dominant society, while "conservatives" were uncooperative and clung to old tribal ways. Under the frustrations of reservation life, Indians often quarreled with each other.

But in spite of the brutality and bleakness which so often characterized the reservation, the Indians survived. While there was disorganization, there was also health and cohesion. Many of the tribes showed an extraordinary capacity to come to terms with new conditions and to combine the old ways and the new. Ancient tribal institutions were adapted to the changed conditions and new ones were evolved. The patterns of accommodation which developed varied widely from tribe to tribe and region to region.

The long and complex process of Indian resistance and adjustment carried out largely in tribal terms reflected the diversity of Indian societies and the differing and fragmented nature of Indian contacts with whites. But all the while another theme was at work, sometimes complementing, sometimes contradicting, sometimes overwhelming the tribal one. This was the effort to find a common ground beyond the tribe, a broader identity and unity based on shared cultural elements, shared experiences, shared needs, and a shared common fate. Most such attempts were confined to a few tribes and local areas, but the most important involved Indians from many tribes and localities.

The Pan-Indian response, like the tribal one, was sometimes military, sometimes political, sometimes religious. In the middle of the eighteenth century, as the French and English struggled for possession of North America, Pontiac and the man known to history only as the "Delaware Prophet" represented a combination of these different strands of Pan-Indianism. According to the Prophet, the land would be returned to the Indians through divine intervention. Meanwhile, they were enjoined to behave as brothers to one another, to take only one wife, to cease all buying and selling, to pray, and to drink liquor only in moderation. Thus, as in similar movements to follow, an ethic of individual and social reform was embedded in the larger Pan-Indian conception. Pontiac, an Ottawa, used the Prophet's message as a basis for organizing military and political resistance to the English among Prairie and a few Eastern tribes, culminating in a war on the Great Lakes frontier. But the effort failed. The Indians were unable to maintain even a limited intertribal unity for long.

Another Pan-Indian effort was made near the end of the century by Joseph Brant (Thayendanega), a Mohawk war chief of the Iroquois Confederacy who had fought on the British side in the American Revolution. Brant advanced the idea that the various Indian nations held their land as common property and were "all of one mind—one heart" as he attempted to organize tribes of the Old Northwest into a political-military confederacy to stop American expansion. But he was unable to persuade the tribes to unite.

In the early years of the nineteenth century, Tecumseh and his brother Tenskwataya, the "Shawnee Prophet," led a movement which combined religious and political Pan-Indianism and which eventually erupted into military action. Like the Delaware Prophet before him, Tenskwataya predicted the return of aboriginal conditions through supernatural means. He advocated a reform ethic combining old ways with new customs. Indians were to stop drinking, to cease marrying whites, to revere the aged, to have compassion for the weak, to live peacefully with one another, and to listen to the voice of the Great Spirit. Tecumseh, who subscribed to the doctrines of his brother, was the organizer of the movement. There is little evidence that he desired war. Rather, he attempted to follow a containment policy. In the circumstances, however, it is difficult to imagine how his objectives could have been achieved without war and even more difficult to imagine a permanent Indian victory of containment.

Tecumseh stressed the common Indian ownership of lands, believing that none had the right to sell land which, as he thought, was the property of all the tribes. He consistently identified the white man as the common enemy and constantly reiterated the close relationship of Indians to each other: "We all belong to one family; we are all children of the Great Spirit; we walk in the same path; slake our thirst at the same spring; and now affairs of the greatest concern lead us to smoke the pipe around the same council fire. Brothers, we are friends; we must assist each other to bear our burdens. The blood of our fathers and brothers has run like water on the ground to satisfy the avarice of the white man." [2]

In this vein Tecumseh time and again addressed Indian councils from Wisconsin to the Gulf of Mexico as he patiently built an intertribal confederacy. But this effort, also, was doomed. The confederation movement received a severe blow when, in Tecumseh's absence and against his orders, the Shawnee Prophet engaged William Henry Harrison's forces at Tippecanoe. In the ensuing battle a major casualty was the Prophet's magical powers which failed to protect the Indians against white bullets. Tecumseh soon joined forces with the British and was killed in the War of 1812. With him died his particular dream of a Pan-Indian confederacy and the last union of religious and political Pan-Indianism. Hereafter Pan-Indian movements tended to have either a primarily secular or a primarily religious cast.

The most significant nineteenth-century attempt to build a secular confederation took place in what is now Oklahoma with the forced migration of the majority of the Five Civilized Tribes from the Southeast following the passage of the Removal Act in 1830. These tribes— the Choctaws, Chickasaws, Cherokees, Creeks, and Seminoles—were "far advanced in civilization," as the phrase ran. Three of the tribes had written constitutions or codes of laws. Many tribal members spoke and wrote English, while Sequoyah, a Cherokee, had invented a system for writing the tribal language which quickly enabled his people to become literate in their own tongue. Over the terrible "trail of tears" the Five Civilized Tribes journeyed to their new lands which both they and many whites believed might eventually become an Indian state. They built schools, churches, farms, small industries, towns, newspapers, and a system of self-government. In Indian Territory there was a remarkable blending of Indian and white institutions, ideas, practices, and genes. Many of the tribesmen prospered. Divisions between rich and poor were not unlike those in white society and some Indians owned Negro slaves. In Indian Territory an aristocracy developed which felt in no way inferior to whites. Here too grew a sense of a common identity beyond the tribe. When land-hungry whites pushed inevitably into what is now Oklahoma, they found an Indian society whose commanding positions were held by Indians rather than whites. Oklahoma would, in time, become a center and focus of modern Pan-Indianism.

In the 1880's an effort to institute an Indian commonwealth was made in Oklahoma—then Indian Territory—through a series of international councils. A resolution addressed to the President of the United States was passed at the council held in 1887, attended by fifty-seven representatives from nineteen of the tribes residing in the Territory. The resolution attacked the Dawes Act from which the Five Civilized Tribes had been exempted and asked that the other Territorial tribes be similarly treated. The resolution, as stated in the *Annual Report* of the Commissioner of Indian Affairs, read, in part: "Like other people, the Indian needs at least the germ of political identity, some governmental organization of his own, however crude, to which his pride and manhood may cling and claim allegiance, in order to make true progress in the affairs of life. This peculiarity in the Indian character is elsewhere called patriotism, and the wise and patient fashioning and guidance of which alone will successfully solve the question of civilization."

The Agent, who was sympathetic to the purposes of the council, reported, "It is much to be regretted that there is so little cohesive power in the Indian character and among the Indian nations. It would go far, in my opinion, to the peaceful, beneficent solution of the change of the Indian nations into a flourishing Indian State of the Union if the tribes could unite, but I do not think great interest was exhibited in this meeting, as but one chief of the five nations was present." [3]

The following year another international council was held in which the "wild tribes" sought help and guidance from the Civilized Tribes. After some days of caucusing, a resolution was adopted favoring "the unification of the tribes" in order to "secure the general good of the Indian race" and calling for "one common government, with common laws, officials and institutions, in which "all the tribes shall have equitable representation," and the transformation of the Indian Territory into an "Indian commonwealth." But the plan was never carried out. As the Agent commented, "The Indians have apparently no power of organization, and instead of centripetal motion and cohesion under dangers alleged, show only centrifugal motion." [4] In the 1890's the lands of the Civilized Tribes were themselves allotted, and the hope for an Indian Commonwealth vanished. Had an Indian state been formed, there can be little doubt that political Pan-Indianism would have been greatly strengthened.

Religious Pan-Indianism in the nineteenth century was manifested through a scattering of Pan-Indian prophetic and messianic movements promising that the Indian dead would return to a land divinely restored to its aboriginal splendor, from which the whites would magically vanish. These movements relied on supernatural agencies rather than political means to accomplish their purposes. The coming of the golden age could be hastened by rituals, dancing, and singing, in which all Indians were urged to participate. Like the followers of the Delaware and Shawnee Prophets, the members of these cults were urged to reform their personal conduct—to eschew alcohol, to lead good and honorable lives, to work, and, often, to send their children to school. In spite of their yearning for a return to an aboriginal life stripped of white influences, the messianic movements frequently incorporated Christian as well as Indian ideas and practices. Their leaders were religious prophets, not political organizers like Pontiac or Tecumseh.

The most widespread of these movements was the Ghost Dance of the late 1880's and 1890's. Like earlier Pan-Indian movements, it contained a personal as well as a collective ethic. The united efforts of the Indians through the Ghost Dance rituals were to hasten the return of aboriginal times in which, presumably, the tribes themselves were again to become supreme, thus neatly combining tribalism and Pan-Indianism. While awaiting the great day, Indians were to observe a strict code of personal behavior. The rituals themselves combined personal, tribal, Pan-Indian, and some white and even Christian elements, emphasizing personal participation, Pan-Indian songs and dances, and tribal adaptations of these.

Wovoka, the prophet of the Ghost Dance of the late eighties and nineties, was a man who lived in and between two worlds, Indian and white. He was a member of the Paiute tribe living in a small valley in Nevada. Upon the death of his father, Wovoka went to work as a ranch hand for the Wilson family who lived nearby. Here he acquired a close friend of about his own age, the Wilsons' son Bill; an "American" name—Jack Wilson; an acquaintance with the Bible and with the teachings of Jesus; and some knowledge of English. He, and some of his initial disciples, also seem to have been influenced by Mormonism. As a young man he journeyed briefly out of his valley to Oregon and Washington where he heard about the Indian Shakers, a northwestern messianic cult, from whom he derived some of the ideas for his movement.[5] Married to a Paiute girl, he was well respected both by Indians and whites.

Wovoka's revelation came, as revelations have come to many other men, during a severe illness. He, and many of his friends, believed that he had died and gone to heaven. His condition during the illness was so near death as to convince his friends and family that such was the case.

"[In heaven] he saw God, with all the people who had died long ago engaged in their old time sports and occupations, all happy and forever young. It was a pleasant land and full of game. After showing him all, God told him he must go back and tell his people that they must be good and love one another, have no quarreling, and live in peace with the whites; that they must work and not lie or steal; that they must put away all the old practices that savored of war; that if they faithfully obeyed his instructions they would at last be united with their friends in this other world where there would be no more death or sickness or old age. He was then given the dance which he was commanded to bring back to his people. By performing the dance at intervals, for five consecutive days each time, they would secure this happiness to themselves and hasten the event." [6]

Wovoka also believed that he had been given magical powers, including control over the elements. An eclipse of the sun which occurred during his illness, and which greatly frightened the Paiute, helped to associate his revelation with supernatural powers. The feats of magic which Wovoka subsequently performed—really just simple tricks—helped to convince many of the Indian delegations who visited him of the genuiness of his message.

Wovoka's chief Indian lieutenant was Grant Left Hand, the son of an Arapaho chief and a former student at the Carlisle Indian School. Throughout his career, Wovoka was also helped by a sympathetic local white storekeeper, who read letters and interpreted for him and performed other friendly services. In these associations, as in so many other ways, Wovoka-Wilson had a foot in both Indian and white worlds.[7]

The movement of which Wovoka was the prophet spread rapidly. Its doctrine and rituals were sufficiently flexible so that it could be adapted to local tribal customs while retaining a strong Pan-Indian flavor. The Ghost Dancers were remarkably pacific, putting their trust in supernatural deliverance. In only one tribe—the Sioux—did the Ghost Dancers take up violence, with results which dealt a mortal blow to the movement.

Many of the Ghost Dancers who participated in the "Sioux outbreak" of 1890–91 were "hostiles" whose leaders, including Sitting Bull, were veterans of the Custer war of a decade before. Their animosity was strengthened by shabby treatment in the negotiation of treaties, land policies, and rations. The "outbreak" was in reality a panic and stampede by bands of Sioux who fled into the Bad Lands when an inexperienced reservation agent called for federal troops to come to his aid on the mistaken grounds that the situation was out of control. In this tragic and and unnecessary escalation the bloodiest incident was the famous Battle of Wounded Knee, which occurred when a group of warriors, together with their women and children, were waiting to surrender, meanwhile guarded by government troops. Most of the Indians wore Ghost Shirts, which the Ghost Dancers of some tribes (though not Wovoka) believed offered magical protection against enemy bullets. Suddenly a young Indian drew a rifle and fired at the soldiers. The unequal battle was joined. It quickly turned into a massacre as the infuriated soldiers, many of whom were new recruits who had never before been under fire, pursued and cut down the fleeing woman and children.

The course and outcome of the "Sioux outbreak" were celebrated in a ballad, written by a black private of the Ninth Cavalry, which rapidly became a favorite among troops and frontiersmen.

The Red Skins left their Agency, the Soldiers left their Post,
All on the strength of an Indian tale about Messiah's ghost
Got up by savage chieftains to lead their tribes astray;
But Uncle Sam wouldn't have it so, for he ain't built that way.
They swore that this Messiah came to them in visions sleep,
And promised to restore their game and Buffalos a heap,
So they must start a big ghost dance, then all would join their band,
And may be so lead the way into the great Bad Land.

Chorus:
They claimed the shirt Messiah gave, no bullet could go through,
But when the Soldiers fired at them they saw this was not true.
The Medicine man supplied them with their great Messiah's grace,
And he, too, pulled his freight and swore the 7th hard to face.[8]

Soon after Wounded Knee the "outbreak" was over. It was the last eruption of Indian armed force fortified by Indian religion. The year 1890 marked the close of Indian military resistance as it marked also the closing of the frontier.

When word of the "outbreak" reached Wovoka, the prophet was deeply shaken, for his teachings were strongly pacificistic and he explicitly counseled against warfare: In spite of his disavowals of violence, the "Sioux outbreak" helped to discredit the whole movement and to weaken Indian belief in the efficacy of the Ghost Dance. Wovoka's influence declined drastically after the apocalypse which he had predicted failed to materialize. Among a few tribes the dance continued sporadically for a time. In some instances, as among the Pawnees, the rituals became institutionalized and eventually emptied of messianic meaning. Probably the growing peyote cult offered Indians a more acceptable alternative Pan-Indian religion combining Christian and Indian elements.

Today messianic movements like the Ghost Dance and its predecessors among American Indians are viewed not simply as exotic local movements but as instances of a common and recognizable type of response to situations of deep cultural stress, and similar movements occurring all over the world have been compared and analyzed. But at the time, the anthropologist James Mooney, whose first-hand study of the Ghost Dance remains the classic work on the subject, was one of the few to suggest such a broad interpretation:

"What tribe or people has not had its golden age, before Pandora's box was loosed, when women were nymphs and dryads and men were gods and heroes? And when the race lies crushed and groaning beneath an alien yoke, how natural is the dream of a redeemer, an Arthur, who shall return from exile or awake from some long sleep to drive out the usurper and win back for his people what they have lost. The hope becomes a faith and the faith becomes the creed of priests and prophets, until the hero is a god and the dream a religion, looking to some great miracle of nature for its culmination and accomplishment. The doctrines of the Hindu avatar, the Hebrew messiah, the Christian millenium, and the Hesunanin ['our father'] of the Indian Ghost Dance are essentially the same, and have their origin in a hope and longing common to all humanity." [9]

Later evidence has confirmed Mooney's view of the Ghost Dance, but his interpretation was largely ignored at the time. To most people then involved in Indian affairs, this wider perspective had not yet opened. The Ghost Dancers were thought of as very peculiar people indeed, at best pathetic and deluded visionaries, at worst ignorant and inflamed savages.

In the Ghost Dance of the nineties and the life of its prophet we can see many influences that were to reshape the recurrent Pan-Indian theme, channeling it in new directions and providing it with new doctrines. In the last two decades of the nineteenth century and the first decade of the twentieth, these forces were to gain in strength, helping to produce modern Pan-Indian movements whose major theme was accommodation to and acceptance of white society as permanent, rather than emphasis upon a vain hope of a return to aboriginal conditions through whatever means.

Some of the factors making possible the extraordinarily rapid spread of the Ghost Dance were also those that would help to foster other forms of Pan-Indianism. The fact that Indians were now largely concentrated on reservations made them more accessible to each other; the development of a system of mass communication—including roads, railroads, and mail service—made it simpler for them to reach each other; the development of a group which had an education in English made it easier for leaders to exchange ideas and exert influence widely. For the Ghost Dancers lived in a practical, everyday world as well as an ecstatic one. They carried their ideas with them over railroads and highways, wrote letters, and discussed problems in the English which was beginning to replace sign language as the lingua franca of the Plains. Among their leaders a number were students who had returned from the non-reservation boarding schools. Such students also served as interpreters and conducted much of the correspondence of the movement. Some leaders were men who were reasonably prosperous and who seemed to be "adjusting" well to the white world. And despite its emphasis on aboriginal purity, the movement encompassed many Christian ideas and some Christian practices.

The major chronicler of the Ghost Dance, in his career and sponsorship, also reflected important forces at work in the larger society. James Mooney, the midwestern son of Irish immigrant parents, was a supporter of Irish home rule and republican movements, a Catholic who remained loyal to Catholicism, an Irish nationalist who eventually became sympathetic to socialism. Thus "Mooney brought with him a personally experienced model . . . which included an awareness of ancient glories, of a sense of wrong and deprivation, and a dream of a golden age returned." [10] The Bureau of American Ethnology, of whose *Fourteenth Annual Report* Mooney's monograph formed a part, was already becoming a major institution in the development of anthropology and the compiling of data about American Indians. The resultant storehouse of information was drawn upon not only by whites but also by Indians.

Of all these factors, perhaps the most important single element in stimulating Pan-Indianism was expanding educational opportunity for Indians. Some Indians attended public schools and a few went to college, where they entered directly into the life of the dominant society. Others attended reservation schools which, until the end of the nineteenth century, were often operated by Catholic or Protestant groups under government contract.

In the eighties and nineties the number of reservation day schools conducted directly by the government increased. One of the more important consequences was the growing use of English as the medium of instruction. Missionary schools were usually conducted in the tribal language, it having been discovered that the Word of God was more acceptable to Indians if it reached their ears and eyes in the tribal tongues. The government, on the other hand, insisted upon instruction in English, maintaining that if the Indians were to become part of the larger society, they would have to be proficient in its language.

Under government auspices the trend to instruction in English gained strength, although many of the mission schools under government contract probably continued to use Indian languages in spite of regulations to the contrary.

The quality of education in reservation schools varied a good deal, consisting typically of the three R's and some industrial or vocational training. Common to all reservation schools was the fact that they drew only on the reservation population. If the school was under religious management, the course of study included strong doses of the particular brand of Christianity held by its administrators. This sectarianism struck many Indians as both bewildering and deplorable.

By far the most influential Indian schools were the eastern boarding schools—Carlisle School in Pennsylvania and Hampton Institute in Virginia. Here students were assembled from a number of tribes from all over the country. Many of them went on to lead or participate in Pan-Indian organizations. This was by no means the intention of General Richard Henry Pratt, the founder of Carlisle and of the Indian Department at Hampton.

A man of indefatigible and uncompromising energy, Pratt is often called "the father of Indian education." As a young army officer,

Pratt had been put in charge of a group of Indian prisoners of war at St. Augustine, Florida. He admired the stalwart virtues of his prisoners and got on well with them, as one warrior with another. He was determined to help those who wanted an education to get one. Consequently, upon their release in 1878, Pratt took a group of them to the Hampton Institute for freedmen in Virginia. Here in the following year a small Indian Department was established and continued to function with government aid until 1912 and without it until 1923. What Pratt really wanted, however, was a school for Indians. He succeeded in 1879 in opening such a school in an abandoned army barracks at Carlisle, Pennsylvania, under the auspices of the Indian Bureau.

Pratt conceived of Carlisle as a way-station for reservation Indians who would then become quickly assimilated as individuals into the larger society. His slogan was, "Kill the Indian and save the man!" One of the devices he invented for furthering this end was the celebrated Carlisle outing system in which students lived in nearby communities with selected families of good Christian character, attended public schools, and were visited regularly by the Carlisle Outing Agent. Pratt considered this the best possible way to "Americanize" the Indian.

A military man of forceful if somewhat narrow opinions to which he adhered with remarkable consistency throughout his life, Pratt hated tribalism, politicians, reservations, government wardship and paternalism, graft, the Bureau of American Ethnology, some missionaries, and most of those who disagreed with him. He was single-minded, dogmatic, intolerant, and undiplomatic.

But perhaps only a man of such unity of purpose could have founded and built an Indian boarding school in the face of widespread indifference and occasionally active hostility. He was sustained by his intense belief in the rightness of his cause, by his devout and simple Christianity, by his devotion to public education, and by his patriotism. Pratt believed deeply in America as the land of opportunity. He constantly used the immigrant experience as the model for Indian emulation, pointing to America's capacity to absorb large numbers of immigrants through public education and easy access to citizenship.

Pratt's prejudices were cultural rather than racial. To him, the Indian was a man like other men. He rejected utterly all notions of inborn racial inferiority. To Pratt, the problem was to strip the Indian of his Indianness and to replace this with a new set of religious and social attitudes and skills in harmony with the larger society. "To civilize the Indian, put him in civilization and keep him there," Pratt said again and again. He strongly favored intermarriage. It was perhaps Pratt's complete lack of any sense of racial Indian inferiority coupled with his deep belief in the capacities of his students which accounted for the enormous respect and admiration in which he was held by Indians of widely differing viewpoints.[11]

Carlisle, contrary to popular impression, was not a college. No doubt the school's renowned football team contributed to this public misconception, as well as the fact that most of the students were over fourteen and many of college age. Carlisle was essentially a grammar school with a primarily vocational emphasis. Pratt summarized the reasons for this in the 1897 *Annual Report*. "Exclusive race schools narrow and dwarf, and no better means of perpetrating tribalism and Indianism can be inaugurated than a system of schools holding the Indians together. . . . The limit of the Carlisle course has been placed at a point where if the student stops, he has been equipped for the ordinary avocations of American life, and where at the same time, if a higher education is desired, the foundations for that have been well laid." [12]

Following the establishment of Carlisle, a number of other non-reservation government boarding schools were founded. By 1887 there were eight, exclusive of Hampton. But Carlisle and Hampton were the only eastern schools, the rest being in or near Indian country in the Midwest, Southwest, and Northwest. After 1890 the emphasis shifted to reservation day schools, where the "civilizing" of the Indian was conducted on home grounds.

Carlisle and Pratt parted company in 1904 after Pratt had made a characteristically blunt public speech calling for the abolition of the Indian Bureau under whose auspices Carlisle was run. The emphasis at the school began to shift, as it was already shifting in the day schools. Francis Leupp, a former official of the Indian Rights Association who had been appointed commissioner of Indian affairs in 1905 by President Theodore Roosevelt, took a view of the Indian and his future almost exactly opposite to Pratt's. In his first *Annual Report* (1905) as commissioner, Leupp wrote: "I like the Indian for what is Indian in him. . . . Let us not make the mistake, in the process of absorbing them, of washing out whatever is distinctly Indian. Our aboriginal brother brings, as his contribution to the common store of character, a great deal which is admirable, and which only needs to be developed along the right line. Our proper work is improvement, not transformation." [13]

Soon a department of Native Indian Arts was added at Carlisle. By 1912, freshman students were learning about famous Indian leaders while seniors were exposed to "sociology applied to the Indian race." At Hampton, too, "native industries" were taught.

Carlisle's impact on its students was set forth in its 1908 *Annual Report:* "The plan of mixing the tribes at Carlisle results in nationalizing the Indian: and after all, that is the great object in our dealings with this primitive people. They see beyond the reservation and more than half our graduates are actually making a success away from the reservation." [14]

However, only about one out of every eight students who entered Carlisle graduated. Many stayed only a few months or years. These "returned students" [15] or dropouts were the subject of much anxious concern to the Carlisle authorities, who feared that they might "go back to the blanket," a phrase meaning a return to tribal ways symbolized by the wearing of Indian rather than "citizen dress." A similar dropout problem existed at Hampton.

Back at home, many returned students found themselves in an anomalous position, torn between the old life and the new, yet unhinged from either. Some did "go back to the blanket." Some became tribal interpreters and acted as bridges between the Indian and white worlds. A few became "informants" for anthropologists. Some adjusted fairly well either at home or off the reservation and were pointed to with pride in Carlisle and Hampton publications. Some went utterly to pieces. An appallingly large number died prematurely.

For many students—graduates and dropouts—Pan-Indian movements provided a psychological home, a place where they belonged. A large segment of the Pan-Indian leadership was educated in the eastern boarding schools. So prestigious was a Carlisle education that a few Pan-Indians who had not attended the school claimed that they had done so. Probably this was also due to the fact that admission to Carlisle was regarded as proof of Indian "blood," which in some Pan-Indian leaders ran very thin indeed.

An education, whether white or Indian or both, opened new possibilities of employment for Indian and new life styles. In the Indian Service, Indians were employed in increasingly responsible positions. Numerous

Carlisle and Hampton graduates entered the Service, in spite of General Pratt's urging to break completely with the Indian past and to compete in the race of life with other Americans. But for many educated Indians, the Service provided the means for using their education in an environment more familiar than the world outside and also seemed a way in which they could serve their people. In addition, Indian Service jobs were almost the only ones available on reservations. A 1912 survey of Carlisle graduates reported that of 514 living graduates, eighty-five were currently employed in the Indian Service, sixty of them "away from home." [16]

Indian employment in the Service had three major effects. First, Indian held jobs that required the development of skills and attitudes similar to those in the dominant society. Second, these men and women were frequently employed in situations where they dealt with Indians of other tribes, thus broadening their Indian horizons far beyond tribal boundaries. Third, Indian Service Indians, like other government employees, often found themselves administering public policies with which they privately disagreed. At times the Indian employee was torn between his duty to the Service and his loyalty to his fellow Indians. The ambiguity of his position produced painful, sometimes irreconcilable, inner conflicts. It is not surprising that many Indian Service Indians joined Pan-Indian movements.

Outside of the Indian Service, a number of educated Indians were making their way to respectable positions in the white world, mostly in the professions, but also in business and farming. Often these men and women had either a superficial or an anomalous relationship to their tribe. By education and avocation they were cut off from tribal life or their relationship to it had changed. Many of them felt the need for a more generalized Indian identity within which a tribal identity might also function. They lived in two, or three worlds, and most of them were not quite comfortable in any.

Few of these Indians lived on reservations, but they felt an obligation to help the reservation Indian and a kinship to other Indians in their own position. Many sought to find ways to use their "white" skills and knowledge to help reservation Indians and at the same time to create a recognized place for themselves in the larger society. This small but influential group, together with men and women from Carlisle and Hampton and some Indians from the Service, constituted the tiny

Indian establishment in the eyes of the whites and of many reservation Indians.

Thus through education a group of Indians arose who shared a common language—English—and who had sense of a common experience in the Indian and white worlds. This education and experience also exposed them in varying degrees and in somewhat different ways to a set of important ideas and images which they used in defining themselves as Indians and working out their relationships with whites.

Of these, probably the most important was Christianity, as refracted through the Indian schools, the various denominational missions, and the Christian reform organizations. Many educated Indians were devout or at least nominal Christians. They reflected the diversity of Christianity as well as such unifying ideas as the brotherhood of man under the fatherhood of God. Differences between Roman Catholicism and Protestantism and the varieties of the latter did not seem as significant as they did to whites. The Christian God was often spoken of as the Great Spirit in an ecumenical manner.

The white Christian Indian defense organizations constituted one of the most critical factors in the rise of modern Pan-Indian movements. They came into existence in the early eighties, largely as a result of the uproar over the forcible removal of the Poncas, without their consent, from their Dakota homeland to Indian Territory. By 1883, three major defense organizations had been founded. The earliest was the Women's National Indian Association, which in 1879 began an effort to mobilize public opinion for the Poncas and which had strong Christian support. In 1882, the influential Indian Rights Association (IRA) was founded in Philadelphia by a group of Quakers and other Christian reformers. The following year a group of persons interested in Indian affairs met at Lake Mohonk, New York, to coordinate the work of the various organizations and individuals in the field, most of them Christian in orientation. The annual Lake Mohonk conferences became an important platform for reform in Indian affairs.

The Christian missionary and defense organizations were the major element of white society interested in fighting cases of specific injustice, and it was largely to them that Indians turned for help. But these friends of the Indian saw little value in contemporary Indian tribal life. They believed in the inherent racial equality of Indian and white, but they saw much evil and little value in contemporary Indian religious and tribal institutions. Nevertheless, they often admired the rugged virtues of the vanished aboriginal Indian.

To Christianize and to civilize the Indian were identical processes, in their view. In adopting Christianity, Indians were expected to give up their barbaric ways of dressing, cut their hair, conduct their family life according to Christian ideals of a patriarchal, nuclear family, live in houses like other Americans, forego their dances, work hard, keep clean, learn the value of money, be thrifty, stay away from liquor, believe devoutly in private property, and live and think like other church-going Americans.

Civilizing and Christianizing the Indians were not only right in themselves, according to this view, but were also absolutely necessary if Indians were to learn to cope with the larger society. Into this society they must disappear without a trace. However, this process should be a just one, and white society must prove its worth to the Indians by honorable dealings. Therefore, the Indian defense organizations fought hard for enforcement of Indian treaties and agreements, for fair payment of allotments and annuities, and against white land-grabs, cheating, sale of liquor, arbitrary actions by agency superintendents, and other such practices. Indian uplift included white uplift as well.

The Indian Rights Association and the Lake Mohonk Conference of the Friends of the Indian were the most important organizations active in the reform of government policy which culminated in the Dawes Act. From a modern perspective, their vision seems limited. To them, the reservation was only a prison from which Indians should be liberated. IRA agents spent a good deal of time traveling in the Indian field making investigations of specific violations of Indian rights and attempting to secure justice, as they saw it, for the Indians. To them the Dawes Act was a way of getting Indians out of prison by allotting the lands to individuals, freeing Indians of paternalistic government control, and securing for Indians the rights and responsiblities of citizenship. This was to be accomplished over a period of time sufficient in their estimation to make the process as constructive as possible. They fought hard for a fair operation of the Dawes Act and for putting the Indian Service under Civil Service regulation, the latter finally being accomplished in 1902. They considered themselves, and indeed were, the watchdogs of Indian rights on Capitol Hill.

The chief failure of the Indian Rights Association and of the Lake

Mohonk conference, at least in the first few decades of their existence, was the inability of most of their members to see anything of real value in the Indian societies as such, any indigenous characteristics or forces on which a bridge to the white society might be built. They were especially intolerant of the various Indian versions of two fundamental institutions—religion and the family. In these areas so critical in the formation of individual and social morale, it was all or nothing to the reformers.

The idea of the melting pot as a process in which the contributions of various groups would combine to form a new product partaking of all, rather than a simple replica of one, was not applied to the Indians. No Indian cultural contribution was expected or desired. The Indian alone was to be melted and was to come out white, in culture if not in color. The name which the reformers gave to this process, of which the Dawes Act and the allotment policy were both instrument and symbol, was significant. They called it the "vanishing policy."

The blindness of the reformers to the viability of anything short of unconditional surrender of everything Indian led them to ignore or oppose some of the efforts made by Indians themselves to develop a synthesis of white and Indian values, some accommodation to white society on terms partially Indian. No blending of Indian and Christian religious elements, as in the Ghost Dance or the peyote cult, was acceptable. All unwittingly the reformers—the Indians' chief friends in court in the white world—thus helped to break down Indian self-respect and Indian attempts at self-help.

Many educated Indians, however, were not willing to turn their backs entirely on the Indian past. Although most were Christians, they did not share the missionary view that they should vanish. On the contrary, they wanted somehow to remain Indians and at the same time to adopt what they felt to be the best in white civilization and in Christianity. Their search for some workable definition of what it meant to be simultaneously an Indian and a member of modern society was one of the primary forces leading to Pan-Indian organization.

Another important idea, closely related to Christianity, was American individualism, the idea of standing on one's own feet, making one's way in the world by one's own effort and exertion without benefit of government handouts. Educated Indians held a variety of versions of this idea, often extending it to group as well as individual self-help. Opposition to the Indian Bureau and governmental paternalism among educated Indians was reinforced by this belief. The desire to create an Indian leadership for "the Indian race" was in part an outgrowth of it.

Ideas about Americanizing the immigrant, of which educated Indians were well aware, formed another complex of ideas and practices to draw on. Educated Indians saw the immigrant experience as a model for the Indian in the manner in which the immigrant became Americanized through public education and the easy acquisition of citizenship. Indians regarded with sympathetic interest the immigrant ethnic organizations which functioned both as bridges to the larger society and as mechanisms for retaining or adapting some of the old ways brought from Europe.

Social science provided another group of ideas. Perhaps the most pervasive of these was the theory that all societies had to advance through predetermined evolutionary stages, from savagery through barbarism, culminating in civilization. This was viewed as a very long process. The Indian saw himself engaged in a slow and painful climb up the evolutionary ladder.

The idea of race was both important and quite ill-defined, sometimes being equated with "nationality," sometimes with "culture," and sometimes with biology. Educated Indians considered themselves a race. On the whole, they drew on social science ideas of the inherent equality of races in the biological sense. Thus racial equality as conceived through Christian brotherhood was reinforced by racial equality as formulated by social science.

Ideas of evolutionary stages and of race were held by anthropologists and sociologists in common. But the impact of anthropology and sociology on Indian thought differed somewhat. On the whole, anthropologists took a more positive view of the actual and potential contributions of Indians to the larger society. In their study of Indian tribes, anthropologists found much to be admired. Some sought for a means which would allow the retention of some characteristically Indian or tribal institutions while at the same time bringing the Indian closer to the white world. The very process of collecting and publishing ethnological data resulted in a certain amount of "ethnological feedback." Some of the educated Indians who acted as interpreters or informants for anthropologists who studied their tribes thereby became acquainted with anthropological field work at first hand. A few well-known and well-respected anthropologists were themselves Indians.

The Christian party viewed most anthropologists with the deepest suspicion, especially those connected with the Bureau of American Ethnology. These men were believed to be conspiring selfishly to keep the Indian in "the blanket" as ethnological specimens for further research. Just as the Christians viewed with horror the proposition that "the only good Indian is a dead Indian," so they viewed with equal horror the attitude attributed to anthropologists that "the only good Indian is a blanket Indian."

A few anthropologists, like James Mooney, were active in Indian affairs. Unlike the Christian party, these men had no Indian defense organization of their own, but offered aid and counsel and in some instances testified in behalf of Indian rights at congressional hearings. A number of Indian anthropologists, such as Arthur C. Parker, J. N. B. Hewitt, and Francis LaFlesche, became active in Pan-Indian affairs, creating a tradition which has continued to this day.

Sociologists, on the other hand, were not professionally interested in the Indian, with the notable exception of Fayette McKenzie, the founder of the Society of American Indians. But some ideas from sociology and its close relative, social work, did affect the thought of a few educated Indians. One idea was the social survey, in which relevant data was gathered in a scientific manner as a basis for social policy. Another was the idea of a defined status, of the desirability to both the individual and the group of having a clearly delineated relationship to the rest of society. Yet another was the social settlement idea, in which more "fortunate" members of society helped less "fortunate" members through localized and organized activities for the development of skills and knowledge needed for full participation in national life.

Another group of ideas came from the law. By the first decade of the twentieth century there was a small group of Indian lawyers who attacked what they believed to be the unconstitutionality as well as the unfairness of the maze of laws relating to the Indian and the unequal treatment of the Indian in legal matters. These men were especially concerned with the vexing question of Indian citizenship, the status of Indian lands, allotment procedures, and the enforcement of treaty rights. They argued for Indian equality before the law.

Quite different was a set of romantic ideas and images evolving from the concept of "the noble savage." Many friends of the Indian who were neither primarily of the Christian party nor primarily social scientists held these views. They thought of the Indian as having been driven out of an aboriginal paradise. The Indian was strong, silent, truthful, poetic, hospitable, open-hearted, trustworthy, nomadic, exotic, and deeply attuned to the world of nature. This was a positive, though not necessarily an accurate, picture shared, at least in part, by many educated Indians. To men and women increasingly conscious of the growing problems of an industrializing and urbanizing society, it had great appeal.

A variant of the noble savage theme was the Indian stereotype exemplified in the wild west show. By the early years of the twentieth century, the popular image of the Indian had become the war-bonneted warrior of the Plains, complete with tepee and horse. The creation of this image took place over a considerable period of time, being fostered by the paintings of such men as George Catlin and Karl Bodmer, the coverage of Plains warfare in newspapers and magazines, and the scores of dime novels and plays about Plains Indians which appeared after 1860.

Probably the most important force for Indians and whites alike in casting the image of the Indian in the lineaments of the Plains warrior was Buffalo Bill's Wild West Show. The first show opened in 1883, and for three decades millions of people in the United States, Canada, and Europe thrilled to the stirring performances. Even the great Sitting Bull himself traveled with Buffalo Bill in 1885, midway between the annihilation of Custer's forces and his own annihilation during the Ghost Dance and the "Sioux outbreak," when he was shot by Indian police attempting to arrest him. Buffalo Bill's spectacular success led to the organization of many similar shows. Not the least function of these was the employment and broadening experience they offered to Indians as well as the diffusion of the Plains costume among many of the tribes. Indians themselves began to conform to the picture popularly held of them.

Many educated Indians resented the wild west show image. They believed that ignorant Indians were being exploited for commercial gain, and they thought that white Americans were being given a false picture of the modern Indian, especially of the middle-class professionally trained Indian. To the Christian reformers, the wild west shows were anathema, a perpetuation of everything they were trying to eliminate. They greatly preferred the Indian exhibitions showing modern Indian accomplishments.

The sensitivity of educated Indians to the Indian image as projected by the wild west show underlines another factor difficult to define but nonetheless crucial—the antipathy or condescension that Indians detected in the attitudes of many white Americans toward them. No body of literature or rationale existed which defined the Indian as a permanent enemy or outcast inferior, as was the case with the Negro. Nor was there a national consensus forbidding intermarriage. Many whites, in fact, boasted of an Indian ancestor. It was much easier for an Indian to become a full-fledged member of American society than it was for a Negro, provided that he was willing and able to shed most of his "Indian" characteristics. Even these did not bar him from acceptance if he conformed in speech and in most customs of everyday life to the ways of the white world. His remaining Indianness might in many instances be considered colorful and be welcomed as a pleasant exoticism. Prejudice against Indians tended to be local, directed against local Indians on local reservations and not necessarily extended to other Indians.

The factor of bias, however it operated, served to divide as well as to unite Indians, for the escape hatch to almost full acceptance was always open to the individual. Through it many Indians—it is impossible to tell how many—were absorbed into the larger society.

By the first years of the twentieth century a group of educated Indians had emerged who no longer looked to the return of an aboriginal paradise but rather to an Indian future to be worked out within the promise of American life. From this promise, many educated Indians felt themselves to be at least partially excluded. They felt themselves, as the "native Americans," obviously to be entitled to the rights held by other Americans.

By this time, also, governmental Indian affairs were again in sad disarray. Like all other Indian policies before it, the "vanishing policy" was not working well. The question of citizenship, further muddied by the Burke Act of 1907 which made the acquisition of citizenship more difficult, was lost in a hopeless tangle of federal and state laws. The bright vision of a sturdy, God-fearing, Indian yeomanry working diligently on their own fields had faded. Much more typical was the picture of the Indian who had lost his lands, either through legal means or through chicanery, and who now faced the world empty-handed. Allotment, which was supposed to secure land for the individual Indian, turned out often to secure it for the individual white. The process of allotment itself weakened the sanctions of the tribe over the individual, thereby contributing further to Indian disorganization. Perhaps most disheartening of all, at least to the proponents of the Dawes Act, was the patent fact that the Indian was not vanishing. While many Indians no doubt continued to disappear into the general population, as they had long before the Dawes Act, a very large number remained. Most still lived on reservations. Despite all efforts of friend and foe, many of the old tribal ways persisted in one form or another, often deeply modified by white and Christian influences.

Against this background there grew in the first decade of the twentieth century two important Pan-Indian movements, one religious, the other secular. Both reached beyond particular groups of tribes or areas. Both rejected the idea of a return to an aboriginal past or of a future in which the Indian would vanish without a trace. Rather these movements sought, through a blending of aboriginal and white elements, to come to terms with modern American society.

I
REFORM
PAN-INDIANISM
THE SOCIETY OF
AMERICAN INDIANS

———————— ✳ ————————

2

THE RED PROGRESSIVES

The reformers of the Progressive Era were inveterate founders of organizations. With an exuberance based on faith in the inevitability of progress, they translated ideas into organizations and organizations into action. Problems existed to be solved, and the democratic promise existed to be fulfilled.

Among American Indians the term "progressive" had long had a special meaning. "Progressive" Indians believed in education, hard work, and in adapting their attitudes, values, and habits of life to those of the larger American society. It was these men and women, sharing in the enthusiasm and faith of the white reformers, who composed the first secular Pan-Indian movement organized on a national basis—the Society of American Indians. They were the red progressives.

At the beginning of the twentieth century, three progressive Indians had seriously considered the idea of organizing other progressive Indians into a national body. They were Dr. Charles Eastman, his brother the Reverend John Eastman, and the Reverend Sherman Coolidge. They concluded, after lengthy discussions, that the time was not yet ripe for such a movement because it "would not be understood either by our own race or the American people in general" and would almost surely arouse "the antagonism of the Bureau," which employed "many of the most progressive red men." A few years later Charles Eastman and Sherman Coolidge helped to start the Society of American Indians. Both served as its president.[1]

The man who took the initiative in the formation of the organization, Professor Fayette A. McKenzie of Ohio State University, was not himself an Indian; yet he epitomized many of the forces which made such a society possible and which guided its development. McKenzie's range

31

of interests was typical of many of the progressive reformers of his day. He was an educator, a sociologist, a Christian idealist and reformer, a supporter of the Dawes Act and a critic of its implementation. Deeply involved in the settlement house movement, public recreation, public education, and Negro advancement, he later became President of Fisk University and was on the staff of the influential Meriam Report in the twenties, which laid the groundwork for basic changes in Indian policy.

McKenzie was born in Pennsylvania in 1872, graduated from Lehigh University, taught in the East for some years, and then spent a year teaching at the Wind River Government Indian School in Wyoming. In 1905 he became a professor of economics and sociology at Ohio State University and received the Ph.D. from the University of Pennsylvania in 1906. The subject of his thesis was "The American Indian in Relation to the White Population of the United States," which he published as a book in 1908.

In his book, McKenzie sought to put Indian-white relations in a strong theoretical framework drawn from social science and to use social science theory in the formulation of a workable program for Indian affairs. McKenzie argued that in American Indian policy, "The real question involved is, can a culture and civilization be transferred from a higher to a lower people? Can one race acquire in a few generations what another race has with difficulty gained through many generations?" McKenzie believed emphatically that it could, and that the results would "demonstrate a method for the regeneration of the populations of the globe." [2]

How was this transformation to be brought about? First, McKenzie argued, it was necessary to analyze the causes of "Indian retardation." The "preponderating" causes, he believed, lay in "the conditions made or allowed by the government," especially if viewed as strengthening "the social tryranny of the tribe." "For the Indian we desire change and progress," McKenzie wrote, "something which is directly opposed to the forces of his tradition and custom. Any considerable change in a short time means the absolute rending of these forces. The tribal organization and the tribal spirit are not compatible with the white man's life and civilization."

We cannot wait for "the conceivably probable progress of five hundred years of evolution through internal forces," McKenzie wrote. Such progress "could be secured in two generations under a constant and consistent policy on the part of the government and society, that is, through the action of proper external forces."

What should government policy be? "The aim of the government, in its political action, should be to remove as rapidly as possible—and that means very rapidly—all differences between the red and the white man in their civil status—to make the red man realize that he has no privileges of any sort not granted to people of other colors, and that he has all the obligations which rest upon his fellow citizens of all colors. There are two words which stand for the policy which is here suggested. One is the 'vanishing policy,' and the other is 'citizenship' " (pp. 21–22). The "vanishing policy" was, of course, the Dawes Act policy, but Mc-Kenzie believed that while sound in conception, it had been botched in implementation. He suggested a compromise which, he believed, would retain its best features and obviate its deficiencies.

"The worst feature of the present method is that after a long period of hot-house protection, a whole community is suddenly pushed pell-mell into the cold atmosphere of the outside world. No one has a chance to profit by the experience of others. It would be a great advance if they were released one by one from their leading strings. The first failure would become an example to the warning of many. Surely when an Indian boy is retained in school until he is eighteen, he should be given his allotment at once, and the rights to draw on his government funds in order to stock his farm, and at twenty-one the patent in fee simple should be made over to him. By such a scheme, even though the twenty-five year law should hold for the older people, the stripes of experience would fall successively upon a few to the advantage of the many, and those few would be best able to stand the test, or best able to strike out anew in case they failed. [p. 32]"

Besides a clear definition of the Indian's legal status, the right kind of education was a pressing need, McKenzie believed, in order to "save the new Indian." Education "should fit him to earn his living in contact and in competition with the white man. But any theory of education that proceeds from a belief in his essential inferiority or that would limit him to the lower ranges of life and of thought, is a libel on human nature and the spirit of American democracy." At the present time, the manual training school best suits the needs of the mass of Indians, while the technical college "will be the need of the not distant future," McKenzie argued. But a higher education, which had already produced a number

of Indian professional men and women, was also needed: *"Such education is practically the one way of creating . . . that racial leadership
which is the chief hope and means of attaining an accelerating progress*
[emphasis added]" (p. 80).

McKenzie praised education in the non-reservation school, but believed that, practically speaking, it ignored the needs of many Indians.
There were two ways of "saving the new Indian," he wrote. One was
"General Pratt's dictum: the way to civilize the Indian is to put him in
civilization and keep him there. This is undoubtedly the most effective
means for the particular individual who is thus persuaded to leave his
own people. . . . But the instincts of the majority carry them back to
the Reserve, from which the older people, too, can never go. These
people are in large measure left out of General Pratt's scheme."

A complement to the non-reservation boarding school was needed in
order to use the skills of returned students to serve their people and
to give them a functional place in society, McKenzie asserted. "Bagehot
calls attention to a principle which is not commonly understood. It
affords an explanation of the wild character and frequent retrogression
of the half-breed, and of the educated native. Both are freed from the
old social control, both are apt to be equally free from the bonds of the
dominant race."

"The secondary way of reaping the harvest prepared in the non-
reservation school is found in many forms of industrial, settlement, and
spiritual work to be carried on the reservation itself" (pp. 54–55). Since
"economic activities not only condition the development of the intellect,
but furnish the only positive framework of support for the moral life,
and provide the basis for the development of both the intellectual and
religious life" (p. 96), it was therefore essential to provide initiative and
an opportunity "for some or many of the returned students" on the
reservations.

McKenzie advocated establishing "industries" on the reservation,
citing anthropologist Lewis Henry Morgan's advocacy of a "factory
system," in which he also included farming. He called for an "Indian
settlement" system, which would have "its religious work, its social work,
its medical work, and its educational work. But all of these should center
around its industrial work. The latter should ensure that diversification of
industries which every progressive community must have." These settlements might be started by societies and churches carrying on missionary

work. They should be in part "self-supporting and self-perpetuating" (p. 107).

McKenzie suggested that the government turn over natural resources such as waterfalls to missionaries or settlements, perhaps for twenty-five years, in order to launch the program. He urged colleges and universities to send student volunteers, like those going into foreign missions, for a year's work on a reservation and believed that financial aid might be obtained through private philanthropy.

McKenzie summarized "the fundamental elements of our Indian policy" as: "(1) The strength of tribal control must be broken. The reservation must go. Gratuities must cease. Distinctions of race must disappear. Closeness of contact with the real elements of civilization must be made wider and more vital. These are within the province of governmental action. (2) Civilization must be carried to the reservation and upheld there. Initiative for industrial and religious life must be carried to the Indian by the social settlement and the missionary. These are the fields of voluntary associational activity. The time for the harvest has come" (p. 93).

Thus McKenzie attempted to put into a coherent system based on modern social science, social work, and Christian idealism a program for "race transformation" which would encompass Indians at various levels of acculturation and would be implemented by the major forces in the Indian field, including educated Indians. His program anticipated many reforms which were to be undertaken decades later.

Although McKenzie was a social scientist, he seems to have taken little interest in the social science most directly concerned with Indians, anthropology. This discipline, which might have provided him with a more knowledgeable and sympathetic insight into existing tribal institutions or Indian life, influenced him little. He was well grounded in the history of Indian affairs and deeply conscious of injustices to Indians, but he saw the Indian past and present largely from a political, legal, or administrative perspective rather than a cultural one. His views were more balanced and sophisticated than those of General Pratt and of many of those in the mission field or in the Indian defense organizations, but he shared their failure to see much of positive value in contemporary Indian societies. He sympathized with the Indian in transition between two worlds, but he had developed no comprehensive way of understanding the world the Indian was leaving. In advocating "transformation" he neglected to analyze the societies that were to be transformed, perhaps because his antipathy to tribalism was so strong. Nor does he seem to have explored the possibility that the "native leadership" which would supplement white governmental and voluntary efforts might develop an ideology which would redefine Indian identity and would passionately assert that the Indian must not "vanish."

The "native leadership" which McKenzie sought was to be based on race rather than on tribe. "Such leadership will come," McKenzie wrote, "when the educated representatives of the race shall organize in the unselfish hope that by combined action they shall create the basis for a future leadership. Personal ambition would ruin such an effort; delay may be equally fatal to racial prospects. The conditions are ripe for organization" (p. 86).

In 1908 or 1909 McKenzie himself set about hastening this process through the organization of an association of educated Indians. After considerable correspondence, a group of six leading Indians gathered at Columbus, Ohio, in April, 1911, at Professor McKenzie's invitation. They included Dr. Charles A. Eastman, Dr. Carlos Montezuma, Thomas L. Sloan, Charles E. Daganett, Laura Cornelius, and Henry Standing Bear. They organized themselves under the temporary name of the American Indian Association and adopted a statement of purposes which in language and viewpoint was thoroughly in harmony with reform movements of the period. "The Temporary Executive Committee of the American Indian Association declares that the time has come when the American Indian race should contribute, in a more united way, its influence and exertion with the rest of the citizens of the United States in all lines of progress and reform, for the welfare of the Indian race in particular, and humanity in general," the preamble read.[3]

At the same time the Temporary Executive Committee was enlarged to include eighteen members. Full biographical data are not known for some, but at least eleven were connected with the eastern boarding schools, eight having graduated from Carlisle, two from Hampton, while one had served as staff physician at Carlisle. By occupation, most were professional people, several were clerks, and at least one was a businessman. Eleven had previously been or were currently employed by the Indian Service. Six had been born or lived in Oklahoma. Almost all were from Eastern, Prairie or Plains tribes: four from tribes of the Six Nations Confederacy, two from the Sioux, two from the Five Civilized

Tribes, three from the Chippewa, and one each from the Blackfoot, Potawatomi, Winnebago, Omaha, Osage, Apache, and Klamath.

During the April meeting the group was invited by President W. O. Thompson of Ohio State, the Mayor of Columbus, and a number of civic and religious leaders to hold the first conference in Columbus. The invitation was accepted and a call issued for a national conference in October, 1911. The call to the conference set forth the reasons why such a meeting should be held:

"1. The highest ethical forces of America have been endeavoring on a large scale and in a systematic way to bring the native American into the modern life. It is well to see whether these efforts have brought results.

2. The time has come when the Indians should be encouraged to develop self-help. This can be achieved only with the attainment of a race consciousness and a race leadership. We cannot predict the race leader, but a gathering of the educated, progressive members of all the tribes is a prerequisite to his discovery.[4]

3. The Indian has certain contributions of value to offer to our government and our people. These contributions will be made more efficiently if made in an authorized and collective way. They will, at least they may, save us immense losses from mistaken policies which we might otherwise follow.

4. The white man is somewhat uncomfortable under a conviction that 'a century of dishonor' has not been redeemed. If in any degree he can convince himself and his red brother that he is willing to do what he can for the race whose lands he has occupied, a new step toward social justice will have been taken."

At the second committee meeting, held in June, the group drafted two letters, one an "Indian letter," one a "non-Indian" letter. The "Indian letter" was to be "sent out to the Indians of the country." But who among them was to be invited? Should the basis of representation be tribal? If so, most of the convenors would have little chance of attending the conference as delegates, since it was doubtful that any of them, with perhaps one or two exceptions, could have been elected as tribal representatives. If the basis were tribal, what might happen if a tribe decided to send delegates who were undesirable in some way? How were the convenors themselves to become delegates?

These problems were resolved by an agreement to ask each tribe "to select and send its own delegate," to whom the Executive Committee would issue invitations "unless for very special reasons their judgment shall dictate otherwise." Non-tribal delegates whom the committee deemed "advisable" to have at the conference were to be invited also.[5]

The letterhead on which the "Indian letter" was written carried the names of the temporary executive committee without tribal designations. Professor McKenzie's name was also listed as "local representative, Columbus, Ohio." The letterhead made clear the status of Indian and white relationship to the new organization, proclaiming in large type: "Memberships: Active and Associate Active: Persons of Indian Blood Only." This was to be an association run by Indians.[6]

The term "blood," and its variations such as "full-blood," was closely linked to the idea of race and was widely used both by Indians and whites during this period to indicate degree of Indian ancestry. It has since fallen largely into disrepute, not only because it is scientifically inaccurate but also because it often came to imply inferiority or to indicate condescension.

The "persons of Indian blood" who were to lead the new Pan-Indian organization of educated Indians came from a wide range of backgrounds. Some were what might be called "first-generation" Americans: men who made the great transition from "wild" to "civilized" life in the span of a few years. Others came from families and tribes who had had decades of close contact with American society. The ancestors of some had fought the ancestors of others. Some were "full-bloods," others had a strong admixture of white ancestry. Most, but not all, used both Indian and "American" names. All were educated professional men. Their variety of Indian experience, which might have divided them, was matched by a similarity of American experience, which helped to unite them.

The most prominent man among the founders of the fledgling Society was the physician Dr. Charles A. Eastman (Ohiyesa), the dean of progressive American Indians, widely known and respected as an author and lecturer on Indian life. He was a lithe and handsome man with the classic features of the Sioux, one who looked as much at home in a Boston business suit as in a feathered Plains war bonnet.

Eastman, although repeatedly referred to by others as well as himself as a "full-blooded" Sioux, did in fact have one white ancestor through his mother, as he reports in his autobiography, *Indian Boyhood*. Eastman's claim to "full-bloodedness" no doubt reflects the respect tinged with envy in which this state was held by educated Indians, if it was combined with education and demonstrated ability to get along in the white man's world. "Full-blood" as applied to an uneducated reservation Indian often had unfavorable connotations as being synonymous with "backward" or "blanket" Indians. In this, as in so many other ways, educated Indians showed deeply mixed feelings about their identification with "the race."

In any case, Eastman as a child was culturally a thoroughgoing Sioux, who spent the first fifteen years of his life as a "wild Indian." His mother, who was the granddaughter of a Sioux chief and the daughter of a white father and a Sioux mother, died when he was an infant. His father, Many Lightnings, had been involved in the Minnesota uprising of 1862. He was captured together with several of his older sons, and his family believed that he had been hanged. Eastman was brought up by his uncle and grandmother, to whom he was deeply devoted, and who represented to him the best of the old ways. From them he learned to hate the white man who had killed his father and whose death, he was taught, he must avenge. Eastman looked back affectionately at his Sioux boyhood throughout his life. For him, being an Indian was never far from being a Sioux.

When Eastman was a young man of fifteen, his father reappeared. He had been held in prison, where he was converted to Christianity and "the white man's road" and changed his name to Jacob Eastman. Eventually, he received a pardon from President Lincoln. For a short time after his release, the elder Eastman had lived on a reservation, but he hated what he felt to be the degrading quality of reservation life. Accordingly, he took up homesteading and when he felt well-established, he sought and found his youngest son.

Jacob Eastman was determined that his son follow the white man's road. He gave him a "white" name, Charles, and for the rest of his life, Eastman used both his "white" and his Sioux names. Eastman reports that his father persuaded him to go to the Santee Indian School, run by the Reverend Alfred L. Riggs, and conducted in both English and Indian languages, with these words,

"I have no doubt . . . that my brother, your uncle, has brought you up with the knowledge and traditions of our tribe, especially those of our immediate band. There is no better band of the Sioux nation in bravery and self-control. Our young men are wont to dare anything. When you leave my log cabin, to go away to school, you may consider yourself on the war-path. You will be seeking eagle feathers, my son. If you should not return, your father will weep proud tears.

I have started in here with some of my people to become farmers and citizens like the white men. This is our school—ours, the old men. I shall stick to it. I shall not go back to the reservation. I want all my sons to follow the trail which I am trying to make for you." [7]

Eastman set out on the warpath for Santee, knowing only the little English he had acquired in the mission school. Riggs was a second father to him, while his own father gave encouragement by writing to him in the Dakota language.

From Santee, Eastman was sent to Beloit only a few days after he received word that Jacob Eastman had died. He later went to Knox College and from there to Dartmouth on the latter college's Indian scholarship. Upon graduation he entered Boston University Medical School.

During his happy student years in the East, Eastman was regarded warmly both by his fellow-students and his elders. He entered fully into the life around him. He loved Dartmouth, he loved Boston, and he made many friends. He graduated from medical school determined to use his skills to help his people. Armed with his own brand of high idealism, in which his version of the Sioux religion and the New England conscience blended with a mystical Christianity, Eastman journeyed to the Sioux Agency at Pine Ridge, South Dakota, as a physician in the Indian Service. He was at this time about thirty-three years old.

Eastman had been at the agency only a few months when the "Sioux outbreak" climaxed the Ghost Dance at Pine Ridge and nearby Sioux reservations. By this time he was acquainted with a number of Indians on the reservation, including members of the Indian police, "progressives," Ghost Dancers, "hostiles," and so on. Eastman did not believe then nor did he ever believe that there was any danger of an Indian "uprising." He regarded the Ghost Dancers as misled and foolish but not dangerous. He believed that his duty lay with the government.

The day after the massacre at Wounded Knee, Eastman attempted to go out to treat the wounded, but was not allowed to do so. Not until three days after the "battle" did he journey out to give medical care. It was one of the most terrible moments of his life when he realized that the "battle" had been a massacre, that many of the dead and wounded were women and children, and that they had been relentlessly pursued and shot down by soldiers.

Eastman's disillusionment was not so deep, however, as it was to become. After his marriage to Elaine Goodale, a white, Massachusetts-born supervisor of Indian schools whom he had met at the agency and who was there at the time of the massacre, the young couple returned to Pine Ridge. Here they discovered that the Indians were being cheated by the local agency authorities and concluded that the Ghost Dance "outbreak" had been grounded in actual grievances that they had not suspected. Their repeated protests to Washington resulted in a campaign by the agent to get Eastman removed. He was finally offered a transfer, which he indignantly refused. Disillusioned with the Indian Bureau but confident of the good faith of the larger society, Eastman resigned from the Service. The Eastmans went to Minneapolis, where he entered private medical practice and began to write the books that were to make him famous. Eastman soon became a field secretary for the YMCA, and traveled widely among the tribes. For several years he represented the Sioux in Washington where he also advised visiting delegations of other tribes.

Eastman later spent some seven years under a special government appointment to revise the family names and allotment rolls of the Sioux nation. Eastman described his work thus:

"It was my duty to group the various members of one family under a permanent name, selected for its euphony and appropriateness from among the various cognomens in use among them, of course suppressing mistranslations and grotesque or coarse nicknames calculated to embarrass the educated Indian. My instructions were that the original native name was to be given the preference, if it were short enough and easily pronounced by Americans. If not, a translation or abbreviation might be used, while retaining as much as possible of the distinctive racial flavor. No English surname might be arbitrarily given, but such as were already established if the owner so desired. . . . The task was quite complicated and there were many doubts and suspicions to overcome, as some feared lest it should be another trick to change the Indian's name after he had been allotted, and so defraud him safely." [8]

In this work, as in so much of Eastman's life, he attempted to interpret each world to the other and to bring each closer to the other.

Perhaps as much as any educated Indian of his day, he had a foot solidly in both camps and felt genuinely at home among Indians and among whites. He loved the old vanished life and sympathized with it, yet he felt deeply that it was doomed. He loved the new life, also, critical though he was of many of its aspects, especially of what he considered the failure of Christians to practice Christianity. Perhaps he was romantic about both. He chose to spend most of his later life in New England with his large family, writing and lecturing. His wife was a writer as well, in later years the author of the standard biography of General Pratt.

Of all the founders of the new society, Eastman probably had least need of it as a way of defining his own relationship to Indians and whites, much as he sympathized with its Pan-Indian purposes. Perhaps this helps to explain his frequent ambivalence toward the organization he helped to create.[9]

At the time of the founding of the Society of American Indians, the highest position held by an Indian in the Indian Bureau was Supervisor of Employment. The man who occupied this position was Charles E. Daganett, a Peoria from Oklahoma where his grandfather, Christmas Daganett, had been agent of the Miami-Peoria reservation.

Born about 1872, Daganett's degree of "Indian blood" is uncertain. Carlisle school records list him as "half" and he is elsewhere referred to as "quarter." Whether or not he had an Indian name is unknown. He entered Carlisle in 1887 at the age of fifteen, learned the trade of printer, and became editor of the *Red Man,* the school paper. Graduating in 1891, he attended Dickinson College and eventually graduated from Eastman College in Poughkeepsie, New York. He married a Miami who was a fellow Carlisle graduate.

Daganett edited a paper in Miami, Oklahoma, for a time and joined the Indian Service in 1894. He worked his way up through the ranks, being successively teacher, disciplinarian, and clerk before his appointment as supervisor of employment about 1907. He was offered a superintendency, but refused it. Like a number of other SAI leaders including Eastman, he was a Mason.

Daganett was an organization man, an executive familiar with the ways of bureaucracy and at home in the organization world. There is no evidence that he was either a mystic or romantic like Charles Eastman nor that he was much concerned with theoretical problems as were some other SAI leaders. He does not seem to have been a member of any religious body. But as the senior Indian in the Service he was on the forefront of Indian advancement in the Bureau. Such a situation is almost inevitably a difficult one, involving delicate and complex relationships with both white and Indian colleagues. Clearly Daganett's status made him the focus of Indian hopes for advancement in the Bureau and Indian fears that working for the Service meant working against "the race." It was probably this position, at once secure and ambiguous, that impelled him to lend his considerable talents to the Society. Thus he established a pattern that was to recur in Pan-Indian affairs: leadership by Indian Bureau Indians.[10]

The anti-Indian Bureau forces in the new organization were well represented by Dr. Carlos Montezuma—"Wassaja" or "Monty"—known as "the fiery Apache." Like Eastman he was uprooted from tribal life, went to white schools, and married a white woman.

In 1871, when he was four years old, Montezuma was captured by the Pima, enemies of the Apache, in a terrible massacre which left an indelible impression on him. The Pimas sold him for $50 to Carlos Gentile, a reporter and photographer of Mexican extraction, who adopted him. Montezuma traveled about the country with his adopted father, attending public schools in Brooklyn; Galesburg, Illinois; and Chicago. Gentile died when Montezuma was still quite young, and the boy became a protégé of the Chicago Press Club.

Montezuma worked his way through the University of Illinois at Urbana, graduating in 1884 at the age of seventeen. He then entered the Chicago Medical College, working his way through over a period of five years. After obtaining his license, he practiced medicine for a few months in Chicago, and then entered the Indian Service as physician and clerk at the Fort Stevenson Indian School in North Dakota. A year later he was transferred to the Western Shoshone Agency in Nevada. "There I saw in full what deterioration is for the Indians," Montezuma wrote. "I watched these Indians, cut off from civilized life, trying to become like Yankees with the aid of a few government employees. Because of my own experience, I was now able to fully realize how their situation held them to their old Indian life, and often wondered why the government held them so arbitrarily to their tribal life, when better things were all around them." [11] Next Montezuma became Indian Service physician to Chief Moses' band of Columbia River Indians and

Chief Joseph's band of Nez Perces. Montezuma greatly admired the two famous chiefs, but he "yearned for civilization," and gladly accepted the call to become resident physician at Carlisle, where General Pratt was then the head. He remained at Carlisle for two and a half years, eventually resigning to return to private practice in Chicago, where he became a well-known physician active in civic affairs. He was a Mason of sufficient eminence that a Masonic monument was erected to him when he died. In religion he was a Baptist.

Montezuma's experience at Carlisle was decisive. Pratt's ideology—"to civilize the Indian, put him in civilization and keep him there"—suited him exactly and he took it over as his own. He admired Pratt deeply, perhaps because he and Pratt were somewhat alike—intolerant men of simple, unchanging, but strongly held views.

Montezuma, like Pratt, hated the Indian Bureau and reservation life. He believed in public education and instant assimilation. He was a self-made man, an individualist, a fiery speaker, and a writer with a polemical pen. But unlike Pratt he was, after all, a "full-blooded" Indian, and in him the conflict between being an Indian and living in the white world ran very deep. He affirmed passionately the value of being an Indian, but he was unclear about what that value really was. Although he often visited reservations, he could not bear to live on one, even in the capacity of agency physician, or indeed, even at Carlisle. But when he was mortally ill, he returned to the reservation to die.

Montezuma was by temperament and conviction a factionalist. He helped to found the Society of American Indians and then spent most of the rest of his life attacking it. Even as a Pan-Indian, he was combative, without any gift for compromise. He was perhaps at his best as editor of *Wassaja,* his personal newspaper to which he gave his Apache name meaning "beckoning" or "signaling."

Although all but forgotten today, during his lifetime Montezuma was one of the best-known Indians in the country. After he died in 1923, his influence continued in a most curious way. Montezuma had visited various reservations in Arizona in 1918, preaching against the Indian Bureau. "The preaching was not wholly anti-White," Edward A. Spicer writes, "it was rather completely anti-Indian bureau; and its positive feature consisted in the assertion of the great value of Indian-hood." Montezuma's message was interpreted by various reservation Indians according to their own lights. Among the Pimas (the tribe which had captured and sold Montezuma as a child), the older men who refused to deal with the Indian Bureau and who in general shunned white ways became known as "Montezumas," while among the Papagos, "Montezumas" were older village headmen who came to identify Montezuma with both Jesus and a tribal deity and believed that "Montezuma would one day return and restore better times and good moral behavior." [12] Thus Pratt's disciple after death became transformed into his opposite.[13]

Montezuma was one of the few men with whom another founder of the SAI, the Reverend Sherman Coolidge, ever quarreled publicly. Coolidge was an Episcopal minister of deep and unquestioning faith. Like Eastman and Montezuma, he was a first-generation American, having plunged directly from tribal to white life when a child and later married a white easterner, Grace Wetherbee. Born into the Arapaho tribe in 1863, he was a "full-blood." When he was seven years old, Coolidge was captured by the army and taken into the family of a white army officer, Lieutenant C. A. Coolidge, who gave him his "American" name. He seems rarely to have used his Indian name, "Runs Mysteriously on Ice." However, in private correspondence with Arthur C. Parker, he frequently signed himself "Arapaho," the name of his tribe.

The elder Coolidge took the boy East where he attended public schools in New York City. Later young Coolidge was sent to Shattuck Military School and thence to Bishop Whipple's Seabury Divinity School, where he received the B.D. degree in 1884. Coolidge became a priest in the Protestant Episcopal Church in 1885, working much of the time in Wyoming among the Shoshone and Arapaho. It was here that he served either as an interpreter or informant for the anthropologist James Mooney when Mooney was making his investigation of the Ghost Dance for the Bureau of American Ethnology. At the time of the founding of the SAI, Coolidge was in charge of the Indian Protestant Episcopal mission field for western Oklahoma.

By temperament, Coolidge was a moderate. He was an easy-going man, fair-minded, rather phlegmatic, with a dislike of bombast or extremism. He had a fund of humorous anecdotes with which he larded his speeches. Of all the SAI leaders, his association with the Society was the longest, possibly because his involvement was serious but never very intense. He seems to have taken life as it came with a good deal of equanimity. In the twenties, after the SAI had gone through many bitter struggles, had splintered into several factions, and lost most of

its original leadership, Coolidge became a leader of fraternal Pan-Indianism, thus helping to launch two of the basic types of secular Pan-Indian
movements. He died in 1932.[14]

When the Society of American Indians was founded, there were few
Indian lawyers. Among the best-known of these was Thomas L. Sloan,
one-sixteenth Omaha, from Thurston County, Nebraska. Born in 1863
and brought up on the reservation by his grandmother, Sloan as a lad
of seventeen, together with his friend Hiram Chase, another future SAI
leader, were imprisoned in the agency blockhouse for protesting alleged
cheating by the reservation agent. Sloan claimed that he had attended
Carlisle, but there is no record of his attendance in the school archives.
He did attend Hampton, however, graduating in 1889. Sloan was a
staunch admirer of General Pratt, whom he credited as the inspiration
of "my life, my present career, my ambition in life." [15]

When Sloan returned to the reservation after graduation, he found
that his friend Hiram Chase had graduated from the Cincinnati Law
School and was practicing law. He read law under Chase and was
admitted to the bar. Eventually, the two men formed a partnership.
Sloan worked for several years in government service on the Omaha-
Winnebago reservation and then returned to private law practice, special-
izing in Indian cases. For a time he was an Omaha tribal delegate in
Washington. Chase served as county judge and as county attorney in
Thurston County, Nebraska.

Sloan and Chase were both adherents of the peyote religion which
among the Omaha attracted the younger, better educated, and more
acculturated members of the tribe, and which was active in combating
alcoholism. Sloan had originally been opposed to the religion and had
drawn up a bill to outlaw it in the state of Nebraska. His change of
viewpoint was evidently due to his belief that the cult provided an effective vehicle for Indian accommodation to the dominant society. To Sloan
and Chase, the peyote faith was "the Indian religion," the Indian version
of Christianity. But these men were viewed with deep suspicion by most
of the white missionary and reformer friends of the Society, largely because of their peyotist associations. Considerable hostility to Sloan arose
also from the suspicion that in his activities as a lawyer he exploited
the ignorance of less educated Indians.

Sloan was active in Indian causes in Washington for many years,
eventually serving as president of the Society of American Indians. He

subsequently retired to Los Angeles where in the late thirties he served as an attorney for the American Indian Federation, the only national Indian organization which opposed the Collier New Deal Indian Administration, and one with ties to a number of pro-Nazi and anti-Semitic groups, including the German-American Bund. Sloan died in 1940.[16]

The youngest leader of the Society of American Indians, Henry Roe Cloud, a Winnebago recently graduated from Yale, was only twenty-five when the SAI was founded. Serious and quietly self-assured, he was one of the most balanced and temperate men in the organization. He was firm but not dogmatic in his opinions and had the ability to sympathize with points of view other than his own. The main concern of his life was Indian education, to which he made an outstanding contribution.

Roe Cloud was a "full-blood" Winnebago born in a wigwam on the Winnebago reservation in Nebraska. Early in life he was befriended—perhaps adopted—by the missionaries Dr. and Mrs. Walter Roe, who were among the most respected and dedicated workers in the Indian field. Roe Cloud attended the Indian school at Genoa, Nebraska, and prepared for college at Mt. Hermon, Massachusetts. He graduated from Yale in 1910, the first Indian to do so. He then prepared for the ministry at the Auburn School of Theology from which he was graduated in 1913. Following this he spent a year studying sociology and anthropology at Oberlin. He was an ordained Presbyterian minister with a strong interest in social science.

Roe Cloud was active in tribal as well as in Pan-Indian affairs. In 1912 he was chairman of the official Winnebago delegation to the President of the United States. Perhaps the fact that in his tribe the peyote religion attracted the best-educated and ablest men accounts for his somewhat tolerant and understanding attitude toward it, in contrast to many other SAI leaders. Personally, however, he was strongly opposed to the use of peyote.

Roe Cloud began his educational activities in earnest when he was appointed in 1914 as a member of a federal commission to survey Indian schools. In 1915, with the help of wealthy friends of the Indian, he founded a college preparatory school for Indian boys. Roe Institute, later the American Indian Institute in Wichita, Kansas, offered academic education to Indians at a time when the schools run by the Bureau were vocationally oriented and confined to the lower grades.

Roe Cloud was assisted in running the Institute by his able wife,

Elizabeth Bender Roe Cloud, who was also an SAI member and a life-long Pan-Indian. She came from a prominent Chippewa family, attended Hampton Institute and later the University of Wichita and the University of Kansas. Mrs. Roe Cloud had a distinguished career, holding important positions in the General Federation of Women's Clubs and other women's groups. She was one of the few persons active both in the Society and in this century's second major reform Pan-Indian organization, the National Congress of American Indians, founded in 1945. For several years she directed the NCAI's American Indian Development self-help program.

Henry Roe Cloud's professional activities on behalf of the Indian went beyond educational work. In the twenties he was the only Indian member of the staff of the Brookings Institution which issued the influential Meriam Report, whose findings played an important role in the reform of governmental Indian policy which culminated in the New Deal. In 1933 Roe Cloud became a special representative in the Indian Service and that same year assumed the superintendency of Haskell, Carlisle's successor as a major producer of Pan-Indian leaders.

Roe Cloud was active in a number of organizations, both religious and secular. He was a Rotarian, a Mason, and an Elk. Greatly respected by both Indians and whites, his role in the Society was a moderating one. Although he believed fully in its purposes and was active in its behalf, he did not commit himself to it as passionately as some of the other leaders.[17]

The man most important in the development of the Society of American Indians was, appropriately enough, an anthropologist with a strong historical bent who came from one of the tribes of the Iroquois Confederacy. Arthur C. Parker was a Seneca who served as the editor of the SAI's magazine, its secretary, and eventually, its president. Parker attempted to set the society within the historical tradition of Tecumseh, to provide it with a rationale based on modern social science, and to devise an organizational format like that of white academic and reform organizations. Deeply committed to education, Parker throughout his life emphasized and developed the educational function of the many organizations and institutions with which he was connected, including the SAI. A prolific writer with a clear and vigorous style, his bibliography includes at least 350 titles, of which fourteen are books.

Parker was an extremely complex man. His colleagues thought of him as quiet, dignified, withdrawn, even secretive. Evidently he had the ability and strength to function on many different and conflicting levels at once. In many of the critical areas of his life there was a deep ambiguity, a sense of conflicts controlled but not resolved. Parker was, as William N. Fenton has said, "in the classic Pan-Indian position." [18]

Parker was born in 1881 on the Cattaraugus Reservation at Iroquois, New York. He was three-quarters white and one-quarter Seneca. The Parkers were a distinguished Christian Seneca family very influential in reservation affairs. The surname "was taken by adoption during the French and Indian wars and was not acquired through intermarriage," Parker wrote.[19] On his father's side, Parker was of mixed Iroquois and white ancestry. One of his forebears, so it is said, was a founder of the great Iroquois Confederacy itself. He claimed descent also from Handsome Lake (Skaniadariio), the Seneca Prophet, whose "Code" Parker translated and published, and whose revitalization movement had developed into the Iroquois "pagan" Longhouse religion of Parker's time. His great-uncle was Brigadier General Ely S. Parker, Lewis Henry Morgan's Iroquois colleague and informant, later the first Commissioner of Indian Affairs under President Grant, and until 1966 the only Indian to hold that office. Parker wrote biographies of both of these distinguished relatives, that of the prophet for the *Dictionary of American Biography* and a full-length study of the Brigadier General. Parker's grandfather was for many years Secretary of the Seneca Nation. His paternal grandmother was a white Congregationalist missionary. Parker's father graduated from Fredonia Normal School and worked as a station agent for the New York Central Railroad. Parker was born into a family that believed "the world is large but I will catch it." [20]

But despite his distinguished Iroquois ancestry, Parker was one of the "outside people," those whose fathers are Iroquois but whose mothers are not. For among the Seneca descent is reckoned through the female line, and thus only persons with a Seneca mother are considered Senecas. Parker's mother was white, a member of an old New England family of Scotch and English extraction. For some years she was a teacher on the Cattaraugus and Alleghany Reservations. Before her son reached manhood, however, he became a Seneca through adoption into the Bear Clan and was given a Seneca name, "Gawasowannah," meaning "Big Snowsnake." Parker used his Seneca name often in private correspondence, sometimes with his clan designation. Occasionally it served as his pen name and on a few occasions he coupled his "American" and Seneca names. By his mid-twenties, Parker had been admitted to the Seneca Little Water Society, the most secret and sacred of Iroquois societies, in which he held a sacred medicine bundle. Throughout his life Parker was extremely proud of his Seneca and Iroquois heritage and his descent from early white American stock. But his relationship to both was permeated with ambiguity.

Parker spent most of his childhood on or near the Cattaraugus Reservation, where he developed three of the major interests of his life: the history and culture of the Iroquois, natural history, and collecting. He was deeply influenced by his grandfather, Nicholson Parker, who "could never completely accept civilization's teachings or wholly reject the philosophy of his fathers," as Parker later wrote.

These interests and attitudes of his childhood continued after the family moved to White Plains, New York, when Parker was still in elementary school. He visited Cattaraugus frequently, keeping in close touch with his Seneca relatives. Living near New York City, he soon began to visit the Museum of Natural History, forming associations which played a crucial role in his future. Some of the great men of natural history and anthropology took an interest in the serious and intelligent Indian boy. "These men were never too busy to identify pottery, fossils or bird's eggs brought in by a wondering youth," Parker wrote. "There was a thrilling world back of the scenes. It smelled of spicy dust and moth balls, but mostly mystery and greatness." [21] Thus Parker's love for museums started at an early age. Eventually, he became one of the most important and influential museum men in the country.

By the time Parker graduated from public high school in White Plains in 1897, his future professional interests were already well developed. But evidently he did not yet regard archaeology, anthropology, and museum work as possible vocations for himself. In 1899 he entered Dickinson Seminary in Williamsport, Pennsylvania, to prepare for the ministry.[22]

Little is known about his seminary career, except that he wrote for the literary magazine. For the first two years, he was in "college preparatory," and for the following year in "special work." In 1903 he left without graduating. Evidently he had lost interest in becoming a minister, though he continued his Presbyterian affiliation and activity. It is highly likely that Dickinson seemed boring to a young man whose interests were so much broader than those of his classmates. And Parker was an impatient and ambitious youth who was in a hurry to get on in the world.

Perhaps Parker's decision to leave Dickinson was connected with the stimulating friendships he had formed in New York. While he was still at school, he often visited the home of Harriet Maxwell Converse and her husband Frank, whom Parker affectionately called "Aunt Hattie" and "Uncle Frank." Mrs. Converse was a poet, journalist, commentator on Indian affairs, and an adopted Seneca. Her home was the gathering place for a lively group of Indians and whites, including such men as Joseph Keppler, the cartoonist for *Puck,* and Mark R. Harrington, a young anthropologist. Both became Parker's lifelong friends.

When Parker left Dickinson, he returned to Mrs. Converse's salon and to the Museum of Natural History. During this period he acquired new friends, among which were two young men who, like Harrington, became eminent anthropologists—Frank G. Speck and Alanson Skinner. Skinner remained a close friend for many years, but a coolness later developed between Parker and Speck, probably due in part to their differing views on the relationship of Indians to the larger society.

Through these contacts at the Museum and the salon Parker's formal career as an anthropologist began. In 1900 Parker was appointed an archaelogical assistant at the Museum. In 1903 he and Mark Harrington conducted an archaeological survey for the Peabody Museum at Harvard under the direction of Professor Frederick W. Putnam, who was then connected with both the Peabody Museum and the American Museum of Natural History in New York.

It is not surprising that Parker was attracted to anthropology and that most of his work was done in Iroquois studies. Not only had he been interested in these subjects since boyhood, but anthropology was in the Parker family tradition. Perhaps most important, it offered him a professional participant-observer relationship to the Iroquois which matched in many ways his personal one. But characteristically, Parker early invested his professional career with an ambiguity from which it never completely recovered.

Parker entered anthropology at a time when the academically trained professional was replacing the self-taught anthropologist like Lewis Henry Morgan, J. N. B. Hewitt, and James Mooney. Parker chose to follow the old pattern. The new direction was both led and epitomized by Franz Boas, whose seminars beginning at Columbia in 1896 produced such men as Alfred Kroeber, Robert Lowie, Edward Sapir, Clark Wissler, and Frank G. Speck. Boas was a bitter and unsparing foe of the "cultural evolutionist" school represented by the followers of Lewis Henry Morgan, the founder of systematic Iroquois studies and one of the giants of nineteenth-century anthroplogy. Cultural evolutionists were, in Boas' view, both naive and ethno-centric in their equation of change with progress and in their emphasis on grand designs in the development of human societies.

For a young man starting out in anthropology, Boas was a magnetic figure and Columbia was the place to study. Boas was interested in Parker and encouraged the young Indian to enroll in the university and come up to anthropology through Columbia College. But Parker was either unwilling or unable to "take the long academic route" to the doctorate. Instead he participated in "the congenial and informal tutorials of Professor Putnam at the Museum." [23] Parker's action was characteristic and typical of a pattern which appeared again and again in his life. If he could not get something he wanted, he invented an equivalent. In this case, informal study with Putnam at the Museum was his equivalent of academic training with Boas at the University.

In 1904 Parker secured an appointment as ethnologist with the New York State Library in Albany. Perhaps his decision to leave New York was connected with his marriage in the same year to Beatrice Tahamont, an Abnaki. But when Parker went to Albany, he broke with Boas, incurred the enmity of the most important anthropologist in the country, and abandoned finally any possibility of traveling the academic route in his anthropological career.

In Albany Parker pursued his career vigorously. He took the competitive examination for the new post of archaeologist and "captured the prize" in 1906. Parker envisioned his new post as "a stepping stone to greater things." [24] At the age of twenty-five he—an Indian—had become the first full-time salaried archaeologist in the museum which housed such great Iroquois collections as that of Lewis Henry Morgan, and which was to become the leading institution in Iroquois studies.

Thus Parker's career was flourishing in spite of his failure to win academic credentials. His reputation was further advanced during this period by several important studies. The best was *Iroquois Uses of*

Maize and Other Food Plants, published in 1910. This monograph was probably Parker's equivalent of a doctoral dissertation and shows clearly the influence of Boas' scientific anthropology.

In spite of the recognition which he received, Parker felt keenly his lack of a graduate degree. He handled this problem by inventing suitable equivalents. Upon assuming his position as archaeologist in the state museum, he began signing his mail with the statutory title "State Archeologist," though such was not his appointment. He allowed himself to be addressed as "Dr. Parker." He may have justified this to himself by recalling that ministers were frequently called "Doctor" as a mark of respect; he had once thought of himself as a prospective minister. Perhaps Parker did not fully realize that it was his claiming earned academic credentials rather than his lack of them which made both him and his colleagues so uncomfortable. This unease was reflected in the remark of the eminent anthropologist Edward Sapir to William N. Fenton that he "wished that someone would give Arthur Parker a doctor's degree and make an honest man of him, that he was skating on awfully thin ice." [25]

Not until 1922 did Parker receive an honorary M.S. from the University of Rochester following the publication of his *Archeological History of New York.* For the doctorate he had to wait almost two decades. In 1940 Union College awarded him an honorary doctorate in science, and in 1945 he received the Doctorate of Humane Laws from Keuka College. By that time he had had a long and distinguished career as a museum man. His outstanding work built the Rochester Museum, of which he became director in 1925, from a small and struggling museum to a major institution. Parker's book, *A Manual for History Museums* (1935), quickly became the bible of the museum profession.

Parker's leadership in the Society of American Indians came at the end of his most productive period in anthropology. During the SAI years he was professionally engaged in building the collection of the New York State Museum. During this time he also conceived and created at the museum the famous series of Iroquois still-life groups which are still popular today.

One of Parker's best-known works, *The Code of Handsome Lake, the Seneca Prophet* (1913), produced an interesting review in the *American Anthropologist,* XVII, 1915, by his friend Alanson Skinner. Skinner's observations are relevant to Parker's brand of Pan-Indianism:

"One point that Mr. Parker does not mention is this: Almost since our first contact with the Indians of North America there has been a constant succession of Messianic or revealed religions. . . . That of Tenskwataya and Handsome Lake in the East, and the Dream Dance, Ghost Dance, and Peyote, in the West, being perhaps the best known. . . . The two to make the most lasting, if not the most profound, impressions were the Peyote (miscalled 'mescal') and the Code of Handsome Lake. Both aim at the suppression of drunkenness particularly, both seem to uphold some ancient practices and to condemn others. The Peyote religion differs from the Code of Handsome Lake in many ways, particularly in that it offers, in the Peyote 'button,' a substitute for liquor, which it is said, successfully kills the desire for alcohol. The Peyote teachings have been far more prosperous and popular than the Code of Handsome Lake, having spread like wildfire over many tribes of the West, and are now working eastward and northward, while that of Handsome Lake has always been confined to the Iroquois. Peyote is, however, still a comparatively young religion."

Skinner went on to point out that "it seems improbable that Handsome Lake was not influened by the Shawnee Prophet."

Parker greatly admired Tecumseh and frequently alluded to him as a precursor of the SAI without mentioning his brother, the Shawnee Prophet, thereby emphasizing the political rather than the messianic or religious aspect of Tecumseh's Pan-Indianism. He never seems to have accepted Skinner's view of the wider significance of his relative, Handsome Lake. Parker was strongly against the peyote religion, over which one of the deep divisions of the Society developed. In any case, it would have been extremely difficult for him to bracket Handsome Lake with either Tenskwataya or the peyotists. Parker's attitude toward the Iroquois had a strong flavor of fileo-pietism about it. Perhaps this helps to account for the fact that he took the historical rather than the structural route in anthropology, unlike Morgan and unlike other students of the Iroquois who came after him. An emphasis on systems would have involved seeing the Iroquois in wider comparative perspective and would have moderated their uniqueness. Among the Iroquois in history, Parker seems to have identified strongly with Red Jacket, the friend of the United States, a stance which enabled him to assert at the same time his Iroquois and his American patriotism.

Despite his lack of interest in messianic movements other than Handsome Lake, Parker was himself somewhat of a mystic and a man who loved ritual. He was a devout Mason and wrote a pamphlet on American Indian Masonry, published in 1919 by the Buffalo Consistory. This and other writings on Masonry exercised an important influence on the development of fraternal Pan-Indianism in the twenties. Parker sought to demonstrate that American Indians—the Iroquois and more especially the Senecas—were "inherent" Freemasons. He shared the view of Ely S. Parker, whom Parker in his biography quotes as stating that Masonry would preserve the memory of the Indian "if my race shall disappear from this continent." Not only did Parker like Masonry for its implicit link with the Indian past, but it also offered upward mobility in the white world. It is significant that in his pamphlet on Masonry Parker used both his "American" and his Seneca names.

Parker was a joiner and a doer. When he saw a need, he characteristically wrote about it and joined or founded an organization to do something about it. Parker's organizational and professional interests, both Indian and non-Indian, were closely allied. Among the organizations which he founded and presided over were the Philosophical Society of Albany and the New York State Archaeological Association.

Parker's role in the Society of American Indians was that of peacemaker among the warring factions which beset the Society almost from the beginning. In his dual capacity as editor of the SAI's *Journal* and secretary-treasurer of the organization, he operated very much like a sachem of the Iroquois Confederacy. William Fenton's description of the Iroquois personality fits him well:

"The Iroquois pattern of restraint allows no outward display of emotion in whatever vicissitude; . . . the pattern consciously suppresses anger in interpersonal relations but exalts amiability and mildness. . . . It is of a piece with independence and individualism which gives sanction to no person to order another around and contributes to a lack of real political authority in chiefs. . . . Conscious suppression of deep emotions, even grief, erected a façade of oftentimes feigned haughtiness. Behind the mask were pent-up unrequited affects that were discharged in various forms of retaliation. To counteract open ridicule, rarely direct, and to suppress a direct show of anxiety, a person might treasure a grievance, or resort to covert slander, combined with judicious use of harmless humor which, since it provoked laughter, was a socially sanctioned means of release. . . . In theory the Iroquois chiefs are even-tempered men, impervious to gossip, to whom the public look with confidence. At home they rule by persuasion, consent, and reason without implication of force. Towards subject peoples the old League chiefs, however, did not hesitate to show authority, and their rule was backed by the sanction of war." [26]

Parker's conception of the Society was decidedly Iroquoian. He thought of it as a forum for the expression of varying views within a Pan-Indian framework. Once the framework was agreed on, no substantial alterations in it could be permitted. Iroquoian, too, was his attitude toward Pan-Indian efforts outside the SAI. Several short-lived organizations sprang up during the life of the Society, and toward these Parker was unrelentingly hostile and deeply suspicious, often beyond what seemed to be warranted.

Parker's activities in the Society involved him in personal and professional ambiguities with the Iroquois which he well recognized. Early in the history of the organization he wrote to Rosa B. LaFlesche, a Chippewa who was working in the Society's office:

"Like you I occupy a peculiar position among my own tribe. My father is a citizen and a leader in great movements for patriotic work near N.Y. City. I am a citizen and without any tribal interests. In working for Indian betterment I expect no profit from it. I can only incur criticism, suspicion and unjust remarks. The Senecas of a certain class will think that I am working to make citizens of them and this they have protested for 60 years. They wish to remain as they are, and today the percentage of adult illiteracy in New York among the Indians is greater than in Oklahoma. In a movement of this kind I am injuring myself in a field which must be my life's work." [27]

Whatever difficulties Parker anticipated, he believed that the Society of American Indians should provide an Indian common ground, a vehicle for the expression of a Pan-Indian identity through an organizational format like that of non-Indian reform and academic organizations. Thus, it published a journal, issued proceedings, conducted conferences complete with papers, and met at academic institutions rather than on reservations. Probably these organizational activities, for which Parker was largely responsible, represented also more of those equivalents which he habitually invented. Editing the Society's *Journal* was Parker's equivalent of editing a learned journal. If Parker could not be on the faculty of a university, or if his relationship to academic life was ambiguous, the organization in which he was so influential could meet in an academic setting. In such circumstances Parker could be an Indian ambassador to academia, operating on equal terms from his own base of power.

Under Parker's leadership, the Society of American Indians eschewed anything which savored of the medicine show Indian, though Indian costume might be worn in certain circumstances, provided these were dignified and controlled. Being an Indian was to Parker an inner quality rather than an outward show. He himself dressed quietly and conservatively like the middle-class New Yorker which, in part, he was. A few years before his death, he wrote on the back of a photograph of the Six Nations at Brantford, Ontario, "Dressed in Sioux costume at 500th anniversary of the founding of the League of the Iroquois. Indians to be recognized as such must 'play' Indian!"

Parker's position between and of two worlds, a position in which his birth and upbringing placed him and which his temperament led him to reinforce, caused him considerable personal anguish, but it was also a major source of his strength. For it gave him a vantage point and perspective from which he generated important insights disciplined by a vigorous, searching, and informed intelligence. The equivalents which he created may well have been much more productive than a standard academic career would have been.

At the time of the founding of the Society of American Indians, Parker had high hopes for the Indian future in the terms in which he conceived it. He was firmly committed to the Indian cause and believed that he was participating in a movement of profound historic importance. Although he was younger than most of the other leaders of the movement, being not yet thirty years of age, he dealt with them on equal terms. He threw himself into the work of the Society with all the great enthusiasm and energy of which he was capable. Of all the leaders of the Society, his commitment seems to have been deepest. Perhaps more than any he needed a Pan-Indian organization which would both match and help to resolve the many conflicting levels of his own identifications with the Seneca, the Iroquois, the Indians in general, and the white American middle-class world.[28]

Thus the founders and leaders of the new movement were Indians sufficiently well established in the larger society to have gained recognition far beyond their local communities. They were well educated by the standards of the day. Through their professional activities they participated in such basic institutions as medicine, the law, the church, government, and education. Most of them were also in close touch with tribal life. But there were no chiefs or tribal officials among them. Their relationship to reservation Indians tended to be defined in terms of professional services rendered and, occasionally, of representing the tribe to the outside world in situations where "white" skills or recognition by whites was needed. Thus they occupied a middle ground, marginal both to the tribe and to the dominant society.

To define their position as marginal, however, is not to imply that it was unhonored, useless, or passive. The particular kind of marginality which these men represented was exceedingly useful both to the tribes and to the wider society, and was frequently honored by both. The position of honest broker between two cultures often involves difficult inner conflicts, but it may also bring prestige, recognition, and the satisfaction of service to one's fellow man.

In an ebullient era in which Americans believed ardently in progress, these Indians looked hopefully to a future of expanding opportunities and creative solutions to social problems. All of them had fought hard for what they had won and expected that gains could not be made without pains. They had a good deal of the psychology of the self-made man and very little of the psychology of the passive victim of circumstance. The organization which they formed was born of hope rather than despair. In their view, it was not the last stand of an embattled people but the first great forward thrust of a significant new force in American life.

3

A NEW BEGINNING

The choice of Columbus Day for the opening of the founding conference of the Indian reformers—October 12, 1911—was no doubt symbolic. It was to be a fresh beginning, as if the record of the previous four centuries was now, at last, to take a decisive new direction. This time the red man and the white man were to rediscover each other and to create a relationship based on the best qualities in each. To accomplish this, the new Indian had also to rediscover himself, defining the common ground for Indian unity out of the rich variety of his historical traditions while at the same time showing himself quite competent to participate fully in modern American society.

Not picturesque feathers and warpaint but sober "citizen dress" was the hallmark of the new Indian. The men and women who gathered at Columbus, Ohio, to launch their movement were an eminently respectable-looking group. The official photograph of the conference shows them attired in the fashion of the day, the Indian clergymen among them wearing clerical collars. There was no hint of "Indianness" in their costume with the exception of Nora McFarland from Carlisle who, wearing Indian dress, was seated at the center of the group. Except for their Indian faces, they might have been one more group of earnest middle-class Americans. As Arthur Parker rather ingenuously put it: "The Indians at Columbus were most truly a superior class of men and women and 'above the class of pale invaders,' I heard one visitor say. Headquarters were at the most exclusive hotel and every Indian had money to burn and used it as cultured people would. Columbus was discovered this time by the Indians and the town was surprised." [1]

The conference members were determined to present as favorable an image as possible of the new Indian as high-minded, thoughtful, and capable of running a conference along the most acceptable American lines.

The conference opened, appropriately enough, with an address by Robert G. Valentine, Commissioner of Indian Affairs. Valentine told the group:

"When I first heard of this proposed meeting, *I felt that a new day had come in Indian affairs.* The public opinion of the country as a whole has its attention so largely taken up with other particular big problems that its reaction on Indian affairs is too spasmodic, too local, or too superficial to be a fundamental help in our work.

I hope this organization will continue to broaden its membership till it includes every critic of the Government, every class and shade of opinion. . . . We need an All-Indian public opinion. This meeting is epochal in that it and its successors *can* bring to us that help." [2]

Thus Valentine urged upon the Society two exceedingly difficult tasks—to bring into its ranks representatives of all Indian viewpoints and from them to produce an all-Indian public opinion. Such an achievement would be difficult for any organization, but particularly so for a people as historically disunited as American Indians. These two aims were often to come into conflict during the history of the Society, but at this first conference, the determination for Indian unity kept incipient factionalism under control.

The working sessions of the conference were grouped under three headings which reflected the major concerns of its organizers: industrial problems, educational problems, and legal and political problems. The formal papers and discussions by the members revealed both signficant areas of agreement on basic issues and other areas of potentially conflicting views.

"Industrial problems" were defined broadly, as was the custom of the time. They dealt with the Indian in agriculture, the Indian as a skilled mechanic, and modern homemaking and the Indian woman. All speakers emphasized the necessity of the Indian adapting himself to modern American life and stressed education, whether formal or informal, as a means of doing so.

Perhaps the most interesting paper, "Industrial Organization for the Indian," was given by Laura Cornelius, an Oneida from Wisconsin, whose proposals foreshadowed the New Deal era in Indian affairs. Miss Cornelius proposed that the reservations be transformed into self-governing "industrial villages" combining "the foreign Garden City with the Mormon idea of communistic cooperation," and organized either along Rochdale lines or with a provision prohibiting any individual from obtaining 51 percent of the voting stock. Since various Indian groups were in various stages of evolution, Miss Cornelius argued, the type of industry should be carefully selected to meet local needs and use local skills, and it should be designed to fit into the market economy. Thus Indians would be able to make a life for themselves where they were, returned students would find employment at home, complementing the "Pratt Ideal," and the "natural clannishness" of the Indian would be turned to advantage. By so organizing themselves, Miss Cornelius argued, Indians could select the best aspects of white society, while rejecting the evils of the factory system, of life in a congested city, and of the struggle between capital and labor. "I have not berated white institutions because they are white, but because all economists have agreed already that they are not as economic nor as equitable as they hope to be. Let us take the natural advantages the race already has in its possessions and make for ourselves Gardens and teach the white man that we believe the greatest economy in the world is to be just to all men." [3]

Due to scheduling pressures, most of the papers on industrial problems were not discussed. Evidently Miss Cornelius' ideas did not strike the assemblage as worth pursing for they were scarcely referred to again, only Fayette McKenzie commenting favorably on her paper in a later summary of the convention.[4] Perhaps the members shied away from a plan which envisaged the reservation, even the reservation suitably transformed, as a permanent rather than a transitional stage in Indian development.

The sessions on educational problems were opened with Arthur C. Parker's paper, "The Philosophy of Indian Education," which incorporated ideas from Morgan, Boas, and McKenzie, from social service, and from the melting pot.[5]

"When the white race sought to teach its culture to the Indian, and when the Indian endeavored to acquire it, both races discovered that there was some fundamental difference that prevented immediate success. The fault lay in the chasm that separates one stage of ethnic culture from another, it lay in a difference of mental texture, in a difference of hereditary influence and in a difference of environment. The fault did not lie in a difference in capacity. In the earlier days no one seemed to recognize these facts. The white race thus regarded the Indian as an inferior and accounted for his failures on that score. Here is made a serious mistake, for the relative position of any race as a higher or lower human group is not measured by their present cultural attainment, but by their capacity for advancement when placed in a favorable environment.

Civilization is a matter of evolution. It is not bred overnight or even in a century. It comes to a race by a well-balanced development of its mental and moral capacities. No race may acquire the culture of another until every incident of that other's environment is made theirs."

Parker next dealt with the position of the educated Indian:

"Until the peculiar elements of the culture of the Indian began to disintegrate there could be little hope of the success of an Indian educated in the white man's way among his own people, and so he went back to the blanket. There was no other place to go. . . . Progress cannot be made any faster than the majority or their ruling element are willing to make it. He who is in advance is alone, unprotected and despised. For very existence he falls back into the group, knowing of things beyond, yet not daring to speak. . . . The solitary educated Indian sent back to his own tribe could do little for it. Moreover, he could do little for himself, for he has lost his skill as an Indian, and his knowledge of most things was of little use to his kinsmen.

With the gradual acculturation of the Indian, and with a changed environment wherein he is dependent for his life necessities upon the commodities of the white man, the field of educational effort has become greatly enlarged. There is not now the impassable gulf between the educated Indian and one who has not received such advantages, for in a general way the external surroundings and necessities of each are the same. With the majority of Indian tribes there is not now the suspicion that the educated Indian is a sort of white man who may betray his people. With this changed condition there is a possibility of greater success than formerly."

Parker then praised the Indian schools for their "elaborate system of practical manual training." But, he pointed out, Indian schools need better students. This might be accomplished by raising the standards on the reservations, where the "leveling tendencies" create serious problems. A new program of adult education was also needed.

The vehicle which Parker proposed for accomplishing these ends was the establishment on the reservation of "social betterment stations" under the supervision of responsible bodies reporting to the state or federal government. Social betterment stations would, he argued, supplement the work of the missionaries whose "limitations in their training and prescribed functions in their callings sometimes prescribed their highest usefulness."

Parker seems to have had in mind an Indian version of two important movements of the time, the urban settlement house—or "social settlement," as it was then called—and the rural agricultural experiment station. Both were helping to transform the communities in which they worked through a wide variety of educational efforts and extensive community participation. The reservation social betterment stations would "teach the necessary things of hygiene and industry," Parker suggested, but would have a more fundamental purpose as well. "The first effort of such an undertaking, I would suggest, should be the teaching of independent action, of a pride that would lead to self-help, of a sentiment that would clamor for abolition of special laws that permitted the operation of tribal customs not consistent with modern progress, and of a lively desire to demonstrate the ability of the race to advance."

The Indian, Parker asserted, must assimilate yet retain his Indian individuality.

"To survive at all he must become as other men, a contributing, self-sustaining member of society. This does not mean, necessarily, the loss of individuality, but the asserting of it. The true aim of educational effort should not be to make the Indian a white man, but simply a man normal to his environment. Every Indian who has succeeded is such a person. Hundreds of Indians have attained honorable positions and are as other Americans, yet they retain their individuality as Indians and in reality are the only Indians who can appreciate the true dignity and value of their race, and they alone are able to speak for it. . . .

No nation can afford to permit any person or body of people within it to exist in a condition at variance with the ideals of that nation. Every element perforce must become assimilated. I do not mean by this that the Indian should surrender things and passively allow himself, like clay, to be pressed into a white man's mold. I do not mean, by assimilation, that his love of the great esthetic ideals should be supplanted entirely by commercial greed or that his mind should become sordid with the conventional ideas of white civilization, for it is by no means established that the existing form of civilization is susceptible of no further improvement, nor that the white man as a type is the ultimate model. I do mean, however, that the Indian should accustom himself to the culture that engulfs him and to the force that directs it, that he should become a factor of it, and that once a factor of it he should use his revitalized influence and more advantageous position in asserting and developing the great ideals of his race for the good of the greater race, which means all mankind."

Parker's paper provoked considerable discussion, for it strongly argued a position which attracted many of the conference members yet which also troubled them.[6] Much of the discussion revolved around the idea of the inherent equality of races. Dr. Eastman opened the discussion by lauding the Indians' "capacity and power to attain," a theme expanded on by Judge Chase who stated:

"I think that a great amount of the natural ability of our people lies still dormant because of a lack of proper educational institutions. I know of my own self that my English has been neglected. I have in trying to acquire this English language and progressed faster by comparing my mother tongue with the English than any other way. . . . Some of our Indian people at home, and some of our old people existing today, have just as good intellects as you or I have, who have been to the white schools, but cannot express their feelings to white men. (Applause.) . . . [Chase praised the work of Carlisle, Hampton, and other Indian schools, and added:] We need a higher education, and if we had been left to conduct our own affairs in the matter of progress and civilization, and not had it left to others that are based on false doctrines, I say again, that our people would be on a higher plane of civilization today."

John Oskison, an editor of *Collier's* and a part Cherokee from Oklahoma, argued that whites as well as Indians wanted to preserve the best in the old Indian life.

"We must not run away from here with the idea that we alone appreciate Indian civilization. Some white people with whom I have talked are anxious to get together in some sort of organization that will help us perpetuate all ideas and organizations that are distinctly Indian, and that are worth preserving. It was suggested to me that the beginning might be made in the Puebloes of Mexico and Arizona. . . . The one idea being to keep for the study of Americans in general those things which are distinctive and which represent an element in human progress."

and trade with the white man next door,' and the white man next
r may be the greatest grafter in town, and that Indian who is starting
in business may have had a vision. He may have understood the
aning of the times. . . . I would suggest that we do everything in
power to overcome this prejudice among our own people, in order
urther these new ideas we have been discussing this afternoon."

Charles Daganett, referring to the Indian school as "a necessary evil,"
lined a plan for higher education for Indians in public institutions.
ganett suggested:

We take those whom it would be desirable to give advanced educa-
and let them be provided for in the public institutions . . . in
ch the children of the people of the country are educated. Let the
ians be educated in these, rather than in special Indian institutions.
cost would be a little bit more—perhaps fifty or sixty per cent
re, but I believe the good would be five hundred per cent more. It
easible to have practically the same plan for our advanced Indians,
ng men and women, as is now in operation in behalf of the Philip-
e students in the United States."

Daganett's plan was attacked by Hiram Chase on the ground that
ians who wanted higher education should obtain it through their own
rts. The non-reservation boarding schools deserved continuing sup-
t, Chase believed:

'I for one belong to that class of Indians that wants to stand upon
ir own feet, upon their own exertions. I don't wish this country to
w that they are maintaining me by any gifts or donations. (Ap-
use.) The government is educating our youth in the fundamental
ciples upon which this government stands. They owe it to us as a
ral obligation, not as a legal obligation. It is the good sense of the
ristian people of this country that has elevated—as my friend Sloan
ntioned a while ago—men like General Armstrong and men like
neral Pratt, to influence congressional legislation to bring about
ropriations for such institutions as Hampton and Carlisle. (Ap-
use.) It was not because we have a right to demand it. The education
t our youngsters are getting, as I understand it, is fully upon the
ndard of any of the public schools, and as thorough, as I understand
There is one failing in these institutions. The Indian should be taught
history of this country more, and of his own race, and of his rights as
itizen—civil government is what he needs in his education more than
ything else.

Thus Oskison pointed to those Indian societies which had most successfully retained a strong internal cohesion in the face of outside
pressures.

Indian education and the education of whites about Indians had been
productive and must continue, Sherman Coolidge argued:

"I think we have reached a time when the white people are pretty
well educated to the fact that the Indian can be civilized, can be
Christianized, can be a good man. We must also educate the white
people to be careful not to make too many false statements about the
Indians in general, or about some, perhaps, in particular. I know a
white man among the Arapahoes who said, 'You can't educate the
Arapahoe any more than you can the Ethiopian,' and I have heard
friends of mine say I was educated because I was an Arapahoe smart
enough to take all the studies and carry them through creditably, including the Latin and Greek languages; that the Arapahoe was the
quickest to catch on; he had a quicker intellect than the Sioux and the
Chippewa who were educated in the same schools. I believe that there
are many Chippewas, many Sioux, just as smart as I am! (Laughter.)
. . . Don't let our people neglect their opportunities; let them realize
that they must compete in life's race, and in the conditions of our
American civilization."

Laura Cornelius, who was the product of white schools, was highly
critical of Indian ones, at least as they were presently conducted.
The idea of the "new Indian" was "a fake," she asserted. "*I am not the
new Indian, I am the old Indian adjusted to new conditions,*" she de-
claimed, to the applause of the members. Indian education takes away
"the traditions of the youth on which all other nations build their hopes,
and then you expect to make him a great man," Miss Cornelius stated.

At Carlisle considerable attention was given to some of these traditions, as Angel-Decora Deitz, a Winnebago artist in charge of teaching
native Indian arts at the school, pointed out in the next paper.[7] Mrs.
Deitz discussed what she believed to be the fundamentals of American
Indian art and attacked the corruption of Indian design in the commercial market.

"The American Indian had two art systems, the sign language and a
decorative art, the two mediums of communication which were almost
universal with the whole Indian race. There were the tribal differences,
but the two systems were well founded and well established. . . . The
nature of Indian art is formed on a purely conventional and geometric

basis, and our endeavors [at Carlisle] have been to treat it as a conventional system of designing. . . .

Manufacturers are now employing Indian designs in deteriorated forms. If this system of decoration was better understood by the designers, how much more popular their products would be in the general market. . . .

The Indian in his native dress is a thing of the past, but his art that is inborn shall endure."

In the discussion that followed Mrs. Deitz's paper, Charles Eastman called for a return to "our old distinctive art." Eastman attempted to reconcile his desire for Indian unity with his respect for tribal differences by declaring that Indian art shows

". . . one basic idea, but it has been very badly confused by our teachers who are white people, who have mixed the different characteristics of the different characteristics of the different tribes, so that you cannot tell an Arapahoe from a Sioux now, and cannot tell a Cheyenne from a Crow. (Laughter.) I hope that in this gathering we will come to some realization of these things in the proper sense; that we will take a backward step, if you please, in art, not in the sense of lowering our standard, but returning to the old ideas that are really uplifting, and are a purer basis for character building, and that we can serve and preserve some of these beautiful principles which were the very inspiration of the North American Indian."

Evidently Horton G. Elm, an Oneida from New York, felt that the discussion of Indian art had too much of a flavor of separatism about it:

"I have tried to find out how other races developed, how other races have been civilized, and it seems to me there is a tendency for us to begin where other people are leaving off. . . . We simply appeal to the outward show, and we forget the manhood of the Indian. I would like to see the time come when every Indian with his idealism and force of character would cut through the mere racial life. *I do believe that the solution of our Indian problem is that he must identify himself with every interest and phase of American life.* I do not believe in this separation. I believe that in this century that the unity of the human race is becoming more and more realized. (Applause.) Nobody appreciates more than I do that this matter of Indian art is important, yet at the same time, we as a race cannot all be artists. The Indian race is like any other race if they are subject to the same environment. . . . I want

the Indian to advance on his merits, not on what he h[...] past. The past is dead. We cannot recall it. The past sh[...] museum, and there we can look back and trace our histor[...]

Other members, including Coolidge and Thomas L[...] with pride of Indian art. A consensus was expressed by [...] Henry Roe Cloud, who stated that "it is the sense of the [...] whatever is purely true native Indian art ought by al[...] preserved."

The next topic, "The Indian in the Professions," evok[...] of white and Indian attitudes toward the educated India[...] son concluded his paper on the subject by stating:

"The professions are wide open to us. We have the s[...] steadiness of will to make good in them. Prejudice aga[...] simply does not exist among the people who can make o[...] Always the climb for the top will be going on. The [...] himself for the company of those at the top will go up[...] swiftly and as surely as his white brother. There is no e[...] up—either for the Indian or for the white man. Conscien[...] training, character, hard work—the formula for success[...] sions is simple. I believe the average Indian would rather [...] than his hands. That has been accounted our misfortune[...] be our salvation."

Emma D. Johnson, a Potawatomi teacher from Okl[...] that Indians had to make their way against white prejudic[...]

"I regret very much that *the majority of the people o[...] race of the United States do not recognize the ability o[...] compete with the white race.* . . . So many people see[...] the Indian is like an animal; that he is incapable of thin[...] common impression among the majority of the people; o[...] the more highly educated class, the broad-minded class[...] class which we must work against, and if we can enco[...] and girls not to be afraid of taking up the professions[...] break down this prejudice."

Indian prejudice against the Indian in the professions[...] was described by Henry Roe Cloud:

"Here is an Indian who has started a store, and the In[...] the street says, 'This man is trying to set himself above[...]

This idea that the government is going to give my children money to elevate him into a profession is not the thing we want. If a man becomes capable of it, instinct will tell him what he is good for and he will strive for it. When I left my home in Nebraska to attend the Law School down here in Cincinnati, I went there with a purpose. Before I went there I made a resolution that I was going for hard work, and I did. In two year's time, although not coming through with flying colors, I maintained my own with my class."

Charles Eastman replied:

"In connection with the words of the last speaker, that there has been a great deal of injustice done to our tribes, I wish to say that really no prejudice has existed so far as the American Indian is concerned. I have found that it lies within us to show the paleface what we can do. . . . You must be honorable and moral, and in this way move up and be of service to your neighbor, for it is only the ignorant, the worldly of the worst kind that turn up their noses at our people. There is no prejudice against our people in the professions."

The meeting closed with a motion proposed by Thomas Sloan and unanimously adopted: "Where there are Indian children without common school facilities under the direction and control of the Interior Department, that we request the Indian Office and the Congress of the United States that provision be made to furnish those children with proper school facilities."

The final topic taken up by the conference dealt with legal and political problems, the major speakers being Sloan and Chase. They presented somewhat different interpretations of a fundamental question which had long been debated: whether or not the tribes were in fact independent nations with at least limited sovereignty.

Sloan took the view that the Indians had never actually been considered separate independent nations by the "dominant powers":

"Since the advent of civilized government on this continent, the Indian has been recognized as the subject of the dominant power claiming and holding the territory. While treaties were made with all the solemnity of international law, still the Indian tribes were within the power and jurisdiction of the dominant government. They were not separate nations in the judgment of civilized governments who among themselves made treaties which they respected. The civilized nations made treaties with the Indians as a matter of expediency.

Early in the administration of Indian affairs it became evident that the Indian could not rely upon the statements of the Indian Service officials, the laws made by Congress for their protection, nor the treaties made between them and the United States of America. The rights to hunt, to fish, to make homes and to occupy the lands of their fathers were never held sacred to the Indian, although declared to be by law or treaty. Public policy and political policy joined in the administration to deprive him of his rights." [9]

Sloan then reviewed a number of instances illustrating his major points that enforced Indian dependence on the government-bred habits of subservience and a lack of initiative and that Indian property rights should be determined by the courts rather than by administrative paternalism.

In the discussion that followed, a number of people rose to relate instances of the confusion which existed under the laws then governing Indian affairs. Sherman Coolidge, for example, stated that he did not know if he was an American citizen, echoing a complaint widespread among educated Indians. Arthur C. Parker strongly protested the tribal inheritance system among the Six Nations of New York. Although Parker did not say so, the system excluded him from inherited tribal membership, which was confined to the offspring of Iroquois mothers. Thus the melange of Indian legislation directly affected two of the areas in which educated Indians were most sensitive: their legal rights in the tribe and their legal rights in the larger political order.

Judge Hiram Chase, in an address entitled "The Law and the American Indian in the United States," took a position somewhat different from Sloan's. He argued that the decisions of John Marshall and James Kent were correct, that an Indian tribe occupying its own territory secured by treaties was a state with sovereignty over its domestic affairs. Any other relationship, including the one which now prevailed, was a violation of the U.S. Constitution, Chase concluded.

Acquisition of citizenship should be on a voluntary basis on the immigrant model, he argued. While stating that he did not wish to "alienate those of the white race whose sympathies are with us, because our interests are their interests, our religion should be their religion, and our aspirations should be the same as theirs," Chase attacked the allotment policy as fundamentally wrong. "I do not believe that the salvation of the Indian rests with the division of tribal lands into separate ownership and alienable titles, and the thrusting on him, while he is unprepared to receive them, of the rights and duties of citizenship," the judge asserted.[10]

Chase's attack on the Dawes Act was contained not in the main body of his speech, but in an elaboration that followed. No doubt he hesitated to advance a position which he knew would offend most of the Indians and all of the whites in his audience. But his attack provoked no direct reply. The members preferred to discuss problems arising from the execution of the policy rather than its basic provisions and purposes.

The outcome of the discussion on legal and political problems was a decision, made at a subsequent business meeting, to call for a commission "to codify Indian law and to determine the precise status of every Indian tribe, its rights, duties and obligations and the rights of individuals of Indian blood whose rights are affected by Indian law." [11] Such a bill, calling for a presidential commission of three men, "qualified by legal and sociological training, as well as by acquaintance with Indian affairs and needs," was introduced into the United States House of Representatives by Congressman Charles D. Carter, a Chickasaw of Oklahoma, on January 19, 1912. By focusing on a general plan for a thoroughgoing review of the legal status of Indians, the society sidestepped the specific question of the Dawes Act, and at the same time addressed itself to the vexing problem of tribal and individual rights under the law.

The business session was attended by Indian delegates only. Several important decisions were made. Sloan, Coolidge, and Eastman were nominated for Chairman of the Executive Committee, and Sloan won. Daganett, who had declined to continue as Executive Committee Chairman, was elected secretary-treasurer. The other Executive Committee members elected were: Coolidge, Chase, Parker, Cornelius, and Standing Bear.[12] The committee was directed to "provide a provisional constitution for a representative convention of all the Indians in the country," recommending that each tribe send at least two elected representatives. A provisional statement of purpose was adopted for its guidance.

The name of the new organization was changed from the "American Indian Association" to "The Society of American Indians" in order to remove it from the category of white-run "Indian associations" (such as the Indian Rights Association) and to stamp it unmistakably as an Indian movement.[13] Washington was selected as the headquarters; the executive committee was directed to watch legislation affecting Indian affairs and to cooperate with the Indian Office "for the welfare of the

Indians to the best of their ability." A committee was set up to recommend an emblem for the Society.

The conference designated three classes of membership in the new
Society: actives, Indian associates, and associates. The first two were
to be of "Indian blood" only. Active members were United States
Indians. Indian associates were Indians from other parts of the Ameri-
cas outside the United States, in itself an interesting extension of Indian
identification. Members of either class could hold office, but Indian
associates were allowed to vote only on matters pertaining to their own
tribal interests. Associates were to be persons of "non-Indian blood" interested in Indian welfare. This general pattern of voting and office-hold-
ing Indian members and nonvoting non-Indian associate members has
since characterized most secular Pan-Indian organizations. The vague
sense of fraternity with Indians outside the United States has also
persisted.

The conference at Columbus took place in an atmosphere of strong
white support for the new organization, both local and national. Locally,
the President of Ohio State University, the Mayor of Columbus, and the
Secretary of the Chamber of Commerce addressed the public sessions.
The Indian clergymen attending the conference spoke at churches in the
city. The Improved Order of Red Men gave a luncheon for the delegates. A number of persons active in Indian welfare on a national scale
also attended, including such men as Matthew Sniffen of the IRA; John
Converse, the Grand Sachem of the Improved Order of Red Men;
Robert D. Hall of the YMCA; Thomas C. Moffett, superintendent of
Presbyterian missions; and Bishop Brooke of Oklahoma. Among the
conference events which evoked wide interest were the display of Indian
art and the musical entertainment offered by Carlisle and Hampton
students.

The delegates themselves were by no mean representative of the wide
range of tribes which had originally been envisioned. McKenzie stated
that there were over fifty delegates, of whom a partial list has survived.[14]
Twenty-one of the twenty-seven whose educational history is known
were graduates, returned students, or employees of Carlisle, Hampton, or
both. There can be no question that the most important single influence
at the conference was that of the eastern Indian boarding schools,
especially Carlisle. The bond among Carlisle alumni was so strong that

it provided the major source of Pan-Indian leadership until finally replaced by Haskell Institute.

Certain common ideas and attitudes seem to have been held by most, if not all, of the participants in the conference.

First, Indians were assumed to have something important in common with each other beyond their peculiar relationship to the government. The terms by which members described themselves reveal what these common bonds were believed to be. "The Indian" was the term most frequently employed, followed closely by "the Indian race" or "the race." If membership in the tribe tended to divide Indians, membership in the race united them. It had the added advantage of stressing a broad Indian unity not only in the present but in the past. Active membership in the Society was limited to those of "Indian blood."

In accordance with general usage, race seems to have included both biological and cultural characteristics. When it referred to an Indian identity, it always had positive connotations. Delegates stressed social science evidence of the equality of races and on a few occasions asserted Indian racial superiority.

In addition to "race," "our people" and "the Indian people" were used. Occasionally people and tribe were synonyms. Other terms included "American Indian," "Indian American," and "Amerindian," thus emphasizing an American identity encompassing an Indian one.

Some available terms were conspicuous by their absence. "Culture" was one of these: only Arthur Parker, who was an anthropologist, used it freely. Another was "nation," which, in reference to the tribes, cropped up only in the speeches dealing with the term as it was used in laws and treaties.

Second, a strong sense of pride in being an Indian characterized the attitudes of the conference members. Indians could and should make valuable contributions to the larger society, it was believed. A number of references were made to the virtues of the Indian past. These sometimes became entangled with the sticky question of present tribalism, which the members were at pains to deemphasize.

Third, the influence of evolutionary thinking was very evident. Social evolution was conceived to be a mighty and inexorable force, and it seems clear that the Indians at the conference viewed "the race" as in the process of working itself up the evolutionary ladder. This process, however, was assumed to be at least partially within human control and specifically within Indian control. In spite of the nostalgia expressed for aboriginal life, "evolution" and "progress" tended to be equated.

Fourth, a persistent theme at the conference was the need for Indians to develop self-help, self-reliance, and initiative. Much of the criticism of the Indian Bureau centered on its failure to further these qualities or its outright stifling of such tendencies when they appeared. Yet the conference numbers seemed to have shown little interest in creating new institutions on the reservation designed to nurture Indian self-help, such as Parker's social betterment stations or Cornelius' self-governing industrial villages. Perhaps this indifference reflected their ambivalence toward the reservation, perhaps their lack of personal experience with such pioneering movements, perhaps a preoccupation with their own immediate problems, perhaps a reluctance to commit themselves to enterprises requiring so much time and energy.

Fifth, none of the delegates seems to have thought of himself as a typical member of his particular tribe. By education, occupation, and experience, all seem to have felt some sense of separation from tribal life. For some, racial identification largely replaced tribal identification; for others, racial and tribal identification were complementary.

Sixth, the delegates were extremely sensitive about their relationship to the larger American society and about white attitudes toward them. A strong note of defensiveness ran through discussions on this subject, even when people were asserting that little or no prejudice existed. White middle-class professionals were believed to be the group most free of prejudice. The details of how reservation Indians were to be assimilated into American life, as it was generally assumed that they would eventually be, remained unclear. Most members seemed to assume that the mass of Indians would in due course follow the path they themselves were taking. But whatever the level of integration—whether as professionals, farmers, businessmen, or skilled artisans—the members wanted association with the most respectable elements, as respectability was defined by the larger society. It was generally agreed that the status of the Indian was confused and that a clear definition was needed.

Seventh, all the delegates strongly favored education for Indian children as well as higher education for those willing and able to take advantage of it. So central was the preoccupation with education that it came up at almost every conference discussion no matter what the topic. In view of the many criticisms which were to be directed against the eastern boarding schools in later years, it is interesting to find these schools so warmly praised by so many delegates. This probably reflects the high incidence of graduates as opposed to dropouts among the participants.

Finally, the Indians at the conference seem to have felt that they were creating a movement of historic importance, marking a new day in Indian affairs. They believed themselves to be the advance guard of this movement. Their decision to call an Indian constitutional convention of elected tribal delegates reflected not only the belief that the base of the organization should be broadened, but the faith that a much larger and more representative organization could be erected upon this base which was directly related to the tribes, and that such an organization could have a Pan-Indian character.

Some of the questions which were to be fiercely debated in future Society gatherings can only be glimpsed at this first meeting. While there were many criticisms of the Indian Bureau, no one advocated its immediate abolition. Dr. Carlos Montezuma, chief future spokesman for this position, was not at Columbus, though he had participated in the preliminary discussions. The workings of the Dawes Act were criticized in some detail, but only Hiram Chase attacked the policy of allotment as fundamentally wrong. Religious issues, including the peyote religion, were not debated. Several sessions were opened with an invocation of the Christian God by one or another of the Indian clergymen present.

That at least some of these issues were being discussed privately is indicated by a letter from Arthur Parker to Charles Daganett written several months after the convention:

"There are many who fear Mr. Sloan. Among these are the various missionary workers, for example A. L. Riggs and Thomas C. Moffett of the Presbyterian Church. They are engaged in fighting the Peyote cult and charge Mr. Sloan with sympathy for the so-called mescal eaters. The Word Carrier you have noticed constantly raps Sloan and Standing Bear. These white interests have a large influence over the Indians immediately affected by them. These views represent the Christian and missionary antagonism to Mr. Sloan and thus to the Society. Again you will find, as I did in New York this week, an element who sympathize with the Indian as an Indian of the old ways. The picturesque features of the Indian ceremonies and Indian social system have become idealized with them and they fear that we are trying to 'white-manize' the redskin, that we are, after all a side branch of a missionary league." [15]

Nevertheless, influential white friends of the Indian hailed the new organization and press comment was widespread and favorable. The executive committee of the Indian Rights Association adopted an enthusiastic resolution of greeting shortly after the close of the conference, while Matthew Sniffen of the IRA wrote to Parker, "We feel that your movement is one of the most hopeful signs of the times; that it is the natural outgrowth of the work that has been done by others, such as our Association, the Boston Indian Citizenship Committee, and so on." [16]

The work of the Society of American Indians was well begun. A start had been made in the definition of an Indian common ground and in the building of an organization which would express and epitomize it. Despite numerous differences among the delegates, the desire for unity and the commonality of ideas and experience were strong enough to overcome them, at least for the moment.

One of the basic problems was summarized by Arthur Parker in a letter written shortly after the conference to Rosa B. LaFlesche, the assistant secretary in charge of the new Washington office of the organization: "This Society of ours is the test of the ability of the American Indian race to fraternize with itself and a demonstration that its various divisions have a common ground for sympathetic interest and mutual consolidation. This has long been a question." [17]

Another basic problem—the source and nature of the leadership of the movement—was analysed by Emma Johnson in a letter to Parker shortly after the conference.

"This Society is composed of several types of Indians. 1st Those who were educated and have lived most of their lives in the midst of civilization and are more 'white man' than Indian, in desires, aims and experiences, therefore know very little of the *real* Indians. 2nd Those who were educated with, and have grown up among Indians, but have received higher education in our Public Schools, mingled with educated and business people and know the conditions, needs etc. of several or many tribes on reservations. 3rd Those who are semi educated but have the Indian's interest deep in their hearts, yet are not broad enough to realize the things which are really best for the Indian. Which of these types is most competent for leading our movement during its infancy? We certainly need the best efforts of all three types, but we need them in the places they are best fitted to serve." [18]

Parker agreed in a letter which showed his concept of the organization's leadership and his sense of its historical importance:

"Your analysis of the classes of Indians who are our members is very good. Those who may handle the work of the Society best are those you name in the second class. . . . We are really dealing with a great situation. The things we do as a society are bound to become historic. Those who are best able to lead should be left free to work and not troubled by forces without or within." [19]

The *Proceedings* of the first conference appeared in April, 1912. The Preface contained a long statement designed to set the new organization in historical perspective and identify some of the important questions it faced.

"For a century at least the thinking American Indian has dreamed of an organization for the purpose of the protection and advancement of his race. There have been many successful attempts in the annals of the aboriginal American race to confederate certain tribes and nations, and even parts of different linguistic stocks have united for mutual purposes, but the idea of uniting the entire race or a considerable portion of it within a large geographical area heretofore does not seem to have impressed any Indian as strongly as Tecumseh, the famous Shawnee.

The common ground which every tribe had in Tecumseh's day was the oppression of the red race by the various divisions of the white race that had invaded America. Much of this oppression was due to pure love of conquest and the consequent destruction of a people possessing inadequate means of defense. Much of it was also due to the natural misunderstanding that exists between races of radically different stages of ethnic culture. It was also due largely to the conception on the part of the white race that it had inherently superior rights and was morally justified in oppressing and exterminating the original occupant of America. Some of these ideas unfortunately persist today. . . .

The Indian is no longer a considerable factor, numerically, even though he forms one of the five great races of mankind. Divided into innumerable bands, each speaking a different dialect and still further divided by scores of radically different languages, the Indian hitherto has been unable to act as a unit."

The Preface then discussed the "anomalous and abnormal" position of the Indian in a "false environment inconsistent with the modern conception of enlightened conditions," a man "neither citizen nor foreigner," without a voice in his destiny, subject to government paternalism, and with his real rights obscured by conflicting legislation:

"The thinking Indian, therefore, asks that he be treated as an *American* and that a just opportunity be given whereby the race as a whole may develop and demonstrate its capacity for enlightenment and progress . . . as an American people in America.

It is with these and other similar ideas in mind that the modern Indian who for a long time has been studying the needs of his race sees the necessity for race organization, and holds it as the means by which many of his vexing problems may be solved." [20]

4

RACE AND COUNTRY

The emerging Indian middle class now had an organization of its own—
the Society of American Indians—which in viewpoint and style exemplified the complex relationship of educated Indians both to American
society and to the reservation. Its ideological common denominator was
the postulate of a non-vanishing Indian race as a vital element in a
democratic and progressive nation. Its organizational format closely
resembled that of other American reform organizations.

The founding conference had laid down the Society's broad principles
and charted its general direction. The task of implementation was left to
the executive committee, which moved quickly to put the organization on
a firmer footing. Shortly after the conference, headquarters were opened
in Washington, D.C. Here, on January 25 and 26, 1912, the executive
committee met to write a provisional constitution as directed by the
Columbus conference.[1]

Before voting on the constitution, the committee accepted Charles
Daganett's letter of resignation as secretary-treasurer. His decision probably stemmed from the debate which had arisen in the Society over
whether Indian Service employees should hold "principal offices" in the
organization. This question, which involved attitudes toward the Bureau
and the Indian employees who formed an important part of the SAI's
membership, was to be one of the most hotly debated—and divisive—
issues in the Society's history. By resigning, Daganett made it easier
for the executive committee to sidestep this problem for the moment.
The committee voted to submit the question to the membership, which
was done at the 1912 conference.

To replace Daganett as secretary-treasurer, the committee selected
Arthur C. Parker, thus achieving an acceptable compromise. Parker was

79

a friendly critic of the Bureau and on excellent terms with Daganett, though he could not so readily be accused of subservience to the Bureau. Daganett's place on the executive committee was filled by J. N. B. Hewitt, the distinguished Tuscarora anthropologist, who was on the staff of the Bureau of American Ethnology of the Smithsonian Institution.

A provisional constitution and by-laws of the organization were drawn up and adopted, subject to ratification and amendment by the next convention.[2] This document set forth the following objectives:

"First: To promote and cooperate with all efforts looking to the advancement of the Indian in enlightenment which leave him free, as a man, to develop according to the natural laws of social evolution.

Second: To provide through our open conference, the means for a free discussion on all subjects bearing on the welfare of the race.

Third: To present in a just light a true history of the race, to preserve it records, and emulate its distinguishing virtues.

Fourth: To promote citizenship among Indians and to obtain the rights thereof.

Fifth: To establish a legal department to investigate Indian problems, and to suggest and to obtain remedies.

Sixth: To exercise the right to oppose any movement which may be detrimental to the race.

Seventh: To direct its energies exclusively to general principles and universal interests, and not allow itself to be used for any personal or private interests.

The honor of the race and the good of the country will always be paramount."

Membership classes and requirements were the same as those voted by the 1911 conference, except for the addition of "junior members" (Indians under twenty-one years of age) and "honorary members" (persons of "distinguished attainment"). The provision of both junior and honorary membership was in line with trends in the larger society, the former reflecting the growth of adult-directed youth organizations and the latter the familiar American device of building the prestige of an organization through identification with illustrious persons, or eminence by association. These memberships had a specifically Indian purpose as well. Junior memberships were directed to students seen as the future leaders of the race. Honorary membership also represented a respectable and up-to-date version of the Indian custom of adoption. The definition of Indian-Associates was expanded to include also "persons not on any tribal roll and having less than one-sixteenth Indian blood," thus taking care of supporters whose "Indian blood" was difficult to trace or possibly imaginary. In effect, full active membership was reserved for all Indians of the United States who had more than one-sixteenth "Indian blood" plus Indians on tribal rolls who had less than one-sixteenth "Indian blood."

In addition, the constitution provided that the conference floor was primarily for "active members and for authorized tribal delegates of Indian blood." Others might speak "on motion" or at special sessions. Thus the constitution was designed to protect the organization against a take-over by either whites or nonmembers. This clause contained the only mention in the constitution of "authorized tribal delegates." Membership was clearly to be individual rather than tribal, just as Indians were to enter American society as individuals rather than through tribal bodies.

Officers provided for by the constitution consisted of a president, first vice-president, secretary-treasurer, and a council of three vice-presidents, each of which were to be in charge of a particular division of the Society's work: membership, legislative affairs, and education. Together, this group of officers comprised the executive council.

The membership division was enjoined to obtain and "pass upon candidates and examine carefully into their claim to Indian blood, and refer any questions to the Executive Council." The names of candidates for membership were then to be certified by the annual conference. Evidently the SAI was determined to keep a close eye on who became a member. Henry Roe Cloud was appointed vice-president in charge of membership.

The legislative division's duties were to keep in touch with congressional legislation on Indian affairs and to communicate with any Indians affected by it, as well as to propose or seek to affect legislation, congressional or otherwise, in line with resolutions or actions of the Society. The Honorable Charles Carter, a member of the House of Representatives from Oklahoma and a Chickasaw, was appointed vice-president in charge of legislative affairs.

The education division was to "compile statistics relative to all Indian matters of vital importance," to investigate problems of Indian education and Indian schools, to concern itself with public health, and with agricultural, manual, and academic training for Indians, and to "encourage the conservation of correct Indian history, art and literature, and the just presentation of these subjects to Indian students." The vice-president in charge of this division was Laura M. Cornelius.

These three activities accurately reflected the major concerns of the new Society and emphasized what the members believed they had in common: a commitment to education, to a broad legislative program affecting all Indians, and to building an organizational vehicle for the expression of common interests.

The format and provisions of the SAI constitution were much like those of other American reform organizations of the period. In this legalistic emphasis the council members demonstrated their commitment to the normal organizational procedures of the dominant society.

As soon as the executive committee had adopted the provisional constitution, Chairman Sloan resigned. Although no reason for his resignation is given in the minutes, probably this was another move for amity. Like Daganett, Sloan was a controversial figure distrusted by a number of Society members. To succeed him Sherman Coolidge, who had been runner-up candidate, was elected temporary president. Sloan was thereupon "endorsed" as the first attorney to be employed by the legal aid committee which was also set up at the meeting.

The formation of a legal aid committee to "examine, pass upon or prosecute all Indian claims" raised problems which were long to plague the Society. There were two underlying questions. First, how deeply was the Society to become involved in specific cases, thereby expending time, money, and energy on matters affecting only a small group of Indians and perhaps diluting its Pan-Indian character? This question was left unresolved. Second, Indian legal cases were notorious for the temptation they presented to unscrupulous lawyers to take financial advantage of their clients. How could the Society guard against this? The council attempted to build safeguards by specifying that legal aid was to be administered by "paid attorneys, who should receive no further fee than that paid by the committee. The fee from the Indian clients should not be more than 3 per cent from the tribe and 3 per cent from the individual, never totaling more than 6 per cent."

Following the meeting of the executive council, the new secretary-treasurer, Arthur Parker, set about his duties energetically. In April,

1912, the *Proceedings* of the first conference were published and sent to the membership. By this time, the organization had approximately one hundred active members and an equal number of associate members. The active members included "full-bloods" and "mixed-bloods," professional people, Indian Bureau employees, Carlisle and Hampton graduates and returned students, Christian ministers and peyote practitioners, men and women with English names, and men and women with Indian names. The associates included leaders from the Indian defense organizations, the Lake Mohonk Conferences, professional and business people, ministers, academics, persons who took a deep interest in the "Old Indian" life, two "tribes" of the Improved Order of Red Men, and a DAR chapter. Apparently the only Negro to be an associate member was W. E. B. DuBois, who, like most of the associates, played no role in the actual affairs of the organization.[3]

Parker wrote to many members encouraging them to attract new adherents and emphasizing the SAI's Pan-Indian nature. Parker wrote to Albert Hensley, a leader of the peyote religion in Nebraska who had attended the first conference, urging him to attend the next convention, and to speak there, and telling him that he would receive the printed proceedings of the first meeting very soon. "You will be very proud of the Society then and you will see that we shall be able to do great good by hanging together and working for the good of the whole race. The tribal lines are taken away in this—we are all Indian brothers fighting together for freedom and justice. Will you try and get one or two new members?"[4]

During this time, Parker was formulating an idea for an American Indian Day to be sponsored by the Society, as

"a nation-wide holiday (official or otherwise), devoted to the study or recital of Indian lore. Picnics, parades, Indian games, music, ceremonies, dramas, speeches, orations, recitals of history, exercises by schools, clubs, societies, and out-door lovers—see the scheme? Every red-blooded American, whether just born or just imported from cradle to dotage, would yell long and loud for American Indian Day. The attention which the red man would command would help him immensely. It should be in June—say the 22nd since then nature has brought the year to perfection and it is the moon of the first fruits."[5]

For Parker's brand of Pan-Indianism, such a celebration was ideal. It would involve both whites and Indians. It would provide an opportunity to celebrate the Indian past and to illustrate the Indian present. Indian achievements would be emphasized. And it was an idea thoroughly in the American grain, at home with the American idea of civic celebrations. So suitable was the observance of American Indian Day to the purposes of secular Pan-Indianism that it has continued ever since as a characteristic Pan-Indian activity.

The second annual conference of the Society of American Indians was once again held at Columbus, October 2–7, 1912. The delegates came largely from the Midwest and New York State. Carlisle, Hampton, and Salem Indian schools were represented. The gathering received a warm welcome from the citizens of Columbus for a second time.

The "Conference Sermon" was preached by that renowned exponent of the social gospel, Washington Gladden, then minister of the First Congregational Church of Columbus.[6] Gladden likened the role of the Indian to that of the "remnant" of the Jews, an analogy frequently used in defining the position of the Indian by later critics. It was Gladden's proposition that democracy needed "race" rather than "class" consciousness.

"The assertion of *class interest* or *class rights* is the repudiation of democracy; but race consciousness is a very different matter. When the Creator puts his stamp upon a race and gives it a character of its own, there is something sacred about that distinction. It ought not to make one hostile or unbrotherly to other races, but it is a reason why we should cherish our birthright and seek to bring to their fullness and perfection the qualities thus assembled and consecrated. . . . Each race has its own contribution to make to the sum total of human values, a contribution that can be made by no other."

The duty of the Indian race, Gladden continued, was to make such a contribution. Gladden did not say what this contribution might be specifically, but generally, he argued, the Indian people should serve their race by serving "all the rest of the world." Securing Indian rights would follow, not precede, this process. "Duties first, rights second," Gladden urged. "That is the law of all organizations, physical and social. . . . I think that you are fortunate in setting forth on this enterprise at a time like this, when the old individualistic ethos is so palpably going to pieces; when it is becoming so evident that the only way of life, for a man or a class or a race, is the way of unselfish service. . . . The weaker you are, the more desperate your case is morally, the greater is the need that you should begin at once to help somebody else." With such a purpose, Gladden concluded, "the consciousness of race will be deepened and consecrated."

The theme of "the remnant" was picked up by President Sherman Coolidge in his opening remarks:

"We have heard this morning of the immense possibilities of an earnest few with conscientious purposes and unselfish motives, and that a few can do a colossal work and bring tremendous results. I believe that this is true when we take into consideration that the 'chosen people' have existed century after century as a peculiar people and not lost so many in comparison with the other people of the earth. We find less than 11,000,000 Jews in the world; less than 1,000,000 in the United States; yet they manage to multiply themselves by many times in their power and influence.

Taking that truth and that idea to ourselves, as a small remnant of a race and few in numbers, with our force of character, with our deep patriotism, with our love for native soil, which was our forefathers' from the earliest generations, to re-establish the land of our forefathers in a higher sense as the land and the home of the free. As a part of the population of this great Republic, it seems to me too weak a proposition in this, our country, to relinquish our land and then 'vanish.' "

In order to make themselves felt, Coolidge argued, Indians must curb their "clannish spirit and stand solid and united." [7]

Unity was of course easier to talk about than to achieve, as the reaction to a discussion of the reservation system showed. Most of the delegates believed that the reservation system should go and the Indian Bureau be abolished with it. But differences of opinion arose over when and how this was to be achieved and what relationship the non-reservation Indian should have to the reservation. Young educated Indians returning to the reservation found themselves torn between the old ways and the new, caught in "the social tyranny of the tribe." Asa Hill, a young Mohawk student at Denison University in Ohio, discussed the differences in attitude toward the reservation between the older and younger generation of Indians.[8] "The future of the race," Hill believed, was dependent on the younger generation:

"I was raised under the reservation system and therefore am wholly in sympathy with the old Indians who have been brought up under that system. They have become accustomed to it. They know no other way and do not look at matters as we do. Consequently, they think we are working to their ruin. Such is not the case. I love the old Indians. I am proud of them. Provisions can be made for them if necessary. At present we are looking to the interests of all the tribes in general and the young people in particular."

It was a great mistake, Hill argued, for the government after the Revolution to have allowed the tribes "to maintain their tribal communism and remain distinct. Such worked to their disadvantage in maintaining independence." Present governmental policy was also wrong, Hill believed:

"Such segregation without effective tribal government and with laxness in the enforcement of civil laws, together with the corrupt influence of wicked white people, means moral death to the Indians. . . . The old Indians speak with a laudable pride of the fact that they have the oldest system of government in America. They believe that it should not be involved with the white man's system of government. They feel they must be kept separate. This position is not taken by the more progressive Indians who realize the state of things and who would like to be liberated from such environment, which will never provide the ideals common among an enlightened people."

Hill advanced a program for dealing with this dilemma, consisting of secular education for young people; finding suitable work for Indians and not attempting to make every Indian a farmer, for which calling he might not be suited; improvement in health conditions; strict enforcement of liquor laws; stricter chastity and marriage laws; provisions of superintendents, teachers, and missionaries who will "help the Indians to become *not white men,* but good Indian citizens"; and the eventual adoption of Christianity by Indians. Thus, while condemning the reservation system, Hill took a gradualist position as to its abolition.

Carlos Montezuma was not interested in meliorative measures. The reservation was a prison, he said: "The object of the meeting of the Society of American Indians is not to discuss the insides of our prison walls or the persecutions of the Indians, but the first thing to do is to consider how to beat down those walls, to destroy them all." [9]

Thomas Sloan continued the discussion, feeling that Montezuma "strikes at the root of our trouble." "If there were no reservations, the things about which we complain would not be in existence and the destruction of the reservation is the ultimate object which we are to bring about. We must win for the Indian recognition as part of this great American world. As long as there are reservations over which the government places men who are scheming, selfish and dishonest in control, just so long will the Indian be recognized as other than a free American." [10]

But unlike Montezuma, Sloan was a gradualist and very much interested in attacking the violation of specific Indian rights. Sloan seldom discussed general ideas and large propositions. His speeches at this and other SAI conventions commonly dealt with specific issues and with illustrations of particular injustices to Indians. It was such day-to-day practical matters which really interested him.

Why, asked Joseph Griffis (Tahan), didn't the Indian citizens gathered here help the people on the reservations? "We all decry the reservation system. Why don't these people go back? Why do you trail among the white people and live in the cities? You can go and come when you please and not ask the Indian agent. Why don't you go back and live there and help these people and tell them of the things you have learned?" [11]

These questions provoked a passionate outburst from Carlos Montezuma, who showed himself extremely sensitive to any suggestion that he should live "among his people." Griffis, Montezuma retorted,

"speaks of a question he doesn't know anything about. He doesn't count the cost. I am a practicing physician. . . . Not that I do not revere my race, but I think if I had remained there on the reservation and not have been captured years and years ago, I would not be standing here today defending my race. I will not go back there. . . . I find that the only, the best thing for the good of the Indian is to be thrown on the world and so I would impress upon the Indian race to go out into the world. Better send every Indian away. Get hold and send them to Germany, France, China, Alaska, Cuba, if you please, and then when they *come back* 15 or 20 years from now you will find them strong, a credit to the country, a help and an ornament to this race." [12]

Thomas Sloan, who was a candidate for the position of Indian Commissioner, urged caution on very practical grounds: "The Indian Bureau has grown to be a necessity for a great many employees in the United States government. In case the reservations were destroyed, jobs would have to be sought for by a great many people who are now in the Indian Service, and it seems that that cannot be done at one stroke." [13]

Why, asked Francis LaFlesche, anthropologist of the Bureau of American Ethnology, did Indians always blame the government for their difficulties, rather than themselves? "If the Indian were to go to work, do like the immigrants who came here, build houses such as the German does that comes from Europe, till the soil as the native that comes from Europe, we will have solved this problem that seems so difficult to us and to the white people. It was some such proposition, I think, as this, which General Pratt had in mind when he established the school at Carlisle." If the Indian will go to work, LaFlesche argued, "we will have no need of the reservation system that we complain of so bitterly, we will have no need for a Commissioner of Indian Affairs, no need for the establishment of Indian agencies, no need for Indian agents. We will be our own agents and commissions." [14]

Evidently Montezuma's impassioned speech affected Joseph Griffis while LaFlesche's suggestion for Indian self-help suggested a compromise position to him:

"There are too many large propositions in the world for us to go back to the reservations. Then don't forget that we are Indians. The trouble is that so many of us go out in the world and pass as white men. At schools and colleges they are passing as white men until they try to forget they are a part of the Indian people. . . . I feel certain the advantage of our having a representative of our own people instead of a government agent [and] it might be the function of our own Indian agent to teach the advanced systems of agriculture, so that the Indians could grow and have every advantage. They would listen more gently and earnestly to those of their own people than they would to those who have been instructing them for the money they receive, for the teacher would have at heart those great reasons of sympathy and affection and heredity, instead of the salary they are receiving." [15]

A version of Griffis' suggestion was destined to become a matter of serious controversy in the Society.

An historical review of the growth of the reservation system and a remedy for present ills was given in a paper by Henry Roe Cloud: [16]

"The reservation came into being through the logic of events. It came as much for the protection of the white man as for the Indian. It was to save the white man his life and additional lands which he desired. It was to save a restricted piece of land toward the setting sun for the Indian. The pressure of the incoming white man was such, that even the restricted tracts of land were lost one after the other. . . . It is a lasting testimony to the stamina of a race and a man's sense of outraged justice that a man such as Black Hawk did not leave his domains east of the Mississippi without first raising the war cry. Whatever our attitude as free men toward the reservation may be these days, the Indians of the past looked upon it as a form of captivity. . . . From that day on, all advances the government had made for the social and economic welfare of the Indian have met with general indifference. . . . It is not in a primitive race to discriminate between the good and bad of one regarded as a foe."

From the Indian point of view, reservation conditions of existence conflicted with his economic, social, religious, and moral codes and training, requiring him to "humiliate himself and renounce his manhood," Roe Cloud asserted:

"Our condemnation should not rest too heavily upon the Indian when we consider his inherited traits, customs and environmental conditions. He was asked to reverse in a day the inherited instincts, customs and manner of thought of generations. Human nature will not stand for this, and the Indian *is* human. He was bewildered and confused. . . . Instead of patiently teaching him where necessity might have at this early stage bestirred him to exercise his native strength for livelihood, *the government stepped in and gave him rations."*

This system of "free schools, free transportation, free board and lodging, free clothing" produced "race inertia," Roe Cloud argued. The confining life of the reservation narrowed "the thought-life of the race." The Indian, cut off from any other people, "had no ideas, knew nothing of the ideas and struggle of others." He developed "a conservative spirit." His dependency was made complete by the vast bureaucracy and the bewildering "mesh of laws" which governed him. "Such a position, together with the complex of interests (Indian and white), on the reservation, fosters a division and competitive strife most harmful to progress of any definite kind," Roe Cloud believed. Segregation "blocks the way to progress."

In spite of this unfavorable picture, Roe Cloud continued, Indians should not be "unmindful of the lofty purpose and intent of our guardian, the United States, and the good we have received by the way. . . . We do not forget that our reservation came into vogue when the country was yet in its early stages of development and growth. If mistakes in policy have been made, it was not because this country did not care, but because the people themselves were in an experimental stage with reference to government. From presidents down to the rank and file of men we have always had hosts of friends. . . . They acted according to their idea of the best practical solution of our problem."

Two of the most serious problems facing the Indian were the disrupting of the family—"the social unit of society"—and the question of land titles. Roe Cloud argued that these problems were intimately connected. The unwritten laws and customs governing family relations disintegrated under the reservation system, while federal regulations concerning Indian marriages were largely withdrawn after the passage of the Dawes Act, he pointed out. The disintegration of family relations, Roe Cloud declared, has resulted in "a vast economic problem, the question of inheritance, lands, property, etc." The uncertainty of land titles threatened the "social well-being" of many tribes. Economic conditions on many reservations were so appalling that people died of hunger, cold, and disease.

The remedy, Roe Cloud asserted, "is our own proficiency in the walks of life." If Indians were proficient in solving economic problems, "our status as wards would cease tomorrow." Indians should not depend on the government schools for education, for in a country "of so great and multiplied facilities for schooling, most all our Indians can earn their own education." The whites would help the Indian who strives, and the Indian would prize what cost him something.

"Who is to do this?" Roe Cloud asked:

"We, in this congress are the ones to do it. We must live the doctrines of endeavor and self-support and preach the same continually. It must be an internal movement. The faster the movement spreads, the sooner the shackles of the system will fall off. Situated as we are now, we must inaugurate a publicity campaign to lay the whole crying evil upon the conscience and judgment of men. We must have discussion and concentrated action. . . . [Each] must individually be inspired by the motive God alone gives for our brother man and follow Him who, two thousand years ago, laid down the great, general principles governing all our social and economic problems."

Thus the discussion of the reservation system revealed the ambivalence of most of the members toward it, an ambivalence which would continue to characterize the attitudes of secular Pan-Indians.

Arthur Parker's speech was an attempt to clarify the operations of the SAI as he saw them.[17] First, Parker said, though few in number the Society might legitimately speak for the Indians. People "very seldom as a body speak for themselves. It is the interested few who do," he added. "If there had been such an organization fifty years ago, the interest of the Indians would have been advanced one hundred years today. It is for us to choose and not the white man whether we shall live on the reservation, and it is for us to continue to pursue the paths of wisdom and to improve upon the knowledge we have gained through our association with the ruling race."

Parker next took up the question of why the Society did not hold its conferences on reservations, as Francis LaFlesche had previously suggested. The white race, Parker said, needed to be enlightened. Indian councils held earlier had brought no results. "The newspaper people were not able to understand what they wanted. The people need not only to express themselves, but to get publicity." Meeting in a distant city, Parker continued, developed "one of the great qualities which is inherent and necessary to leadership—that of sacrifice." In addition, "on any one reservation an excess of local delegates could swamp the conference and create an unbalanced condition of organization." Finally, "the Indian does not need to be taught as much as the white race needs to be awakened to our needs."

However, Parker warned, the organization's value did "not lie in our ability to kick. . . . If we would win recognition, when we complain of a wrong we should at the same time offer a sane suggestion for a better condition, if possible, to replace it. . . . I believe in the long run fair play and a square deal will come if the American people are once awakened, but we cannot get a square deal unless we tell them how to give it to us and then work to get it."

Parker was determined that the SAI should be run by Indians. He intervened several times during the conference when it seemed that associates might be given the privileges of active members. When Dennison Wheelock, a Wisconsin Oneida and Carlisle graduate, suggested that the platform committee be composed of three active and three associate members, Parker successfully opposed this on the ground that "if we allow our associate members to formulate our platform, then we are no longer primarily an Indian Society giving vent to Indian ideas." [18] When Judge Hughes of Columbus took the floor to comment on a speech by Thomas Sloan, Parker promptly rose to object, saying that "this is the Indian's Congress, and we are the senators and the delegates entitled to the floor, and we are reserving for ourselves the right to speak. I wish it distinctly understood that this floor and this meeting is for papers on the Indian question by persons of Indian blood." Full opportunity for others to speak would come at the joint active-associate meetings, Parker added. Hughes then apologized, saying that he had not understood the situation, while the abashed Wheelock, who was in the chair, insisted that he was "to blame if anyone was." [19]

On another occasion during the conference, Parker reacted against still a different type of relationship between Indians and associates: adoption of a white as an Indian. After hearing a stirring tribute to General Pratt by Carlos Montezuma, President Coolidge in a burst of enthusiasm moved that "we adopt General Pratt as an Indian." Parker objected, saying, "We do not need to adopt General Pratt as an Indian, as he is already one—none better." After some discussion, the motion was declared out of order.[20]

General Pratt, who was one of a number of whites present at the conference, made a major address in which he developed some of his favorite themes in characteristic old-warrior style.[21] Calling the SAI "the wisest undertaking the Indians have developed to my knowledge," Pratt stated: "This convention would never have been but for the association of your members with the mass of our intelligent citizens, and the practical training in our affairs you received during that association. . . . If the circumstances of your lives have brought such happy results and so entirely removed you from the problem condition, what a pity like circumstances have not been permitted, and even enforced, on all Indians long ago, and thus all differences between the races and the disabilities of your people removed."

Pratt compared the situation of the Indian with three other groups: ancient Hebrews, immigrants to the United States, and Negroes:

"Let me recall to you Joseph, the tribesman who was sold into slavery and became a part of the country in which he was enslaved, its second in authority and its saver, and the saver of his tribe in their greatest crisis. Had Joseph's brethren followed his example and amalgamated with the Egyptians, their hundreds of years of slavery would have been impossible. Their insistence on holding on to racehood has driven them out and made them unwelcome in many lands through all the centuries.

America is full of eminent men, who though foreign-born, have quit their many countries, languages and relatives and crossed the ocean to join hands with and become a very part of us in making the greatest composite people in the history of the world.

Ten millions of aboriginal black men from darkest Africa, forcibly brought to America, scattered into contact and usefulness among our people, have become English-speaking American citizens. Thirty-five negroes for every Indian in our borders. The 'camel' negro swallowed, but the 'gnat' Indians a constant strain.

The 'curse of slavery' taught usefulness, made their lives valuable and gave American citizenship to the negroes, while at the same time, by the same nation, the device of segregation on reservations enforced idleness, which gave disease and death and denied fitness for and withheld citizenship from the Indians."

Pratt then bitterly attacked "the reactionary government policy established eight years ago," which "schemed" to destroy the non-reservation schools and "established a plan of peonage and mass labor for Indians in contact with our lowest labor classes." [22] The General also denounced the Bureau's "encouragement" of Indian participation in wild west shows. These "wicked acts," Pratt declared, were "calculated to promote and prolong bureau domination." They "stayed progress and brought the Indian race more and more into contempt, and made the purposes of this organization [the SAI] far more difficult of accomplishment." The effect of government policy, including education in the government day schools, Pratt argued, had been to keep the Indian tribal. "The autonomy of the tribes which we have nursed for generations has long ago proven to be the enemy of individuality and the promoter of most of the Indian's ills, and is the very entrenchment of bureau control over him." By refusing "the hire" and overcoming "the allurements to tribalism," an Indian may enter fully into American life. "My observation is that when he heartily does this his being an Indian is an advantage. (Prolonged applause.)"

Another deeply felt address by an associate was made by W. E. "Pussyfoot" Johnson.[23] Johnson had served as a special officer for the Indian Service charged with the duty of breaking up the liquor traffic among Indians, and had extended these activities to the suppression of peyote. He attacked Acting Indian Commissioner F. A. Abbott for "undermining" his work against "the liquor evil" and for "treachery" against former Commissioner Robert Valentine. "It was Mr. Abbott who broke up my campaign for protecting the Indians from peyote which had become so successful that its use had been practically annihilated. The headquarters of the peyote cult was in Nebraska and the politicians wanted to control the Indian vote in that state," Johnson charged. Whether or not he knew it, several important leaders of the Nebraska peyote cult were present in his audience.

Johnson concluded this oration with a ringing tribute to "the Indian," from whom whites had much to learn, including "his sense of truthfulness," "sense of logic," "instinct for poetry and art," and above all, "his reverence for sacred things."

On the motion of Carlos Montezuma, Acting Commissioner Abbott, whom Johnson had so bitterly attacked, was also invited to speak. Abbott's remarks were made during a discussion of the government subsidy to Hampton, which had recently been withdrawn by congressional action. Abbott strongly supported the reinstatement of the Hampton subsidy. However, he added that "Indians ought to push for a position to get Indian children into public schools." But Indian school attendance would raise certain problems, Abbott declared with unerring tactlessness: "It has come down to this, a question of your home conditions. I know there is no selfish prejudice, so far as I am able to find it. They claim I took my girl where they can't bring an Indian boy or girl into. Now, the only prejudice in that school, the only reason why the Indian children on the reservation do not attend the public school, is because their home conditions are such that the children are not as clean as the average white children. . . . At some places, the home conditions are better than the home conditions of the white children. Clearly there is no prejudice." [24]

At this, Dennison Wheelock and Frederick E. Parker, Arthur Parker's father, rose to defend Indian cleanliness. Rosa LaFlesche favored public schools for Indian children but cited instances in her own experience in attending public school where the Indian children's habits were not the same as the white children's due to their home environment. Charles Kealer of Wyoming strongly advocated reservation day schools where "Indian children will learn more" from an Indian teacher, and attacked reservation boarding schools as "the curse of the United States." Whereupon Sherman Coolidge defended government boarding schools. Carlos Montezuma declared that in Chicago public schools where there were children from poorer homes, "all attending the school are receiving instructions in personal cleanliness. . . . I see no reason, why our Indian boys and girls are not as quick to learn as these white children are."

Acting Commissioner Abbott then attempted to extricate himself, but succeeded only in compounding the confusion. He favored, he said, the reservation day school rather than the public school because the curriculum included training in domestic science and agriculture, as was not the case in public schools. "It is not because of the uncleanliness of the Indian children, but because the home conditions do not furnish the industrial training, and that is why we want to have the Indian children in the schools where they receive that training that fits them to be with the children of these schools. I want you to understand the office of the Indian Commissioner is open at all times to the Indian Society."

As if to round out the list of white fellow-antagonists who spoke at the conference, Superintendent of Carlisle Moses Friedman delivered an address.[25] Friedman's administration of Carlisle was not viewed with favor by its founder, General Pratt.

Friedman addressed himself to the role of the Society of American Indians whose members constituted "the progressive, highly educated and most successful of the American Indians. . . . What a jolt the old idea, that the various Indian tribes could not be brought together, has received," Friedman asserted. "Even now it is not too early to discern the development of intertribal leaders, and another myth will be exploded when an Indian leads his whole race with all its 250 tribes."

Some in the Society, Friedman said, counsel "harmony and compromise." These people "advocate the most intimate relations between the Society and the Government, and are not adverse to prominent whites having a hand in its affairs." The danger in this view was the possibility of domination by the government or by whites, Friedman believed.

Another group in the SAI who "champion the radical course" wish to "force the hand of the Government and meet the white man with a militant, uncompromising front." Here the danger was of straining the improved relations between Indian and white and arousing opposition "by the claim that the Indians were impatient to control their governmental affairs before they were ready or competent."

Friedman advocated a middle course. The Society should not alienate the white man "because for a solution of the Indian problem red and white must live side by side in mutual respect. But it should be said with even more firmness that the Society of American Indians must never be dominated by white men or controlled by the government. It is an Indian society—of Indians for Indians. The surest way of preventing this calamity is for the Society to keep out of politics."

A number of other whites spoke, including the Reverend W. H. Ketcham of the Catholic Bureau of Missions and the Reverend Robert Hall of the YMCA. Others from the Indian defense organizations also attended.

Professor McKenzie, the "father" of the Society, characteristically kept in the background, speaking only briefly, but working assiduously and quietly to help the organization help itself. As chairman of the associates, he offered in their behalf to assist the organization "in any way without infringing upon the independence which is so characteristic of your organization and so essential to the vitality and usefulness of your Society." [26] In point of fact, the white friends of the Society were divided among themselves and not averse to lending aid to one or another faction within it. But despite arguments among white friends as well as among themselves, the Indian members of the Society were in agreement on a broad range of issues. These views were reflected in the constitution and in the platform of the organization. Both were to affect deeply the future direction of Pan-Indianism.

The provisional constitution was adopted with only minor changes. In the discussion there was no mention of the 1911 conference plan to obtain representatives from each tribe and thus to set up a federated intertribal body. Such a course would probably have had little or no chance of success in any case. The tribes as yet had little basis for unity in culture, language, or common experience. In addition, deep divisions existed within individual tribes. Clearly the SAI was to be the expression of an educated and acculturated elite. Although a few Indians who attended the conference spoke English poorly, they were in a distinct minority. The Society was a town meeting of educated English-speaking Indians rather than a representative confederation of tribes.

The election of officers erupted into an argument which was in the future to become increasingly bitter. Coolidge, Parker, and Sloan were elected without opposition as president, secretary-treasurer, and first vice-president respectively. Each represented somewhat different, though not yet incompatible, tendencies in the Society. None were employees of the Indian Bureau, and all took a gradualist position on it, believing that the Bureau's activities should be phased out over a period of time.

It was the nomination of Charles Daganett as second vice-president on membership which provoked the debate, for Daganett occupied the most senior position held by an Indian in the Bureau.[27] Daganett strongly defended the role of Indian Bureau employees in the Society and their right to participate. "If the Society declares itself against Indians in the Indian Service, it is going to drive a good many Indians from the Society and cause them to lose interest. There are hundreds of progressive honest men and women in that service who are loyal to their race first of all," he asserted.

Daganett's nomination was strongly supported by Thomas L. Sloan. Before the nomination was considered further, a vote was taken on the question of whether employees of the Bureau might be officers of the Society. The result was 30 for, 31 against. At this point Parker intervened, pointing out that "there were sixty votes reported from over 150 who were asked to vote. The vote is not conclusive evidence since it is not complete, some members here not voting; this by way of explanation." Nevertheless, Daganett was then elected second vice-president by a much smaller vote of 16 to 9, and in this case no question was raised as to whether the vote was representative. Obviously the active members were deeply divided on the general question, and Daganett himself did not have much support. Whether Daganett's unpopularity was due to his position in the Bureau, or to other causes, is impossible to determine. The remaining officers chosen were Dennison Wheelock as vice-president on legislation and Laura Cornelius Kellogg as vice-president on education. Both were Oneidas.[28]

The most notable absentee from the convention was Charles Eastman. For some years Eastman, after his initial activity, took little hand in the affairs of the Society, though he remained a member. Evidently he did not believe that the organization was sufficiently representative, for he urged that it be transformed into an elected intertribal body, an Indian congress of official tribal delegates.[29]

The conference adopted a platform which dealt with six major areas: status, the relationship of Indians to the Bureau, the investigation of complaints, education, health, and American Indian Day.[30]

First, the Society demanded a clarification of Indian status through the creation of an Indian Code Commission which would codify Indian law and set forth clearly "the privileges and disabilities of the several classes of Indians in the United States." This closely followed the provisions of a bill previously introduced in the House of Representatives by Congressman Carter. Such a review and clarification of the status of all American Indians was believed basic to any rational Indian policy. Nor would it commit the organization to any specific plan. The confusion in Indian law, and resultant uncertainty about the Indian's status, deeply affected both the personal situation of educated Indians and their efforts to help less acculturated Indians on the reservation.

As for the Indian Bureau, the conference urged that efficient Indians be given more and better jobs in the Indian Service wherever possible, a policy "entirely in accord with the general policy of the Indian department to put the Indian on his feet." In short, the conference favored the expansion of opportunity for educated Indians in the most important single field of their employment. It also recommended that if the Board of Indian Commissioners were retained, there should be "equal representation of Indians" on the board.[31] Finally it demanded that the soon-to-be-appointed commissioner of Indian Affairs be a man "with whom the uplift and promotion of the Indians shall be his first, his last and his only concern." A letter expressing this view was dispatched to the President of the United States, emphasizing the desirability of an appointment on merit without regard to political affiliation and explaining the nonpartisan nature of the Society. Two SAI members, Charles A. Eastman and Thomas L. Sloan, were being widely mentioned as candidates for the office. Neither was endorsed. Members were wary of any possible effort to use the Society as a vehicle for the advancement of particular individuals, however worthy they might be.

With regard to Indian complaints, the conference urged that all investigations of Indian affairs be conducted through public hearings "where affidavits can be submitted by Indians." The president of the Society was authorized to investigate specific allegations of unfair treatment, and the President of the United States was requested to aid in furnishing "the necessary information and facilities to make such investigation." Since it was often difficult for a nongovernmental body to obtain information on specific cases or to investigate freely on reservations, such presidential authorization was felt to be necessary.

More and better education was sought: the provision of school facilities for every Indian child; the standardization of curriculum in Indian schools to conform as closely as possible to that of the states in which they were located; careful examination and selection of teachers; and provision for more advanced teacher training. The boarding versus day-school dispute was not mentioned in the platform, nor was the controversy over Hampton.

By separate resolution the conference urged the government to provide student transportation to and from nonsectarian Indian schools. This resolution grew out of a debate over the future of the Indian department at Hampton arising from the withdrawal of governmental subsidies. Indian students at the Institute had chosen to stay at their own expense. Michael Wolfe, a Hampton student attending the conference, asked the group to support an appropriation for Hampton or at least to press for student transportation. Although the delegates were willing to endorse federal aid for transportation, there was clearly another question which they hesitated to discuss: the education of Indians with Negroes. Both Arthur Parker and Marie Baldwin privately opposed Hampton strongly for this reason and welcomed the termination of congressional financial support.[32] No doubt others felt the same way. The only conference member to discuss the issue directly was Sloan, who was himself a Hampton graduate:

"I was present and spoke before the Indian Committee of the House when the privileges, circumstances, etc., of Hampton were discussed. One member of the committee said in the presence of other members that Hampton school was higher in many ways than any similar white school, that it was modern and up to the highest standards, but he opposed it on account of the mingling of the races. There might be a question of miscegenation, but during the thirty-four years of Indians being at Hampton there has never been a case. The Indian students hold themselves proudly as Indians and I think it is a credit to the Indians that they do."[33]

It was Sloan who moved the resolution asking for government support for the transportation of Indian students, though not for a reinstatement of the Hampton appropriation. In opposing the proposal, Montezuma said, "This is a doubtful question, very doubtful in propriety, yet on account of it being so delicate a question it is very hard to decide publicly, but it is a very easy thing to decide in your own minds." Probably Montezuma was troubled on the one hand by General Pratt's strong support of Hampton, and on the other by private doubts about Indians and Negroes attending school together. Sloan's resolution, which was passed, was a compromise on which most of the delegates could agree.

After calling for the improvement of health conditions in Indian communities and the provision of sanitary facilities, the platform vigorously endorsed American Indian Day and urged its widespread celebration by "schools, colleges, churches, historical and fraternal organizations and by the body of citizens generally." American Indian Day "should be devoted to the true history of the Indian, his true character and habits before the coming of the white man and to his present social and economic condition today." Apparently, American Indian Day was conceived primarily as a means of educating the American public about the Indian. It was not thought of as a celebration to be carried on by the tribes on the reservation.

In retrospect the conference aims seem moderate. They accurately reflected the most important immediate concerns of educated Indians and the application of more general reform interests, such as health and sanitation, to the Indian situation. On potentially explosive issues, the delegates had been able to find a common ground on which to unite. In two other actions the convention sought to further strengthen Indian unity.

One was the selection of an emblem—the American Eagle. The committee on selection had sought for "a badge that should be peculiarly and typically American Indian and be some object held in common by all tribes of all periods of aboriginal history. . . . Almost every known tribe uses the eagle symbol." The specific eagle suggested was one found in a mound in Peoria, Illinois, by Major John Wesley Powell, the founder of the Bureau of American Ethnology.[34]

Originally, the selection committee had identified the copper bird found by Major Powell as a "thunder bird." But J. N. B. Hewitt had criticized this identification strongly, saying that it was "unfortunate that the figure was not identified with the eagle, for this is far more dominant in the arts, adornment and symbolism of the American Indian than the chimerical beast called the Thunder Bird." [35] Hewitt's identification of the symbol as an eagle was accepted and was thereafter frequently used as a Pan-Indian symbol. No doubt its popularity was due not only to its aboriginal origins but also to its similarity to the national emblem.

The other conference action designed to strengthen the Indian common ground was the decision to publish a quarterly journal. Arthur Parker's resolution on the journal stated that its "primary aim" would be "to present and to carry out in a dignified way the objects of the Society and to keep before the public the social, ethical and industrial needs of the Indian and his achievements." The journal would "not engage in religious or political controversies" nor be "subverted to personal interests." It would focus on contemporary Indian affairs rather than on history, and would publish papers presented at the conferences of the Society. A committee on feasibility was appointed with authorization to proceed with publication "if advisable and useful for the Society."[36]

The SAI's second conference thus carried forward the work of the first. The members faced much more directly than they had in the earlier meeting the vexing question of the future of the reservation and of Indian relationships to the Bureau. The moderates were firmly in control, but the organization encompassed fairly comfortably such radicals as Montezuma. The Indian members seemed to be less divided than the white associates. But the fact that the SAI attracted the support of whites who disagreed with each other bespoke the importance attached to the new body by diverse friends of the Indian.

An interesting and significant development at Columbus not reported in the conference proceedings was the formation within the SAI of a semi-secret organization called the "Loyal Order of Tecumseh," in all likelihood on the initiative of Arthur Parker. To Parker, it seems to have represented the secret inner core of the Society. The Order was set up to provide a place where members of less than one-sixteenth Indian "blood" could participate in ritual with men and women of fuller Indian ancestry, uniting them firmly in support of the Society and providing the group with a further source of funds. Apparently it was not designed to influence SAI policy. Each member of the initial council was authorized to swear in "four other members and only four." Four members together could form a local council and swear in other members who would be "mutually agreeable." To the initial council members, Parker wrote:

"It is advisable to ask people of remote Indian ancestry who come into the Society and wish to advance their social standing thereby by registering in the new patriotic order, the Loyal Order of Tecumseh, to which a fee of at least $10.00 will be given. This will enable us to create a sustaining fund with which we may do as seems best. There are, as you probably know, hundreds of people whose Indian blood is from one-sixteenth to one two hundred fifty six who are extremely anxious to have it recognized. Many of these people are well educated and cultured people and would find the $10.00 a comparatively small amount in comparison with the good that would be theirs from wearing our colors." [37]

Another organization in the SAI, the "Descendants of the American Aborigines" which was "especially designed to bring together those of more remote Indian ancestry" was probably invented by Parker at or soon after the Columbus conference. It seems to have been envisioned as a Pan-Indian DAR or SAR. Parker described the two "orders" in this manner: "We believe that to be able to display the colors of this society gives one a better right to boast American descent than even the Cincinnati Order of Washington's time. We antedate everything." [38]

Neither of these organizations seems to have been active. They are of interest chiefly because they reveal important attitudes and foreshadow the fraternal Pan-Indianism of the twenties. At the second SAI conference, they were a minor note in a strongly reform-oriented convention.

The first issue of the *Quarterly Journal,* which had been authorized at Columbus, was published on April 15, 1913. Its masthead carried on one side the Society's emblem, the American Eagle, and on the other a lighted torch. Underneath was the legend, taken from the Society's statement of purposes: "The honor of the race and the good of the country shall be paramount." Arthur C. Parker was the editor-general, while contributing editors included Sherman Coolidge, Henry Roe Cloud, Howard Gansworth, Carlos Montezuma, and John M. Oskison.

The *Journal* marked "a new departure" in "the history of the race," an editorial declared in the first issue:

"There have been, it is true, several periodicals published by Indians and even now there are several printed in the language of some Indian tribe, but these papers have been limited in their appeal. There are many splendid school journals, also, published by the government in the interest of the Indian race or a division of it. Never before has an attempt been made on the part of a national Indian organization to publish a periodical devoted to the interests of the entire race. That heretofore this has not been done, points to reasons beyond the mere conservatism of the race and the drawback of hundreds of native dialects. This venture is therefore more or less an experiment based both upon the faith of the Society in its own integrity and the essential pride of the race in its position as the native race of America." [39]

The role of the Society and the problems confronting it were discussed at some length in several editorials. "The open plan is to develop race leaders," the *Journal* explained. "These leaders will not come from those so merged in American life that they have forgotten they are Indians or from those so 'bound by lack of education' or 'reservation environment' that their vision is narrow, but from the small company of Indians of broad vision." The active members comprised "an all-Indian organization" largely composed of "self-supporting men and women drawn to the Society because of their interest in their race," and including "every shade of Indian opinion." The organization was free from any connection with political bodies, churches, or the government. "Nobody may say what we shall do or say, save the Indian people themselves." [40]

Unity of the Indian race was essential if success was to be achieved, another editorial counseled. "Do not get your Society mixed up with any other Indian brotherhood, council, congress or association. . . . *You can only hurt the Indian race by helping split up its forces.* . . . The worst enemies of the race . . . will do everything to push factions into being."

These warnings referred not only to the historical problem of Indian factionalism, but to several existing short-lived groups, among them "The Brotherhood of North American Indians" and the "Grand Council of American Indians." [41] Both were evidently Pan-Indian organizations. "Remember, success is coming to the Indian only as he can command the respect of the forces of the country that influence his destiny. We have commanded that respect," the editorial concluded. [42] Elsewhere in the issue were listed the names of a number of prominent white and Indian supporters of the Society.

The first issue of the *Quarterly Journal* also contained articles by SAI leaders on various subjects, in keeping with the conception of the magazine as an open forum for Indian opinion. Greatest emphasis was given to education. An essay contest for students in Indian schools, which soon became a yearly venture, was announced on the topic "Why the Indian student should have as good an education as the white student."

Throughout Parker's editorship of the *Journal,* education continued to be a major subject. Parker often commented editorially on the various Indian school journals and frequently printed pieces by Indian students.

The eminent Indian anthropologist J. N. B. Hewitt contributed an article strongly advocating the teaching of "anthropology, or at least, the elements of American Indian ethnology" in Indian schools.[43] Only "a very few persons in every tribe" know "what the characteristic culture of his tribe is and was," Hewitt wrote, adding that, "We have Irish, French, Italian, Swedish, Norwegian, and numerous other organizations formed to perpetuate the traditions and culture of the several people forming these bodies."

If the Society of American Indians was to promote the advancement of the American Indian race, "conserving and developing what is congruous to their attainment and eliminating what is not, . . . the past history and culture of that people must be known," Hewitt declared. "Before the Society can intelligently undertake to carry out the enormous task outlined in its statement of purpose, its membership and its officers must know accurately and succinctly the main and peculiar cultural attainments of the various tribes and stocks of American Indians throughout the entire western hemisphere," he wrote.

Unlike most other Society members, Hewitt believed that heredity was more important than environment:

"It is true that a good environment has its advantages, but the inherited capacity or ability to take advantage of these opportunities to make profitable use of the favorable environment, are by far the most dominating factors in the grade and kind of success attained. In large measure, these cannot be imparted by training and education. On account of these differences in inherited traits or tendencies, abilities or capacities, great differences appear everywhere in all conditions of society. *While great attention is bestowed on improving the environment, none is given to the improvement of the inherited man—the more important factor of the two.*"

Hewitt proposed that the Society sponsor

"a suitable textbook of American Indian ethnology, not prolix or controversial, but summary and comparative in character, which shall fearlessly embody the facts of American Indian culture and achievement in the past, without distortion or unfounded self-adulation. There is nothing in the past of the American Indian race for which we need apologize to any other race. . . . *A live race of human beings should not merely absorb the wisdom and culture placed before it, but it should digest what it absorbs, and should therefore grow to a higher and broader life in all departments of thought and mentation, in its entire psychic expression."*

Thus Hewitt believed that Indian improvement should be predicated on a scientifically based knowledge of the past history of the race. Probably his article was aimed primarily at those who would romanticize the Indian past, thus implying that it was something to be ashamed of.

While most of the *Journal's* articles were by educated Indians, the first issue contained a speech made at the 1912 conference by Joe Mack Ignatius, Chief of the Prairie Band of Pottawatomies of Kansas.[44] Chief Ignatius was a member of the SAI and attended a number of its annual meetings. His views on education and on the position of the Indian differed somewhat from those of most other members and were expressed in quite a different mode from the customary speeches and papers:

"I don't know whether you can understand me. I can't understand white man's talk myself. I am glad I'm not educated. I would forget I was Indian.

I suppose you have heard about those three tribal brothers, Chippewa Indian is oldest; Ottawa is second brother, Pottawatomie is youngest brother. They were three brothers before white man landed in our country and they were told there is something white going to come such a day to take care of red man, so they went to the shore. Sure enough they saw ships coming and that is the reason they did not head them off in the first place because they were told. . . .

[Later, Ignatius related, the whites negotiated for the Indian's land.] White man said, 'I pay you long as sun shines, long as star shines, long as Mississippi runs, long as grass grows.' He raised his right hand when he said this, and that include to all the Indians. . . .

[The government, Ignatius said] is very busy taking care of himself. He wants all the money and all the land. Even he don't look at the white women and white children. There are lots of poor white people in this country. Of course he forgets us Indians entirely.

This white man has disappointed us from the time when he raised his right hand, from generations on to this last day. I don't know what he meant when he pointed out that Indians keep that suggestion and consent in his mind. From generations white man he write piece of paper and he put it away and forget it. . . .

[The three brothers, the Chief continued, didn't know what they were doing when they gave up their land.] They thought just one place four hundred miles square. They didn't know it was going to be United States. The government told us Indians he was going to leave us alone on our reservations, but now he is breaking them up. Whites settle in. Where is that little Indian girl's children going to live. They will be thrown into the ocean. . . .

[Reservation Superintendents don't help Indians, Ignatius asserted.] I think Indian ought to do for himself. His welfare will be better. Of course we will be under the government forever. We ought to have our own Indian employees, Indian teachers, Indian blacksmiths, Indian wagonmakers, Indian clerks, Indian superintendents and Indian inspectors. We don't have to have high, well educated man to be Superintendent, just so he is honest and has a good head. These smart men they know how to do wrong and they know how to get out of it. That is the way these high educated men like [Congressman] Charles Curtis do.

I don't know who we call government. Whoever he is, if he comes through that suggestion and obligation I think will be good friend white man forever, if he don't, we will have to correspond to our other government [political party]. So we don't care who will take, the Democrats or the Republicans. Democrats may do better. . . .

The reason Indian didn't make no complaint he look at white man's children in this country. White said Indian got no sense. Indian got good heart. We don't want to be afraid this government just because he shoots fifteen miles. This common for our other friend. Then you can't tell this White nothing. He has to see something with his own eyes before he can believe anything. An Indian can never wear white man's coat.

I guess this government is getting tired having fun in this country, and enjoyment, the reason he don't go through with his promise."

The *Journal* also carried articles by Fayette McKenzie, who continued to develop his ideas about the relationship of the Indian to American life. In an important article in *The Journal of Race Development* which was reprinted in the *Quarterly Journal,* McKenzie characterized three major views of the Indian centering around the "nature-nurture" controversy and examined their implications for education.[45]

The first view McKenzie characterized as the "pessimistic biological," that of the "old-school Darwinian conqueror who believes that this world belongs to the strong and that the melting of the primitive races before the arms and business spirit of the 'civilized' peoples, is a heaven-decreed justification" of conquest. Such perspective holds that "the fate of the dispossessed is pathetic but inevitable and necessary, if not directly deserved."

The second—"laissez-faire ethnological"—view is more humane, McKenzie asserted. It "would practically waive the question of superiority and inferiority and would merely say the Indian is different. Civilizations are natural products and are of slow development. They are the outcome of internal forces and can not be transferred by external means, no matter how benevolent." Those who hold this view believe that "we should keep our hands off the native race for two reasons," McKenzie wrote. Indians "constitute a museum of great interest and of very great scientific value" which should not be destroyed and, in any case, genuine progress must necessarily come from internal forces.

Both these views are often advocated by Indians, McKenzie maintained, and both "tend to make rapid progress improbable or impossible." Practically speaking, isolation of the Indian is impossible. The Indian can not remain uninfluenced by the white. "The group that would live must adapt itself to the larger culture that surrounds it."

The third viewpoint, held by certain anthropologists and sociologists, provides "the ground upon which an optimistic statesmanship can build a positive and progressive program. We may recognize lack of achievement in the Indian, we may even recognize the natural development of individuals and groups through internal forces, and yet see how progress may be accelerated through outside influences," McKenzie wrote.

"The problem leads to the question: Is culture a product of biology and blood, or one of psychology and tradition? The pessimist and the indifferentist work from the former premise, the optimist from the latter. If the mind, individual or social, is built up out of the environment and experience, we have great possibilities of racial mutation. We have only to effect a considerable change in circumstances (material and psychic) to bring about a corresponding change in ideas and culture."

The fundamental institution for bringing about such a "social mutation" was education, McKenzie believed. Indian schools should be staffed by highly trained teachers and standardized so that Indian children might enter white schools "without loss of grade or time." Indians should also go on to higher education.

The most desirable course, in McKenzie's view, would be to get considerable numbers of Indians into white colleges. But due to the "gap between the Indian school and the white college" and the reluctance of Indians "to enter into daily competition or comparison with a large group of whites," some intermediary step was needed.

McKenzie advocated turning one of the present Indian boarding schools into a combination secondary school and junior college from which some students might go on to white colleges. Such a school would provide training for future Indian teachers. It would pay special attention to "Indian history" and "Indian problems." The school "might be opened to Indians from the countries to the south and so work to international unity as well as start a movement for the welfare of millions of natives still surviving on this continent," he suggested.

McKenzie's interest in starting an Indian junior college was shared by Parker as well. But nothing came of the idea. Had it been implemented successfully, there can be little question that such an institution would have profoundly affected the development of Pan-Indianism, if the role of Carlisle and Haskell in the production of Pan-Indian leaders is any guide.

Besides publishing the *Journal,* the Society engaged in other activities and services for its members. While the Society was primarily a vehicle for educated Indians, many uneducated Indians turned to it seeking help or wishing to discuss problems which troubled them. Many letters came into the Society's office from reservation Indians, often dictated or written by an interpreter. Parker answered them with great care attempting to make his replies clear and understandable. He spent a good deal of time bringing individual cases to the attention of the Bureau and interceding for Indians who could not get "a square deal" and had no one to speak for them.

Another SAI activity was legal assistance. Providing legal aid to Indians at low cost had been one of the first aims of the Society. The legal aid committee attempted to raise money for this purpose from the associates, but proceeds were scanty and it proved impossible to hire prominent lawyers with the modest commissions which could be offered. President Sherman Coolidge therefore appointed Fayette McKenzie and Arthur Parker as a new legal aid committee to draft a bill for the settling of "certain types of cases through the legal machinery of the government." After consulting a number of authorities a bill was drawn up for submission to the next SAI conference. The committee expressed the hope that when and if the bill was passed, the legal aid committee could serve as an advisor to the tribes, provide attorneys at nominal fees, and review contracts between tribes and their attorneys, thus contributing to the solution of one of the most difficult problems faced by Indians— that of getting honest legal advice at fair and reasonable cost.[46]

Thus in its first two years, the Society of American Indians had refined its program and developed the techniques of persuasion which it would use to enlist the active participation of educated and "progressive" Indians, to "advance" the reservation Indians and to present its case to the American people. Its organizational techniques were those of reform movements of the period: holding annual conferences, issuing statements of principles and goals, maintaining a Washington headquarters, advocating remedial legislation, publishing a journal, celebrating a "Day," and offering legal aid and general advice to persons in need. Its leadership, like that of many other reform groups, was drawn from the educated middle class. In principles and program the Society showed its deep commitment to the reform ideals of the time: to a vision which would transcend petty selfish interests, to a belief in progress, to the necessity for self-reliance and self-help, to expanding education as a vehicle for expanding opportunity, to government intervention on behalf of the weak, to uplifting the less fortunate, and to defining American nationality as a continually renewed and reinvigorated product of the best characteristics of the diverse American population. As the Progressive Era neared its crest, its Indian wing in the Society of American Indians was carried forward on the full tide of reform: "The honor of the race and the good of the country will always be paramount."

5

THE CAMPAIGN FOR REFORMS

By the middle of 1913, the Society was flourishing. Its membership had increased to more than two hundred actives. The states with the largest memberships were Oklahoma, Montana, South Dakota, Nebraska, and New York. The center of gravity of the Indian membership was already shifting westward. There were SAI members in most of the non-reservation boarding schools.[1] The associate membership had grown to over four hundred, including men and women from the Indian defense organizations, missionaries and clergymen, anthropologists and other academics, and businessmen. A number of white Indian Bureau employees and persons on the staffs of the Indian schools had also joined.[2] The future of the organization seemed bright.

It was thus in an atmosphere of buoyant hope that the third conference of the Society of American Indians met in Denver, Colorado, October 14–20, 1913. The conference theme—"What the Indian can do for himself, for his race and for his country"—stressed self-reliance, optimism, and patriotism. The conference's location in a western city demonstrated the organization's desire to move closer to Indian country while remaining independent of the reservation.[3]

The conference membership reflected both its broadened base and the weakening of the role of the eastern boarding schools. While still dominated by educated middle-class Indians, a larger minority of reservation Indians participated. Photographs of groups of members taken at the convention show some in Indian dress and others in the modified dress worn on many reservations. The largest group of delegates came from Nebraska, closely followed by Oklahoma. Kansas, South Dakota, and Colorado were well represented, while the number of Indians from the East dropped sharply. As to the tribes, the Sioux were the most numerous. Other tribal members present in some strength included Potawatomi, Omaha, Winnebago, and Arapaho. Altogether, members from twenty-nine tribes attended. While the location of the conference doubtless influenced this shift, the growth of membership west of the Mississippi was also important. No Indians from either Carlisle or Hampton were present. This was probably due not only to distance, but to the fact that affairs at Carlisle were in an uproar over a congressional investigation of financial irregularities, while Hampton students, who were no longer supported by government appropriations, could not afford the trip. But perhaps most important was the fact that the eastern boarding schools, which had educated so many SAI members, had had their day.[4]

The Denver meeting followed closely the original Columbus, Ohio, pattern. The Indians were welcomed by various leaders, including the governor and the mayor; a "mass meeting" for the citizenry was held; there was an evening of "Indian entertainment" featuring both Indian and non-Indian songs; and Indian speakers were supplied to various churches in the city on Sunday.

Most of the speeches at the convention were reiterations of positions taken before. Perhaps the absence of Carlos Montezuma was responsible for the fact that there was no sharp debate over the Indian Bureau. At any rate, in an editorial on the conference, the *Quarterly Journal* reported that:

"Dominating the entire conference was one great thought. It was that of putting aside personal ambitions, opinions, and differences in order that the great purpose of the Society might be achieved. In the Denver conference there was unity of purpose and harmony of action. There was debate, of course, and a clash of individual ideas, but there was nothing to indicate anything but honesty of purpose and a desire to arrive at the truth.

The conference expressed the hope that the American Indian might now reach out and beyond mere tribal consciousness with its limitations, and lay hold of the vital things that the great nation has to give to every man." [5]

The most interesting speeches were made by three very different men: Oliver Lamere, a Winnebago who was a leader of the peyote religion in

Nebraska; Fayette McKenzie, the "father" of the Society; and Chief Henry Roman Nose, a Cheyenne from Oklahoma. Each, from his own perspective, attemped to define the future of the Indian in America.

Lamere, who was descended from French ancestors on his father's side and Winnebago on his mother's, was a Pan-Indian *par excellence.* A former Carlisle student, he was at once a man deeply respectful of the old Winnebago way of life, a leader of the progressive wing of his tribe, an active peyotist in the strongly Christianized Winnebago version of the peyote religion, and a reform Pan-Indian. By trade Lamere was a dairy inspector. Lamere was also a thoughtful amateur anthropologist strongly influenced by Paul Radin, for whom he served as interpreter in the latter's classic study *The Winnebago Tribe.* At the time of the conference, he had recently collaborated with Radin on an article on Winnebago funeral customs for Volume XIII (1911) of the *American Anthropologist.*

Lamere attempted to define a position which would encompass the most positive and usable elements of Indian life and of the larger American society.[6] If absorption into American culture meant either "the complete disappearance of what is worth preserving in our Indian culture," he declared, "I would prefer to stand with the romantic elders of our race and die. But it does not mean that, and the fact that our Society of American Indians could be organized is the best proof that it does not mean that."

Absorption, or "better, *union with the civic life of America,* is inevitable," Lamere asserted. What then, should the Indian take from America?

"Her practical sense, her energy, the courage with which she faces the problems of life and conquers them, considering no work too low or beneath her, . . . [and] ethical ideals, even though she has failed lamentably far from practicing them. . . . In so far as she brings us into contact with the arts and culture of Europe, she can teach us more, much more.

What of the old life must the Indian give up? Certain things like the 'open life' conditions compel us to give up; other things like the part warriors and warfare and superstitious rites played in our life we should be glad to give up."

Indians must seriously consider what means "should be adopted by us here present, and by the individual tribes at home, to keep before the young those elements of Indian life which we wish to incorporate into the future American civilization." This was a most urgent matter, Lamere argued, for "in twenty years it may be too late, and our younger generation will have grown up completely demoralized, having neither absorbed the worthy features of American life nor preserved those of their ancestors."

What features of Indian life would we wish to incorporate into our future culture? "They are a love of nature and an acquaintance with nature which few whites know; ethical and moral teachings fully as high as those of Christianity, and in fact coinciding with them, but which we can more effectually teach, not as borrowed Christian, but as old Indian ideals; and lastly, but not least, Indian art, whether in the form of decoration, sculpture or wood carving, or whether in that of music or literature."

Absorption, Lamere argued, did "not mean that American elements and Indian elements will have become so mixed up and interwined that it will be impossible to separate one from the other. This will unquestionably be the fate of some. But there are other elements that possibly cannot unite with the American culture of today or will be in the future; and these we must try to keep side by side in the American characteristics."

Lamere did not doubt that this was possible. "For as men become more and more enlightened and nations grow larger and larger, and more and more complex, it will be recognized that there can be a union of parts and still a separate individual existence of those parts, and that although they form one distinctive culture, still the parts composing it may likewise retain their distinctive life and ideals," he concluded.

Fayette McKenzie addressed the first part of his speech to whites, the second part to Indians.[7] To the whites, he pleaded for support for a new "comprehensive and comprehending policy carried out with adequate funds by competent men" and based on equal rights, opportunities, justice and efficient administration. The "vanishing policy" had failed, McKenzie asserted, "because its administrators have not believed in it, or have not been big enough to carry it out." The first steps in the development of a new policy should be the codification of Indian law and the opening of the Court of Claims to Indian cases. A "strong active leadership was essential," McKenzie argued, and whites should support the Society of American Indians as "a great experiment of altruism and self-help."

McKenzie then appealed to "my friends, the Indians. Indians have duties to the white race" also. "Just as the white man must believe in the capacity of the Indian, so the Indian must believe in the kindness of the white man. We must both learn to judge a man's ideas, not by the color of his skin, but by the value of the ideas."

"[As members of the Society,] . . . you must in the first place maintain your high ideals [which will be] your chief source of power. . . . [If] anybody is trying to get office or position or influence or lands or money out of the organization, it is losing power. . . . Remember that you want the best for your people, not that you want your friends to have good jobs or high positions. . . . When you are looking after the interests of your children, get the highest trained and best trained leader in the market. Don't sacrifice the education of your children just to give a job to an Indian. Demand highly trained men of good sympathies in all positions affecting Indians, and you will command respect and get what you want. Demand positions for Indians, and you will lose public respect. . . . Let nobody fool you into thinking that you are so different that second best is good enough for you."

Support the Society by active work and appreciate its officers, McKenzie urged. "You probably do not know how completely the Society owes its very existence to the labors of its chief officers," McKenzie asserted. Charles Daganett and Rosa LaFlesche had put "tremendous energy" into the first temporary organization. The Society was signally fortunate in "your first permanent officers," Coolidge and Parker, he asserted, thus neatly bypassing Thomas L. Sloan.

"Remember your own people," McKenzie pleaded:

"Your people are not here. They cannot afford to come. . . . You have seen a vision of the restored nation. Who will open their eyes to the same splendid sight? . . . The man who rises above his race and is willing to forget those less successful than he is not the man he ought to be. You are not that kind; but do you remember that you are the ones who can get closest to your people? . . . You cannot all go back to the reservation, but you can all plan and work for those who are there.

[Finally,] . . . be just and generous to the white man. Be just and stern if you will, to every rascal of every race, but do not think that a rascal necessarily is a white man, or that a white man is necessarily a rascal. . . . [Counsel with whites who have proven that you can trust them. Such a course is not only wise but necessary for] because of the great difference in numbers, you will secure public policies to your advantage only as you can interest the white race in those policies. Any attempt to 'go it alone' is doomed to failure. The Indian in the nation is like a man in society. No man either liveth or dieth to himself. You must let us help you, as we must let you help us. . . . The strong race must remember that responsibility is proportional to power, and the weaker race, as it aspires to power, must remember that duties come when power comes. Each race must remember that rights and duties rise and fall together."

The third speech, by Henry Roman Nose, a highly respected Cheyenne chief, was expressed quite differently.[8] Roman Nose was an "educated Indian" who had attended Hampton, but his facility in English was much poorer than that of SAI leaders who had also attended the eastern boarding schools and probably much more typical of the average students of those schools. Roman Nose told the conference:

"Now, my brothers and sisters, all the different tribes in this town: I am very glad to see you here. It looks like peace. The first thing, you boys and girls, your parents, your people, send you to school. That is the first thing to get knowing about the white man's way, and it is true, and you get knowing, you boys and girls, and you are to be a man and a woman and come back home to your people, and you sure what you know and you sure what you to do work by white man's way, and second thing now same way; you get up here and you try to do best you can for your people, and your people watch you what you do, and your people want you to help them—all tribes in the United States. . . . You talk English. I know something about six or seven years ago, if I remember it or not, I see. Some great friend give it to me in great big book called Bible. Long time ago when I was at Hampton Institute. So that big book tell all how you, my friend, white men, settle Indian problem. I don't see you follow it, but I believe Sermon on the Mount, if you follow it, settles all troubles men have with one another. So I read long ago, 'Therefore all things whatsoever ye would that men should do to you, do ye even so to them, for this is the law and the prophets.' Now you try to follow that rule, everybody, and nobody have trouble."

Henry Roman Nose's speech typified the attitude of many reservation Indians who joined the Society and who themselves were struggling in an unfamiliar language to assert an Indian common bond.

The platform of the Denver conference reiterated and strengthened positions taken in the past and added new ones. To Arthur Parker it represented the best thought of the Society. In later years Parker often referred to the "Denver Platform" as the ideal statement of the organization's goals.[9] The Society urged the passage of two basic pieces of legislation. One had been advocated earlier: the Carter Code Bill to define Indian status. The second was the opening of the United States Court of Claims "to all tribes and bands in the United States" through the passage of the amended Stephens Bill. Treaty-based tribal claims against the government were treated like those of foreign nations; that is, a special act of Congress was required before an Indian claim could be presented to the court. This procedure was highly unsatisfactory: it was time-consuming, expensive, and frustrating.

The platform plank on education was more sweeping than previous ones. "Realizing that the failure of the Indian to keep pace with modern thought is due to the inadequacy and ineffectiveness of Indian education," the conference demanded "the complete reorganization of the Indian school system," to be headed by "a superintendent of education, of the broadest scholastic attainments" with "the authority and power to improve and to standardize the system in its every part."

These demands anticipated by decades important Indian reforms: a major reorganization of the Indian school system in the late twenties, the codification of Indian law in the thirties, and the opening of the Court of Claims to Indians in the forties. But one plank looked backward to the Dawes Act, although the act was not specifically named. For the first time, the platform urged "the prompt division in severalty [among members of a tribe] upon the books of the nation of all funds held in trust by the United States for any and all Indian tribes" and the payment of these individual accounts "at as early a date as wisdom will allow. Annuities and doles foster pauperism and are a curse to any people that intends to develop independence and retain self respect as men." Thus the Society took a transitional position which incorporated some elements of the old "vanishing policy" but pointed to the outlines of new policies to be realized long after the Society had passed out of existence.

In a summary statement, the platform affirmed that:

"We realize that hand in hand with the demand of our rights must go an unwavering desire to take on new responsibility. We call upon our own people to lay hold of the duties that lie before them, to serve not only their own race as the conditions of the day demand, but to serve all mankind. . . . We have no higher end than to see [the race] reach out toward a place where it will become an active, positive, constructive factor, in the life of the great nation, [to regain] a normal place in this country of free men."

In the balloting for officers, Coolidge and Parker were reelected as president and secretary. William J. Kershaw, a Menominee who was an attorney in Milwaukee, Wisconsin, became first vice-president, replacing Thomas L. Sloan. Charles Daganett was elected second vice-president in charge of membership. Congressman Charles Carter was chosen third vice-president (legislation) and Emma Johnson Goulette of Oklahoma, a Potawatomi school teacher, fourth vice-president (education). Henry Roe Cloud continued as chairman of the advisory board. On the whole, the changes in officers do not seem to have had much ideological significance, except for the replacement of Sloan. The vote was largely a vote of confidence in the existing leadership. Fayette McKenzie was reelected chairman of the associates.

A significant change took place at the Denver conference in the relationship between the active and associate members of the Society. The *Journal* reported that "the Society at this conference found itself organized and crystallized firmly enough to open the floor discussions to its entire membership," adding that "no associate ever sought to sway the Society for any individual interest or opinion." [10]

The Denver conference was probably both the most representative and the most amicable in the history of the Society. The members felt a sense of exhilaration and pride that the organization had been able not only to survive, but to grow. For a golden moment, it seemed that the Society had been able to achieve a balance among the differing viewpoints of its members, that it had been able to concur on a realistic program of legislation acceptable to everyone—legislation which would put "the Indian problem" well on the way to solution.

In the flush of enthusiasm following the Denver conference, the executive committee held its winter meeting in Philadelphia in more elaborate fashion than usual. The session included a banquet. The *Quarterly Journal* reported: "The aim of the committee was to hold a banquet that might be regarded as equal to any in polite society. . . . The entire evening affair was a brilliant one. The ladies were tastefully gowned in evening dress, and the gentlemen carefully groomed in full accord with polite society. The red men from farm or college met on an

averred, showing "parallels in some respects to the corresponding stages in Old World history." Knowledge of them, Speck declared, arouses first respect, then admiration, and finally, "the reactionary sentiment, where comparison between these aboriginal cultures and our own modern and complex one, with all its faults and weak places, as well as virtues, leads to the conviction that questions of superiority in culture, represented, of course, by beauty of language, wealth of expression, poetry, music, art, philosophy and industries, is largely a question of reference. It is only when one has come broadmindedly to a point where he can realize the good underlying the spirit of all types of culture that he can be considered rational and impartial in judging race qualities without any egotism. So with the Indians."

Speck then discussed some of the Indian's "native virtues," including bravery, magnanimity, hospitality, racial pride, original moral purity, manly bearing, athletic prowess, knowledge of nature, complex social and rich ceremonial life, love of truth, respect for womankind, art techniques, designs and symbolism, picturesque garb, perfection of devices for hunting, fishing and transportation, and achievements in plant domestication. "This summary," Speck continued, "exaggerated as it may seem to some, is indeed only a partial one." Believing in this "catalogue of native virtues," Speck asked, "are we then to try to emasculate them and educate them out of the institutions and traits that we admire them for? By what authority are we called upon to deculturate them, to transform them completely to the likeness of ourselves? It can only be out of self-pride in our own institutions. . . . Education is not deculturation—education should be constructive, using as a basis the spirit of tribal life which every race should possess for its own strengthening."

Speck then turned to the question of Indian languages which, he stated, "are much more beautiful in grammatical structure than many of the European languages." These "native idioms" should not be permitted to be lost as "the result of misdirected educational enthusiasm." "We might as well prate to the Germans or the French people in America about dropping their own languages in their homes, and then send them to school to re-acquire, by the present imperfect means of teaching languages in our schools, the advantage of their own languages, and even Latin and Greek. Even further, what would it sound like if our spirit of self-conceit were so strong as to induce us to urge the Swiss, the German or Italian peasants to conform to the superiority of our own language and ways?"

The Indian, Speck argued, "could serve himself and his country best by standing upon his own institutions, with, of course, modifications which are unavoidable nowadays, as the exponent of outdoor life, the ideal of the Boy Scouts movement." The Indian should pursue outdoor occupations "with all that goes with these clean, natural pursuits, rather than becoming a sweat-shop, factory or office slave in our already crowded industrial sphere. The Indians should, of course, preferably marry within their own race and raise their children in a full knowledge of their respective dialects, traditions, and institutions."

"[The] native who can neither speak his own language nor answer questions on his own tribal customs . . . is almost an outcast among cultured and intelligent white people because he is holding on to a mere bubble of racial pride. . . . An Indian with no native individuality is to the public at large merely a dark-skinned man who passes casually in the busy work-a-day American world, most unfortunately, as either a mulatto, Japanese, Chinaman, Italian or Syrian. Moreover, the shame of it is that when thoroughly decultured the Indians often lose their pride enough to mingle and marry with their social inferiors among certain classes of negroes or whites.

Now, how can we, in truth and honesty with ourselves and our friends, the Indians, ask them to lower themselves socially to the level of our heterogeneous dark-skinned masses? The thing which holds the Indian up to his Indian-ness, so to speak. . . . The ethnologist never takes his stand against native cultures in which he sees so much good, by contact, that he objects to educating the Indian down to the level of the average community white man."

Speck also strongly condemned tribal disintegration:

"Anybody who advocates total tribal disintegration is manifestly advocating race murder. For the moment that any band of Indians gives up at least some semblance to tribal organization, whether it be an actual tribal government or merely even an incorporated body bearing a tribal name, on a par, for instance, with some fraternal or social orders, at that moment it seals its own fate. As each tribe or group of tribes is a unit, so they must hold out or else fade away. And what tribe wants to fade away? Might as well some powerful foreign nation establish propagandist centers in the States, trying to convert us to some foreign idea that we should dissolve our national feelings for the sake of assimilating its higher life. To be candid, the Indian tribes have as much right to their native patriotism as a British subject has to his or the American to his own. Ought we not to encourage the Indian in his own patriotism as we admire it in ourselves?"

It is necessary, of course, Speck argued, "for the Indians to build themselves up by all possible means in education and adaptation, basing their growth in this land, which is their own, upon their own splendid abilities and judgment, each tribe gradually selecting its own process along the line of least resistance in accordance with, and framed on, its own historic past. Under this process of upbuilding under the tribal sense of pride in lineage and institutions the minor details as to what these may include will take care of themselves automatically, because all evolution in culture, as well as in life, takes care of its own details of adjustment."

Speck's position, with its positive recognition of the values of aboriginal life, its negative judgment of the dominant society, its implied hostility to groups other than the Indian, its invocation of science, and its use of such terms as "emasculation" and "race murder," presaged in many ways a mid-twentieth-century approach to minority problems in American life. Montezuma's viewpoint stemmed essentially from a nineteenth-century base. They were not delivered from the same platform, as it happened, but Parker placed them side by side in the *Quarterly Journal,* no doubt with malice aforethought. Perhaps he enjoyed seeing two positions which he considered extreme thus juxtaposed in the magazine, with instant assimilation being championed by an Indian and indefinite separatism advocated by a white.

The *Journal* continued to deal with the educational issues of special concern to its members. By the spring of 1914, Carlisle, the school so beloved by so many of the SAI members, was under heavy congressional investigation for financial irregularities and poor administration. The *Quarterly Journal* advanced a number of suggestions for reform of the school, the most important of which were athletic deemphasis and upgrading the curriculum. "Industrial training is not enough" the editorial stated. Carlisle should become "something more than a mere eighth-grade grammar school" by raising itself "to the grade of normal and preparatory schools." The student body should be chosen with more care and preference given to "the full-blood Indian student," the "real Indians for whom the school was devised." The "mixed-bloods," raised in "more or less civilized surroundings," did not need federal schools as much. The *Journal* urged the appointment of a superintendent "of high educational ideals" who would command the respect of the students. Carlisle should not be moved to the West, for "the opportunities for work and acquaintance with American life are not excelled elsewhere," and "an outing system is not possible elsewhere as it is at Carlisle." If such reforms could be achieved, the editor felt sure that Carlisle would "advance and become the means of a great change in the intellectual status of the race." [16]

The same issue carried the *Journal's* first story about the peyote religion, summarizing the history of its use and present importance.[17] Aside from the title—"A Drug-Induced Religion"—and its references to "addiction" and "intoxication," there was little in the article for a peyote follower to object to. On the whole the tone was reportorial rather than hortatory, far different from the attitude the Society would take in the future, and far different from a strong editorial attack upon "the curse of alcohol" in the same issue.

"Peyote has had a tremendous influence during the past decade among the Indians west of the Mississippi, [among whom] the peyote religion has spread like wild fire," the *Journal* reported. "More than all the labors of the missionaries, perhaps, it has led to an abandonment of the old native religious customs." The article pointed out that "to govern the use of peyote 'religious societies' are formed. A medley of Christian and native songs are sung to the sound of the peyote rattle. . . . Many Indians claim that peyote is a cure for alcoholism. As a matter of fact, many former drunkards now leave liquor entirely alone using peyote, periodically, instead. Others use both forms of intoxication, neither curing the other."

"It is of interest to know that many intelligent Indians are addicted to peyote eating and that they participate in the peculiar religious ceremonies. White men are often seen with them, but it is to be suspected that these men are low grade and that they have a reason for getting on the right side of the Indians. . . . The peyote cult is well organized in congregations, and even has a fund and 'missionaries' for spreading its doctrines. . . . [Noting that peyote was] an intoxicant producing hallucinations, [the article commented that] missionary societies for some time have been laboring to prevent peyote eating, and now the Indian Bureau will endeavor to suppress its use on the grounds that it falls in the classification of an intoxicant."

The attention of *Journal* readers was called to a "valuable article" in the *Journal of Religious Psychology* by the anthropologist Paul Radin discussing the hostility of the conservative Winnebagos to peyote when it was first introduced by John Rave, and the introduction of Christian ideas and practices into the cult by Albert Hensley, who brought them from Oklahoma. The SAI article did not mention the fact that Hensley was a Society member. "The use of peyote is rapidly extending and its effect upon the mental and physical quality of the children born to its users ought to be noted with interest," the article concluded.

Although the *Journal* continued lively discussions of affairs of importance to educated Indians, the Society as a whole did not prosper. In spite of the enthusiasm generated at the Denver conference, interest in the organization waned during 1914. The reason for this, as the *Journal* saw it, was the failure to spread "the gospel of service" among Indians following the Colorado meeting: "Members seeing every evidence of success accepted it as an assurance that all was well, forgetting themselves to serve. The work fell on a small group, and the membership seemed to feel that no effort was needful on their part. To appeals for funds and for help in other lines the active officers had almost no response." [18]

Those who assembled at the University of Wisconsin at Madison, for the fourth conference, October 6–11, 1914, were "almost in gloom. The question seemed to be, 'Can we solve our problems; and if we do, will it all be worth while?' " Active members at the conference were fewer in number and less widely representative than a year before. The largest delegation came from Wisconsin, followed by Nebraska, Minnesota, and Kansas. Only Angel-Decora Deitz attended from Carlisle. Oliver Lamere, Hiram Chase, and Albert Hensley were on hand, evidently not seriously antagonized by the *Journal* article on peyote.[19] A good deal of time was spent "in deciding questions of organization, policy, and finance," and there was "less discussion of Indian affairs as a whole than in previous years." [20]

The Madison conference reaffirmed the Denver policies with certain additions.[21] First, the conference extended its Pan-Indian interests southward as it affirmed its sympathy "with our blood brothers, the struggling peons of Mexico, and we express our profound sense of gratitude to the President of the United States for his attitude on the Mexican situation. The cause of the Mexican Indian is our cause. They are attempting by force of arms, we by force of public opinion, to obtain equality before the law."

The conference also commended "much of the good that has been accomplished by the present administration of the Indian Bureau" and praised Commissioner Cato Sells, while adding that "great needs" were not yet relieved on the reservations and "great fundamental changes" were necessary in national legislation, policies, and administration. Whether Carlos Montezuma, who was present, openly attacked this resolution cannot be determined from the truncated account printed in the *Journal*. Also adopted was a measure for "assistant secretaries to represent each considerable tribe in each state" who would "serve in a measure as field agents, with the special object of enlisting new members in the Society." This decision, however, does not seem to have been implemented.

To advance its legislative program, the conference sought a meeting with President Wilson to place directly before him a memorial on Indian affairs. Dennison Wheelock was made chairman of the memorial committee which included Professor McKenzie, Henry Roe Cloud, Hiram Chase, and William J. Kershaw, plus the executive committee.

All incumbent officers were reelected, including several who did not attend. Charles Daganett had resigned in September because he believed that his activity on behalf of the Society was being misconstrued as evidence of Indian Bureau domination. Apparently the Society chose to disregard this abdication. Arthur Parker also sat out the Madison conference. He gave his reasons in a letter replying to a congratulatory message at his election:

"It is an honor that I did not anticipate to have been called again to serve in the capacity of general secretary. The work during the past year has been extremely arduous and required practically all of my time. With such heavy responsibility and only slight response and encouragement from the vast body of the membership, I almost felt that my administration was not to the liking of the Society. Mr. Daganett, myself and a few others, including of course, our good president, have shared very largely in the financial responsibilities. My personal feeling was that if matters went entirely smooth and I appeared at Madison with the encouraging report, the Society would not have risen to the crisis as they did do in my absence. It was for the purpose of making our membership feel that each individual had his own responsibilities that I remained away, hoping thereby to test the strength." [22]

As on previous occasions, the associates in attendance consisted of those active in the Indian defense organizations and schools, such as Fayette McKenzie, Caroline Andrus of Hampton, Superintendent Wise and Elmer Lindquist of Haskell, Robert D. Hall of the YWCA, Matthew K. Sniffen of the Indian Rights Association, and Thomas C. Moffett of the Home Missions Council.

The conference obviously tried to rally its forces to rebuild on areas of strength. The projected meeting with President Wilson would, it was hoped, help the legislative program and the work of the legal aid committee, further reinforced by the SAI's kind words for the Bureau. The moderate tone of the platform would commend itself to the white friends of the Indian most active on its behalf. The decision to enlist assistant secretaries would bring the organization closer to the tribes. But friendliness to the Bureau and moderation would inevitably further antagonize those who believed the organization was only a puppet of the Bureau and the missionaries. The appointment of tribal secretaries would inevitably accentuate tribal interests and perhaps antagonize those who so staunchly fought "tribalism." The Madison conference offered a little something for everyone, but probably not quite enough for anybody.

A few days after the end of the Madison meeting, several SAI members—including Marie L. Baldwin, Henry Roe Cloud, Charles Daganett, John Oskison, and Arthur Parker—made a point of attending the Lake Mohonk conference. One of the leading topics of discussion at Lake Mohonk was "the peyote menace." Only a year before peyote had not been mentioned; yet by 1914 it was considered so serious a problem that the conference recommended "that the Federal prohibition of intoxicating liquors be extended to include this dangerous drug." [23]

Parker and other SAI leaders were certainly well aware both of the antipathy to peyote prevailing among many of the white associates and also of the extent to which other SAI members were adherents of the peyote faith. For the moment the *Journal* avoided the controversy and decided not to carry the text of the Lake Mohonk platform, thus reversing its policy of the previous year. Instead a short report of the conference appeared which merely listed the names of active and associate members who had attended. "Nearly all of our members [present] associate and active, took part in the Mohonk discussions," the *Journal* reported. "It must be said however that our associates represented primarily other interests than ours as a Society." [24]

The meeting with President Wilson was duly scheduled for December 10, 1914. The memorial itself was drawn up in the office of Gabe Parker (Choctaw), register of the treasury and a member of the SAI advisory board. The memorial stressed the Society's two major legislative demands: appointment of a code commission and bestowal of jurisdiction over all Indian claims to the Court of Claims. "We believe that you feel, with the progressive members of your race, that it is anomalous permanently to conserve within the nation groups of people whose civic condition by legislation is different from the normal standard of American life," the memorial stated.[25]

The delegation which waited on the President consisted of almost the entire SAI leadership except Sloan, Montezuma, and Eastman, as well as a number of white friends of the Indian.[26] The President "was instantly impressed" when he heard the memorial—but he made no commitment. The event, described as a "new beginning in Indian progress" which "proclaimed a new day for the red race" was described enthusiastically and in detail in the *Quarterly Journal*.[27] It was followed by a banquet, at which the toastmaster was Congressman Charles Carter and the principal speaker Cato Sells, Wilson's Indian commissioner.

The memorialization of the President was a splendid success in bringing together a prominent group of Indians and whites under the SAI aegis, in demonstrating "the Society's unity and purpose," and in "establishing a deeper confidence of the public in the capacity of red men to reach out for higher things," the *Journal* reported. In fact it succeeded in everything but its central purpose: the enactment of fundamental remedial Indian legislation. On this it seems to have had no effect whatsoever.

Nor was the plan for an American Indian Day faring well, despite the Society's diligent campaign in the pages of the *Journal*. The idea itself received considerable publicity, however, through the efforts of Red Fox James, an SAI member, described in the *Journal* as "a part-blood Indian." James, who was later to develop a brand of romantic fraternal Pan-Indianism different from that of the founders of the Society, and who would finally inherit its remnants, was a rancher from Montana. By riding his pony to various state capitals, he was able to collect numerous gubernatorial endorsements for American Indian Day. His trip was climaxed by a meeting with President Wilson, to which he was escorted by Washington Boy Scout troops. His visit to the President was "backed by the officers of the Society," so the *Journal* reported. But in reality James acted on his own and the Society made the best of it.[28]

The emphasis on educational reform in the *Quarterly Journal* continued during 1915. The subject of the annual essay contest open to students at Indian schools was "The Value and Necessity of Higher Academic Training for the Indian Student." In the prize essay, Lucy E. Hunter, a Winnebago studying at Hampton, revealed some of the problems which Indian students faced when they returned to the reservation.[29] Better educated than most of the tribe, they were thereby called on to perform all sorts of services, from interpreting to helping with government claims; but their education was too narrow to enable them to perform these services competently.

Indian students needed higher academic training, Miss Hunter believed, not only to help their fellow Indians on the reservation, but for other reasons as well. All occupations, whether in the professions, business, farming or trade, increasingly demanded a trained mind as well as trained hands. Indians must also share a common language if they were to work together for their mutual benefit and for the good of the country; in fact, the lack of a common language prevented them from "pulling together as a people." The Indian race required the trained leadership of men of superior education, cultivation, and strength of character. All Indians must be prepared for the new problems and opportunities which would arise when they were thrown on their own without government aid, a prospect already in sight. In summary, the essay concluded, the Indian would not be able to obtain or protect his rights or to participate fully in the national life until he was educated.

In the following issue, Arthur Parker presented an extended program for the reform of Indian industrial and vocational education, set within the context of major contemporary trends in American educational thought.[30] We need a "new view of the purpose of education," he wrote. "It should no longer be thought that a schooling will lead a man away from the burdens of actual labor. It must be recognized that the ditch-digger is as important a man as the law clerk, and entitled to as much respect and consideration."

Classical education, as practiced in Greece, and passed on to Rome and Europe, taught "contempt for industry." But today "there is an awakening," as men begin to see "that there is as much 'culture' to be derived from the pursuit of agriculture as from the absorption of Aristotle, if not more." Industry was the "real factor that brought civilization to its present height," yet industry had been neglected by the schools.

Indian vocational schools, like other schools, should enlist the interest and cooperation of the communities they serve: "the labor unions, the granges, the women's organizations, the chambers of commerce, the railroad companies and manufacturers." They should begin to take stock of themselves, making a survey of assets and liabilities: the number of graduates; the occupations chosen by those leaving school; the reasons why pupils left school; and the value of school training.

Pupil training should include both vocational preparation for specific occupations and broader training as well. Vocational education should be geared to the leading occupations in the area and should include practical work with which broader training should be incorporated. The Indian student should learn English, industrial geography, mathematics, drawing, the elementary sciences, history, elementary civics, and other related subjects "both to the extent valuable to the student's future trade" and to give him "a hunger for greater information along these lines." School conditions should be like those of the home, farm, shop, or business for which pupils are preparing. Skilled workmanship and good citizenship should be emphasized, and training should be of such high quality that graduates will be in demand.

Indian vocational schools required personnel of high professional competence fitted for their jobs by education and temperament. The nonvocational teacher should have enough knowledge of the industrial world so as to be able to relate the subjects taught to the vocational training of the student, and to his role as citizen, Parker wrote.

Graduates of "the various noted schools of civics and philanthropy" should be asked to prepare teachers for the Indian Service. The cooperation of schools training teachers for vocational education should be secured. The leaders of the Student Volunteer Movement should be apprised of the need for "a high quality of education and refined men and women" for both the teaching and clerical force of the Service. Teachers in Indian schools should have a regular course of reading, in which they met periodically with the Superintendent for discussion.

Pupils who desired and possessed the capacity for a more liberal education should be both encouraged and enabled to achieve it. "There must be a percentage of men and women in every generation and among every group of people, Indians not excluded, who will make themselves acquainted with all the arts and sciences they can master. . . . Highly educated men are a necessity and are the only guarantee of civilization. The mere industrial worker will ruin the world and bring it down to the depths of savagery."

The Indian race must have leaders, "men and women of its own blood who are able by reasons of their highly-cultivated intellects to understand the plight of their race, the remedies that must be applied, the ultimate destiny of their race, and how to lead it to its inheritance," Parker wrote.

Parker's program was an Indian version of many of the most important educational reform ideas of the Progressive Era, encompassing a broadened view of the mission of the school, of the potentiality of the student, of the relationship of school to community, and of the purpose and clientele of high education, all undergirded by a sturdy commitment to a modern democratic and industrial society.

His attack on classical education and his celebration of the dignity of labor were thoroughly in accord with advanced educational thought, which included the conviction that classical education had a narrow class bias and basis, reflected the needs of an aristocratic rather than a democratic social and political order, and ignored the immense forces of science and industry that were transforming American life. Parker's definition of "culture" in education was consistent not only with his anthropological views, but also with the reformers' attack on an elitist conception of culture which they believed dominated much of the educational enterprise. Such a narrow conception, the reformers argued, had resulted in the teaching of a few literary and historical works, with the major emphasis on the mastery of Latin and Greek, and in the virtual exclusion of science, civics, and other subjects relevant to a modern society. The ancient breach between culture and vocation must be healed, the reformers insisted. This required a "reconstitution of culture," a process which necessarily involved reconstituting the curriculum to stress commonalities rather than class and association rather than exclusiveness.

Parker was like many progressive reformers in his view that training for a vocation must be infused with a general awakening of intellectual capacities. His proposed curriculum for Indian vocational schools would abandon a curriculum designed merely for the acquisition of technical skills. His choice of subjects and of the manner and spirit in which they should be taught, the connection he wished to establish between education for a vocation and the world outside the school, his program for recruiting and professionally training teachers and for their continuing self-education, were thoroughly progressive measures.

Parker's suggestion for involving a wide range of community organizations in the schools reflected the national movement to bring the school and the community into closer relationship, a movement which included the rural as well as the urban school. The Indian vocational schools were doubly isolated. They had little contact with the Indian communities and even less with the non-Indian community. By opening the schools to systematic study and participation by a variety of representative community groups, no doubt Parker hoped to end both their isolation and their parochialism, thereby making them responsive to forces beyond the Indian Bureau which presently controlled them.

Parker, like many other progressives, believed that a liberal education should include the arts and the sciences and should be made available to those who could not afford it but were competent to absorb it. Therefore Indian vocational education should be so organized as to encourage the promising student to acquire a liberal education while society should provide the means for him to do so. Parker had little confidence in race leadership by the uneducated, no matter how great their natural abilities. Rather, race leadership could arise only from men and women of broad vision and of "highly cultivated intellects."

But several Indians with highly cultivated intellects were far from satisfied with the Society's remedies. Charles Eastman continued to view the SAI with coolness. Some of his misgivings were shared by Fayette McKenzie. In a *Journal* review of Eastman's new book, *The Indian Today*, McKenzie wrote:

"Dr. Eastman renders a signal service to the public and to the Society of American Indians [by declaring] his belief that the Society should do 'intensive work among our people, looking especially toward their moral and social welfare,' rather than concerning itself with governmental affairs. In this, Dr. Eastman meets the views of many friends of the Indian, views which the present writer has ventured to express at great length in public addresses before the Society. It is important that Dr. Eastman should use his great influence at the annual conferences, in securing the policies he advocates. It is important that the Society carefully consider Dr. Eastman's advice on this subject." [31]

Thus, no doubt, McKenzie hoped to bring Eastman into more active relationship with the Society, and to induce him to attend the annual conferences, every one of which McKenzie himself had attended.

Another Society critic was J. N. B. Hewitt, who wrote to Parker strongly protesting various SAI policies:

"First, I share the view of those persons of Indian blood who believe, and rightly so as events have shown, that the Society of American Indians embarked on a viciously impractical policy when it decided to hold its annual conferences at various State Universities, located far from the haunts of the very persons of predominantly Indian blood, who are and have been most interested in the success of the published program of the Society of American Indians. The negative results of this policy greatly outweighs any individual minor accomplishments that may be credited to the activity of the Society's officers and friends.

This evil policy has not taken the American Indian, the Indian whose blood is dominating that of his native ancestors, into the confidence of the Society." [32]

It was Hewitt's conviction that the reservation Indian more than any other needed "efficient legal services." This had been a professed sentiment of the SAI from the beginning; it held out hope that "trustworthy aid was at last at hand," and that hope also "gave an impetus to the growth of the Society." It was the duty of the Society, then, to "fulfill this profession as soon as possible, especially as to the organization of an efficient legal department in Washington D.C., the only logical place for such a department." Hewitt argued that "The conferences should have been held on different central reservations in the east and west alternatively to enable the 'full' bloods and the mixed bloods to become acquainted not only with one another but also with the needs of one another. . . . There would have been personal contact with the people who need the help of an organization with the purposes of the Society of American Indians and the so-called leaders among the Indians would become better acquainted with the actual conditions which should be bettered and improved, for these leaders are for the most part quite unacquainted with the general Indian situation." Such a policy, Hewitt maintained, would have been the best possible way of advertising the aims and purposes of the SAI among Indians, "because, for one thing, they would have regarded it as 'something belonging to us' and not an adjunct of the Indian Office . . . as many of them now think."

A thorough reorganization of the Society was necessary, Hewitt wrote. The SAI "should elect as its President a man such as Thomas L. Sloan, who has under the most trying difficulties shown that he can successfully fight the Indian Office and have the Courts enter judgments against it and its policies; he is the one man not subservient to the wishes of the Indian Office, and he is not afraid to tell the people the truth about Indian affairs; he has the brains, the courage, the Washington residence, the personal character, and the abiding love of his fellow Indian, to make an ideal President of the Society of American Indians."

As the Society's fifth conference approached, the campaign for reforms was faltering badly. Nevertheless, the SAI had a number of solid achievements to its credit. It had proved itself capable of defining an Indian common ground and formulating a thoughtful program for the present reform of Indian policy which anticipated important future reforms by decades. It had provided, through its conferences, meetings, and its *Journal,* a forum for the serious discussion by Indians of Indian affairs. It had presented its case to the president of the United States. It had held the loyalty of many dedicated, middle-class Indians and a number of reservation Indians. It had enlisted the support of many friendly whites.

But the Society had not been even remotely successful in bringing about the changes which it advocated in governmental policies. It lacked the resources to meet the pressing legal needs of reservation Indians and to handle adequately their complaints against the Bureau. It was a reform organization which could not achieve reforms. And as in other reform movements unable to deliver concrete results, its members began to vent their frustrations upon each other, and conflicts hitherto minor began to assume major proportions.

6

THE GROWTH OF
FACTIONALISM

The divisions emerging in the Society of American Indians centered around three basic issues. The first and eventually the most destructive to the organization concerned attitudes toward the Indian Bureau. The second involved the peyote religion and the third the question of the Society's responsibility in the handling of specific complaints put forward either by a tribe or a tribal faction. All of these conflicts were evident at the fifth annual conference held at Lawrence, Kansas, September 28–October 3, 1915.

The selection of Lawrence as the conference meeting place was probably an attempt to reassert a broad Pan-Indian unity. Lawrence was sufficiently close to Indian country so that it was possible for many reservation Indians to attend. It was the site of the University of Kansas and of Haskell Institute, and sessions took place at both institutions. By meeting at a university, the Society's bonds with academia were emphasized. By meeting at Haskell, the organization demonstrated its continuing interest in Indian education. Haskell was already replacing Carlisle as the leading non-reservation boarding school. Like Carlisle, it soon began to produce Pan-Indian leaders.

Members from twenty-five tribes attended the conference. The largest number were from Oklahoma, followed by Kansas, Nebraska, Minnesota, South Dakota, and Montana. Thus the distribution of the delegates was much more like the Denver than the Madison conference, and the attendance was much larger than had been the case at Madison.[1]

A number of the Oklahoma delegates were important peyotists. These included Nahwats and Howard White Wolf (Comanches), Paul

135

Boynton (Cheyenne), and Cleaver Warden (Arapaho). William F. Springer, an active Omaha peyotist, also attended.

Many of the delegates came to the conference "to present claims and complaints." Among them were Comanches, Crows, Chippewas, Pimas and Papagos (Carlos Montezuma, though an Apache, was a representative of these two tribes), Cheyennes and Arapahoes, and Pawnees. The Pawnee contingent included James Murie, author of *Pawnee Secret Societies,* and Stacey Matlock, who was later to be the anthropologist Gene Weltfish's informant.

In its report on the conference the *Journal* viewed the situation with alarm and warned of the danger of making

"the Society a Clearing House or Court of Review of special cases [which] will stamp its membership as prejudiced and hasty in judgment. The easy way in which special cases and complaints were put up in the Conference without debate or evidence showed on the part of some a lack of understanding that the Society especially states as one of its objects, 'to direct its energies exclusively to general principles and universal interests and not allow itself to be used for any personal or private interest.' There was danger also in over-riding all rules, principles and laws by individuals bent on personal ends. Members ought not to be admitted without some investigation if the Society is to guard its welfare. It must also be understood that the stated principles of the Society constitute its real groundwork and that worthy members, both associate and active, who apply for membership, do so because of their belief in the principles and policies of the Society as they have been given. No individual or group of individuals in a conference has a right to attempt to overthrow those principles, also a Conference does not and cannot express the aims of the Society. In the hands of honest men the Society cannot but succeed, as is shown by the results of the Lawrence Conference." [2]

The published proceedings of the Lawrence conference do not indicate more specifically what the controversies were about. The peyote religion was probably one, since the conference included persons with diametrically opposed views on the subject. The peyotists may have come to the meeting to seek aid in protecting their religion from the increasing pressure of the Bureau and the missionaries. Another probably revolved around a highly polemical attack on the Indian Service by Carlos Montezuma, in which he advocated its immediate abolition.

The address, which Montezuma later published and circulated as a pamphlet under the title "Let My People Go," [3] became one of his favorite weapons in the abolitionist campaign.

Coolidge was reelected president and Parker as national secretary, but Charles Daganett was replaced as first vice-president by W. A. Durant, a Choctaw who had long been a leading member of the Oklahoma legislature. Never again was Daganett active in SAI affairs. Thomas L. Sloan, whom Hewitt had favored for the presidency, was elected vice-president in charge of legislation. Daganett's exit and Sloan's election probably reflected a hardening of attitudes toward the Bureau and a desire to assert independence of any possible Bureau domination. Henry Roe Cloud became vice-president in charge of education. Estaiene De Peltquestangue, a Chippewa nurse, was chosen vice-president on membership, and Mrs. Marie L. Baldwin, also a Chippewa, treasurer.[4] William J. Kershaw, a well-known Milwaukee attorney who was one-half Menominee, replaced Roe Cloud as chairman of the advisory board. Fayette McKenzie was again elected chairman by the associates, and Thomas C. Moffett became associate secretary.

The platform of the conference was a restatement of previous demands with several additions which concerned matters on which all factions heartily agreed: education, citizenship, and "the liquor evil." [5] The platform urged that "graduates of Indian schools, or of private or public schools of similar grades," be given "such proportion of their treaty or trust funds" required for their further education in private or public schools. The assemblage also called on Congress to organize the administration of Indian affairs on a non-partisan basis and urged that "citizenship of the Indians may be made to conform as far as possible with the same laws that govern the citizens of the country."

The conference allied itself with the growing national prohibitionist sentiment by demanding "the fulfillment of all treaties promising the suppression of the liquor traffic in the Indian country and the prohibition of the traffic entirely by state and national legislation." The plank noted that "the first law enacted by Congress looking to the curtailment of the liquor traffic was enacted through the efforts of Mechecunnequa Little Turtle, the Miami chief," and that "the Indians for two centuries have pleaded for the elimination of this curse," thus crediting the Indians in the pioneering of prohibitionist efforts. This conference stand received wide and favorable publicity in the press.

One of the most promising actions of the conference was the inauguration of an activity aimed at the reservation Indian—"a community center movement to be instituted on the various reservations as soon as practicable." It was hoped that the movement "would become a strong factor in bringing the reservation Indians into a better understanding and more harmonious relationship with the civilization of the country." [6] Some leading members of the Society had long advocated the estabishment of "social betterment stations" on the reservations which would perform services similar to those of the settlement house among the urban poor. Community centers might constitute the modest beginnings of a parallel movement among the Indian poor.

No doubt the community center movement was designed to serve several other purposes as well. It would help to allay the fears of men like Eastman and McKenzie who believed that the Society should devote more energy to social service. It would engage Indians in a meliorative activity characteristic of many reform movements of the period and offer educated Indians a specific way to help in the uplift of their less fortunate brothers. It would provide an area in which the Society could achieve concrete results.

The first center was to be opened at Fort Duchesne, Utah, among the Utes, and was placed in the charge of Gertrude L. Bonnin (Zitkala-sa), a Sioux writer and poetess whose husband, also a Sioux and a member of the Indian Service, was stationed at the Agency. Mrs. Bonnin was to play an important role in Pan-Indian affairs over the next two decades. Of mixed French and Siouan ancestry, she had been brought up in a family opposed to white influences but nevertheless had managed to attend Earlham College, a Quaker institution in Indiana, as well as the New England Conservatory of Music. She had also taught at Carlisle for two years. Later Mrs. Bonnin published several books of Indian stories and legends as well as articles in such periodicals as *Harper's* and the *Atlantic Monthly*. She was active in a number of women's organizations, including the League of American Pen Women and the General Federation of Women's Clubs.[7] But at the time that the community-center movement was launched, she was only at the beginning of her career as a Pan-Indian leader.

Mrs. Bonnin lost no time in embarking on her duties as a hopeful pioneer in a new phase of Pan-Indian reform. The same issue of the *Quarterly Journal* carrying the report of the Lawrence conference contained her "Christmas letter" describing the work of the newly opened center.[8] Its main activities consisted of sewing classes for women, the serving of inexpensive lunches on "Ration Day" when the Indians gathered to collect their rations, and the provision of a "Rest-room" for the Indians.

Mrs. Bonnin also reported that she had been "very sad to see that these Utes are beginning to fall victim to that terrible stuff"—peyote. This was the start of Mrs. Bonnin's campaign, carried on with increasing vigor, against peyote. The Society, however, had not yet taken a position against it, though it was shortly to become a major issue, one of a number which fed the growing factionalism in the organization. The Lake Mohonk conference which followed the Lawrence conference affirmed its stand against peyote, though with far less discussion than there had been the previous year.

The first issue of the SAI journal for 1916 appeared with a new name—*"The American Indian Magazine* published as the Quarterly Journal of the Society of American Indians." The front cover proclaimed it as "A JOURNAL OF RACE IDEALS Edited by Arthur C. Parker." In a succeeding issue, Parker explained that the change of name might "enlarge our sphere of usefulness. A Journal of a particular Society appears too clannish many times for the general reader." [9] Probably Parker wished to build a separate constituency for the magazine so that he could continue to edit it independently of the Society if need be. Probably also he knew of Carlos Montezuma's plan to publish a periodical of his own and wished to put the magazine in a stronger competitive position. Parker chose the name after the model of "The National Geographical Magazine, which while published by the National Geographical Society does not embody the Society in the title of its publication." [10]

The newly named magazine carried an article entitled "The Editor's Viewpoint: The Functions of the Society of American Indians" in which Parker attempted to restate the basis for unity in the SAI.[11] The Society, Parker wrote, "exists for the inspiration and encouragement of a race in the process of adjustment," bringing together "the more advanced and patriotic men and women of Indian blood." Its "aim is to attain harmonious action along the lines of great principles. In details, men will ever differ. Indians have ever differed, but through the instrumentality of the Society . . . differences may be laid aside and a mutual understanding of diverse views be attained."

The white associates, Parker continued, "in a degree constitute the background upon which the ideas of the red race are projected. They are the guarantee that the Society is not primarily a race organization selfishly devoted to the interests of one race alone. The future of the Indians is with the white race, and in a civilization derived from the old world." The Indian must adjust to this fact, or perish.

The Society contains men and women of extremely diverse views, Parker went on. Some consider the problem of race adjustment and assimilation purely from the political side, others from the religious. Some may wish the Indian to remain as he was four centuries ago, others think only in terms of his social and economic problems. The Society must consider all these elements of race welfare. Honorable men and women honestly disagree on the role of the Indian Bureau, on temperance, on taking up individual complaints. None of these, however, is fundamental, Parker wrote:

"This is patent when it is realized *that there will be men and women of Indian blood who need guidance and inspiration whether the Indian Bureau is abolished or not, or whether political corruption exists or not.* Let the rumblings heard at Lawrence serve as a warning. Ambition for self elevation will prove fatal. Insistence on a certain political policy not general in its application will be fatal. Desire to promote actions for or against anyone or any organization for motives of revenge will be fatal. To turn the Society into an organization for voicing complaints will be fatal. . . . *A confused notion of the Society and an attempt to use it for purposes for which it is not by its very nature intended will bring destruction, no matter how valuable and how pressing the desired reforms may be.*"

As if to underline the open forum nature of the *Magazine,* in the same issue Parker carried Montezuma's "Let My People Go" and an article by Father Phillip B. Gordon, a Chippewa who was a close friend of Montezuma and a supporter of Thomas L. Sloan. A long poem by Gertrude Bonnin called "The Indian's Awakening" also graced the pages. One stanza gives a glimpse of Gertrude Bonnin's romantic brand of Pan-Indianism, as well as of her talents as a poetess.

> I've lost my long hair; my eagle plumes too.
> From you my own people, I've gone astray.
> A wanderer now, with no where to stay.
> The will-o-wisp learning, it brought me rue.
> It brings no admittance. Where I have knocked

Some evil imps, hearts, have bolted and locked.
Alone with the night and fearful abyss
I stand isolated, life gone amiss.[12]

American Indian Day, Parker hoped, might be a unifying activity around which all factions in the Society could rally. In an unsigned article on "the real purpose of the proposed holiday," Parker wrote:

"Heretofore Indians have considered only tribe and reservation. To them the tribe was mankind and the tribal area this world. Today there is a growing consciousness of race existence. The Sioux is no longer a mere Sioux, or the Ojibway a mere Ojibway, the Iroquois a mere Iroquois. Today as perhaps never before all men of the aboriginal peoples feel themselves members of the red race or of aboriginal ancestry. No man should seek to destroy the special genius that race ancestry gives him. The God of nations did not give races distinctive racial endowments and characteristics for naught. And now with a coming race-consciousness the American Indian seeks to go even further and say, 'I am not a red man only, I am an American in the truest sense, and a brother man to all human kind.' " [13]

The article suggested that American Indian Day celebrations be held throughout a weekend: in schools on Friday, historical and patriotic societies on Saturday, and churches on Sunday. Programs for schools and literary and historical societies were outlined, together with a bibliography, questions for discussion, and a list of organizations ready to supply information about the Indian.

The *Magazine*'s program for schools or literary societies suggested opening with "The Star-Spangled Banner," closing with the salute to the flag. The program might include selections from Cadman's or Gilbert's Indian songs, tableaux, addresses on "The American Indian as a Patriot," "The Indians of our State," or "The American Indian in Literature," readings from Indian legends, declamations from famous Indian oratory—such as the speeches of Red Jacket, Logan, Black Hawk, Osceola, or Tecumseh—and the singing of an Indian folksong.

The promotion of American Indian Day met with considerable success. Three states—New York, Connecticut, and Wisconsin—held school celebrations. "Every state with an Indian population was reached, and in most cases there was a cordial response," the *Magazine* reported.

But the celebration of American Indian Day met with scorn from Carlos Montezuma. In April, 1916, the first issue of Montezuma's personal publication, *Wassaja,* appeared. It was billed as a successor to Father Gordon's suspended *War Whoop.* In this and subsequent issues of the monthly *Wassaja,* Montezuma passionately attacked the Society of American Indians as being in league with the Bureau. American Indian Day was "a farce and worst kind of a fad. It will not help the Indians, but the Indians will be used as tools for interested parties. To the Indian it is a laughing mockery because he does not enjoy freedom, but is a ward and is handicapped by the Indian Bureau," Montezuma wrote.[14]

The *American Indian Magazine* was the target of Montezuma's "Arrow Points," as he called one of the columns in *Wassaja.* "The Journal of the Society of American Indians has turned into a magazine. Now it can straddle any old thing that comes along. Like all magazines, it cannot have any definite object but to tickle its readers at the expense of the Indians. Buffalo Bill and P. T. Barnum used the Indians. Now it is the American Indian Magazine's turn."

Montezuma was equally unsparing in his attack on the Lawrence conference of the SAI:

"Clear Cut Attitude of Procedure of the Society of American Indians at the Lawrence Conference, as seen by Wassaja. The sky is clear and we meet only to discuss. There is nothing wrong. We meet only to discuss. It is so nice to meet and discuss. We can meet and discuss as well as the Mohonk Conference, the Indian Rights Association, Indian Service Teachers' Association and the missionaries. We will show them we can meet and discuss. What is the use of worrying, we are only going to meet and discuss. There is nothing like meeting and discussing. Meeting and discussing are so soothing and smoothing. Sh-! Sh-! Don't whisper about the Indian Bureau. We are to meet and discuss." [15]

Parker replied with a restrained but nevertheless cutting answer in the pages of the *American Indian Magazine:*

"Dr. Montezuma has a splendid sense of humor and luckily for the rest of us we have also. Dr. Montezuma and all the rest of us at Lawrence said all the things in our systems about the Indian Bureau and nobody stopped us. The only limit anybody had was the time we spent 'showing up the Bureau.' As to the Magazine, if we are using the Indian like a Barnum or a Buffalo Bill, dear readers, please show us how and where.

And American Indian Day—why we quoted Montezuma on that day until everybody wanted to 'let that Indian go.' We were glad to give publicity to his views just as we have done in these pages more than once. Montezuma is a vigorous fighter—no one will accuse him of lack of purpose or of intentionally trying to hurt his people. His heart is all the other way. We wish him every success in every noble purpose he undertakes. We wish him power to present without rancor, prejudice or unkindness, in a manner that will appeal to all for its logic and justness, the great truths that will make for efficient, loyal citizenship for the American Indian." [16]

The masthead of *Wassaja* summarized Montezuma's conception of its role and his relationship to it. On the left stood a brick, prison-like building with a heavy door labeled "Indian Office." In the center was Montezuma himself, grasping the front of a huge log pointed at the door. On the log was the legend "Freedom's Signal for the Indian." Several Indians in overalls but wearing hair and hat in Indian fashion were helping Montezuma hold the log, while supporting the end of the log was another Indian in full Indian dress. Far in the background on the right was a tepee. Underneath the drawing appeared the statement, "Edited by Wassaja (Dr. Montezuma's Indian name, meaning 'Signaling') an Apache Indian."

Wassaja's message was simple and may be summarized briefly: The Indian race is not vanishing but changing. Race pride and simple justice require that the Indian be treated just like anyone else and given the full privileges and responsibilities of citizenship. He must stand on his own feet. The reservation system kills his manhood. The Indian does not desire to preserve his distinctiveness. Education in the public school is therefore the best education for the Indian. The solution to the Indian problem is simple—abolish the Bureau and free the Indian. Anyone who opposes this program is by definition a hypocrite or a traitor to the race. Essentially, *Wassaja* restated General Pratt's position, adding to it a strong dose of race pride and considerable hostility to whites. Its constant attacks on the Society and its constantly reiterated demand for the abolition of the Bureau deepened the divisions within the organization.

Further conflict arose over the attitude Indians should take on specific legislation. The Society was divided over bills in Congress which would abolish the Bureau and would provide for the nomination and election by tribes or bands of their own agents and superintendents. Parker and Coolidge opposed these bills strongly, while Sloan supported them. However, the *American Indian Magazine* dealt cautiously with the proposed legislation, stressing the wide difference of opinion among both Indians and whites but giving somewhat more emphasis to the negative arguments. "Perhaps the time is not yet ripe for this revolutionary legislation, but certainly the time must come when there is a greater order, more justice, and more efficiency in Indian administration," the *Magazine* stated.[17]

An editorial warned again of the necessity for "a united front":

"Two divergent ideas are advanced as the primary purpose of the Society of American Indians. One is that the Society should become active along lines of particular legislation and advocate certain bills having more or less political ends; and the other is that the Society should concern itself with intensive measures affecting the education, social standards, morals and inspiration of the Indians and keep clear of political or legislative controversy. . . .

[A voluntary society supported by voluntary contributions] cannot hope to compete with political factors or factions backed by large interests and supported by adequate funds. A society composed of men and women of various degrees of education, conditions of environment, of religious, social and political beliefs, cannot expect unity of action in political measures. Realizing, however, the value of a mutual interchange of ideas, the society invites a free discussion on all matters affecting the welfare of the race. In full confidence as to the essential loyalty of its members, the Society can and ought to unite on certain first principles, such as are laid down in our statement of objects, our annual platform and in our basic legislative program."

Honorable men may disagree on specific legislation, the editorial continued. But in the heat of battle, controversy becomes intense and the effect will be to disrupt the Society, thus bringing disorder to the ranks and delighting the enemy. "Which shall it be with us, disorder or order? The weakness of contending forces, or the strength of united action? We ask these questions because our Society as an internal movement of men and women of Indian blood is the most important action ever taken by American Indians in the United States." [18]

Having made a plea for unity on the basis of fundamental principles and cautioned against becoming involved in specific legislation, Parker proceeded to raise an issue which he must have known would be deeply divisive—the use of peyote in Indian religious ceremonies. He did this by reprinting an anti-peyote article written by Gertrude Seymour and entitled "An Indian Cult and a Powerful Drug." It had originally appeared in *The Survey*.[19]

In preparing the article, Miss Seymour had written to Parker asking whether the importation of peyote from Mexico had been interfered with following a Department of Agriculture ruling bringing control of peyote under the food and drug laws. She had also asked Parker to send her data concerning the effect of peyote on children. Parker had replied that so far as he could determine nothing had been done to restrict the dealing in peyote:

"The Federal Government has sought to bring legislation into being but the peyote advocates, many of whom are wealthy men, have endeavored to represent that the ceremony is a religious rite and therefore cannot be disturbed. So far as I have been able to determine, thru questioning the Superintendents of Indian schools it appears that the use of peyote by pupils is destructive to the ability of a pupil to concentrate upon a subject or to carry on his studies with continuity. Before the traffic in the button became commercialized, the use of the drug was carefully restricted by ceremonies and to a certain extent this is true today. The native religious concept, however, has been largely eliminated and a form of Christianity such as the uneducated Indian leader deducts is substituted. . . . [Parker also referred Miss Seymour to the use of peyote] as a purely native ceremony in a work on the Kiowa by James Mooney." [20]

Miss Seymour's article did not refer to the introduction of Christian elements into the peyote religion. She reviewed briefly the history of its use by Indians, some of the scientific evidence about the effects of peyote, and recent attempts to control the drug, including pending legislation. She distinguished sharply between its use aboriginally, and the present

"obvious degeneration of peyote worship. The younger ambitious Indians have seen in the position of mescal leadership an opportunity for personal and party prestige and have not hesitated to take it, for it is a matter of vision real or so-called. . . . [Regulating peyote] under the law of habit-forming drugs or under a special law, is beyond question an immediate necessity; but even granting that physical and mental gain will follow the enforcement of such laws, the measure is but negative. . . . [The religious, idealistic, poetic, and aesthetic nature of the Indian] cannot be satisfied with negatives, cannot perhaps be "industrialized," cannot find complete satisfaction in schools and manual training or instruction in agriculture. The wider education that shall provide for philosophy and aesthetic culture, as well as a religion—this, and not less, is involved in the problem of peyote—which is, after all, only a part of the whole problem of the Indian."

Parker was personally opposed to peyote, but he hesitated to push strongly issues which he knew would further divide the Society.[21] By publishing Miss Seymour's article, he could take account of the increasing hostility to the peyote religion while not committing the magazine editorially. He may have believed that an article on the subject written by a white would cause less difficulty than one by an Indian and at the same time would appease the growing concern over peyote among the whites most friendly to the Society, especially Thomas C. Moffett, the associate secretary, who was bitterly opposed both to peyote and to Thomas L. Sloan. Parker may also have seen the issue as one which could be used to discredit Sloan, or to divide the forces of those who were veering toward a position like Montezuma's on the Indian Bureau.

These two issues—the abolition of the Bureau and the peyote religion —were hotly debated at the Society's sixth annual conference held at Cedar Rapids, Iowa, September 26–30, 1916. As in the past, some of the conference sessions were held at a college, in this case Coe College. But while the welcome to the delegates was warm, it was not as extensive as in previous conferences, and the meeting itself was not well attended. The Society was in serious financial difficulties and the meeting was poorly publicized. No list of delegates was published, but a group picture shows twenty-eight members, including associates. Fayette McKenzie did not attend, perhaps because of a serious operation early in August or perhaps because his duties as president of Fisk University were channeling his interest in other directions. This was unfortunate, because McKenzie's quiet influence had frequently in the past calmed excitable members, both Indians and whites.

However united the members were on certain very general positions, they were by now bitterly and passionately divided on specific ones. President Sherman Coolidge, in his opening address, pleaded for "union and strength and harmony," expressing the hope that what might be done at this session "will not be to the destruction and shame of the Indians or the country":

"Both the white race and the Indian race have expected a great deal more from us than we are able, either through money or by workers, to accomplish. . . . We have practically undertaken to do work that the Indian Rights Association, the Indian National Association, and indeed the United States Government, as well as the different denominations of religion in our country have tried before. We have in this endeavor tried to do the work of literary people, of people who write stories, legends, history, and indeed who write music; and also to study the handicraft of our people, and, what is more important to see and understand, if possible, the problem into which the race has been thrust by the white race and our own nation. As a race we are in a state of chaos."

Coolidge pleaded for more orderly proceedings, according to parliamentary law, and less "destructive criticism, muckraking, or abolishing." He also called the group's attention to a suggestion by one member that the associates be allowed "to vote in some cases, for instance, in case of the officers. They have tremendous interest as to who represents them as well as those who represent the active membership." [22]

Carlos Montezuma, leader of the "radicals," as the abolitionist wing was beginning to be called, continued his attack on the direction the Society was taking. "We cannot work side by side with the Indian Bureau and do any good for the Indians," Montezuma declared. The Society was not progressing, Montezuma argued, because the Indians in the field knew that it was working with the Bureau and they did not like it. Montezuma also attacked the *Magazine,* American Indian Day, and the Society's lack of activity. "I am not here to fight. I would like to see the Society grow. But when it comes to doing anything radical, when it comes to the point of whether it is right or wrong, they crawfish, they duck," Montezuma declared, urging the members to "get out of the talking business" and "get into the right road." [23]

Father Phillip Gordon, Montezuma's ally, took a similar stand. The Society, he declared, should be "opposed to this idea of keeping us Indians, in making us to prolong our Indian life." Father Gordon asserted that Indians should be placed "under those laws which every pure-blooded citizen enjoys and which we do not enjoy and let us go about and be white men legally speaking." What Father Gordon meant was not entirely clear, however, since in the same speech he reported that "Just a few weeks ago I was declared a competent Indian. . . . I didn't want it because now I have to pay taxes." [24]

A heated and somewhat confused debate took place over whether one could at the same time be an employee of the Indian Bureau and loyal to the Society or "the race." [25] Sherman Coolidge maintained that it was perfectly possible for a "Government Indian employee" to be "equally loyal to his race and to his Government," and that "the Indian Bureau has its work to do and we have our work to do." Father Gordon retorted that it was not possible for "a member in the employment of the Government [to be] at the same time loyal to this Society." Coolidge replied, "I did not say this Society; I said the Indian race. The race may be helped by this Society. That is not what I am talking about. Before this Society ever existed I was a Government employee." Montezuma maintained that his opposition to the Bureau "as a system" did not mean opposition to the Government or to the Commissioner, which Coolidge had earlier implied. But the Indian in the Service was, he asserted, a "hireling."

Mrs. Marie Baldwin, SAI treasurer, defended Bureau employees in the Society:

"I am one of those Government clerks that my brothers have been speaking of today. I do not know where at any time the Government clerk does not dare to say just what he thinks about the Indian Bureau. . . . *I am sure that very many times I have told Indians that I feel and I want the Indian Bureau to be abolished, but I do not believe that it ought to be abolished on the instant.* I think the Indians know that there are many Indians who are not ready now to be put out in the world to take care of themselves. . . . You may not know it, but it is a fact that the Indian Bureau is striving to that end, when some day there will be no need of an Indian Bureau. (Applause.)"

Gertrude Bonnin argued that many Indians who could make their way in the world at large remained in the Service "from a sense of duty," not for the small salary involved. By "all the ties of the heart [they] stay in the wilderness," she asserted, to "give the kind of help that money could never buy."

Ancient tribal animosities flared during the debate on the Bureau. According to one newspaper account, Montezuma became so angry with Coolidge that he "jumped to his feet, waving his arms wildly. 'I am an Apache,' " he shouted to Mr. Coolidge, " 'and you are an Arapahoe. I can lick you. My tribe has licked your tribe before.' " " 'I am from Missouri,' " replied Mr. Coolidge, a tall and powerfully built man who towered over the small, compactly built Montezuma. The paper reported that this remark "broke the tension by creating a laugh and what promised to be an exciting incident soon simmered down and the discussion continued." The exchange was widely reported in the press, to the distress of the *Magazine* editors.[26]

The peyote debate also revealed deep divisions. A strong attack on its use was delivered by Henry A. Larson, an associate and Indian Bureau official, in an address on "The Indian and His Liquor Problem." Larson's attack on "the liquor traffic" evoked no criticism—on this the members were united—but Larson characterized peyote as "a species of drunkenness" which was developing into a "rather dangerous" situation among the Indians. He urged the Society to go on record "not only against the use of peyote, but in favor of congressional and state legislation to eliminate that kind of business." [27]

General Pratt, whose instinct for self-parody was remarkable, delivered a typical Pratt blow against peyote, while admitting that his experience with it was limited: "The information I have has come from those who have had experience. . . . This thought has come to me as I have listened; no father of a family who saw evil creeping in among his children would hesitate to take it up and do to it that which was necessary to drive it out. The United States is the family. There ought not to be long consideration of a thing like that. . . . It requires too much talk, too much legislation to do things; we ought to have a czar who would say and do the thing that put an end to vodka of Russia; quit it right now. There should be more of that sort of government."

The General then moved that the conference urge the passage of the Gandy Bill to outlaw peyote. His motion was carried. The Society had come a long way from the time when Arthur Parker had rebuked an associate for even speaking during a debate.[28]

The only defense of peyote reported in the *American Indian Magazine,* came from Delos Lone Wolf, a prominent Kiowa peyote leader from Oklahoma, whom Pratt had earlier mentioned favorably as a successful farmer and a champion football player at Carlisle.[29] Lone Wolf stated:

"I have been among the Indians, among my people, ever since I graduated at Carlisle in 1896. What I want to say is not what Indians tell me
or what I learned from the Quakers. I am going to tell what I know from
personal experience. . . . Now you Christian people who are trying to
civilize the Indians, why don't you take your civilization and your Christianity to the lost Indians who are using peyote. Right there is where the
fault comes in. This thing of talking about peyote killing the Indians,
there is no such thing. I used peyote for fifteen years. I have been right
in with those 'lost Indians' as a Christian Indian. There is a certain
time when the Indians reach out, a certain time about three o'clock
when the influence comes on them, they naturally reach out to get hold
of something, their worship, right then I have been brave enough to go
there, not what the Christian people or missionary or anybody else say,
but I talk Jesus Christ to them and through my influence and through the
instrument of peyote some of the hardest cases that the missionary or
anybody else could not reach they have been converted and introduced
into Christian churches."

Lone Wolf then turned to the question of the Indian Bureau. "I feel
just like Montezuma about freedom but because *of the conditions I
could not recommend turning the Indians loose today,"* he declared.
The government should "leave our land and our restrictions just like
they are until the trust period runs out which is about nine or ten years
from now, but give us more liberal use of our funds." Such a policy
should apply to "the younger people, say people about fifty years and
down. But over that, of course, the Government will have to take care
of them." If those who have been given their money "blow it in" then
they "will have to go to work, and that is the only salvation. *Work is the
solution for Indians,"* Lone Wolf asserted. If Indians were allowed to
lease their allotments, he argued, "practical experience will teach us
better and quicker than any of the best teachers and instructors you
can send out among us. . . . Let us have what is ours and give us a
chance to work."

Other questions discussed at the conference did not arouse the kind
of intense feeling that surrounded the issues of Indian Bureau abolition,
the loyalty of Indians in the Service, and peyote. The Supervisor of
Indian Education, H. B. Peairs, described reforms in Indian education
in the light of a "genuine campaign now throughout this country being
carried on in favor of what is termed vocational guidance," and asked
the Society's aid in "establishing extension courses among the young

people who have gone out of Indian schools" and in urging young people to attend school, either on the reservation or in public school.[30]

Mrs. Bonnin reported on the work of the Community Center at Fort Duchesne, Utah, so bravely begun at the previous conference.[31] The center, which operated in a room provided by the reservation agent, conducted sewing classes and offered inexpensive weekly lunches for Indians visiting the government offices, she stated. In the spring, when the people were busy with farm work, these activities had been discontinued. Instead, a local branch of the SAI was organized, meeting monthly for evening discussion and trying to promote school attendance, a tribal fair, and child health work. These activities were carried on without funds from the national office.

"The question naturally arose [Mrs. Bonnin reported] of the National organization of Indians diverting their energy upon a line of work already taken care of by able bodies. And perhaps there would be some to whom such an endeavor might appear as an interference with the workers in the field, more especially, since there were phases of our problem that urgently demanded our undivided attention. The thought of any interference with any good work is wholly foreign to our high motive; nor do we presume any superiority to those already in the field."

The Community Center was nonsectarian and nonpartisan, Mrs. Bonnin explained. For this reason, she said, it could aid unobtrusively "toward uniting and welding together the earnest endeavors of various groups of educators and missionaries."

Thus the community-center movement had not spread to other reservations, nor was it performing any significant service not already performed by other groups. From Mrs. Bonnin's defense, it may be suspected that it was resented as a competitor. And it is difficult to see how the results could have been otherwise. One person working in an isolated area without outside support, whose work depended on the goodwill of the agent and competed with that of long-established agencies, was hardly in a position to launch a movement. Nor was a Society preoccupied with factionalism, drained of new ideas, and beset by financial woes able to do so. The Society's social service efforts thus had very limited success.

Nor was the Society making headway in its efforts to promote other activities in the field. A new plan formulated by the conference to organize state councils was evidently designed to replace the one adopted at the Madison conference for tribal secretaries. It was equally unsuccessful. Neither seems to have been implemented.

The platform of the Cedar Rapids conference differed somewhat from previous ones.[32] Its preamble, which stated that the Society was "more conscious than ever of the complex situation in which a kindly and benevolent Government has placed the Indian of the United States" thereby spoke more highly of the government than it had in the past, no doubt to soften the first plank, called "Closing the Indian Bureau." This plank obviously represented a compromise between the abolitionists and the gradualists. It did not call for immediate abolition, but stated: "The time has come when we ought to call upon the country and upon Congress to look to the closing of the Indian Bureau, so soon as trust funds, treaty rights and other just obligations can be individualized, fulfilled or paid. . . . With the progress and education of Indians, they should be invested with the full privileges of citizens, without burdensome restrictions. As its jurisdiction is removed, the books of the Bureau should be closed until there is a final elimination."

The platform also commended "the preparation and introduction in Indian schools of the new vocational courses of study" as marking "an epoch in Indian education." Provision should be made by Congress "to make use of the Federal schools merely as stepping stones to the attendance of white schools, where contact with other American youth makes for patriotic, competent citizenship." All Indian pupils over twenty-one years of age, "having completed a prescribed course of study, should be deemed fully competent, given control of their property and thrown upon their own resources," the conference urged.

For the first time, the Society went on record condemning peyote and calling for legislation to outlaw it. The conference linked this position with opposition to alcohol. In a plank on the "Liquor Evil," the conference commended the Bureau for suppressing the liquor traffic among Indians, called upon Indians to adopt "habits of total abstinence," and urged "unequivocally upon Congress the passage of the Gandy Bill to prohibit the commerce in and use of peyote among our people, because of its known baneful effects upon the users in mind and morals."

By its actions and through the force of circumstance, the SAI was cutting away its bases of support. The fight over the Bureau and the "race loyalty" of its Indian employees had already largely eliminated them from active participation. The compromise plank on "Closing the Indian Bureau" did not satisfy the abolitionist wing, which was probably more vocal than numerous in any case. But enough had been said to make a number of Indians fearful of the Society as "Bureau dominated." The support of the Gandy Bill outlawing peyote served to alienate the adherents of the peyote religion in the Society. Lack of funds was probably the most important factor in the Society's failure to accomplish much in the way of providing impartial and honest legal aid, a service which would have appealed to reservation Indians. The community-center movement was a failure and was forthwith abandoned. The major broad congressional planks—the Carter Code Bill and the amended Stephens Bill—did not have sufficient public support to win enactment. The magic of Carlisle and the loyalty and *esprit de corps* of its alumni was fading, as Carlisle itself, which had "nationalized" so many Indians, was dying in spite of administrative and educational reforms. And with the rise of Father Gordon to prominence in the Society, indications began to appear of some Protestant-Catholic conflict.

Nor did the white friends of the Society represent a sufficiently broad spectrum of white opinion. Those most loyal were also those who tended to be deeply partisan, both about policies and individuals. With Fayette McKenzie devoting most of his energy to Fisk University, the influential white associates were officials of the Indian Rights Association and missionaries like Thomas C. Moffett and Robert D. Hall. Except for a few anthropologists like Alanson Skinner, who for a time served as the Society's New York representative, there was little interest among social scientists. Nevertheless those white associates who were active were resented by some Indian members.

It was in this rather chilling situation that the Society's new officials took office. Sherman Coolidge was named honorary president and Arthur Parker was elected president. First vice-president was John M. Oskison; vice-president on membership, Margaret Frazier (a Sioux); vice-president on legislation, William J. Kershaw; vice-president on education, Gabe E. Parker. Mrs. Bonnin was secretary and Mrs. Baldwin was treasurer. Father Gordon was elected chairman of the advisory board, replacing Roe Cloud, who for the first time held no office in the organization. Three of the vice-presidents—Oskison, Kershaw, and Gabe Parker—were not at the meeting.

The officers, with the exception of Gordon, were moderates in their views on the Indian Bureau, and also those most acceptable to the small loyal group of white associates. The *Magazine's* report on the convention referred to the new officers as a "cabinet." But actually they were more like a caretaker government of an almost nonexistent country in the throes of civil strife.

7

THE EFFECTS OF
WORLD WAR I

When Arthur Parker became president of the Society of American Indians, the national tide of reform on which the movement had been launched was ebbing rapidly, carrying with it the hope of Indian reform as well. As the threat of American involvement in the European war grew more ominous, the country's mood became less hospitable to Indian demands. The Society itself was wracked by internal conflicts.

Few men would have been able to function effectively in such a situation, but for Parker, the conflicts it entailed were especially painful. Hitherto he had carried a major responsibility for the development and presentation of the Society's philosophy and program, and for many of its day-to-day activities as well. In his capacity as editor of the SAI magazine and as its erstwhile secretary, he had occupied a position well suited to his temperament and experience, a rather conspicuous power behind the throne. Such a stance enabled him to function as an important and recognized figure in Pan-Indian affairs and, at the same time, in a more Iroquoian fashion as a mediator and broker who made things move by indirection.

But now Parker was the titular leader of the Society, the man in front, the public spokesman. Perhaps if he had assumed the presidency of the SAI in happier circumstances, he would have moved much more confidently in his new role. No doubt he could have functioned well as president of a white reform organization or even as a chief of the Iroquois Confederacy. As president of the Society, he seemed to try to be both and had the heart for neither. Characteristically, as he had so often done in his life, he moved in several directions at once.

As SAI president, he dispatched a message to Congress attacking the "segregation" of the Indians, calling for the dissolution of the tribes as "social, commercial and political entities" and stating that "the Indians must come into the nation as individual units." He outlined a legislative program along familiar SAI lines for accomplishing these purposes. Such a program had, of course, no prospects whatever of enactment. He seems to have done very little beyond this to speak for the organization.

As a broker of ideas, Parker moved in another direction. This was the creation of a broader framework in which to view the position of the Indians. He did so in the form of an article entitled "Problems of Race Assimilation in America, With Special Reference to the American Indian," which appeared in the October–December issue of the *American Indian Magazine* for 1916. In it he attempted to open a wider perspective on the Indian situation by comparing the conditions of assimilation of the Indian, the Negro, and the European immigrant. Although reform Pan-Indians and their friends frequently invoked the immigrant model and occasionally made reference to the Negro, such comparisons were offered rather flatly, unaccompanied by a more probing analysis. Parker's article, despite some prejudices, was the most searching statement produced on the subject of assimilation by an Indian during this period and may have been the only attempt to undertake a systematic comparison of the conditions of assimilation of the three groups.[1]

Parker's essay started from the basic premise that America is a "great melting pot of nations," and that for all "races" the same end is sought—assimilation in America civilization. Parker defined assimilation as giving

"the various racial elements the common national ideals. The Americanism of which we surround ourselves and in which we believe, is of Anglo-Saxon origin, but its flavor is no longer European. We have developed the original ideals of government and freedom, of social relations and methods of commerce along distinctly American lines. We expect all that come to our shores to embrace these ideals and to cherish them as we do. We expect all to pledge their lives and fortunes to the support of American ideals. When immigrants, Indians, Mongolians, or Negroes lay hold of these ideals, they have become assimilated."

Parker distinguished between assimilation and amalgamation; the latter takes places "when by intermarriage any one or all the racial elements have fused their blood." The problem of race assimilation, Parker wrote, is generally discussed in terms of "a single race, as the Chinese, the American Indian, or the Italian. Generalizing from their observations of one race or one group of racial elements, writers have often stated that the problem of incorporation of one race is the same as for another." Thus it is suggested that if the Indian were treated like the immigrant, he would be as easily absorbed. He is often "contrasted with the immigrant in his ability to take on 'civilization.' " The fact that the Indian is not absorbed is variously blamed on "racial incapacity" or the failure of the government to "treat the Indians exactly as it treats immigrants. Some critics of Indian progress will say that the Negro slave has been absorbed into civilization and lost all traits of his fathers in Africa, even though grievously handicapped. Therefore, it is asked, why has the Indian not been absorbed?"

Assimilation depends on two basic factors, Parker suggested. One is the "initial condition of the race" at the time it comes in contact with American civilization. The other is how American civilization conceives of and treats the newcomer. Parker then proceeded to examine the European immigrant, the Negro and the American Indian in the light of the two basic factors mentioned above.

The European immigrant, Parker wrote, came to America either for liberty, for money, or for both. "Liberty to him means greater freedom of action and the escape from tyrannical laws; money means the ability to have greater ease, desired possessions and land." Both *"mean the expansion of self and the realization of dreams."* The problems of breaking home ties and entering a strange land "are overcome when the prospective immigrant is told that in America he will find friends of his own race, that American customs were derived from Europe, that the churches are the same and that the same general institutions prevail. *The immigrant knows he will not have to abandon utterly things with which he has been familiar and in which he believes."*

He comes from one civilized country to another in which the economic system is basically the same. In spite of his often exaggerated and erroneous ideas both about liberty and money, "he understands, generally speaking, what is expected of him." He knows that he must obey the laws, that directly or indirectly he must be a taxpayer, and that he must work. He understands "the meaning of money and how to handle it," and among his traits are "frugality and thrift." Therefore, assimilation of the European immigrant is not difficult because "he has already the elements that make him easily incorporated into our national life."

Foreigners segregate themselves in colonies because *"men of like cultural traits seek association with themselves."* These "race colonies and the persistence of foreign tongues become formidable barriers to assimilation. Thus, we find churches and schools catering entirely to a foreign element and perpetuating foreign ideals. This is against public welfare but in a free country is tolerated because we are optimistic of the final outcome."

The successful immigrant, Parker wrote, comes of good stock and brings with him some money and often a certain degree of training. He becomes a worker, a part of "the industrial fabric." His children go to the public schools and become part of the social fabric.

"The longer the immigrant stays in America, the more his interests are allied to it and when he has acquired the language, becomes a citizen and becomes familiar with our institutions, he has Americanism pretty well ingrained in his system. The children of the immigrant have even a greater chance, for the ideals they form are American and the desires they have for homes and social life are American. They become assimilated—they are Americans.

The European immigrant is a white man from a civilized country. His transformation is not a radical one and once he is Americanized we have no prejudice against his ancestry. Native born Americans intermarry with the foreign born and their children and so the race is blended. The white immigrant becomes amalgamated as well as assimilated."

Next Parker considered the situation of the American Negro, "brought to America in bondage" and subjected to the utmost cruelties:

"The African negro was a savage who was cruel to his own race and superstitious in the extreme. The slave catcher was likewise cruel. The negro saw in the white man that came to enslave him a representative of the master race. . . .

Two things made the Negro consent to adopt the ways of civilization—that is such ways as made him passable. These were his natural *servility* and his *imitativeness.* The Negro admired his master and wanted to be like him. To make his own lot easier he served with reverence and obedience. Gradually the Negro forgot his African home, his customs and his tribal affiliations. He learned English because he had to. Nevertheless this did not civilize the Negro, though it put him into communication with civilized men and domesticated him. . . . Imitation is never civilization, for civilization is an inward growth during the process of which, there is much of the old nature retained. . . . [Imitation is] an evidence of feeble character and inferiority."

Parker next sought to distinguish between the mass of Negroes and those Negroes who were in the forefront of "race regeneration," declaring that "many of the African race . . . have manfully striven to cast out the traits that must have made then a people apart from other men. Great schools have inculcated great ideals and splendid Negroes have gone forth to bring about race regeneration. In this lies the promise of a better race. The credit belongs to a few enlightened leaders, who seeing in its full enormity the plight of their people, cry out for a widespread forward movement. The work of Fisk University, of Tuskegee and of Hampton is telling work, for it leads to sober realization, to real culture and to productive activity along intelligent lines."

Parker considered that the chief factors contributing to Negro segregation were "the Negroes' own desire to remain apart, their economic condition and the prejudice of whites living with or near them." Furthermore, Parker argued that:

"Normal society, with its intelligence and its taste, as well as its prejudices, objects to Negroes who offend the standards of etiquette, of living, of conduct and of morals. It objects to *any people* who offend its taste and its standards. . . .

The white man by instinct desires to preserve his racial type [and] intermixed with the Negro he cannot do this. [The white man] therefore does not admit as a white person any person having negro blood. . . . As a group, or more accurately, as a mass of people, the Negroes will not be amalgamated in the white race. The fact that Negroes are growing whiter, decade by decade, through the absorption of white blood, constitutes a danger to the white element in the nation, and at the same time a bitter reproach."

The problem of Negro assimilation is therefore far different from that of the European immigrant, Parker believed. In his view, the Negro must first "undergo a personal regeneration. This is a difficult process, for the Negro in his endeavor for cultural transformation must think even more clearly and realize even more deeply than the white man what the elements of civilization and enlightment are. And he must be even more magnanimous than most of his white mentors. Before he has full social freedom the Negro must pay a heavy price and achieve goals that command universal respect . . . [demonstrating] his equality and capacity. Until then, civilization will hold the Negro in social and economic bondage and count him an element to be exploited."

Very different from either the immigrant or the Negro was the "primary mental attitude" of the Indian. The immigrant came because he "desired to rule," the Negro because he was "compelled to serve." But the Indian was here, occupying two continents, "a product of long centuries of American environment." The Indians felt themselves free, and fought in defense of their rights. The Indian was a *"landowner and independent of any ruling power save of his own chiefs."*

As large numbers of Europeans came here, Indians gradually came into contact with civilized institutions, but were "not dependent upon them. Except as Indians lived in or near white communities they were not compelled to conform or even understand civilized law or custom." Indians could not see in civilization any great blessing. They had not the cultural development that would lead to an appreciation of the forces that civilization controlled." Only gradually through trade did Indians "begin to get an inkling into our economic system. It was different from theirs. Indians were communists and frequently worked co-operatively. They could not conceive of actually selling land any more than of selling blocks of the air. . . . [They differed from Europeans also in] the idea of occupation of land, in the idea of property ownership, of government, and of punishment for crimes."

Parker argued that the Indian is conservative rather than imitative in "his racial makeup," loving best "the things he himself has developed and created." Even though Indians took over some of the white man's material culture, "in a large measure the internal form of their culture remained." Some tribes "clung to their native superstructure" and "steadfastly assert their desire to 'remain Indians.' "

"By being an Indian, they mean the right to live in the same way, dress in the same manner and believe in the same religion as their ancestors, and what is more insisted upon is the privilege of remaining free from taxation. These are extreme cases but the fact is evident— *Indians are proud of their racial extraction and count it no virtue to imitate other races. . . .* They argue that, we have our way, you have yours; each is suited to his own plan of life. The Indians proved that their young people who had been educated among the whites and then returned to them were unfitted for anything—neither successful as white men nor good for anything in the Indian life. Indians made the fatal mistake of thinking that because they loved a certain environment they could retain it and continue the habits of life that characterized the old life."

Thus, Parker wrote, their segregated localities were surrounded and they were engulfed without being absorbed.

Today, Parker argued, the conservative Indian is economically dependent. Although he may be a rancher or farmer, he can neither produce the manufactured goods he uses nor can he control their production. To pay for them he gives up his land and resources. He is cut off "from the vital life of the country and comes to think that this life is hostile to him. He realizes bitterly that he is being exploited." To some extent, Parker reported, this has acted as a spur to endeavor: some Indians have themselves become businessmen.

"Segregation has done more than bullets to conquer the red man, and has cost the Government less," Parker believed. Segregation isolated the Indian from civilization and *"he was able to get only that form of civilization that was brought in to him."* He was passive while the white man was active, a condition which "does not tend to produce a people characterized by energy. The method has not been successful as yet in assimilating the Indian and as one examines the Indian law as it stands, the reasons are not difficult to find," Parker wrote.

The red man was first segregated "to protect the country," and the segregation was continued "to protect the Indian," Parker asserted. The attempt was made to civilize, educate and "make him understand how to support himself by manual work" in isolation. "Until non-reservation schools were established whereby Indian youth were allowed to mingle in white communities, this educational process was a slow one." The reservation system "continues to corrupt the Indian," he maintained.

In spite of this, Parker said, "many Indians have become successful in farming, stock raising and in certain business pursuits, even on the reservations. Many have gone far from the old tribal home and entered trades and professions." Parker pointed out that even though little more than half the Indian population was literate, Indians have produced able men and women in all lines of endeavor: in law, medicine, teaching and theology alone, they "have more representatives than whites in proportion to the total number respectively," he asserted.

Indian character has been variously described as "almost entirely vicious" and as "heroically ideal," Parker stated. "An impartial analysis will probably reveal that Indians had many worthy qualities of mind and morals, as well as some weak and inferior traits. On the whole, among enlightened people the Indian is honored because of his love of freedom, his native honesty, his reverence for his Creator, his refusal to be enslaved and his fighting qualities. In the popular mind, however, there will be a prejudice against the savage traits which he has exhibited and people will always look for the lapses of 'Indian blood' expecting evil outcroppings."

These views, Parker believed, give the Indian "a certain incentive" to live up to the "reputed high character of the 'noble red man' " and also to "give heed that his conduct does not lead to the belief that he is still 'an irreclaimable savage.' " The modern educated Indian who "has entered fully into the life of the nation is closely watched and frequently criticized for doing things that in a white man are passed by with a wink. He is expected to be even more 'civilized' than his fellow associates," Parker observed.

Due to intermarriage with both white men and white women, the number of "full bloods" is diminishing rapidly, Parker reported. "While much has been written concerning the low-grade half-breed it is found as a matter of actual observation that where healthy whites of good morals marry Indians, the children of the unions are not inferior, but most frequently possess the good traits of each parent. Unions between the inferior and diseased of the races produce progeny greatly handicapped in the race of life," he declared. Regardless of race, Parker argued that *"there is always prejudice against the economic nurseling, the low grade incompetent, the filthy and the unlike in purpose and custom."* Social discrimination exists against

"tribal Indians who fit these descriptions and who have otherwise degenerated [but] there is not strong prejudice against the competent, educated Indian of sterling character, who is engaged in the world's work. As a well-bred Indian, who is familiar with modern culture recedes from the reservation he feels less race prejudice directed against him. Often there is none at all even in a community where the two races touch one another. There is not the prejudice against good Indian blood that there is against some foreign bloods *because of race*. Indians so assimilated and amalgamated constitute no grave social or race problem. Their aims and methods of thought are thoroughly American."

Parker believed that intermarriage was producing "a mixed race and a new type of Indian." Indian blood was diffusing "through the veins of the white race" while at the same time the Indian was being absorbed. However, there still remained thousands of helpless Indians in need of protection and it was "contrary to the national policy to allow these people to be ruthlessly exploited." Parker advocated federal rather than state supervision of these Indians, citing the "evil effects" of the latter in Florida, New York, California, Louisiana, Oklahoma, and Mississippi. "The Indian is a special problem because of his character, his history and because of obligations of the country to him assumed under treaties and other contracts. *The obligations of the Government are definite facts and these facts must be met, not ignored in pointing out the remedy.* In helping the Indian to citizenship today, we must pay the Indian what we owe him before we send him on his way alone. We must take the Indian as we find him, and not assume him to be what he is not."

Most important, the Indian "must be allowed to feel he has the principal part in his struggle for a true adjustment. *If we would give the Indians civilization, we must first awaken his moral energy and provide a clear incentive,"* Parker declared.

The situations of the immigrant and the Indian were quite different, according to Parker's analysis. Unlike the immigrant, *"the assimilation of the Indian means the blotting out of nearly all that was previously his in lines of culture."* While the immigrant at first lives in "a foreign colony," like the Indian on his reservation, "he has no property holdings that bind him to segregation." The Indian is a property holder who lacks the experience and perspective to manage his property and therefore he dissipates it, while the immigrant, who is not a property holder, knows out of his experience in civilization the value of land as a resource and acquires land out of savings. The labor power of the immigrant alone becomes the object of exploitation by society, while the Indian because of his vast property holdings is used as a source of profit by other men, Parker wrote. However, he pointed out, both Indian and immigrant were examined for competency. "Congress provides laws that govern the Immigrant Bureau just as it does for the Indian Bureau, and the aim of both is or should be to examine the qualifications of future citizens and to encourage that citizenship."

Parker summarized his argument by stating that even if "our ultimate intention" toward all "the various racial elements that go to the making up of our country" is the same, our "greeting is unlike." We welcome the European immigrant, already like us, as a "commercial asset." The Negro brought here against his will is tolerated as "a convenient laborer" who "may do even more for us, in time." But we tell the Indian " 'You must be segregated until you can understand us. You have a great deal of land and mineral wealth and although we will try to protect you, our sharper citizens are going to try to get everything from you that they can. You'd better understand that first as last, because that is the way we do business. Listen to your friends and learn to think and live like us or—well, you'll become extinct.' "

Thus Parker sought to demonstrate that there was *"an unequal basis of assimilation"* among immigrants, Negroes, and Indians and that *"the various elements will come into the full life of the nation only after the training suited to their special needs* and their previous condition." For, he asserted, "the assimilation of any race depends measurably upon the characteristic and education which it already has which are similar to those of the country into which the group is to be incorporated."

The chief factors which make assimilation possible, Parker concluded, are as follows:

"1. Desire of the potential citizen to become like the native born and to uphold American ideals.
2. Ability to speak and to read the English language.
3. Familiarity with the same body of facts. This comes through a common education.
4. Common religious ideals and a charitable toleration for the beliefs of others.
5. Everyday association with native born and other completely assimilated Americans.
6. Participation in the productive activities of the country in participation with other Americans.
7. The realization of cherished hopes makes the potential citizen loyal to his new country.

When the native Indian, the foreign born south European, the Teutonic north European or even the Asiatic through the equal possession of the seven requirements we have enumerated calls upon us to recognize his qualifications for complete citizenship we need have no fear of granting him political equality and the privilege of the ballot."

Parker's article was probably aimed primarily at Montezuma and that school of thought voiced by General Pratt, who constantly used the immigrant experience, in simplistic fashion, as a model for the Indian. But Parker clearly had other viewpoints in mind also.

Obviously he was deeply concerned with the comparison of Indian and Negro experience, especially since many whites were "friends" of both. Parker, though he tried to keep his prejudice in check, was, like many Indians, rather hostile to Negroes. This feeling was no doubt aggravated by the presence in his own state of tribes, like the Shinnecocks, who had a strong admixture of Negro "blood." Parker seems to have been torn among his own bias against Negroes, his conviction that the Negro had been exploited by society, his admiration for some Negro achievements, his desire to differentiate sharply between the Negro and the Indian, his obligations as a social scientist, the views of his white friends who did not share his adverse opinions about the Negro, and his sense of justice. He does not seem to have considered the question of why the white man's "desire to protect his racial type" against Negroes did not also operate against Indians. He omitted Negroes in his concluding paragraph from those who could safely be granted political equality, and it is difficult to suppose that this was simply an oversight. Probably Parker's analysis went as far as he was psychologically able to go in view of the conflicts about Negroes which beset him.

Perhaps, also, Parker wished to tell his white friends some of the inner difficulties which beset a man in his position, and at the same time to interpret to them more sympathetically the position of the reservation Indian. Parker knew from his own experience that "it costs the other man something" to meet the demand for assimilation into American civilization and believed that "just what this cost is we should know." While in reality Parker had mixed feelings about recent immigrants and certainly even more mixed feelings about the Negro, he was most sympathetic when he discussed the psychic cost of assimilation which they had had to pay.

Parker was also speaking to those friends of the Indian who believed that Indians were better off trying to remain as nearly as possible in their aboriginal state. To them, he was attempting to point out that this

effort was not only impracticable but that it made the Indian extremely
vulnerable to pressures in society which he was not able either to understand or deal with.

Parker attempted to make his analysis from the point of view
of American society as a whole. The "we" of the article is a generalized
American "we," while American Indians are "they." This tension between the identity of "we" and "they" was at the center of his own relationship to society. Probably the article was directed as much at himself,
in an attempt to place the Indian problem in a broad perspective, as to
the other viewpoints mentioned. Thus he also tried to bring the analytical
tools of the social scientist to bear on his own situation.

Parker's article produced little reaction. As might be expected, Montezuma commented adversely. In the January, 1917, issue of *Wassaja* the
fiery Apache called it "a choice selection of wide generalizations (not
always true), meaningless conclusions, bad reasoning. It is an ebullition
of the Census-enumerator type, characterized by a lot of pretended philosophy, as senseless as it is shallow," but "well meant, no doubt." If
Parker's fellow social scientists reacted to his article, they did not do so
in print. Nor was it picked up by white friends of the Society among the
reformers or missionaries. Except for Montezuma's attack, Parker's
major effort to examine the question of American Indian assimilation in
broad perspective was greeted by silence and indifference.

No doubt the reception—or lack of it—accorded Parker's article
contributed to his despondency and growing bitterness. The fact that
the article had failed to include any definition of a positive basis for
Pan-Indianism may have been due to a belief that he had already done
so in his other writings, or he may have thought it inappropriate. But
it is more likely that Parker no longer had the intellectual or emotional
energy to attempt a formulation adequate to the rest of the analysis
which he presented. Certainly his hopes for a Pan-Indian reform movement were running out. And since he had long believed that the Society
offered both a test of the capacity of the race to advance through mutual
cooperation and an answer to those who believed Indians incapable
either of sustained joint action or of initiative and self help, his dis-
appointments and doubts went deeper than simply organizational ones.

In any case, the outlook for Pan-Indian unity was exceedingly bleak.
The mood of the country was conducive neither to reasoned debate nor
to compromise. As military preparedness and the European war replaced

domestic reform as an overriding concern of the American people, discussion of public issues became more heated. Public and private tempers grew more irascible and less tolerant. People feared plots and spies. The feverish climate encouraged drastic solutions, high-flown hopes, and quixotic crusades. The spirit of moderation languished.

The atmosphere of the country reinforced and accentuated a similar atmosphere within the Society of American Indians and the pessimism and bitterness of its president-editor, who was in such deep conflict as to what course the movement should take and so torn between differing conceptions of his present role in it.

Parker's conception of the Society had always contained a strong Iroquoian element transmuted into a Pan-Indian one. Like the old Iroquois Confederacy, the Society should provide a forum for discussion within a framework of agreed principles and procedures but it should not be permitted to change either principles or procedures in any drastic fashion or to act in ways which would seriously endanger them. Leadership should by right continue to be vested in those who adhered to the basic consensus and denied to those who did not. Those unwilling to continue to accept the consensus were thereby enemies who no longer merited the protection of the organization. Such a conception was of course by no means exclusively Iroquoian, but it seems to have been the one which largely guided Parker in the ways in which he sought to counter the efforts of the dissidents.

Parker moved against them on two fronts, the one public, the other private. In the first issue of the *American Indian Magazine* for 1917 Carlos Montezuma and Dennison Wheelock, who was currently in Montezuma's favor, were summarily dropped as "contributing editors." A new "Board of Managers" appeared on the masthead with Coolidge as President of the board. Mrs. Coolidge and Mrs. S. A. R. Brown, both of whom were white, replaced Wheelock and Montezuma.[2] For the first time the direction of the Society's publication was not entirely in Indian hands.

At the same time Parker was maneuvering to scuttle the Society of which he was president in order to create a new organization subservient to the magazine. He wrote Coolidge [3] that he was casting about for an acceptable alternative to "the real work we set out to perform" which was "a moral task which consisted of bringing about an awakening of the race from within. . . . Certainly we have demonstrated that it is impossible for us to have a legal division to correct by force or by law reservation abuses. We can only hope to expose the abuse." With "large sums of money, the Society might have done good work and have had a permanent Secretary." But even with sufficient funds, "under the present system of organization I doubt that we could have succeeded. We are too open, too free and our members have the power to wreck us if they set out to do it."

Parker suggested that:

"The solutions of these difficulties lies in an independent publication not under Society control. . . . [Some time ago, Parker wrote], I saw that . . . [the magazine] could not continue, at least as a Society publication. As far as the Society is now concerned it is not supporting it financially. Our plain right is to withdraw it as a Society organ and start out as a periodical issued by another set of individuals. . . . As for management I would have an organization named the American Indian Publication (or Press) Association, or similar name and have a President, a Secretary-Treasurer and an Editor. Chairmen of various committees could be named. Not all need be Indian. I have in mind Mr. Coolidge as President of the movement, Mrs. Brown as Treasurer, and as a live board of editors men and women like Mrs. Coolidge, Mr. Oskison, Yellow Robe, Roe-Cloud and the like.

As for policy I would not condemn the best in the old life or shut the pages from the picturesque. I would fight cleanly and in the open the various enemies and show just why they are trying to protect or to destroy their pet aversions or perversions.

As for support our membership ought to give at least $5.00 a year and added to this would be donations of yours and others.

The Society could go on out or otherwise. It is an 'unfinished experiment' indeed and it has been too optimistic and trustful of dangerous elements."

Obviously what Parker was proposing was a new organization built around a magazine with a point of view free of the present constraints. No doubt Parker had been deeply wounded by the constant attacks on him in *Wassaja* and particularly by his inability to reply while staying within the bounds of the Society as he conceived them.

"Personally I have been working at low pressure and amid great discouragement. Of this I need not say more but it is certain I cannot continue to ostensibly head a Society that is constituted so vulnerably. I have been too ill to bear the weight of discord and the pitiful appeals of my kinsmen without being able to assist them, not to have it effect me vitally," Parker wrote Coolidge.

Parker also confided his great discouragement to Gertrude Bonnin. Addressing her as "Dear Sioux Secretary," Parker wrote:

"I almost feel that I ought to give up . . . the presidency of the SAI. I am constrained to hold on however by the fact that we are under fire and because a new society, The Grand Council of AM Indians has formed in Washington.

Several fights are doing us no good but tending toward destruction. The first is the fear of government employees who are Indians, the second is the consciousness of some of the membership of religious affiliations, and the third is the secret opposition of the government. We must be broader than politics, above suspicion of the treachery of our Indian brothers and sisters in the service of the government and Christian without being in the least sectarian. Some of our most able Indians, in the clergy or otherwise, are hurting us by spreading the dissension that springs from suspicion." [4]

Probably this referred to the activities of Father Gordon and possibly to the treasurer, Marie Baldwin, who Parker feared was under "undue [Catholic] religious influence." Evidently Protestant-Catholic rivalries were also plaguing the Society.

A bitterly intemperate attack in the *Magazine* on "the peyote poison" and its advocates, further contributed to the divisions in the Society. "There are some ethnologists and some lawyers that make money by standing in with the drug users who defend it and say it does no harm," an editorial warned. Among the defenders of peyote were Thomas L. Sloan, who represented peyote users in court, and ethnologists like James Mooney and Francis LaFlesche. The magazine seems to have been quite willing to treat them as enemies. "The fact that some users of peyote do better than before they used it is no argument for its virtue. The fact that most users of peyote suffer nervous and mental breakdowns and that most are impoverished and rendered inefficient and immoral is proof of its evil effect," the publication proclaimed.

The Indians are "menaced by a new form of danger" in "the rapid spread of the peyote cult," the editorial continued. "The false advisor and secret foe must be exposed. . . . This is an age of enlightenment. Stupefying gases, narcotics and peyote must be banished. The God must be perceived by a clear, clean moral vision and not by a crazed dream of a drug eater's brain." [5]

As a unifying theme, the *Magazine* now stressed the patriotism and loyalty of Indians and noted the number of Indians serving with the Allies. "When the country calls for men the native sons of America, the Indians, will respond with all the patriotic fire that characterized their ancestors in the earlier days," an editorial declared. Although Indians in the past often fought against troops of the United States and have, in addition, fought many "verbal battles," this should never be interpreted by foreigners as disloyalty. Some Indians have been approached by representatives of "a foreign government" but "when history shall have been written . . . not a single case will be found wherein the Indian was a traitor to his country. . . . Someday the foreigner will understand that Indians are Americans who take the right given by a free country to discuss their affairs and even their grievances without a single thought of disloyalty to the country." While condemning the Kaiser and "the Prussian autocracy," the Indian has sympathy for the German people and admires greatly persons of German extraction in this country who are "proud, sensitive and patriotic," the editorial concluded. [6]

The divisions in the Society were further exacerbated by controversy over a new proposal: the organization of a separate regiment in the army consisting of Indian soldiers. The chief support for such a regiment came from Edward Ayer, a member of the Board of Indian Commissioners, Francis LaFlesche of the Bureau of American Ethnology, and Dr. Joseph K. Dixon, former leader of the Wanamaker Citizenship Expedition, a romantic venture which the *Journal* had once attacked as using "methods that smack of fakery." According to Mrs. Bonnin, Montezuma and Father Gordon also supported the proposal. [7] Another advocate was Red Fox St. James, who had once ridden a pony on his personal crusade for American Indian Day, and was currently the head of a romantic fraternal Pan-Indian youth organization called the Tepee Order.

The editors of the *Magazine* strongly opposed the formation of any type of separate Indian units in the army on the grounds that this would constitute a species of segregation, and would interfere with the Indian's freedom of choice. The chief arguments for such units were described in a manner which left no doubt where the publication stood:

"The idea of separate Indian units arises from several sources and as many arguments are brought up to support the idea. First, the Indian is thought to be superior in some ways; second, he is thought to have a lower social station in some ways; third, he is thought to be a separate and peculiar race that has a noble and warlike history, which reputation for war and nobility must be maintained on the battlefield by regiments of the surviving members of the race; fourth, it is thought that Indians since they are not white should be segregated and placed apart from other Americans.

Much of the clamor for a spectacular Indian regiment or battalion arises from the showman's brand of Indian as seen in the circus." [8]

Affairs in the management of the Society were also strained by the personal animosity between the secretary, Mrs. Bonnin, and the treasurer, Mrs. Baldwin. Mrs. Bonnin had by this time left the Community Service Station among the Utes and gone to Washington, D.C. where she set up the Society's office in her apartment, much to the chagrin of Mrs. Baldwin, who also lived in Washington. Parker attempted to keep peace between the two, whose conflicts were both personal and religious. Both were Roman Catholics, but Mrs. Bonnin feared that Father Gordon was unduly influenced by Montezuma and that the Catholic Bureau of Indian Missions was hostile to the Society. Writing Parker about a visit she had paid to the Catholic Bureau, she said that "I left, feeling in my inmost heart that I would stand by the SAI to the end, that I would not go back on the efforts of my race, even if I had to quit my church." [9] She was deeply worried about furnishing the SAI membership list to Father Gordon, as Parker had instructed her to do.

The Society's 1917 conference was scheduled to be held in Oklahoma City. The announcement in the *Magazine* stated that this decision was taken "with some reluctance," since the first plan had been for a Minneapolis conference as recommended by Father Gordon. "Due consideration of the best interests of the Society and for the purpose of reaching the largest number of Indians prompted the decision," the announcement stated, adding that the invitation to meet in Oklahoma had been held out to the Society for three years.[10] No doubt "the best interests of the Society" also precluded holding a conference in Father Gordon's bailiwick.

Unlike previous conferences, this was not to be held in connection with a university. It therefore represented a retreat from Parker's idea that through its conferences the SAI should continually seek links with the academic community.

But the 1917 conference was "postponed," the major reason given being "the conditions of the country due to the war." Few of the officers would be able to attend, the *Magazine* stated, due to their involvement in war work. Therefore the executive committee "determined that no conference should be held until a further determination by the membership. The greater needs of the country have overwhelmed the needs of the Indian people, but only so far as the holding of a conference affects the needs of the red race. The vital issues of our people will not suffer by our deferring the conference."

But other reasons were suggested in the announcement of the conference cancellation:

"The destruction of our organization would be easy in the hands of those who did not know its full history. . . . Only those who know the principles of effective organization should be entrusted with the life and safety of such an organization. . . . The weaknesses of our own Society have existed because there was to much of a belligerent spirit and even personal animosity, instead of a friendly spirit of cooperation. Those who have looked higher and who have seen the broader meaning of our movement alone are to be credited with holding the Society together." [11]

It seems quite likely that the Society's officers feared defeat or, at a minimum, bitter dissension and preferred to call the conference off rather than risk losing control of the organization. Probably the officers were going ahead with a modified version of Parker's plan to make the Society an appendage of the magazine. As Parker wrote to Coolidge: "Our best interests would be served by holding conferences every three years and by spending our money in propaganda work through a vigorous magazine calling our people to loyal cooperation with the better things in this country. It has been demonstrated that certain malcontents and peyote-drug defending lawyers prevent a real fraternal bond within our organization. We who are heart and soul of the real Indian stripe without ulterior motives have borne a heavy burden." [12]

The final issue of the *American Indian Magazine* for 1917 was a special "Sioux Number." For the first time a whole issue was devoted to a single tribe. Perhaps this was an effort to reenlist the interest of Charles Eastman. In all likelihood it was an evidence of Gertrude Bonnin's Sioux patriotism. For as Parker took less interest and devoted less time to the affairs of the Society, Mrs. Bonnin gave more. No doubt Parker had thought she would serve as a secretary carrying out his orders. The tone of her letters to him at first confirmed this view. But Mrs. Bonnin was an energetic and ambitious woman with a mind and will of her own. She was by no means willing to sit by and watch the Society expire or allow it to become merely an adjunct of the *American Indian Magazine*. While she agreed with Parker on many issues, being especially vehement against peyote, she was increasingly inclined to take a stronger line against the Indian Bureau than he did. The lead editorial in the "Sioux Number" denounced the Indian Bureau as "an un-American institution" and called for its "elimination." The emphasis on the glories of one tribe and the bitter attack on the Bureau represented a shifting direction in the Society's publication. Parker himself had begun to shift his position on the abolition of the Bureau, or at least to couch it in terms more acceptable to the abolitionists. In an address to a conference of "Friends of the Indian" held in Philadelphia in January, 1918, Parker stated: "We shall never get anywhere until we break the grip of the Indian Department in its repressing hold upon the lives and the development of the Indians. . . . If we can do nothing else let us say that the Bureau shall be limited to be a Department of Indian Disbursements charged with paying out that which treaties, contracts and Congress order." Parker further urged Congress to assert without further delay "that all Indians within the United States of America are citizens or candidate citizens of the land." [13]

However much Parker might have wished to put off an SAI national conference, Mrs. Bonnin was determined that one should be held in 1918. Accordingly, she and a reluctant Parker called a "business meeting" of the Society in February, 1918, with a program arranged by herself and her fellow Sioux, Dr. Eastman. Plans were made for the 1918 conference to be held in Pierre, South Dakota, in the heart of the Sioux country. Parker favored their choice largely "because [Delos] Lone Wolf told in the recent meeting that the peyote people of Oklahoma did not approve the stand of the SAI on this matter, any place in Oklahoma would not be desirable." [14]

The controversy over peyote which so divided both Indians and their

white allies moved into a new and more critical phase with the introduction of an Indian Bureau bill by Representative Carl Hayden (Arizona) dealing with the suppression of the liquor traffic and peyote
among the Indians. Hearings on the bill were held in February and
March, 1918, before the House Subcommittee on Indian Affairs. (See
Chapter 10.)

At the hearings members and former members of the Society argued
on both sides of the question. The major Indian testimony against the
peyote cult was given by Gertrude Bonnin and Charles Eastman, while
Indians supporting the peyote religion included Thomas L. Sloan, Francis LaFlesche, Cleaver Warden, and Paul Boynton.

The anti-peyotists argued that liquor and peyote were twin evils to
be fought vigorously. They contended that the peyote religion was only
a cover-up for drug-taking, that peyote was harmful physically and
degrading morally, and that it was an addictive drug. Those defending
the peyote religion insisted that it was a genuine Indian religion with
many Christian elements, that peyote was useful in curing diseases and
was not addictive, that the religion had cured many Indians of alcoholism, and that it was morally and socially beneficial to Indians. The
medical evidence was contradictory and inconclusive. On one point,
however, there was general agreement: the peyote religion's greatest
appeal was to younger, educated Indians.

That peyote paraphernalia had already become symbolic of Pan-Indianism was inadvertently shown by none other than Mrs. Bonnin. The
SAI secretary had unwittingly been sporting a peyote fan as part of the
"Indian dress" which she frequently wore, a circumstance which James
Mooney of the Bureau of American Ethnology, testifying on behalf of
the peyotists, solemnly pointed out, no doubt with a good deal of quiet
satisfaction. Mooney referred to an interview with Mrs. Bonnin which
had appeared in the *Washington Times*. In the accompanying picture,
Mooney said, Mrs. Bonnin was dressed "in Indian costume. The dress is
a woman's dress from some southern tribe, as shown by the long fringes,
the belt is a Navajo men's belt, the fan is a peyote man's fan, carried
only by men, usually in the peyote ceremony." Evidently Mrs. Bonnin
was a more eclectic Pan-Indian than she intended to be.

However devoted to Pan-Indianism she was, during this period of
stress the SAI secretary was attempting to build a strong center of the
Society in her own tribe, the Sioux. Arthur Parker also, as his Society

activities dwindled, turned increasingly to the affairs of the Iroquois. Tribalism was not as unimportant to either as they had thought. Parker wrote the declaration of war of the Onondaga against "The Austrian and the German Empires" and urged the Seneca to adopt a similar one. Such an action, he wrote to a Seneca leader, would "establish your independent right to act as a Nation and not as a ward-bound tribe that had no powers of a Nation. The Senecas have lost none of their sovereignty since 1812 and a war declaration would serve to emphasize your status. The fighters could then enter the U.S. Army the same as now." Evidently the abolition of "tribalism" was not to include the Iroquois.[15]

Nevertheless, plans for the Pierre conference went forward, perhaps spurred by attacks on the SAI in *Wassaja* for its failure to meet. "Organization is the power that rules the world today," *Wassaja* stated. "Our race is weak because of our distant relation with each other. If we wish to be a power for good and influence in the world we must have a great Indian organization." In the next issue, Montezuma urged attendance at the conference. "Leave your ill-feeling at home and attend the meeting," he wrote.[16]

The Pierre conference, held September 25–28, 1918, represented a victory for the radicals in calling for the immediate abolition of the Indian Bureau.[17] Other platform planks were much the same as in previous years, with the addition of a strong statement in support of the war and of Indian loyalty. Interestingly enough, the platform did not mention the closing of Carlisle, which had been taken over in the late summer by the War Department for military use. Mrs. Bonnin, as secretary of the Society, had earlier written to the War Department requesting a reconsideration of the decision and had received a negative reply. The need for the buildings for military purposes was probably a convenient and face-saving excuse to close a school which had never been able to recover from the scandals concerning financial mismanagement which had wracked it. With the passing of Carlisle, the era of the eastern boarding schools came to an end.

Arthur Parker did not attend the Pierre conference of the organization of which he was president. Thomas Moffett and Matthew Sniffen, who went as associates, reported to him that though the attendance was small —between twenty-five and thirty active members—"there was really a very good spirit, and the discussions were animated and in the main harmonious." While Moffett and Sniffen were not enthusiastic about the officers elected, they felt that "the thing to do now is to preserve the good name of the Society, if possible, during this year, with the confident expectation that as soon as peace times permit a good strong conference the organization can be put in shipshape and more wisely officered." [18]

The new officers of the Society were Charles Eastman, president; Father Gordon, first vice-president; Gertrude Bonnin, secretary and treasurer; Henry Roe Cloud, vice-president on education; DeWitt Hare, vice-president on membership; and Charles D. Carter, vice-president on legislation. Sherman Coolidge (who had been defeated for the offices of both president and vice-president) was named chairman of the advisory board. The associates did not elect any officers, since there were so few present. Moffett, the associate chairman, resigned while Robert Hall, associate secretary, was already in the army and was "excused from continuance." [19]

Parker was asked to remain as editor of the *Magazine* should he desire to do so; otherwise, Mrs. Bonnin was to become editor, as she informed him shortly after the conference. In addition, the incoming president "was instructed to appoint a board to approve all articles before they may be published in the Magazine." [20]

Parker was of two minds about continuing. He objected especially to the veto power of the new editorial board. While he hesitated, Mrs. Bonnin acted, notifying him that since she had received no reply from him, she was assuming the editorship herself.[21] Meanwhile, Carlos Montezuma, in the October issue of *Wassaja,* greeted the new turn the organization had taken with great enthusiasm. He praised all the new officers as those "most loyal of the Indian race."

Arthur Parker was finished as the most important intellectual influence in the Society and as its most consistent and creative organizer. The conflicts rending the Society had also wracked Parker's mind and will, numbing his desire and his ability to attempt a reformulation of a Pan-Indian position and paralyzing his capacity to act as a leader of Pan-Indian reform. His departure from leadership in the Society was an ignominious one, humiliating to a proud, ambitious, and sensitive man, not the least because it was forced on him. His own sense of a relevant and functioning Pan-Indian identity was rapidly dissolving. In the future he would define himself as simultaneously more Iroquoian and more "white."

Whatever Parker's shortcomings, his vision had been a spacious one: a Pan-Indian organization which would unite educated, middle-class Indians around an ideology and program sufficiently broad to encompass them all and through which, he believed, they could provide "native leadership" to their fellow Indians. The Pan-Indian rationale which he advanced and which the Society advocated was a blend of elements from social science, progressive reform, Christian idealism, education, Indian history and culture, and faith in the openness and flexibility of American society, all infused with a strong sense of the possible. But by the end of Parker's leadership of the SAI, many elements in the blend were separating out, and within each there had appeared new strains and new tendencies at variance with the older conceptions. No longer was there a sense of a coherent developing whole, of an ideology and program whose parts complemented and reinforced one another.

The conflict in the Society over the "race loyalty" of Indian Bureau Indians had virtually eliminated one of the Society's major constituencies, while the fight over peyote eliminated a minor one. But the division over the immediate abolition of the Bureau cut the Society to a small band of true believers. In the end most middle-class Indians, much as they resented the Bureau, could not reconcile themselves to a policy which they feared would deliver older Indians into the hands of rapacious enemies and destroy forever the possibility of protecting the Indian land base.

The abolition of the Bureau was a goal of the Dawes Act ideology. In this sense, the Society's adoption of the demand for immediate abolition was a logical culmination of the Dawes policy. Indeed, Carlos Montezuma, the chief proponent of abolition, was probably the SAI leader least affected by the changes that had taken place since the early promise of the Dawes Act, in this matching the intellectual rigidity and narrowness of his idol, General Pratt, as in other ways Montezuma matched Pratt's frequent generosity of spirit.

But the abolition of the Bureau had been seen as part of a larger process in which the termination of Bureau control would be the logical outcome of the termination of Bureau "protection" of Indian lands, these lands having been individually allotted to Indians. By the end of World War I the allotment process was far advanced, but substantial lands remained under Bureau control. Many of the individual allotments which had been made had quickly passed from Indian to white hands, leaving penniless Indians unable to cope with the pressures of the dominant society. Despite the efforts of the Indian educational system, many Indians had not yet acquired the skills of modern life. Thus the basic preconditions envisaged as essential to the abolition of the Bureau had not been achieved.

In advocating the immediate abolition of the Bureau, the Society adopted a simplistic solution to a complex problem. It was doomed to failure. Not only was there no practical likelihood of the immediate abolition of the Bureau, but even if by some miracle this solution had come to pass, it could by no stretch of the imagination have solved the Indian problem. By committing itself so wholeheartedly to an unworkable solution, and by consigning all those with whom it disagreed to outer darkness as traitors to the race, the Society was left with a remnant of followers, united by an impossible demand but in other respects deeply divided. "Abolish the Indian Bureau" was a slogan with considerable appeal but little practicability.

The Society now had a different tone, more romantic, less rational; at once committed to instant solutions but at the same time less confident of the country's capacity to offer any solutions; more sentimental about Indian life and less closely in touch with it. The Society's new leaders would lead it in new directions.

Arthur Bonnicastle (Osage), a former Carlisle student who served in the American army during the Boxer Rebellion, testified in defense of the peyote religion at the 1918 congressional hearings on the Hayden Bill outlawing peyote. Photo 1905. *Smithsonian Institution National Anthropological Archives, Bureau of American Ethnology Collection*

A future Society of American Indians leader, Thomas L. Sloan (Omaha), as a student at Hampton Institute. Sloan was both a reform and religious Pan-Indian, a lawyer who defended peyotists in court, incurring the hostility of the anti-peyotist reformers. Date not recorded. *Smithsonian Institution National Anthropological Archives, Bureau of American Ethnology Collection*

Dr. Charles A. Eastman (Sioux) was probably the most famous Indian of his day; a physician who wrote popular books on Indian life, a reformer active in many causes of the time. Eastman was a red "Progressive," one of the founders of the Society of American Indians who later served as its president. Photo 1897. *Smithsonian Institution National Anthropological Archives, Bureau of American Ethnology Collection*

Quanah Parker, the "last great chief of the Comanches," one of the most influential proponents of the peyote religion, friend of President Theodore Roosevelt, and spokesman in Washington for Indian interests. Date not recorded, ca. 1895. *Smithsonian Institution National Anthropological Archives, Bureau of American Ethnology Collection*

Wovoka (Jack Wilson), a Paiute who was the messiah of the Ghost Dance. James Mooney, the Bureau of American Ethnology anthropologist who conducted the earliest studies of the peyote cult, took this photo in 1891 during his investigations of the Ghost Dance. *Smithsonian Institution National Anthropological Archives, Bureau of American Ethnology Collection*

Chief Henry Roman Nose (Cheyenne), a reform Pan-Indian and former Hampton student who addressed the 1914 conference of the Society of American Indians, urging Indian boys and girls to learn the white man's ways in order to help the people of all tribes. Photo 1899. *Smithsonian Institution National Anthropological Archives, Bureau of American Ethnology Collection*

Carlos Montezuma, the "fiery Apache," leader of the radicals in the Society of American Indians, a Chicago physician who once served as school physician at Carlisle and who idolized General Pratt. Photo 1896. *Smithsonian Institution National Anthropological Archives, Bureau of American Ethnology Collection*

Francis LaFlesche (Omaha), a distinguished Bureau of American Ethnology anthropologist and the son of an Omaha chief. LaFlesche was active in reform and religious Pan-Indianism and was treasurer of the Omaha Peyote Historical Society Church. Date not recorded. *Smithsonian Institution National Anthropological Archives, Bureau of American Ethnology Collection*

Albert Hensley, a Carlisle student who introduced specifically Christian rituals into the Winnebago peyote cult. Hensley was also a reform Pan-Indian who attended a number of Society of American Indians conferences. Photo 1909. *Smithsonian Institution National Anthropological Archives, Bureau of American Ethnology Collection*

Louis McDonald (Ponca), for many years treasurer of the Native American Church. A former Carlisle student, McDonald was selected to be a pallbearer at General Pratt's funeral in spite of Pratt's hostility to peyote. Photo 1909. *Smithsonian Institution National Anthropological Archives, Bureau of American Ethnology Collection*

"Indian Printer Boys" at the Carlisle School. Paul Boynton (front row, second from left), whom Mooney called "a particularly bright Carlisle student," participated in the Ghost Dance of 1890–91 and later became leader of the Native American Church. He was also a reform Pan-Indian. Date not recorded. *Smithsonian Institution National Anthropological Archives, Bureau of American Ethnology Collection*

The Reverend Sherman Coolidge, president of the Society of American Indians and a leader of fraternal Pan-Indianism in the twenties. Photo 1902. *Smithsonian Institution National Anthropological Archives, Bureau of American Ethnology Collection*

Cleaver Warden (Arapaho), a former Carlisle student who became a leader of the Native American Church and who was a reform Pan-Indian as well. Photo 1909. *Smithsonian Institution National Anthropological Archives, Bureau of American Ethnology Collection*

J. N. B. Hewitt (Tuscarora), the eminent Bureau of American Ethnology ethnologist who sought to bring the Society of American Indians closer to the reservation. Date not recorded. *Smithsonian Institution National Anthropological Archives, Bureau of American Ethnology Collection*

Marie L. Baldwin (Chippewa), Society of American Indians treasurer, was a lawyer and suffragist employed in the education division of the Bureau of Indian Affairs. Photo 1914. *Smithsonian Institution National Anthropological Archives, Bureau of American Ethnology Collection*

A group of Navajos from New Mexico as they arrived at Carlisle. The school's founder, Richard H. Pratt, leans on the railing above them. Date not recorded, ca. 1880's. *Smithsonian Institution National Anthropological Archives, Bureau of American Ethnology Collection*

Six months later the Navajos in Carlisle uniform. The variety in age was typical of the student body. Date not recorded, ca. 1880's. *Smithsonian Institution National Anthropological Archives, Bureau of American Ethnology Collection*

Arthur C. Parker (Seneca), the most important intellectual influence on reform Pan-Indianism before World War I, an anthropologist who served as editor of the Society of American Indians *Quarterly Journal,* as secretary of the Society of American Indians, and eventually as its president. Parker's work in Indian freemasonry was often cited by fraternal Pan-Indians in the twenties. Photo ca. 1906–11. *Rochester Museum and Science Center*

8

TRANSITION IN THE
TWENTIES

In the period immediately following World War I, new themes began
to appear in the Society of American Indians, reflecting currents of
thought now flowing strongly in the wider world. One was the idea of
self-determination as enunciated by President Woodrow Wilson. Another was its domestic counterpart, the idea of cultural pluralism in
American society, of America as a "nation of nations." Another was the
growth of an American nativism which viewed the American past as
exclusively an Anglo-Saxon product and foreigners, immigrants, and
non-whites as lesser breeds—the domestic counterpart of imperialism.
Yet another was the shift of focus from the individual to the group,
the growing belief in a rugged American groupism, and the waning
strength of the idea of rugged American individualism.

All of these conceptions were, of course, older than the postwar
period, but following the war they grew mightily in strength. All were
hostile in varying ways to the old conception of the melting pot as a
producer of a new American; as a unifying process to which individuals
from many and diverse backgrounds contributed, resulting in an American product which was different—and better—than any of its com-
ponents.

It was this idea of the melting pot, and of the Indian contribution to
it, that had been one of the major unifying forces in the Society of
American Indians. As the idea weakened in the larger society, so it
did in the Society of American Indians. In groping about for some new
and usable position, the leaders of the Society employed fragments of all
the ideas mentioned above. The new emphases were not the result of
a systematic attempt to rethink the position of the Indian in relation to

179

the dominant society, and they were even cloudier in the Indian version than in the original. The resulting mix was a melange encompassing a stronger tribal emphasis; a conception of Indians as a separate ethnic group like other American "minorities," as they were beginning to be called; a continued appeal to Indian racial consciousness; a new antagonism to other groups in the "nation of nations," especially the "new" immigrants and, on the part of some, the Negro; plus a continuation of many of the older ideas.

The most explicit statements made by leaders of the Society concerned self-determination, though they were by no means clear as to what it meant. What seems to have been happening is that a catchword was picked up and added to the older ideology of individual assimilation without much thought as to its implications. But in using the slogan of self-determination, the Society's leaders also began to use some of the ideas which adhered to it. These ideas suited Charles Eastman's tribal patriotism and disillusionment with the fruits of civilization, Gertrude Bonnin's romanticism, and Carlos Montezuma's fitful belief in Indian racial superiority.

The lead editorial in the Winter, 1919, issue of the *American Indian Magazine* dealt with self-determination in connection with the World War I Peace Conference then sitting in Paris:

"Under the sun a new epoch is being staged! Little peoples are to be granted the right of self determination!

Small nations and remnants of nations are to sit beside their great allies at the Peace Table; and their just claims are to be duly incorporated in the terms of a righteous peace. . . . Labor organizations, . . . women of the world, . . . the Black men of America . . . [seek] representation at the Conference. . . . A large assembly of New York men and women . . . [have requested President Wilson's] aid in behalf of self-government for the Irish people.

The Redman asks for a very simple thing—citizenship in the land that was once his own—America. Who shall represent his cause at the World's Peace Conference? The Indian, too, made the supreme sacrifice for liberty's sake. He loves democratic ideals, what shall world democracy mean to his race?

There never was a time more opportune than now for America to enfranchise the Red man!" [1]

Thus despite the editorial emphasis on self-determination, the *Maga-*

zine did not demand for the American Indian what that slogan meant in Europe, but rather for full citizenship. The same issue, however, contained a reprint of an 1830 speech by Senator Theodore Frelinghuysen of New Jersey, vigorously proclaiming the "political sovereignty" of the Indian "nations" as the basis for the inviolability of treaties made with the Indians. Perhaps the Society's leaders were searching for some historical basis for the ideas they now struggled with.

The Society's new president, Charles Eastman, analyzed three bills then before Congress, all of which would have the effect of speeding up citizenship for the Indian.[2] These were bills introduced by Senator (later vice-president) Charles Curtis of Kansas, Senator Carl Hayden of Arizona, and Representative Charles Carter of Oklahoma.

Eastman judged the best bill to be Carter's, which provided for immediate full citizenship for every Indian in the United States. However, the bill also called for "the individualizing and removal of restrictions upon all property and moneys belonging to adult mixed blood Indians of less than one-half Indian blood." This, Eastman argued, would create two kinds of citizens, some with a clear title, but others whose "rights" were still to be administered by a bureau without their consent. "If we should apply this rule to Irish, Bohemians, Swedes, Poles, et al. what an outcry would follow! I fear there is bound to be much injustice in such an arbitrary ruling, which will be felt keenly if applied to the many Indians of full or nearly full blood who are stronger, more able and intelligent than many of their half-blood neighbors," Eastman wrote.

Under the bill, competency of those of one-half or more "Indian blood" was to be determined by three commissions, each composed of an Indian member ("an excellent provision," Eastman commented), a member of the Board of Indian Commissioners, and an officer of the Indian Service. Eastman proposed that the commissions immediately decide on and thereupon grant the Indian "freedom to control his own property" instead of having the recommendation go from the reservation agent up to the Secretary of the Interior. He urged that any "hopelessly incompetent" Indian or one "not desiring to be freed" either be "turned over to the respective states" or cared for by "a minor division of the Indian Bureau left in existence for the purpose, the Bureau being otherwise abolished."

In the same issue, Mrs. Bonnin addressed a letter to "the Chiefs and Headmen of the tribes" whom she called "my friends and kinsmen," citing the Americanization movement as a model for Indians. Mrs. Bonnin had taken to writing *red* and *white* with a capital first letter:

"Since the close of the great war, in which our Indians fought so bravely, there is much talk among our White brothers about the importance of all Americans learning to speak English. There are many languages among the White people just as there are among our different Indian tribes. Plans are being made and our government is supporting this new movement to educate all foreigners who now are American citizens, in the study of the English language. . . . Friends, if the White people have found it worth while to do this, isn't it even more worth our while to renew our efforts to speak English . . . how often I have wished that you could write to me in a language we would both understand perfectly. I could then profit by your advice in many things, and you would know you were not forgot."

Mrs. Bonnin also urged her kinsmen to hold "permanently a small portion of their inherited land" for "we cannot really be happy unless we have a small piece of Out-of-Doors to enjoy as we please." Her letter was signed, "Yours for the Indian cause." [3]

The changes in editorial personnel evident in this issue of the *Magazine* reflected the realignment of forces—and of personalities—which had taken place at the Society's Pierre conference. Gertrude Bonnin was now the editor. Montezuma and Gordon were members of the "Review Board and Editorial Staff." Elaine Goodale Eastman (Charles Eastman's wife who, it will be remembered, was white) was also a member and contributed several articles. The other board members were Margaret Frazier, Ben Brave, and George Tinker. Mrs. Frazier and Ben Brave were Sioux.[4] Thus the Society now had a Sioux president, a Sioux secretary-editor, and several Sioux on the editorial board—representing a more exclusive emphasis on one tribe than ever before in its history.

During the spring of 1919, President Eastman made a lecture tour to stump for Indian citizenship. Eastman, Father Gordon, and Carlos Montezuma traveled through Wisconsin together, addressing gatherings of Indians and whites, advocating the abolition of the Bureau and citizenship for the Indian.

Carlos Montezuma described the tour in *Wassaja,* representing it as a triumph. One incident marred the trip: the group was not allowed to enter the Menominee reservation by order of the agent. However, the meeting was held instead at a Catholic school, and on the following day, another was held at a U.S. government school, *Wassaja* reported. Interestingly enough, Montezuma's account of the incident was much more temperate than that which appeared in the *American Indian Magazine*. The latter stated: "Indian Bureau autocracy forbade these educated, leading Indian men to hold any meeting on the Indian reservation! Though the riffraff of the white people from the four corners of the earth may enter Indian lands and homestead them, thus permitting daily contact with the very scum of other races, the educated, refined, and patriotic Indian, teaching the highest ideals of democracy is forbidden to meet with his own race, even for a day." [5]

Montezuma was now most anxious for unity in the Society. "All Indians should stand together," he proclaimed. "In the cause for freedom and citizenship by the abolishment of the Indian Bureau, we Indians must all unite and be of one mind on the matter; the churches of all denominations must help us. The same motive must prompt the Christian people as it did for the black race, to free the Indian race from the corrupt and enslaving system of the Indian Bureau." In the previous issue he had written: "We may differ in opinion on many things, but we must see as one on abolishing the Indian Bureau." [6] Thus, at this time, Montezuma conceived of the fight for the abolition of the Bureau as the Indian common ground.

The summer, 1919, number of the *Magazine* again emphasized self-determination in an article by Mabel Powers, a white writer who was very much interested in the Iroquois, having been adopted by the Senecas. Entitled "Self-Determination, the War Cry of the Iroquois," the article dealt with a conference held in New York State between federal and state officials and Iroquois chiefs from the various reservations. [7] "The problem of little peoples is not a problem and experiment confined to the world across the big sea water, nor south of the Rio Grande. It lies at the very door of New York State," Mrs. Powers wrote. *"Let all the men and women get together in the council houses and discuss the needs of the people, the problems of self-determination, and the meaning of citizenship, discuss both sides of every question in an open fairminded way."* Let citizenship be "granted to those who wish it," Mrs. Powers suggested, pointing out that "strong opposition to self-determination will be raised by the citizenship group." She urged the government to "confer citizenship upon those who want it. Give those

who do not the opportunity to reestablish an independent government
—if they can," she concluded.

In another article in the same issue, Charles Eastman declared,
"Every other race in the United States has a voice in public affairs.
There are 300,000 Indians in the country today and the majority of
them are educated, but we have no right of self-determination; the
fourteen points seemingly do not apply to us."

Eastman's conception of the Society's role had always been somewhat
more tribally oriented than that of the other leaders. Exactly what Eastman meant by "self-determination" is not clear. But he does not seem to
have been talking about the type of self-determination that Mrs. Powers
advocated, that is, independent tribal government.

The new direction in the Society included growing hostility to immigrants and Negroes, now increasingly referred to as "blacks." Perhaps
such shifting attitudes were in part responsible for the growing role of
Red Fox St. James in Society affairs. St. James was both anti-immigrant
and anti-Negro. He, Eastman, and Montezuma organized a white auxiliary of the Society in Chicago. St. James was also busy building the
Tepee Order of America, whose program included granting "the Indian
people full citizenship and the abolishment of the Indian Bureau," as
Wassaja reported in its winter issue. The American Indian Magazine
did not carry news of the Tepee Order, possibly because Mrs. Bonnin
may have seen it as a rival to the Society. Perhaps it was to undercut
the influence of the Order that Mrs. Bonnin, urging SAI members to
attend the next conference, stated, "the Society of American Indians is
the National Teepee for all our tribes." [8]

The Society's eighth annual conference was held at Minneapolis,
Minnesota, October 2–4, 1919. The slogan for the meeting as given in
the call, was "American Citizenship for the Indians." [9] Prior to the
conference, Thomas Moffett wrote to Parker asking him to become active again in the Society to counteract the influence of Gordon, Eastman,
and Montezuma and urging him to get in touch with Fayette McKenzie
for help. Parker replied that he doubted that he could get to Minneapolis
because of the pressure of work in Albany and the Indian work in
which he was engaged; in New York he was a member of the State
Indian Commission representing the Education Department, of which
the State Museum was part. But his reasons went far beyond these:

"From the time of the Lawrence conference until I withdrew my active participation I had less and less time to give [to the Society]. To me it was a tragedy for I saw what we all had hoped for slipping through our fingers. Rather than give a half hearted service it seemed better to withdraw entirely. I am quite sure that this has been highly pleasing to nearly all the Indians who are interested in the Society's work. I am convinced that our educated Indians as a class as well as the Indians of lesser development have no appreciation of the value of adhering to a definite set of principles and in associating every action they take with an individual principle. . . . [Parker added that he would be glad to appeal to McKenzie] to do something, though it seems that Indians are always appealing for someone to get them out of a predicament into which they have often placed themselves."

Parker also told Moffett, "You may be sure that I watch with great interest the progress of the Society, for to my mind it forms a test of the qualities of the race." [10] Clearly, he was disillusioned and hurt. Parker had no hope that his brand of Pan-Indianism, which in his view was the only type with a chance of success, would prevail. The class of educated Indians in whom he had placed his confidence had, in his mind, failed the test. The "qualities of the race" were not yet equal to the situation confronting them. And Parker himself was losing faith in the promise of the melting pot on which he had earlier based his Pan-Indian hopes.

Charles Eastman gave the opening address at the Minneapolis conference, describing his conception of the Indian contribution to America, revealing a highly romantic notion of Indian history.[11]

"We are part of this great American Nation [Eastman said], and we must be some good to the country. This country is composed of hundreds of representatives of different nations and they are all contributing materially in its progress. . . . We Indians started the whole basis of Americanism. We Indians laid the foundation of freedom and equality and democracy long before any white people came here and those who took it up, but they do not give us credit—that this country is absolutely free, to whatever race. . . .

Our Indians had little differences but these differences were no more than athletic games. We did not take anybody's land, we never enslaved anybody. . . . We developed man, man was man, and he loved his God. . . . We all believe in one God. That too was our contribution to this country . . . we were that character, the original American character," he declared.

"The only thing we lacked was organization," Eastman stated. The "big organizations now rule everything. . . . Organization has been the trouble with the white man. It is all right, but it has gone too far":

"We must stand by this country, we Indians. Poles have their societies, Norwegians have their societies. Swedes have their organizations. The French club together; Greeks club together; Armenians club together; Italians club together and so do the English and all the others and yet they say they are Americans. They say they are. But we are Americans. . . . The Indian became part of civilization. We are not going to live in teepees all our lives. We are not going to continue our hunting. The white man's hunting is business. We must conform to this life, this new life, and we have. I do not know of any Indian who has come into this civilization but what his nature is like the white man's—dollar, dollar, dollar. Civilization is formed on that. . . .

[The Indian] will save this country. The day when an Indian becomes leader of this country will be the day when civilization may come on a more stable foundation. Not that he is going to take this people back to the woods and the teepees. . . . There must be a guiding hand and God will take from a small people a man who can do that work. . . . The greatest reformers are from the smallest peoples. It is not necessary that that man should have an education. From Moses to Abraham Lincoln it has been the rule. What would be more likely than God would choose one possessing the sturdy characteristics of our race and thrust him into civilization as its leader? . . .

We must keep our heads and our hearts together. Keep our old characteristics that we have contributed to the country—those characteristics that have been put into the Constitution of the United States itself. . . . Among the influx of European people who come in here, some are trying to destroy that which is real American—the equality of man. And our country is trembling—nobody will be safe because it is composed of several different races."

The Indians, Eastman continued, "have no racial prejudices. We are color blind. . . . Rules and laws make no difference to a white man. . . . But we do not say that the white man is all bad. . . . There are good people among the white, good people right with us." Eastman concluded his address with a strong plea to abolish the Indian Bureau, respect Indian treaties, and give citizenship to the Indian.

Father Gordon advocated practical steps in the campaign to eliminate the Bureau. "We should draft a bill to abolish the Indian Bureau. We must propose a plan to take its place. We must appoint a committee to go to Washington and do some lobby work," he urged. Indians have to be practical, Gordon warned. "It is very fine to tell the white people what is in us and what was in our forefathers, but we are here to eliminate the Bureau, and we mustn't be purely idealists." [12]

Robert Hall, the former associate secretary, called for immediate citizenship for every Indian who served in the armed forces and for a broader Indian franchise as well, buttressing his remarks with an appeal to Social Darwinism:

"I maintain that if it is the desire of the Indian race to have citizenship and they are willing to not only seek the privileges but accept the responsibilities and suffering, then a conference like this should pronounce itself in certain terms, stating that the majority of the Indians who are capable of exercising citizenship is so large that they should be considered rather than the incompetent. In other words, we can commmit ourselves to the necessity of revering that rule for the Indians that has always been true among other peoples—the survival of the fittest." [13]

Thomas Sloan attacked Hall's position:

"[Hall's] statement that only those Indians who have shown themselves capable or equal to certain requirements should have the right of citizenship [is wrong]. The Indian is a native of this country and it is a universal rule of civilization that a person shall be a citizen of the country of which he is a native. The Indian is a subject of the United States Government, a native, and of right is or ought to be a citizen. . . . The backward subject Indian needs citizenship more than the advanced Indian."

Sloan further pointed out that "the suggestion of our associate member [in regard to citizenship for Indians who served in the military or naval forces] comes too late." Such Indians, Sloan stated, "are already declared to be citizens." [14]

The question of citizenship provoked a heated debate. Thomas L. Sloan introduced a resolution calling for SAI endorsement of the Carter Citizenship Bill. Some opposed the bill because it set up several classes of Indians and was therefore judged to be discriminatory, while others feared that it did not offer enough protection for older and less acculturated Indians. Although a number of SAI members favored the bill, which also had the support of the Bureau and of the Indian Rights Association, dissension was so apparent that Sloan withdrew his resolution and the conference took no action on the matter. Moreover no conference platform was published and perhaps none was adopted. The conference which had been convened around the slogan "American Citizenship for the Indian" was unable to unite in support of it.

Thomas L. Sloan was named president, defeating both Eastman and Captain Bonnin, Gertrude Bonnin's husband. After almost a decade, Sloan at last headed the Society in which he had so long been a controversial figure. After being nominated by Sloan's ally Father Gordon, Theodore D. Beaulieu, a fellow Chippewa from Minnesota, was elected vice-president. Mrs. Bonnin declined to continue serving, ostensibly for reasons of health though her opposition to Sloan was probably the real reason. After considerable pressure, Thomas G. Bishop, a Sound Indian from Washington State, became both secretary and treasurer. The office of editor of the *Magazine* was left open. Coolidge continued as chairman of the advisory board and Carter as vice-president on legislation. John Carl, an Indian from Minnesota,[15] became vice-president on membership, and James Irving, a Sioux, who was publisher and editor of the *Woodstock News,* also from Minnesota, became vice-president on education. Among the officers, there was thus a heavy concentration of Minnesota Indians, perhaps reflecting Father Gordon's activities in that state as well as the location of the conference.

A number of the Society's earlier leaders were relegated to the advisory board, including Parker, Roe Cloud, Emma Johnson Goulette, Charles Kealer, Henry Standing Bear, and Chauncey Yellow Robe. Montezuma and Gordon were also members.[16] Charles Eastman and Gertrude Bonnin were not; so far as can be determined, they gave up all SAI activity, evidently disenchanted with the direction the Society was taking.

The new officers set about transforming the Society into a political pressure group with patronage interests. A major enterprise was the attempt to have an Indian appointed as commissioner. In the past, the Society had deliberately avoided any such effort on the ground that it did not wish to be a vehicle for personal advancement for anyone, however well qualified.

James Irving, vice-president on education, wrote Parker asking him for suggestions for the nomination.[17] "The Jews had their Moses; the negroes their Booker T. Washington," Irving wrote. "I believe it is now time to have a real Indian leader for the next Commissioner of Indian Affairs." Thus Irving's view of the place for "a real Indian leader" was at the head of the Bureau the Society was working so hard to abolish.

The next president of the United States, Irving predicted, would be a Republican. Therefore since the job of commissioner "will still be a political plum," the Indian candidate should be a Republican "experienced and highly educated, with the very best of reputation, morally as well as to other points." An ex-soldier might also be a good choice, Irving suggested.

"When I was thinking about this matter I had you and Mr. John Oskison in mind," Irving declared, inquiring also whether Parker knew of any Indian majors and asking his views on "our Indian senators" for the post. "I am going to take this matter up with the Republican State central committeemen in every state where there are Indian voters and will also take the matter up with the National Committeeman in Washington," he concluded. Irving was following a standard American pattern in his efforts to get an Indian Indian Commissioner, as fully in line with the practices of the dominant society as the earlier efforts of the Society had been in behalf of different ends.

Parker's reply was cautious. He did not comment on the propriety of the Society's effort but commended John Oskison as a candidate, stating also that, "Perhaps Mr. Carter or Senator Curtis would consider the nomination, but under the circumstances the position of commissioner is one with so many difficulties that no one intimately acquainted with the work would care much to take it up." [18] Perhaps Parker was speaking of himself.

In a further letter to Irving, Parker spoke harshly of the *American Indian Magazine* and of a proposal to change its title:

"Our society and its magazine have departed so radically from their intended purposes that apparently little remains to be said. I do believe that the Magazine should retain its title. Libraries and collectors will be confused by changes and impute to us a vacillating spirit. It may be that the present officers wish to depart from everything that I did and thus deliberately desire to change the name of the magazine. It is a poor piece of printing and the spelling is far from scholarly. The entire tone of the magazine is shoddy and the hysterical writing of men who are supposed to be educated brings only discredit upon us. However, since I am not in position to be of constructive service it ill becomes me to criticize." [19]

The following month Thomas G. Bishop, the new secretary-treasurer of the Society, wrote Parker describing the current emphasis of the organization. "We have not had time to give the Magazine attention, because of the great amount of work before Congress, and in aiding delegations who are here [in Washington]. The work has taken a new line—up in Congress. We hope to work some reforms during this and the next session of Congress," Bishop reported, adding that negotiations were under way to revive the *Magazine*.[20] Thus the functions of the Society had become those of a normal American lobbying group.

It was precisely to such activities, however, that some of the older leaders of the Society objected. Both Parker and Henry Roe Cloud resigned from the advisory board in the fall of 1920, and M. K. Sniffen of the Indian Rights Association congratulated Parker on his withdrawal. The break between the Society and the white friends of the Indian represented by such groups as the IRA was now complete. By this time Parker was president of the New York Indian Welfare Society. His major activities with Indians were by now Pan-Iroquoian rather than Pan-Indian. The Welfare Society was set up very much along the lines of the old SAI, with a distinguished white advisory board which was probably the equivalent of the SAI associates.

The *American Indian Magazine* which Parker had found so "shoddy" did not appear again until August, 1920. In form and context, the August issue was a radical departure both from the magazine as Parker had edited it and from those issues edited by Gertrude Bonnin. Evidently, the Society leadership had thought it advisable to put out a highly respectable magazine, quiet in tone, aimed at Americans who had a somewhat romantic view of Indians or who were interested in popular ethnology. None of the signed articles were written by Indians. It was not to be, like its predecessor, a magazine of Indian opinion written largely by Indians, but rather a magazine about Indians written mostly by whites, and yet at the same time the official publication of the Society.

The first—and only—issue with the new format and approach was handsomely produced on glossy paper, liberally and beautifully illustrated, and obviously intended for a new audience. Most of the articles were by such distinguished white anthropologists as Clark Wissler, curator of anthropology in the American Museum of Natural History; Stewart Culin, curator of ethnology of the Museum of the Brooklyn Institute of Arts and Sciences; and Walter Hough, curator of ethnology of the United States National Museum. They dealt in popular fashion not with the Indian of the present but with Indians of the past.

The lead article was by the well-known writer Mary Roberts Rinehart, identified as a Blackfoot by adoption.[21] She paid tribute to the "fundamental racial characteristics of the Indian": loyalty, dignity, and generosity:

"It is not possible to alter the racial characteristics of the Indian to fit our civilization. Government errors in the past have been largely because of a failure to understand the lack of adaptability to change of the Indian mind. And why should we change them? The Indian has an ethical creed of his own. When he is unspoiled by the attempt to graft on him a civilization he neither understands nor desires, when he is uncontaminated by the vices of a dominant people, he is sturdily honest, loyal and upright.

[For the 'full-bloods'] . . . paternalism in the best sense is the only solution. . . . But it must be a generous and kindly paternalism, not a grudging one. We must cease to think of our Indians as a menace, as an inimical element to be restrained only. They need encouragement and support. They need our interest as well as our government funds. They represent our romance and our history. . . . To the visitors to our shores from other lands, the single unique element is the American Indian. Other lands have great cities, mountains, lakes and roads. Only America has the Indian."

The "full-blood," Mrs. Rinehart wrote, must be protected not only from white "encroachments" but also "from some of his own people, who have acquired by a mixture of other blood the white man's cunning." Mrs. Rinehart hastened to say that she meant "by this no reflection on the many splendid men and women who pointed with pride to their admixture of Indian blood, and who have devoted themselves to the service of their people with intelligence and knowledge." Indians "with an admixture of white blood can and do assimilate our civilization, and although our school system is still inadequate, they will eventually find their places in the country. Many have already done so," she wrote.

Thus Mrs. Rinehart appeared to believe that the ability to assimilate was biological rather than cultural and that "pure Indians"—by which she obviously meant tribal Indians—must be protected in their unique ways of life by a kindly government.

Despite the strong ethnological and historical emphasis of the new magazine, its aim and that of the Society was proclaimed to be "to enlighten the American people on the present-day Indian and by sane, impartial methods to give the American Indian his rightful place in modern society." The magazine's stated purpose was "the perpetuation of a people, the original American race." The Indian of Cooper and Remington was "a vanishing race." The modern "Red man faces problems which, unless solved speedily, threaten his extinction as a race." These problems "cannot be solved by him alone"; national "understanding of his needs" was necessary. The *American Indian Magazine* would henceforth be a medium to "impress upon Americans the fundamental qualities of Indian character and the worthiness of a people which sent 17,000 of its young men overseas to fight and to suffer for a democracy in which they are not even entitled to the elementary rights of citizenship." [22]

The editorial page was exceedingly staid. Nothing was said about abolishing the Indian Bureau, the lead editorial confining itself to the observation that the annual Commissioner's Report had neglected to deal with a number of Indian complaints. "The Indian situation is full of complexities that cannot be unraveled without a thorough and impartial understanding on the part of the Public," an editorial stated. "Without bitterness, without sensationalism and with impartiality it will endeavor to press to serious-thinking, fair minded American readers . . . the various aspects of a many-sided problem.[23]

The issue also contained laudatory biographies of Thomas L. Sloan and Senator Charles Curtis of Kansas, the latter a member of the Kaw tribe. Aside from a few notes, including an announcement of the next convention to be held in St. Louis, there was little SAI news. The organization was described, however, as "composed of representatives of the tribes in the United States and of 'palefaces' who are interested in Indian welfare," thus vaguely suggesting an intertribal confederation.

Thomas L. Sloan was editor-in-chief of the magazine. The associate editors included such well-known white anthropologists as Clark Wissler, Frederick W. Hodge, Stewart Culin, and Vilhjalmur Stefansson, as well as the poet and lecturer Lew Sarett. No Indian anthropologists were listed.

This was the last issue of *American Indian Magazine* ever published. The *American Indian Tepee,* started in 1920 by Red Fox St. James's Tepee Order, became for a time something of an unofficial organ of the Society of American Indians. It staunchly and unsuccessfully supported SAI President Thomas L. Sloan for the post of Indian Commissioner and reported SAI news, including the St. Louis conference.

The St. Louis conference was a sad affair. Its sessions, held November 15–19, 1920, were distinguished chiefly by wrangles over the fate of the Society's *Magazine,* on which the organization had taken a financial loss. A proposal for the magazine to be put out by a "syndicate" was defeated on the grounds that the Society would then lose control over its own journal. The new approach and format were criticized for not standing four-square on Indian rights.

Much of the remaining conference time was taken up by the complaints of a delegation from several Arizona reservations led by Carlos Montezuma, who had been spending a good deal of time advising Arizona tribes. Only Sherman Coolidge, Thomas Sloan, Thomas Bishop, Father Gordon, and a few others attended the meeting. Clearly, the SAI had lost all sense of direction and was in rapid disintegration.[24]

If the St. Louis meeting was disappointing, the "convention" held the following year at Detroit, October 26–November 2, 1921, was, according to Thomas Bishop, the SAI's secretary, a "fiasco." Billed as an "International Convention of the American Indians," the convention call, signed by Bishop, urged members of the "American Indian Tepee Association [a branch of the Tepee Order], and Tipi Order of America, Society of Indian Ancestry [a Pittsburgh organization], Indian Rights Association and Federation Society of Mission Indians, and all other Indian organizations, to attend this convention, for the purpose of solving the problem of the best interest of the Red Race. We also would like to see some members of the Improved Order of Red Men. Let us all go to this big Indian pow wow and show that American Indians (natives) are much alive." [25]

In a letter to his old colleague Charles Daganett, Arthur Parker angrily attacked the forthcoming meeting and the Society's leadership:

"Francis Fox James, alias Red Fox J. Skuishuhu [St. James] wrote me a letter stating that he 'had nothing against' me and inviting me to 'come and be a man, putting aside petty things and personal feelings.' 'I am an ordained minister,' he goes on to say, and proceeds to preach my duties to me. I told him where he could go.

So far as the conference is concerned, I had no desire to go. I have been spending some time in the medical college lately looking over cadavers. I can stand only so much odor of carrion and no more.

I never think of the Society without thinking also of the work you and I did in company with the hard heads that helped us. Then, thinking of the present state of things, I develop nausea. That bunch of bolshevists could never have started the Society; now they are living on the reputation we made for it." [26]

The "convention" was hardly worth Parker's ire. Only eight active and associate members attended, including Sloan, Coolidge, and St. James, the latter officiating at a program which included "Indian songs and recitations" by members of the Improved Order of Red Men. Sloan made a speech calling for the abolition of the Indian Bureau and for Indian citizenship.[27]

A few months after the disastrous Detroit convention, Parker made a slashing attack on the whole melting pot theory. His intellectual and emotional commitment to Pan-Indianism had run out. His disillusionment extended not only to Pan-Indian activity but to the theoretical basis of the Pan-Indianism he had helped to create.

Parker summed up his case against the melting pot in an eloquent speech to the Albany Philosophical Society in which he did not even mention the American Indian directly: [28]

"During the past few years we have waged a wordy war over such phrases as, 'The League of Nations,' 'making the world safe for democracy,' 'government by consent of the governed,' 'the rights of minor nationalities' and 'self-determination.' In earlier days we heard that 'all men are created free and equal' and that this is 'a free country.'

Now many a phrase has made a man and a nation, but such potent things are quite as apt to ruin both. Let us take the phrase, 'America, the *melting pot* of the world.' What a beautiful simile . . . and yet there are some of us who are skeptical enough to think that the myth of the 'melting pot' has all gone to pot."

The solid colonial stock of the country was "Nordic-European," Parker argued. These "hardy settlers" had the moral and physical stamina to establish the Republic. The "national philosophy of the commonwealth, as expressed by our Nordic-Aryan forefathers of the colonial days" demanded the following:

"1. a common political ideal, and loyalty to our form of government; both in spirit, principle and detail;
2. conformity to established institutions and customs;
3. speaking the common language—English;
4. an education of the average standard;
5. a common moral standard; but wide religious liberty;
6. a common standard of living;
7. similar modes of behavior and a democratic etiquette."

These seven points were similar to those enumerated in Parker's article six years before in the *American Indian Magazine*. But the tone had changed. Parker's new formulation implied a rigid conformity. Omitted were the crucial factors of the willing participation of those to be assimilated in the process of assimilation, of the desirability of their everyday association with other Americans, and of the necessity for "the realization of cherished hopes." Significantly, also, Parker now added a further curious point:

"8. the preservation of the physical type—that of the Aryan white man. So important was the latter demand that when our national constitution was formed there was a lengthy debate as to whether the European white man alone should be eligible to citizenship, to the exclusion of the Asiatic, Negro and native red man."

In Parker's manuscript, "and native red man" is crossed out, thus eliminating his only reference to the American Indian.

The "agricultural tendencies" of the Nordic Europeans coupled with "their moral qualities" had made the settlement of America possible, Parker alleged. But with the rise of industry, a new "fortune-hunting" immigration of eastern and southern European peoples began. The "native white stock" was threatened, Parker believed, by these new immigrants as well as by Negroes and Jews.

"What do we mean by melting?" Parker asked. "Is it only assimilation and not amalgamation? If assimilation only is meant, then we may become a crazy-quilt nation full of racial patches, some black, some white, some yellow, some brown." The new "motley peoples" have never proved "any capacity whatever for self government." They "came from chaos and proclaim new social orders and plans for revolution here." Amalgamation is dangerous unless "between like types. . . . Each [race] has hereditary tendencies that are quite fixed and are repeated in the offspring. Students of Eugenics have much to say of the results of racial blendings, especially those of different blood stocks. In general such blendings are discouraged," though a few, such as the Scotch, English, and early Athenians and Romans, may be "advantageous."

Parker advocated a ten-year staying of "the tide of immigration" while America concerns "herself with the elimination of race poisons, feeble mindedness, the sex diseases, tuberculosis and cancer" and builds up "a higher intelligence standard."

Parker ended his speech with a solemn warning:

"If we fail to heed the plain, clear voice of experience as it points out the fatal results of indiscriminate blood blending and inharmonious race contacts, we shall only build a nation to be known for its glorious industrial achievements, and finally for its blindness, its palsy, its leprosy and its death by fire upon a bed of scented silks. And in that day the yellow man and the Mediterranean and the son of Abraham will shake dice for the mulatto servants and the estate of the idealist who built his house upon the sands of mawkish sentiment. As a monument these three will erect an ornate melting pot of lead in which will be placed grinning images of bronze, iron and gold."

Parker had ended his earlier article quite differently: "When the native Indian, the foreign born south European, the Teutonic north European or even the Asiatic through the equal possession of the seven requirements we have enumerated calls upon us to recognize his qualifications for complete citizenship we need have no fear of granting him political equality and the privilege of the ballot." [29]

If Parker had been white, his attack on the melting pot would be only one more example of a stream of thought important in the twenties. If Parker had not previously attempted to fit the Indian into a theory of American nationality based on the melting pot, his omission of the Indian would not even be noticed. But Parker indeed was an Indian and had been the most important of Indians in developing a theoretical framework for Pan-Indianism. As he had once used social science to develop a concept of Indian assimilation, he now used eugenics in the service of a theory of exclusion. By projecting a new vision of America in which the Indian was simply ignored, he betrayed himself. For a man with Parker's intellectual gifts, such a fateful omission could come only out of a deep inner turmoil. For a decade he had found a spiritual home in the Society's Pan-Indianism. The bitterness of losing it still rankled.

The Society of American Indians contrived a precarious existence into the mid-twenties. In 1923, the organization held a convention in Chicago. The invitation to meet in that city had been issued by Carlos Montezuma, but by the time it was necessary to begin planning, Montezuma was mortally ill and had decided to go back to the reservation to die. Before leaving, Montezuma "with tears in his eyes" begged a white friend, Miss M. Austine Stanley, to organize the meeting. "They'll fight you and try to tear down every time you build up, but don't give up. See the convention through, promise me that," Montezuma told her. "I am going away and may not be well enough to come back, but I leave everything in your hands." [30] Montezuma and his wife left Chicago shortly thereafter for the McDowell Reservation in Arizona, where he died on January 31, 1923, in a primitive hut on the reservation. After so many years of asserting that he would not "go back," he did indeed "go back" to die among Indians. Montezuma was still deeply committed to Pan-Indianism, but he chose to die an Apache. In the end he tried to honor his devotion both to the Indian race and to the Apache.[31]

Montezuma's warning proved well founded, for Miss Stanley had great difficulty in obtaining local support in Chicago for the convention. Eventually, she got a group together to organize the conference, but according to her account, it was taken over by a group of white and Indian Christian Scientists and Republicans who "excluded other denominations and the Democrats." The trouble began, Miss Stanley reported, when she suggested that "the government cannot be ignored, we must ask its cooperation." Attitudes toward the Indian Bureau thus continued to be a source of division in Pan-Indian ranks, including those of white supporters.

Arthur Parker, whom Miss Stanley had consulted for advice about the selection of speakers and program arrangements, wrote her a consoling letter which revealed his disillusionment with the prospects of Pan-Indianism. "To go into the work too deeply only brings a heartache," he told her:

"One must realize that there is no such being or race today in America as 'the Indian.' To the contrary, there are between 300,000 and 340,000 persons of more or less Indian blood, each one of which has his own vital individual interests. Few have any very deep interest based on the idea of race. If there is such an interest it is historical or sentimental and does not lend itself to strong association. In other words there is no idea of race. If there is such an interest it is historical or sentimental and the blunting of the former ideals of the old red man conspire to prevent the floating of any great Indian organization.

The Society of American Indians lived when a few idealists dominated, but when it fell into other control it became an invalid. Then came a rush of Indian societies. My mail every week brought me circulars from one or other Indian association. There is lack of coherence. Why? Because as before stated, there is so much individual interest and so little community of interest. This is quite natural while the red men are undergoing transition." [32]

Despite the factionalism which developed in the preparations for the conference, it was held September 24–30. It seems to have been run largely by the local committee, which included such distinguished citizens as the anthropologist Ralph Linton and Mrs. Harold Ickes, with Thomas L. Sloan as "Honorary Chairman."

The Chicago conference was less a conference than a series of events in which Indians were featured attractions. A reception for the Indians was held at the Chicago Historical Society and a banquet at the Hotel Sherman. The *Chicago Tribune* reported that Mrs. Rockefeller McCormick "will entertain twenty-five Indian chiefs" and "Mrs. Archibald Field and Mrs. Frank O. Lowden [wife of Governor Lowden] will have a table."

Thomas Sloan, accompanied by an Indian delegation, visited the Chicago Bar Association and attempted to drum up interest in Indian affairs. But the meetings in Chicago were far overshadowed by the Indian encampment held in connection with the conference in a forest preserve near the city. Thousands of Chicagoans journeyed to the camp to see the Indians "in full regalia" and to watch Indian dances and ceremonials. Obviously the citizenry was much more interested in the exotic Indian past than in the reality of the Indian present. William Madison, a Minnesota Chippewa who was treasurer of the Society, "expressed his regrets that it is only when he exhibits Indian war dances and ancient ceremonies that the public evinces any interest in the Indian." [33] The Pan-Indian message that reached the public was the powwow rather than the conference. The image of the Indian projected by the Society was very different from the one of a decade earlier, when the picturesque Indian past had been deliberately subordinated to debate on the Indian present and future.[34]

No doubt the *Tribune* stories tended to emphasize the "color" aspects of the conference. However, it seems clear from contemporary accounts that the Indian participants were swamped by their white sponsors and that the Society had little to offer in the way of a program for Indian affairs beyond criticism of the Bureau and interest in the acquiring of citizenship.

By the mid-twenties any basis for a significant reform Pan-Indianism had melted away. All attempts to unify the Society around differing ideas had failed. The abolition of the Bureau was a hopeless cause which only alienated most of the able leadership and failed to provide an Indian common ground. Already dead in spirit, the Society dragged out a precarious existence for a few more years with Father Gordon as president.

The final effort to make the Society function as a national political pressure organization was doomed to failure, if only because the Indians did not possess the power or the willingness to act together as a significant pressure group. A substantial number of Indians lacked the right to vote. Many of those who did have the vote were unwilling to use it for fear of losing their property rights or their special relationship to the tribe. Even if all the Indians had been able to vote in both national and state elections, political action would necessarily have been based largely on reservation Indians who were concerned primarily with local or tribal rather than national issues except as the latter affected them directly.

During the twenties, the clearest tendency in the Society was an increasing emphasis on the tribe, on separate Indian cultures rather than on an inclusive Pan-Indian perspective. The Society's leaders were themselves peripheral to their own tribes which in any case were usually riven by factions. Not so much tribal animosities in particular as the tribal culture emphasis in general weakened the force of a Pan-Indian viewpoint in the Society.

In the preceding decade, the national commitment to the melting pot was sufficiently vigorous to sustain a Pan-Indian version based on race. This position was strongly held by white friends of the Indian with whom the Society worked most closely. By the early twenties, faith in the melting pot was faltering, under attack from diverse quarters. Some believed that America could absorb only immigrants from certain countries and that those from eastern and southern Europe were virtually unassimilable or at least only in small numbers. Extremists darkly predicted the triumph of "bad" genes over "good," and talked of race suicide, bolstering their arguments with references to eugenics. Others believed that it was highly desirable for ethnic groups to remain together as groups, preserving as much as possible of their "native" cultures. This, they maintained, would give spice and variety to American life and would minimize the psychic cost of adjustment to the larger society.

In the specific case of the Indian, a new group of reformers, more interested in tribal than in Pan-Indian development, were becoming involved in Indian affairs. They were not necessarily hostile to Pan-Indian development, but merely gave it a low priority or ignored it. Perhaps this was due in part to the circumstances in which the great debate over Indian policy in the twenties arose. The public uproar which forced a reformulation of Indian policy grew out of three events, two of which brought together old and new friends of the Indian of rather divergent views while the last was the cause of bitter controversy among them.

The first event concerned the ancient Pueblos of New Mexico, who had maintained a strong internal cohesion as self-governing societies for hundreds of years. Each Pueblo owned lands communally and unconditionally under grants from the King of Spain later confirmed by the United States Congress. Despite this, numbers of squatters had moved onto Pueblo lands over the opposition of the Indians. In 1921, Senator H. O. Bursum of New Mexico introduced a bill whose effect would have been to divest the Pueblos of large portions of their lands in favor of the trespassers. By 1922, Secretary of the Interior Albert B. Fall was strongly backing the Bursum Bill as an administration measure.

Fall's Pueblo policy was part of a larger administration attempt to take away or exploit Indian lands. In 1922, the Secretary ruled that "Executive Order Reservations," that is, reservations set aside by Presidential order rather than by treaty or an act of Congress, were "merely public lands temporarily withdrawn by Executive Order" and that the General Leasing Act of 1920 dealing with oil and gas deposits thereby applied to these lands. The Executive Order Reservations which were thus put in jeopardy comprised two thirds of the unallotted lands, some twenty-two million acres. For three generations the Indians had believed that their tribal titles to this vast estate were secure. Now they faced the possible loss of a large portion of it.[35]

These flagrant attempts to lay hands on Indian lands resulted in an aroused public opinion and renewed activty in behalf of Indian rights. Not only did the old Indian defense organizations like the IRA enter the fray, but such influential non-Indian groups as the General Federation of Women's Clubs, long interested in Indian affairs, became increasingly active.

To their ranks was now added a group of writers, artists, social scientists and reformers who had been working in Indian affairs on a local basis, but who had not participated actively on the national Indian scene. They were organized by John Collier into the American Indian Defense Association in 1923 with Collier as executive secretary. These men and women possessed substantial influence in public and academic circles, and all were deeply sympathetic to Indian tribal cultures. Impressed with the insights to be gained by social science, they were immediately interested in applying the lessons of "indirect rule" emergent from the experience of colonial powers and in the problems of developing a sense of community and neighborhood in a swiftly urbanizing culture. They were an important new force in Indian affairs.

All of the reform organizations, old and new, united to oppose the Bursum Bill and Fall's ruling on the Executive Order Reservations. But another action—the Dance Order—was supported by the IRA and the missionaries and opposed by the newer reformers. The Dance Order was a circular issued by the Commissioner of Indian Affairs in 1923 directing superintendents to discourage the "give-aways" which were part of the ceremonials of a number of tribes, as well as any dances the agent deemed immoral, indecent, or dangerous. The missionaries and the IRA had long deplored what they considered excessive time spent in ceremonials and had opposed the "orgies," as they termed them, so "shocking" that "the practices indulged in by those participating in the dance are unprintable." [36] There seems little question that the Dance Order was issued in response to pressure from missionaries and the IRA.

The issuance of the order was strongly protested by a number of persons and groups, including the American Indian Defense Association, on the grounds that it represented an interference with the constitutional right of the Indians to religious freedom. Those opposed to the order maintained that the secret ceremonials to which the objections were made could by no stretch of the imagination be considered immoral or indecent, but were, on the contrary, beautiful and moving rituals of a deeply religious character.

Thus by 1923, Indian governmental policy was under attack from both the older and newer reformers. Although many tribes were endangered by the fateful direction of administration policies, the Pueblos emerged as the symbol of the Indian and of the injustices forced upon him. The coherence and dignity of the Pueblo societies and the reverence of their ceremonials evoked widespread public sympathy and support which might have been less easily extended to tribes whose ways of life were not so colorful and appealing. In any case, public support for the Pueblos helped to focus attention on the values of tribal culture.

In the wake of intense pressure from so many and so diverse forces, the new Secretary of the Interior, Herbert W. Work, who had replaced Fall in 1923, invited an eminent group of Americans to review and advise on Indian policy. The group summoned to Washington by the Secretary consisted of some of the most distinguished men and women in public life. The Committee of One Hundred included Bernard M. Baruch, Nicholas Murray Butler, William Jennings Bryan, David Starr Jordan, General John J. Pershing, Mark Sullivan, Roy Lyman Wilbur, William Allen White, Oswald Garrison Villard, and many others. Invited also were the leaders of all the Indian defense organizations, including M. K. Sniffen and John Collier, a number of clergymen, and such old friends of the Indian as Fayette McKenzie.

Most of the Indian members of the Committee of One Hundred had been leaders of the Society of American Indians in its heyday: Henry Roe Cloud, Sherman Coolidge, Charles Eastman, Father Phillip Gordon, Arthur C. Parker, Thomas L. Sloan, and Dennison Wheelock. But only Sloan and Gordon were still active in the Society.

One of the more interesting aspects of the committee's composition was the strong representation of anthropologists, a factor both indicating and foreshadowing the increasing importance of anthropology in the formulation of Indian policy. There were nine anthropologists in the group, including such eminent men as Frederick W. Hodge, Alfred L. Kroeber, Warren C. Moorehead, and Clark Wissler.[37]

The Committee of One Hundred, after a series of smaller preparatory meetings, met on December 12 and 13, 1923, in Washington. Arthur Parker was selected to preside over the committee sessions, while Fayette McKenzie was made chairman of the resolutions subcommittee.

Despite the wide variety of opinions represented, the Committee of One Hundred agreed on a series of resolutions. The group strongly urged better-quality Indian education, admission of Indians to public schools, and the provision of government scholarships in high schools and colleges for able Indian youth "with a view to fitting them for positions of native leadership." More adequate health and sanitation facilities were advocated, as was the opening of the Court of Claims to the tribes.

On the delicate question of Indian dances and ceremonies, the committee stated that "all lawful ancient ceremonies, rites and customs of the Indian race" might be cultivated as the "privilege and liberty of the Indians, not to be curtailed or infringed." But if the ceremonies were unlawful or contravened "the interests of morality" they should be "discontinued and discouraged." At the same time, the committee urged the encouragement of "the characteristic native arts and crafts."

The committee took up several other controversial matters. On the subject of peyote, the group recommended a National Research Council study. If peyote were thereby shown to be "fundamentally detrimental" to the health or morals of the users, appropriate congressional legislation should be enacted prohibiting its use, sale, and possession. Unfortunately, the study was never made.

The committee flatly recommended the suspension of all court proceedings under the "Executive Reservation Order" and the enactment of legislation to secure Indian title to their lands. This problem was later partially resolved by a ruling of the Attorney General that Fall's original order was illegal. On the question of the Pueblo lands, the committee urged "the most prompt and vigorous action by the Department of the Interior and the Department of Justice to hasten the rendering of decisions" of certain test cases affecting Pueblo land titles in the courts, and just compensation to the Pueblos and to settlers who had occupied the lands in good faith. The Bursum Bill, which had originally set off the controversy, had already been defeated.

The Committee of One Hundred did not take a position on Indian citizenship, evidently because it was feared that the immediate acquisition of citizenship would endanger the status of Indians protected by the federal government.[38]

The results of the committee's deliberations showed that it was now possible for persons of widely varying views, whether white or Indian, to arrive at reasonably satisfactory compromises on important aspects of Indian policy. The shaping of a new consensus had begun.

Commenting on the resolutions of the Committee of One Hundred, Fayette McKenzie wrote, "It would be interesting to compare the platform of this conference with the positions taken in earlier years by the Society of American Indians. In general it was a summarization of those positions but in more general terms and in places with less accuracy of statement or policy." [39] McKenzie was right. The reformulation of Indian policy began from a position very much like that of the old SAI. The reform Pan-Indianism of the preceding decade came to partial fruition in the twenties. But the process thus begun would result in a position quite different from its starting point.

Some of the old SAI leaders, like Parker, who helped to launch this reexamination of policy were themselves disillusioned with Pan-Indianism. Eastman's position had always been somewhat equivocal. Sloan and Gordon still labored ineffectively and unsuccessfully in Pan-Indian affairs. Sherman Coolidge had now become involved in a different brand of fraternal Pan-Indianism characteristic of the spirit of the twenties.

Of all the old SAI leaders, the man who most deeply affected the reformulation of Indian policy was probably Henry Roe Cloud. Roe Cloud, together with the Society's founder, Fayette McKenzie, was a member of the Brookings Institution research group which in 1926 began a massive and authoritative study of the administration of Indian affairs. The study was an outgrowth of the Committee of One Hundred's activities and was undertaken at the request of the Secretary of the Interior. The report was issued in 1928.[40] Known as the Meriam Report after its chief, Lewis Meriam, the study helped to lay the groundwork for the reform administration of Commissioner Charles Rhoads and Assistant Commissioner J. Henry Scattergood under President Hoover, as well as for the Indian New Deal under the commissionership of John Collier.

How radically the viewpoint of informed persons interested in Indian affairs had changed was demonstrated in a debate and symposium which appeared in the pages of *Forum* magazine in the spring of 1924. Two opposing articles on the Indian question were published, one by Flora Warren Seymour, upholding the early Dawes Act perspective in uncompromising fashion, and the other, by Mary Austin, strongly favoring governmental policies which would preserve Indian tribal cultures.[41] Both articles were extreme statements, as M. K. Sniffen noted, thus revealing that even he did not wholly subscribe to Mrs. Seymour's argument.[42]

The "great volume of letters" received as a result of the *Forum* debate represented a wide variety of emphases and nuances. The majority opinion on "segregation vs. absorption" indicated a growing sentiment for a new approach. The *Forum* editors summarized the major viewpoints as follows: "Opinion is greatly divided over the question of whether the Indian should be encouraged to preserve his individuality, tradition, arts, and customs, or be received into the melting pot. The majority prefer the former course, although many think it impracticable if not entirely impossible; while a few wish to see the Indian civilized, Christianized, and absorbed by his conquerers as quickly as may be."

But however divided friends of the Indian and the Indians themselves might be over "segregation vs. absorption," they were largely united on the desirability of Indian citizenship. The major stumbling block had been the problem of how to grant citizenship and still retain federal protection of Indian lands and other rights. This problem was solved by the provisions of the 1924 Citizenship Bill. The result was a smooth passage through Congress with the support of all major Indian defense organizations.

Passage of the Indian Citizenship Bill, which was signed into law on June 2, 1924, might also be regarded as the symbolic date of the demise of the Society of American Indians. It was by this time almost completely inactive—but one of the most important goals for which it had fought so long had been won.

The bill passed quietly—very quietly indeed for a piece of legislation which represented the achievement of one of the crucial objectives of the Dawes era. Perhaps the lack of general public interest in the bill indicated how far the country had moved from the Dawes Act perspective. Perhaps also the concentration of public attention on the Quota Act restricting immigration was in part responsible for the scant notice given to Indian citizenship, for the Citizenship Act was approved only a week after the passage of the Quota Act. There seems to have been little connection in the public mind between these two measures dealing with American nationality; at least none was discernible in the debates on either bill.

The Indian Citizenship Bill (HR 6355) was introduced in the House by Representative Homer P. Snyder of Little Falls, New York, the chairman of the House Committee on Indian Affairs. Snyder's bill originally provided for the issuance of certificates of citizenship by the Secretary of the Interior to any non-citizen native-born Indian who applied, without affecting any rights to tribal or other property.

The bill was reported out of the Senate Committee on Indian Affairs by Senator Charles Curtis acting in behalf of the chairman of the committee, Senator John W. Harrold of Oklahoma. The Senate version eliminated the issuance of certificates and simply declared all native-born Indians citizens, while substantially retaining the other provisions of the House bill.

Debate was limited to the question of whether or not the bill meant that Indians would have to fulfill state suffrage requirements in order to vote. Upon being assured that they would, the House promptly agreed to the Senate version without further discussion. None of the members who spoke briefly on the bill in either House linked it with the Quota Act. Nor did they do so in debate on the immigration bill. The Citizenship Bill's House sponsor, Congressman Snyder of New York, voted against the proposed immigration quota on the ground that the 1890 basis was discriminatory, while its Senate sponsor, Senator Harrold of Oklahoma, voted for the Quota Act.

A parallel between the situation of immigrants and Indians was drawn by an editorial in the New York *Times,* July 7, 1924, hailing the passage of the Indian Citizenship Act.

"Thus in the one hundred and forty-eighth year of the independence of the United States it has pleased Congress to admit the descendants of the original American people to the same legal status as aliens who have gone through the necessary procedure after five years of continuous residence here. . . .

What material advantage the Indians will obtain from their new status as citizens it is hard to say. Presumably they will become subject to local laws, at least when off the reservations, although there is no reason to suppose that their tribal form of government will be interfered with. In due time we may expect to hear that the 'Indian-American' vote has been mobilized behind a candidate pledged to this or that issue. This might strengthen their position technically, and make it easier for them to maintain their rights. But not even the new legal status affords them practical protection from the jealousy and ignorance of white men determined to 'civilize' them by gradual elimination.

If there are cynics among the Indians, they may receive the news of their new citizenship with wry smiles. The white race, having robbed them of a continent, and having sought to deprive them of freedom of action, freedom of social custom and freedom of worship, now at last gives them the same legal basis as their conquerors."

Two years after the passage of the Indian Citizenship Act, a new secular Pan-Indian reform group was founded, having as one of its primary purposes the organization of Indian voters for political action. Defining as its objective "a constructive effort to better the Red Race and make its members better citizens of the United States," it called itself the National Council of American Indians. Its president was none other than Gertrude Bonnin, while her husband, Captain R. T. Bonnin, was its secretary-treasurer. The Council participated in several political campaigns in Oklahoma and South Dakota during the congressional elections of 1926, but does not seem to have attempted subsequently to organize voters.[43]

The National Council attempted to be a body representative of the tribes. In practice it seems to have been a small and struggling group owing its existence to the devotion of the Bonnins. Mrs. Bonnin's outlook on Indian affairs remained very much what it had been in Society days, though she no longer advocated immediate abolition of the Bureau. During the twenties and thirties she worked closely with John Collier, in spite of their differences over the peyote religion, to which she remained staunchly opposed.[44] She also participated in the Indian work of the General Federation of Women's Clubs and cooperated with the IRA.

The letterhead of the National Council proclaimed as its purpose: "Help Indians Help Themselves in Protecting Their Rights and Properties." To this end, Mrs. Bonnin sent out an informational newsletter reporting on legislation and other matters affecting Indian rights, and aided tribesmen who came to Washington. But the amount of cooperation she secured from other Indians for "the Indian cause" was discouraging. As she wrote in a newsletter to her "Indian Kinsmen":

"Too many individual Indians ask help for themselves only, and seem to forget the TRIBE'S welfare as a whole. This spring I heard Assistant

Commissioner of Indian Affairs, Mr. Scattergood in a public speech here in Washington, D. C. Among other things, he compared the Indians with the Negros [sic] saying he was sorry that the Indians did not have as much race consciousness as the Negros. Right there, Capt. Bonnin asked, 'What do you mean by race consciousness?' Mr. Scattergood tried to explain that educated Negros went back to their own people, to give them the benefit of their education, while Indians did not, as a rule. He did not tell his audience that Indians were not enough educated to pass the required Civil Service examinations, while the Negros have '77 colleges and universities' while Indians had no real High School in the entire Indian Service. Mr. Scattergood left the impression that Indians today are not trying in any way to help their tribes. This is not true as far as the NATIONAL COUNCIL OF AMERICAN INDIANS, Inc. is concerned. Our ancestors had enough race consciousness to protect, feed and teach HONESTY to the Indian race of their day without white men's schools. However, today, with printed books in our hands, Indian people are rated below the Black race in the matter of race-consciousness. Think about this. Whose fault is it?" [45]

But the tribes to whom Mrs. Bonnin addressed her appeals did not respond, and the educated Indian elite took no interest in Mrs. Bonnin's work. Personal faction and jealousies were ever the bane of Pan-Indian organization, and Mrs. Bonnin's tendency to run a one-woman show no doubt virtually precluded the active participation of other educated Indians. The National Council lasted into the mid-thirties as the only functioning Pan-Indian reform group organized on a national basis.

Thus reform Pan-Indianism in the twenties led a precarious existence, kept alive by the commitment of a few hardy souls who had acquired their Pan-Indianism in an earlier time when the movement was creative and vigorous. Yet the middle-class and professional group on which the reform Pan-Indianism of the Progressive period was based had not disappeared but was, in fact, increasing. Moreover, during the twenties a whole new wing of white reformers led by John Collier entered the field in response to such threats as Fall's Executive Reservation Order. Both the newer and the older white reform organizations were able to take cooperative action in spite of their underlying differences. But the attacks on Indian rights which united white reformers did not evoke any widespread or effective Pan-Indian reaction. Protests there were, but on a tribal rather than on a Pan-Indian basis.

The reasons for the quiescence of reform Pan-Indianism in this period lay in a number of factors. One of the most important of these was the circumstance that governmental Indian policy was undergoing a period of transition. It had lost the old coherence of the Dawes Act policies and had not yet developed the new coherence which would characterize the Indian New Deal. Evidently such a confused transitional period did not furnish the impetus required to overcome traditional Indian differences nor to unite Indian reformers. From a historical perspective, each of the two major Pan-Indian reform movements of the twentieth century—the Society of American Indians in the second decade and the National Congress of American Indians in the fourth—arose some years after a fundamental change in governmental policy had taken place, when the effects of the new policy were clearly evident, and when the policy itself was in trouble. None of these conditions existed in the twenties.

The unifying bond of Carlisle had also grown more tenuous, or at least had changed its character. While former Carlisle students continued to man all the varieties of Pan-Indian movements, their ties were no longer to a living institution, but to the memory of one. They were alumni without a school. No new generations of Carlisle students were available to inherit or reshape a reform Pan-Indian tradition. No fresh inspiration for a vital Pan-Indian reform movement could arise from the now abandoned barracks in Pennsylvania. Haskell, which would partially serve these functions in the future, was only just beginning to do so.

But perhaps the most basic reasons for the decline of reform Pan-Indianism in the twenties lay in the more general decline of interest in reform in the larger society and in the weakening of the ideology which had earlier united the Indian reformers. Without the sustaining power of a national reform impulse, Pan-Indian reform withered. The old unifying ideas, based on the concepts of the melting pot and the Indian race, had lost much of their potency. The newer ideas which emphasized tribal cultres helped to weaken reform Pan-Indianism, though such was not the intent of those who advanced them.

Pan-Indianism in the twenties developed in ways more compatible with the spirit of the age than political reform. In its secular manifestation, the characteristic type of Pan-Indianism in this period was not reformism, but fraternalism. Like so many of their fellow countrymen, Pan-Indians found themselves more attracted to the delights of high-sounding rites and rituals in the lodge hall than to the enunciation of high hopes for political and social transformation.

II

FRATERNAL
PAN-INDIANISM

———————— ✻ ————————

9

INDIANS IN THE CITIES

Insofar as America of the twenties was characterized by a flowering of numerous fraternal orders and clubs, fraternal Pan-Indianism was a true reflection of the times. Having as its dynamic factor the desire of Indians living in towns and cities to retain an Indian identity, fraternal Pan-Indianism took various forms. In some cases it displayed an elaborate ritual enveloped in an impressive air of mystery. In others it featured ritual without secrecy. In yet others it resembled the usual good-and-welfare social clubs. Although usually led by Indians, it also frequently included whites in its membership, even in its leadership. Unlike reform Pan-Indianism, its primary purposes were fraternal and social rather than reformist and political.

One of the earliest of the fraternal Pan-Indian organizations and one which encompassed all the above variations was the Tepee Order of America.[1] It first appeared in New York City around 1915 as a youth group, and only gradually did it develop into an adult movement. Its founder was Red Fox St. James, and its first head chief was Charles Eastman.

The Tepee Order was originally a secret organization for native-born Protestant young people from fifteen to thirty years of age, and its avowed purpose was "studying the early history of the natives of America, its languages, customs, and to put into practice the activities of Indian outdoor life." The Order was primarily for boys but there was also to be a branch for "young ladies." Its governing board was composed of *"real American Indians* and selected Boy's Work Experts exclusively," and it was to be "directed by Indians, assisted by white men." Officers held such titles as Head Chief, Medicine Man, and Scribe. Provision was made for initiation, degrees, badges, and ceremonials which were "strictly Indian, real not imitation." Each member was to get an "Indian name," and was to wear "real" Indian dress.[2]

The Tepee Order followed the general pattern of the Boy Scouts and similar youth organizations. It seems to have been envisioned as an Indian-led alternative to scouting, addressed largely to white youngsters. In its emphasis on secrecy and exclusiveness, however, it differed sharply from the Boy Scouts. These characteristics were retained when the Order became an adult organization.

The Order's founder, the Reverend Red Fox Francis St. James Skiuhushu, was a man with an almost classically marginal life history and with a series of names that exemplified it.[3] St. James' father, James Thomas St. James, was an American of Welsh descent who claimed one-sixteenth Indian "blood," while his mother was a Northern Blackfoot who left the reservation when she married. St. James was "one-quarter degree Indian blood and more white." He "never had any connection with the Reservation" and was "raised the same as any child born of white people." [4]

St. James claimed to have attended Carlisle, but the school archives have no record of him. About 1909 he joined the Roman Catholic Church and acquired the name Francis. After several years of Catholicism, he not only reverted to Protestantism but became anti-Catholic in the bargain. He also disliked immigrants, believing that they brought crime and degeneracy to this country. Unlike SAI leaders, his anti-immigrant bias was evident long before the First World War. He was active in the YMCA, and seems to have worked with a Boy Scout troup at Carlisle.

In 1914 St. James first appeared in the pages of the SAI's magazine with a letter in support of the western cattle industry which he signed "Francis Fox James, Western Range Rider." [5] The letter did not discuss Indian affairs nor was St. James identified as an Indian. It was during his cow-herding days in Montana, however, that he acquired the "Red" part of his name as a nickname given him on the range. St. James shortly reappeared in the pages of the *Journal* as "Red Fox James," riding from capital to capital of various states collecting endorsements of American Indian Day.[6] At this time he was an active member of the Society of American Indians.

Several years after he had launched the Tepee Order in 1915, he became an ordained minister of the Disciples of Christ and founded a mission of that denomination, called the American Indian Christian Tepee

Mission, on the Yakima Reservation in Washington.[7] Around this time he added "Skiuhushu" to his name, which, he explained, "means Red Fox in the Indian tongue." St. James made his living largely by lecturing on Indian topics and running camps for white boys.[8]

Throughout his career, St. James was deeply troubled by his degree of Indian "blood." From his photographs, one would not recognize him as an Indian, though he may have looked somewhat different in person. He attempted to resolve his identity problems in a number of ways. One, as we have seen, was his progressive adoption of a number of names and titles both Indian and non-Indian. Another was his theory that the Welsh were in America before Columbus and that Indian "blood" had at this early period been mixed with Welsh. Presumably, St. James' own mixture of "blood" had thereby a pre-Columbian legitimacy. Yet another was his hostility to Negroes, with whom he was ever fearful of being confused. But most important was the Tepee Order itself, with its rituals which combined Indian and non-Indian elements, its rigid exclusion of Negroes, and its plethora of available Indian and non-Indian titles. If St. James belonged neither in the Indian world nor in the white, he would create a third: a Pan-Indian society which offered a solution to his precarious status by legitimizing it.

Throughout the life of the Order which he founded, the Reverend Red Fox St. James Skiuhushu served as its chief mentor and most peripatetic champion. The cloud of Christian earnestness, Indian mysticism, exalted schemes for Indian improvement, and just plain hokum which emanated from St. James also characterized the organization. So did the confusion and quantity of names. Like St. James, the Order was continually uncertain as to just what it was.

By 1920 the Tepee Order had become an adult secret fraternal organization with its own publication, the *American Indian Tepee.*[9] It was a curious blend of ideas and rituals from Masonry, the Improved Order of Red Men, and Indian life, while still showing traces of its youthful origin.

In the beginning Boy Scouting had contributed to the Order's idea of the Indian. In its adult phase, the Order drew heavily on the Indian image as refracted through the ideas and practices of the Improved Order of Red Men. Thus its Pan-Indian view was much more strongly influenced by popular and romantic white attitudes toward the Indian than was reform Pan-Indianism. No doubt this was due in part to its lack of contact with reservation life.

The Improved Order of Red Men which served as a model for the

Tepee Order was a white fraternal organization with a history reaching back to the early days of the Republic. It was an outgrowth of an earlier Society of Red Men, founded in 1813, which claimed descent from the Sons of Liberty. During the anti-Masonic agitation it disintegrated and was revived in 1833 on a nonpolitical and temperance basis, thereby becoming "improved."

The purpose of the Improved Order of Red Men was to conserve the "history, customs, and virtues of the aboriginal Americans—the Indians." It featured an elaborate system of degrees and titles. Locals were called "tribes," each taking the name of an Indian tribe. "Tribal" officers included a Sachem, Senior Sagamore, Junior Sagamore, Prophet, Chief of Records, and Keeper of Wampum. State lodges were known as "reservations." The head of the national IORM was called the "Great Incohonee." A special calendar which referred to "Great Suns" and "Moons" was used by the organization. A ladies' auxiliary, which also featured degrees and elaborate titles, was known as the "Daughters of Pocahontas." [10]

Although dedicated to the preservation of Indian virtues, the IORM barred Indians from membership. This circumstance did not prevent the Red Men from strongly supporting the Society of American Indians at its inception, nor did it prevent the Society from welcoming IORM support. The Red Men helped with the arrangements for the first two conferences held at Columbus, at one of which they tendered a luncheon to the delegates. A number of IORM tribes also joined the SAI as associates.

John W. Converse, a national leader of the IORM, published an article in the Society's *Quarterly Journal,* hailing the Indian's "capacity to advance" on rather curious grounds:

"It may be reasonably inferred only from the mere existence of the Improved Order of Red Men that the Indian has capacity to advance. The Order admits to membership none but white citizens of this country found upon investigation to be physically, mentally, and morally sound. It bars liquor dealers and gamblers. It numbers half a million. Its ultimate goals are mutual assistance and self-improvement by emulating North American Indian characteristics. . . .

It is hard to believe that a half million white citizens of this country in striving for self-improvement have made the error of adopting for their prototype and the emulation of his characteristics a man or people wanting in capacity to advance." [11]

Converse's article was the last mention in the *Journal* of the Improved Order of Red Men. Perhaps Arthur Parker had second thoughts about an organization which barred Indians. At some point, apparently, Sherman Coolidge attempted to join the Improved Order and was turned down because he was an Indian.[12]

Evidently the IORM ban on Indian membership was not too strictly enforced. St. James did join the Red Men even though he was presumably an Indian, and, in turn, a number of Red Men joined the Tepee Order.[13] The *American Indian Tepee* frequently attacked the IORM for its Indian exclusionist policy:

"When Red Fox Skiuhushu [St. James] appeared before the Great Council of the I.O.R.M. of the United States for a plea for them to help in getting the Indians citizenship, they requested him not to say anything of his being a member of that order, because Indians are not allowed or supposed to be in that Order. It is strictly for White men. The excuse was, that they do not encourage Indians in the Order, because they do not know the difference between the Indian blood and Negro blood. There are many Indians, besides Red Fox, members of that Order.

We recommend that this order change its name. They would do well to do it, for they have no real love for the Indians as a whole. Call themselves 'Sons of Liberty,' or anything, but not Red Men. We are too proud of a people, too proud of native Americans, to have such order ashamed of our Indian blood.

There is just as much danger of this order getting Negro blood into their order through white's membership, as through Indian membership. In the Great Masonic Order, or other secret orders, they are proud to have the Indians as members, and to sit in their council chambers." [14]

The membership qualifications of the Tepee Order were an ingenious and somewhat bewildering combination of those of the IORM and the Society of American Indians. Indians and whites of the United States, Canada, and Latin America were eligible for membership. "Degree" and "active" members were "those who have a voice in all the affairs of the organization," while "associates" were "those who wish to be affiliated with the organization in promoting the interests of the Indian." [15] Thus the somewhat unclear division between active and associate members was not to be on racial lines, as had been in the case of the Society of American Indians. Rather, the intention seems to have been that the core of the organization would consist of those members who participated in the Order's secret-degree work, while associates were outsiders interested in the Indian cause. Negroes were barred.

The Order's government was vested in a Supreme Grand Council Under Great Buffalo Totem Pole, including elected members, representatives of local groups, and others whom the council might choose to add. Both Indians and whites were eligible. But it was stipulated in the constitution that "no amendment can be made to place a man of pure white blood as head of this Order and its official staff. He must be of Indian blood, to represent fully his race of America." [16]

The Order had a full complement of symbols, emblems and mottoes. The "National Emblem" was the "Golden Eagle"; the "National Totem" the "Buffalo"; the colors "Cardinal Red and Orange Gold"; and the mottoes "Love and Help Thy Brother" and "In Great Spirit We Trust as We Turn Our Faces to the East in Prayer." [17]

Like many fraternal orders, the Tepee Order had a series of degrees. These were originally composed by Charles A. Eastman.[18] The highest was the ninth, described by Eastman as "the ceremony of the Sun Dance rites—into the Ranks of the Eagle Lodge under the Maltese Cross with a most selemn rite put in it as one enters in it. This is somewhat on the idea of a 33d Scottish rite. The American Indian Order [i.e., the Tepee Order] is using every effort, and sincere learned, educated men of the red and white races to bring back again many of these beautiful native ceremonies." [19] Eastman made it clear that this ritual was patterned after a Sioux ritual as he remembered it from his boyhood. The eagle, Eastman stated, is "the sacred emblem of the American Indian." It will be recalled that it was also the emblem of the Society of American Indians.

The organizational format of the Tepee Order was much like the IORM. In both cases, the local organizations took the name of an Indian tribe. While the IORM locals were called "tribes," the Tepee Order locals were known as both "tribes" and "councils." The latter were further divided into "clans" or "bands." In both organizations a member received an Indian name. State IORM bodies were "reservations," a term ardently repudiated as inappropriate by the Tepee Order, which used "councils" instead. The ladies' auxiliary which matched the IORM Daughters of Pocahontas was the Daughters of Sacajawea, named for an Indian woman who was a guide on the Lewis and Clark Expedition. The Tepee Order also adopted the IORM Calendar, first using only references to months as "moons" and later adding "Great Suns," followed by "A.D."

Many of the high-flown statements, rituals, and titles of the Tepee Order seem ludicrous to an outsider, but by those in the organization they were taken very seriously indeed. And they were very much in the American grain. In the 1920's thirty million Americans were active members of some eight hundred secret orders. A description of their general appeal could apply equally well to that of the Tepee Order:

"Lodge night in a thousand towns and cities: Centre Hall a blaze of lights, its chandeliers festooned with paper bunting. Guards at the gates —a blowsy veil at the mystic shrine—crossed flags above the booming organ—row on row of folding-chairs, wax-yellow, cushionless, but upholstered with rich memories.

From the street outside you climb a flight of well-worn stairs to the second landing. There is a door of varnished oak, behind which stands the Lord High Seneschal. It is just an average door; but beyond lies mystery, drama, opportunity to share great names and take a hand in deeds well done, the satisfaction of 'belonging.'

You knock three times; pause for a heart beat; knock three times again. . . . The panel opens wide enough to disclose a lawn tie and two waist-coat buttons. . . . 'Advance, stranger, and give the countersign!'

A whispered word. . . . The door swings slowly on its hinges.

It will continue to swing as long as life is drab enough for grown men to play Indian." [20]

How much more delightful if you were an Indian who was not quite sure just who he was—or a white about to play Indian with real Indians.

The rise of the Tepee Order coincided with the disintegration of the Society of American Indians. For some time St. James was active in both, and the Tepee Order magazine carried the proceedings of several SAI conventions. The early advisory boards of the Order (later replaced by the Supreme Grand Council) included at various times such SAI stalwarts and ex-stalwarts as Montezuma, Eastman, Bishop, Irving, and Sloan.

The Tepee Order, like the SAI, also tried to enlist the support of eminent whites. In 1920 the advisory board included such distinguished names as Dan Beard of the Boy Scouts, Governor Samuel R. McElire of Nebraska, Governor Frank Lowden of Illinois, Senator Miles Poindexter

of the State of Washington, several clergymen, and the cowboy movie
star William S. Hart. By 1922, all the whites listed above except Dan
Beard had disappeared from the board's roster, while Hart for one issue
appeared as "associate editor" of the magazine.[21]

The Tepee Order engaged also in a favorite SAI activity—the celebration of American Indian Day. A proclamation calling for its observance
was issued in 1920 by St. James, who for this purpose called himself the
Reverend Chief Red Fox Skiuhushu. In its anti-foreign emphasis, however, it differed markedly from the old SAI proclamations:

"The American Indians of this land have a right to call upon the
people of this nation to honor their past, as we must honor your noble
men that made this country a republic and free. To America the Indian
has given his life, in all the wars for the Stars and Stripes, and out of
300,000 American Indians in the United States we have given 9,000
young braves to the colors, and have given over 12,000,000 [dollars]
for the American Red Cross, and invested over $50,000,000 in Liberty
Bonds. The Indians' souls were in the cause of the world's war. *We
know not the hyphen—we know not the pro this or that; we are one
hundred per cent American.*" [22]

Following the SAI's dismal 1921 Detroit convention, the Tepee Order
attempted to incorporate some SAI members into its ranks. Sherman
Coolidge was elected "Great Incohonee," and the name of their journal
—*American Indian Tepee*—was briefly changed to *American Indian
Advocate,* which was described as "a national Indian journal of North
and South America." Judge James J. Irving, a Sioux who had been vice-
president of the Society, was to be the editorial chief of the publication,
a plan which failed to materialize. William Madison, a Chippewa from
Minnesota who was later secretary of the SAI, became its associate
editor.

Another move probably designed to attract SAI members and others
unlikely to be interested in participation in a secret fraternal organization
was the formation in 1922 of an American Indian Association—the
name initially used by the SAI—as a branch of the Tepee Order. Sherman Coolidge served initially as "Head Chief" of both and Dr. Alonzo
E. Austin, a white physician, was "Honorable President" of the Association.[23] Membership was open to Indians and whites, but Negroes were
explicitly barred. For a fleeting moment, it was announced that officers
of the Association were to be white.[24] This provision was not taken too

seriously, however. Within a year, Chief Joseph Strong Wolf, a Chippewa, was "Most High Chief" of the Association, while Austin continued to be active in the Order.

The platform of the new Association was much like that of the old SAI, with a few additions. It stressed citizenship, legal rights, admission of tribes to the Court of Claims, "Americanizing the original American," the celebration of American Indian Day, and "religious liberty for all Indians." No mention was made of abolishing the Indian Bureau; rather, the organization urged decreasing the number of "unnecessary employees" and upgrading salaries. In some respects the platform looked forward to the thirties in advocating "giving the Indians a voice in reservation affairs," giving land to homeless Indians and increasing the holdings of those with insufficient or poor quality land, and creating a system of "old age compensation or pension for elderly dependent Indians." [25] These latter positions were an important departure from the old SAI policy and reflected the new concerns of the twenties. However, in practice little effort seems to have been made to lobby for the program.

In time the American Indian Association came to be referred to by its members as if it were the Society of American Indians with a changed name. For instance, 1911 was given as the date of its founding, and the early SAI officers were listed as those of the Association. Long after references to the Society by name had disappeared from the magazine, it often reprinted without credit statements lifted from the pages of the Society's *Journal.*

The *American Indian Tepee* (under various names) was sponsored by both the American Indian Association and the Tepee Order, whose affairs quickly became inextricably entwined. Its readers were served up organization news, items about Indians, romantic accounts of Indian history and lore, and pleas for financial assistance coupled with warnings about the unauthorized collection of funds.

Not the least of the magazine's attractions were the numerous advertisements and news stories about schemes undertaken by its officers. These included several outdoor Indian camps for white boys. One of the most endearing of these was the "Kitchemanitous Ozark Camp," which also offered a home to Indian boys and young men as well as to "older folks." In actuality, the camp was a poultry farm, presided over by George C. Stagg (Flying Eagle), the Second Junior High Priest of the Order, as "Head farmer" and "Supervisor," and "Professor Chester N.

Schrock (Black Hawk), professor of Fine Arts and director of Poultry Department." The camp was identified as "Under the Direction of the American Indian Association." [26]

Another dream which found expression in the pages of the magazine was a proposed "American Indian Tipi Institute" in Colorado, to be launched under the auspices of the Order and Association. This was envisioned as a place to train Indian leaders in a home "under good Christian moral influence" of a "non-sectarian" variety. Plans included a camp and sanatorium. All facilities were to be open to both Indians and whites.[27]

Aside from such matters, the magazine often dealt with the problems of defining an Indian common ground. One of the ways this was done was identification by exclusion, especially in the early and mid-twenties. Thus Indians were 100 percent American patriots, as opposed to the foreign-born and "subversive" elements. In 1921, an article stated: "America to-day is greatly interested in Americanization—Good suggestion! Why not round up all the undesirables, and with the aliens, coming from other shores, place them on reservations, have men like Indian agents over them until they become Americanized, and give to the native Americans, the same privileges all good Americans enjoy. For we are all Americans!" [28]

It is interesting to compare this view with the often expressed earlier suggestion of Carlos Montezuma that Indians be rounded up and allowed to reenter the country under the same procedures open to immigrants. For Montezuma the immigrant was a model, while for St. James he was an enemy. In the preceding decade, some Indians had advocated treating the Indian like the immigrant: in the twenties some Indians were advocating treating the immigrant like the Indian.

This anti-foreign and chauvinist bias continued into the mid-twenties. In 1924, the magazine called on the Ku Klux Klan "which believes in 100 percent *Americanism* and *Justice*" not to "overlook the *real* 100 percent *Americans—who* are the *Red Indians* or *American Indians—* who are pleading for Justice and liberty in their *own native land 'America.'* " [29] Indians, the magazine proclaimed, "are justly entitled to full citizenship, more so than the IWW or Red Element and others from European stock, or southern Europe, who come to this country and are non-citizens and can hardly read or write English." [30]

This overheated view soon cooled, however, and attacks on the foreign-born ceased. By 1926, the magazine was echoing the words of the old SAI in appealing for members, stating that the American Indian Association "affords both the native American [i.e., the Indian] and the American who became so because he has found on these shores a land of freedom, the means of cooperation. It makes every Indian a participant in a great race movement, and it provides the awakened social conscience of the country the means for making better Americans." [31] The Order's reasons for barring Negroes from membership took on a somewhat defensive tone. "We have nothing against the black race, but we do not allow any member of Negro strain to be a member of our organization. We take the same stand, very strictly, regarding this point that the white race does in white organizations. So long as the white race holds this, we will. However, long before Columbus came, the Incas, the Maya and the Aztecs had Negro slaves and used them as servants only. They were never permitted to intermarry." [32]

Occasionally, the magazine attempted to explain this position more fully. In an article entitled "God's Law and Races, and Mixed Races," described as "written for the benefit of those who have been wondering where the black race belonged, and why perhaps there are mixed races," a white member of the Order, Dr. Thomas M. Stewart (Black Bear), tried to clear up this question, with an assist from the occult.

"The human species is the only species which, however unequal in its races, can breed together. This is the reason for the mixture of races.

The Atlanteans were more mixed than Europe today, according to some of the remnants of the ancient teachings. There were red, yellow, brown, white and black races.

The original races were yellow-white, golden-yellow, red and brown. These latter became black because of sin. I think it was breeding with some laggards of a preceding race—animal-like man—but it is a spiritual and not a physical matter. The how is a mystery to me, at least. . . .

Since the beginnings of the Atlantean race, many million years have passed, yet we find the last of the Atlanteans still mixed up with the Aryan element 11,000 years ago. This shows the enormous overlapping of one race over another succeeding race. . . . Now occult philosophy teaches that even under our very eyes the new race and races are preparing to be formed, and that it is in America that the transformation will take place, and it has already silently commenced. . . . By means of legends and traditions of the Red man, we can gently help to carry over the grand concepts of the ancient teaching with which he had much to do in Atlantean and later times." [33]

From the high point of the mid-twenties the Order's hostility to Negroes gradually declined. While Negroes continued to be barred from membership, their exclusion was no longer so strongly emphasized. The relationship between Indians and whites was a favorite subject. The organization stood firmly for friendship between the red and white races. But now and then doubts were expressed about the wisdom of racial intermarriage. Thus Chief Flying Eagle (George C. Stagg), the general secretary of the Order, in an article entitled "Why Preserve Their Indian Blood?" decried marriages between Indians and whites. Flying Eagle was himself a "mixed blood," being "part-Algonquin." [34]

"The blood should be preserved by marrying within their race," Flying Eagle urged. "The Hebrew teachings, that they are not allowed to marry into other 'families' of the white race, in this way they preserve the Hebrew blood. It is sad indeed, here in the United States, to see so many Indians marrying into the white race; thus the Indian Blood in time will become absorbed in the white blood," he asserted.

"The Great Spirit has created diversity in the faces of humans, animals, and all nature. A bunch of flowers is more beautiful for its variety and exquisiteness of coloring than if there were a deadly sameness in leaf and petal. So it is with nations and races. All are needed, and all should be permitted to work out their own destiny, with assistance if necessary, and with the best equipment in education and all that makes for achievement, but it must be along their own particular lines. It is quite easy for a man to be nothing. Any fool can do that. It takes a strong and brave man to become an individual, something, a somebody. I admire any person, I salute him for his courage, that loves his race, loves his tribe, and is not afraid to wear his national garb.

Reverend Henry Roe Cloud, full-blood Indian, can be admired for his courage when he married a few years ago an Indian lady, former teacher at the United States Indian School of Carlisle."

Roe Cloud would have been surprised to learn that his marriage to Elizabeth Bender had required "courage." Perhaps Flying Eagle's article, which was written in 1924, reflected the mood of America in the mid-twenties. At any rate he did not return to this theme, nor did the magazine discuss it further.

The source for the Pan-Indianism manifested by the Order and its branches was clearly the idea of an Indian race. But in the early and mid-twenties the Indian race was, as we have seen, frequently defined by what it was not. The Order's exclusionist emphasis reflected trends in the larger society; as these broader trends subsided, so did their manifestations in the Order. This process coincided with a decreased emphasis on the IORM, an increased emphasis on Freemasonry, and a growing habit of referring to the organization as the American Indian Association rather than the Tepee Order.

From its inception the Order had extolled the Indian past and Indian virtues, both past and present. In the mid-twenties, greater attention was paid to "Indian Freemasonry" as an interpretation of aboriginal life. Arthur Parker's articles on the subject were reprinted in the magazine and included in a pamphlet published by the group.[35] The periodical also carried articles on Indian history and lore with panegyrics to Indian spiritual qualities. Prayers to the Great Spirit abounded, and "The Indian Ten Commandments" was a perennial favorite. In these ways the organization attempted to provide its members with a positive image of the Indian past and present.

Aside from such vaguely Pan-Indian articles, the periodical sometimes took a position on legislation affecting Indians. Thus sympathy was expressed for the Pueblos, the "Dance Order" was opposed, and the Snyder Bill providing for Indian citizenship received the organization's backing.[36] The passage of the Indian Citizenship Bill in 1924 was hailed by Chief Joseph Strong Wolf in an editorial which also emphasized the need for Indian racial consciousness.[37] Strong Wolf wrote in a spirit reminiscent of the SAI a decade earlier:

"The hardest part of the work is now to come, and that is to arouse a feeling of racial consciousness in the breast of every Indian, whether full blood or not, in our country, and to teach him to take his place in our civilization, to teach him his value to the community, to live in his mode of reservation or in some small village, and to teach him also that there are many white men and women who are willing to help him if he will only help himself in taking his place in the white man's world.

This does not mean standing on the corner in some of our large cities selling snake oil, or dressing up in the Indian headdress and painted face, and going to some white man's house and saying I am an Indian; loan me a few dollars. They must be taught that they are no better than anyone else because they are Indians. . . . And it must be remembered that no white man has been able to take from us OUR STRONG BELIEF IN 'KITCHIMANITO' (Great Spirit), and my prayer is— let us go down the trails of life, hand in hand, with faith in the Great Spirit." [38]

While unusual pieces of legislation, such as the Indian Citizenship Act, received considerable attention in the magazine, discussion of ordinary Indian measures was spasmodic and limited, often confined to small news items. Clearly the organization was fraternal and social rather than political or reformist in its major interests.

Such interest probably reflected grass roots sentiment. By the mid-twenties, there were a number of local councils, clubs, and ladies' auxiliaries in various cities of the East and Midwest, including Philadelphia, New York, Minneapolis, Detroit, and Cincinnati, with a "New England Council" as well. Thus the organization covered somewhat the same territory as had the SAI in its earliest days. There were also councils in Denver, Colorado, and Long Beach, California.

The Tepee Order and its branches offered something for everyone, and there seems to have been considerable variation in the local groups. Some were primarily concerned with ritual and degree work, thus emphasizing the Tepee Order aspect of the organization, while others leaned to an American Indian Association approach and showed little interest in ritual.

Since in the cities where the locals flourished there were always Indians from a number of tribes, including some who were unsure of their tribal origins, the branches were almost unavoidably Pan-Indian. The members were reasonably satisfied by the blend of Indian ceremonials, the Red Man, Freemasonry, Boy Scouting, Christianity, and old-fashioned American hokum which was served up to them. In the urban clubs, a person could be an Indian and a member of a fraternal order of a type familiar in the wider society. Every member could have an assured status: there were plenty of chiefs and princesses, wampum keepers, messengers, and guides of the forest. The usual pattern of president, vice-president, secretary, treasurer, and executive committee was followed with appropriate Indian titles for these offices.

The clubs also served as a common meeting ground for Indians and whites in a situation where the very fact of being an Indian carried a built-in advantage. For white members the clubs provided both a romantic variation on the American fraternal order and an opportunity to help the "Indian cause."

In spite of the variety in the local organizations, certain common themes ran through most of them, including activities drawn from earlier reform Pan-Indianism. The celebration of American Indian Day was continued, and efforts were made to encourage its observance in schools, churches, and civic groups. American Indian Day was proving to be a hardy favorite and an ideal vehicle for Pan-Indian activity.

A commitment to education continued as a basic Pan-Indian emphasis. Some groups raised scholarship money for deserving Indian youth, and the national body raised money for a student at Haskell. In at least one case, a local group maintained a fraternity house—the "Indian Koska Tipi"—near the University of Minnesota campus with the object of serving "Indian students attending the State Universities and the city High Schools." [39] The locals attempted to educate their members in Indian history, Indian lore, and current Indian affairs, frequently sponsoring talks on such subjects, often of highly dubtful accuracy. The Indian past was viewed with a strong dash of romanticism.

Some of the urban clubs also attempted to aid members who were ill or otherwise in distress, occasionally sent gifts of clothing to reservations, and extended a welcome to Indians newly arrived in the city. Powwows and Indian celebrations were held. In New York City, for instance, a clubhouse sponsored by the American Indian Association was opened in 1926 with a program of social and charitable activities, lectures, lantern slides, and Christian and "Indian" religious services.[40]

Most of the local groups seem to have mushroomed, flourished for a time and then faded away, sometimes to rise again in new forms. Throughout its history, the organization, both nationally and locally, was wracked by a series of indignant resignations and expulsions which seem to have been caused largely by personal conflicts. St. James continued to play a leading role in the organization, but by 1927 he had become deeply discouraged about its prospects:

"There is no unity among our people of the Red Race; there is overmuch jealousy and tale bearing; everyone would be the Big Chief or some kind of princess; each is jealous of the publicity his neighbor gets, and so on and on, worlds without end. . . . The Indians themselves are giving practically no support to Indian organizations, whatever they may be. . . . Yet they expect the white people to help; and if it weren't for the kindness of our white friends, all these organizations for the good of the Indian would go. Many such groups I have seen spring up and pass away in the last fifteen years. But by the Great Spirit's help and the kindness of our white friends, the American Indian Association has kept the breath of life since 1911." [41]

Actually, a good deal of white support had by this time melted away. A suggestion by a leading white member that all Indian organizations be merged into one was firmly rejected.

Resentment of the role of whites in the organization was also growing among the Indian members. Toward the end of 1927, the national officers decided that "no person of the white race could hold a National Office in the Association. All the National Officers must be of Indian blood." St. James thereupon tendered his resignation because "he was taking up other work with his church and will be unable to give all his time to the association." [42] The next issue of the magazine following the announcement of St. James' resignation carried his assurance of continuing support, but this evidently did not last for long. The American Indian Association–Tepee Order faded into obscurity. Only a few more issues of the magazine were published.

In the early thirties, St. James reappeared as the "Chief Executive" of a new organization—the Indian Association of America. By this time he had dropped many of his earlier names and was using the name Barnabas Skiuhushu. The president and "Assistant Executive" of the new group, being respectively Father Phillip Gordon and Flying Eagle (George Stagg), were veteran Pan-Indians. [43]

The Indian Association described itself as a "non-sectarian, non-political, non-profit body; organized by Indian leaders and prominent White Men and Women who are deeply interested in the spiritual and temporal welfare of the Indians of North and South America, and in the principles of Justice to all Indians; and to promote a friendly relationship between the Indians of North and South America. Although Indians of divers nations, they are ONE RACE—the RED RACE of the American Continents."

The Indian Association's program included "scientific research work and studies on all phases regarding the Red Race—remembering to acknowledge in science the Mysteries of the Great Spirit"; support for American Indian Day; upholding Indian rights; religious toleration for "both tribal and Christian beliefs"; cooperation with Christian missionaries; and conservation of forests and wildlife. It also included several new variations, carrying forward older themes in a more extreme form. Among these were the establishment of an Indian Indian claims commission "so that the Indians themselves may have their own representatives, to sit in Council, to hear and settle all legitimate Indian claims"; Indian representatives in the Senate and House elected by the tribes; approval of the Commissioner of Indian Affairs and local agency superintendents by "Reservation Indians themselves, taking Indian affairs out of politics"; and giving Indians jobs as guides in national parks and rangers in national forests.[44] Thus the organization combined the Pan-Indian idea of the unifying force of race with its own version of tribal self-determination, reflecting more general ideas which had been growing in the twenties and early thirties.

Membership in the group was open to both Indians and whites. A special membership fee for missionaries and for Indians living on reservations was provided, thus indicating the hopes of its founders for a new constituency. Indian Council Clubs were to be formed as well. Both active and associate memberships were available but undefined. Little is known of the actual functioning of the association, which was probably largely a paper organization with a few local branches including a group in New York City.

While national Pan-Indian superstructures rose and fell, local groups often continued, to some extent mirroring the fortunes of national bodies but also having a life of their own. The transmutations of Indian local organizations in New York City illustrate how an organization like the Tepee Order–American Indian Association survived in various groups in a specific locality.

In the early twenties in New York City, several local councils of the Tepee Order were organized including a Blackfoot Council (for men) and a branch of the Daughters of Sacajawea.[45] Initially, the stronger emphasis seems to have been on the rituals of the organization. In 1926, St. James and Princess Chinquilla, a Cheyenne who was at the time Great Sacajawea of the Daughters of Sacajawea, took the initiative in planning an Indian clubhouse in the city.[46] The clubhouse was conceived of as a combination of lodge hall and Indian center, and from this circumstance serious difficulties arose, which were described by St. James and Princess Chinquilla in the pages of the magazine.

Some problems were financial. The club was besieged by impecunious and "disreputable-looking" Indians asking for loans. Other problems were religious, revolving around Protestant-Catholic antagonisms. Although the association was supposed to be nonsectarian, in practice Catholics were barred, and New York Catholic Indians evidently resented their exclusion from an Indian clubhouse. Yet others may have been racial, in all likelihood due to the presence in New York of Long Island Indians who were part Negro.[47]

Following the decision of the national officers to bar whites from holding national office and the subsequent rapid decline of the organization, Princess Chinquilla continued to work with a group of women in New York City known as the Ojistah Council, which sent clothing to reservations and discussed "Indian history or news." The aim of the council was "to help Indians help themselves." [48]

Pan-Indian activity in New York also continued in other forms. Following a celebration of American Indian Day at Inwood Hill Park in 1933, an Indian Confederation of America was organized "to uplift generally the Indian, and to acquaint those not of his race with his sterling qualities and to indicate to the world at large the beauties of the Indian arts and crafts." The titles of the officers—including "Sachem," "Sagamore," "Keeper of Records," "Guard of Wigwam," and "Collector of Wampum"—were much like those of the Tepee Order. The office of "Collector of Wampum" was filled by Leon Miller, a Cherokee graduate of Carlisle who had been active in the affairs of the Tepee Order and American Indian Association and was an old friend of St. James.[49]

Indians from a number of tribes belonged to the organization as active members, while associates were persons "not of Indian extraction" and had no vote. Thus the Society of American Indians' membership pattern reemerged.[50] In practice, most of the members were Indians.

As time went on, the Confederation extended aid to Indians coming to New York City and helped to find jobs for them, raising money with semi-annual powwows, the programs of which often contained memorials to Indians or friends of the Indian like Gertrude Bonnin and General Pratt.[51] Thus the Confederation drew on a number of Pan-Indian organizations and traditions of the past and, like the urban clubs of the twenties, functioned as a fraternal and social body which kept city Indians in contact with each other.[52]

The Confederation was not the only Pan-Indian organization in New

York in the thirties which grew out of the clubs of the twenties. St. James' Indian Association of America, "composed of Indians as active members and whites as associate members," had a clubhouse in Queens and celebrated American Indian Day with "Indian dances and ceremonials.[53] Another celebration of American Indian Day by the "United Tribes of America" was held under the leadership of Harold Davis Emerson, the "head chief," formerly active in the Tepee Order.[54] It is probable that similar developments took place in other cities where the Order had been active.

This process of dissolution and reformation of Pan-Indian groups evidently went on in many localities. A continuing Pan-Indian urban tradition thus took various forms according to the needs and interests of its members, many of whom had belonged to earlier Pan-Indian groups.

The Tepee Order–American Indian Association was probably the most active of the national fraternal Pan-Indian bodies in the twenties. There were, however, a number of other organizations, come quite short-lived. For example, in the early twenties an attempt was made to organize a Pan-Indian veterans' organization, "American Indians of the World War," with headquarters in Minneapolis, Minnesota. The group was nonpartisan and nonpolitical and was hostile to the current SAI leadership. Among its officers were such Pan-Indian activists as George W. Peake, president, and Anderson W. Cash, secretary. Little is known of the activities of the organization. Its significance lies in the tendency so marked in Pan-Indian affairs to form an Indian counterpart of an important type of organization in the larger society.[55]

The organization with the most staying power was the Grand Council Fire of the American Indians, founded in Chicago in 1923 as "a National Organization Devoted to the Advancements of the Indian Race and to the Interests of Indians." Unlike the Tepee Order–American Indian Association, the Grand Council did not organize local groups, though it was active in the Chicago area.

The purposes of the Grand Council Fire were as follows:

". . . to revive faith of the Indian in the Great Spirit and transmit it unalloyed to posterity; restore old customs, usages and traditions and keep them uncorrupted; engender confidence among the tribes and encourage their co-operation; extend the hand of fellowship to the Paleface and show him Indian hospitality; strive for better laws touching rights and property of the Indian, and for their enforcement; awaken the American conscience to the wrongs heaped on the Indian, and to right them; prevent waste in Indian affairs, and punish unlawful practice; promote the general welfare of the Indian; secure his enfranchisement; fit him for citizenship; enable him to cope with the hardships of Caucasian civilization; encourage the Indian in all artistic pursuits and maintain unconquered his Indian character that the American Indian shall not perish from the earth." [56]

The officers of the Grand Council Fire held familiar titles: "Chief of Chiefs," "Chief Wampum Keeper," "Chief Medicine Man," "Chief of Lodge," and so on. The first "Chief of Chiefs" was Frank Cayou, who held the office for two years and who was active for many years thereafter in Pan-Indian affairs, including the peyote religion.[57]

During most of the twenties and early thirties the "Chief of Chiefs" was Scott Peters, a Chippewa from Michigan who had attended Carlisle and who owned a small business near Chicago.[58] A number of other officials had a Pan-Indian history. From the old Society of American Indians came Oliver Lamere, also a leader in the peyote religion, and Asa Hill, who had spoken at one of the early SAI conferences. A. Warren Cash had been active in the Tepee Order. George Peake, a Chippewa who was a Grand Council Fire member from the beginning, later became head of the Indian Confederation in New York City. Both Peake and Cash were officials of the Pan-Indian veterans' group mentioned above. National officers of the Grand Council Fire in the twenties included members of the Chippewa, Oneida, Winnebago, Pueblo, Sioux, Navaho, Omaha, and Ottawa tribes.

Most of the officials of the Grand Council Fire were Indians, but a few were white, including the "Chief Story Teller," or secretary, Marion Gridley, an adopted Omaha. The Grand Council Fire's program was much like that of other fraternal Pan-Indian organizations of the period. One of its chief concerns was the celebration of American Indian Day, which was promoted in schools, churches, and civic groups in the Chicago area and in the state.

The Grand Council Fire had a deep interest in education. It strongly supported Indian enrollment in public schools wherever possible, as well as the improvement of the Indian school system. Scott Peters, the Chief of Chiefs, advocated adding a four-year high school course to Indian schools and strengthening the Indian schools academically so as to encourage more Indian young people to enter the arts and professions. He urged "doing away with the policy of making all Indians mechanics and laborers." [59] The organization also raised money for scholarships for Indian students. The group was concerned about the fair presentation of American Indian history in the public schools, petitioning the Mayor of Chicago for more equitable treatment of Indians in textbooks.[60] One of the most interesting of the organization's efforts was its promotion of a bill to make it "a crime for one NOT of Indian blood to claim to be an Indian." [61]

The Grand Council Fire engaged in a number of social and charitable activities. It gave assistance to ill and needy Indians and sent gifts of clothing and other articles to reservations. It sponsored social activities and dances in the Chicago area.

The Grand Council Fire thus combined elements of fraternal and reform Pan-Indianism, but with much more emphasis on fraternal and educational matters than on reform issues. While a good deal of its activity was concentrated in and around Chicago, it reached out to the surrounding region, and some of its officers lived outside the area. It was not as geographically widespread as the Tepee Order–American Indian Association but more national in character and influence than many of the other Pan-Indian groups of the period.

In 1932, the name of the organization was changed to Indian Council Fire. The following year, in connection with the Chicago Century of Progress, the group initiated the Indian Achievement Awards given annually by the organization for the purpose of focusing attention on "Indian ability through the attainments of the individual." During the thirties, three of the awards went to former leaders of the Society of American Indians: Charles Eastman (1933), Henry Roe Cloud (1935), and Arthur C. Parker (1936). In the mid-thirties the organization published *Indians of Today,* a Who's Who of American Indians, which had several subsequent editions. It was edited by Miss Gridley.

During the twenties there were other local Pan-Indian urban clubs which sprang up in various cities. Many of them billed themselves as national organizations but in practice were confined to local areas. For example, Los Angeles had three "national" Pan-Indian groups in the twenties. The American Indian Progressive Association was composed of "younger Indians" concerned with presenting, studying, and trying to understand the problems of all American Indians." Its educational work consisted of "setting forth the value of citizenship and of exercising the rights thereby implied, such as voting and taking part in civic and social affairs." The members worked to break down "abnormal race consciousness" and "to have the Indians put behind them customs and practices that bar them from the benefits available to the dominant race." [62]

A similar organization, the Wigwam Club, was founded to help Indian boys and girls, "supplying all aid within its means to worthy Indians, and to assist in the education of Indians of rare talent." Both clubs sponsored monthly dances exclusively for Indians, while the Wigwam Club had a large annual picnic featuring "adaptations of Indian dances," Indian costumes, the sale of Indian curios and objects of art, and speeches by Indian leaders and "other men prominent in public life." [63]

Los Angeles also had during this period an Indian women's organization—"Wa-Tha-Huck (Brings Light Club)," affiliated with the General Federation of Women's Clubs, and a War Paint Club. The latter was the only one of its kind which from the very first was planned as purely local. It consisted of Indians in the movie industry and was concerned with "guarding Indians from exploitation in their work and with trying to supply a large number of genuine Indians to play Indian parts that are now often played by Orientals, Mexicans and others in Indian costumes.[64]

Other Pan-Indian groups flourished in towns and cities during the twenties, often taking their flavor from the local tribes. Some, like the National Society of Indian Women (State of Washington) were actually local or regional despite their aspirations to a wider constituency.[65] Others, like the Society of Oklahoma Indians, were avowedly local or regional.[66] News of such groups was carried in such Pan-Indian periodicals as the *American Indian Magazine,* a lively monthly magazine published in Tulsa, Oklahoma, from 1926 to 1931. It printed, in addition to much local news, articles of more general Indian interest. Another, *The American Indian Bulletin,* reported general Indian news. It was published in the late twenties and early thirties in Pipestone, Minnesota, by Judge James Irving, a former vice-president of the Society of American Indians.

Thus by the early thirties, fraternal Pan-Indianism could be clearly identified and had emerged as a continuing force in American Indian life. Like reform Pan-Indianism, it used the idea of "the Indian race" as the Indian common ground and emphasized past Indian virtues assumed to have been held in common by all Indians. Direct social science influence, evident in the Society of American Indians, was minimal. Instead, reliance was placed on a more romantic and popular version of the Indian past.

The organizational format of fraternal Pan-Indianism was drawn from a variety of sources in the larger society but given an Indian flavor. Models included secret fraternal orders, good-and-welfare clubs, and women's organizations. The elaborate ritual and secrecy of the Tepee Order of the early and mid-twenties does not seem to have been fully copied by the clubs outside the Order. But modifications persisted— especially in the system of using "Indian" versions of the titles of officers and members of executive committees. "Chiefs" and "princesses" were common.

The activities of the various clubs tended to be quite similar, being fraternal, social, and educational. Often dances and powwows were featured. The celebration of American Indian Day continued as a favorite activity of many clubs, and better education was a perennial theme.

The leadership of the clubs was both Indian and white, with Indians predominating. The only two fraternal Pan-Indian organizations which in this period could lay claim to any national scope were both partially led by whites. Some local clubs were entirely Indian while others continued the old SAI active-associate pattern.

With few exceptions, the leadership of fraternal Pan-Indianism, whether Indian or white, was not college educated. Carlisle and Haskell continued to furnish leaders for this variety of Pan-Indianism. In a few instances, claim to Carlisle attendance seems to have been more wish than fact. Not surprisingly, most college-trained Indians and the more prominent Carlisle and Haskell alumni tended to act as if fraternal Pan-Indianism did not exist. Neither the Indian elite nor the white Indian defense organizations took much interest in the urban clubs. The latter were, on the whole, composed of people in modest circumstances— workers, small businessmen, and sometimes Indian entertainers.

The Indians who participated were removed from the tribe in varying degrees. Some were unsure even of their tribal origins. Others had left the reservation to make their fortunes in the world outside. Some traveled back and forth between reservation and city. In spite of the many claims to "full-bloodedness," it is highly likely that most were partly white. Many leaders in the fraternal organizations were perennial Pan-Indians, continuing their participation in a number of Pan-Indian bodies and in the process diffusing Pan-Indian ideas, organizational forms, and activities.

Fraternal Pan-Indianism, in all its variety, arose in response to a need felt by Indians in the city who wanted to remain Indians and at the same time participate in the larger society. Despite factionalism and personal rivalries and jealousies, the desire of many urban Indians to identify themselves as Indians was strong enough to keep fraternal Pan-Indianism alive. In the process, a Pan-Indian subculture grew, drawing on Indian and non-Indian sources, setting a pattern for Indian urbanization.

Although the evolving subculture was influenced by the reform tradition and while a few fraternal Pan-Indians were peyotists, Pan-Indian reform had only a minor impact on Indians in the cities and Pan-Indian religion had virtually none. The renewal of reform Pan-Indianism would follow a more general revival of reform interest in the wider society. Pan-Indian religion developed far from the urban centers and engaged the loyalty not of city but of country folk.

III

RELIGIOUS
PAN-INDIANISM

※

10

THE PEYOTE CULT

Near the end of the nineteenth century, a new movement, religious in character, arose among Indians of the Plains recently confined on reservations. The movement was the peyote cult, which was to become the most significant and widespread Pan-Indian religion of twentieth-century America. As reform Pan-Indianism was the organizational vehicle for the educated middle-class Indian elite who had left the reservation, and fraternal Pan-Indianism the organizational expression of humbler Indians who had moved to towns and cities, so the peyote faith was the Pan-Indianism of the reservation.

Of all the modern varieties of Pan-Indianism, the peyote religion involved the largest number of active participants. It arose earlier than reform or fraternal Pan-Indianism, evolved more slowly than either, remained closest to reservation life and was the most strongly Indian.

Like reform and fraternal Pan-Indianism, the peyote cult was a movement of accommodation. It abandoned the messianic hopes of earlier Pan-Indian religions and instead developed ideology and procedures more in harmony with the reality of the Indian as part of modern society. While strongly rooted in traditions of the past, the peyote religion was also a religious reform movement which sought to come to terms with the present.

As the organizational model for reform Pan-Indianism was the reform movement, and that of fraternal Pan-Indianism the fraternal order and social club, for religious Pan-Indianism, the model was—or became—the Christian church. But the peyote religion deviated more sharply from its model than did other types of Pan-Indianism.

The most obvious reason for the deviation was the fact that the peyote religion had its setting on the reservation, and it drew much more directly on aboriginal sources than did the other varieties of Pan-Indianism. But probably of equal importance was the nature of the opposition to the peyote religion. On the one hand it incurred the hostility of traditional tribal religions and on the other the hostility of the organized Christian churches, who came to regard it as a rival, a thinly disguised form of paganism. The Indian Bureau, which looked with fitful favor on reform Pan-Indianism and largely ignored fraternal Pan-Indianism, also frowned on the peyote religion as a barrier to the "civilizing process," seeing it as a disquieting if not dangerous form of independent Indian activity. Faced with such formidable opposition from quarters so influential, the peyote religion gradually adapted itself to the church model as much for defensive reasons as out of admiration. By so doing, it put itself under the protection of the guarantees of religious freedom in the larger society.

The most vocal and influential friends of the peyote religion in the white world came not from the ranks of its model, as was the case with the other varieties of Pan-Indianism, but rather from a small group of anthropologists who had studied Indian life and who sympathized with Indian efforts to create a Pan-Indian religion. These men had no organization suitable for adaptation to Indian religious purposes. Moreover, at the time that the peyote religion began to spread beyond a few localities, anthropologists were struggling to establish their discipline as a profession. Their professional interests lay in studies of the aboriginal characteristics of individual tribes or in the analysis of more general patterns of aboriginal cultures. Only a handful paid much attention to a new movement reaching beyond the tribe and exhibiting a blend of Indian and white ideas and practices.

The ancestry of the new movement reached far back into pre-Columbian times. The use of peyote in religious ritual is an ancient practice among the Indians of Mexico.[1] Its first appearance in the United States seems to have been around 1870, when it was acquired from Indians in northern Mexico by the Mescalero Apaches who used it to reinforce the traditional religious values of their own tribe.[2] However, the religion soon took on a Pan-Indian character and in the process became radically transformed from a tribal to a societal religion. The Comanche acquired it around 1873 or 1874 and the Kiowa about 1875. Both tribes were important in its subsequent diffusion among Indians in the United States.

The Kiowa-Comanche rite became one of the major forms of the religion, representing the least Christianized type.[3]

The peyote religion was already established but not yet widespread at the time of the flowering of the last great Pan-Indian messianic movement, the Ghost Dance of the late eighties and early nineties. Peyotists differed in their attitudes towards the Ghost Dance, some participating in it, some opposing it. For a time, both religions flourished. But the hopes of the Ghost Dancers were doomed to disappointment, and the religion languished. The Ghost Dance, however, with its message of peace and amity among the tribes, had opened up "channels of friendship" among the Indians. Through them flowed the good news of the peyote religion which spread rapidly as the Ghost Dance subsided.[4]

While generally friendly to Christianity, peyotists differed in their attitudes toward the incorporation of Christian ideas and practices into the religion. In some peyote groups, Christian elements were an integral part of the religion. In others, they were peripheral or virtually absent.

In one respect at least, peyotists and Christians agreed. Both recognized alcoholism as a major evil in Indian life. Opposition to alchohol was a fundamental tenet of the peyote religion, and the cures achieved were one of the cult's chief sources of strength. Indeed, the peyote religion may legitimately be viewed in part as an Indian temperance movement whose anti-alcohol activities were set, as was largely the case in the temperance movement among whites, in a religious context. But this circumstance increased rather than ameliorated official Christian hostility to the cult. Christian spokesmen believed that the use of peyote was no better than drinking whiskey, and in fact, was a more insidious evil. The success of the peyote religion in combating alcoholism was thus viewed as a blow to the temperance cause rather than a victory for it.

The biographies of two important early peyotist leaders illustrate these varying tendencies, show the process by which the religion was disseminated, and reveal some of the forces at work in the growth of the cult. In many ways the lives of these men parallel those of the leaders of reform Pan-Indianism.

One of the leading exponents and missionaries of the peyote religion was Quanah Parker, celebrated as the "last great chief of the Comanches," a man noted for his strength of character, shrewdness, and magnanimity. Parker was born about 1852, the son of a famous Comanche war chief. Parker's mother was a white woman who had been captured as a child and brought up as a Comanche. Quanah was deeply devoted to her. She was later recaptured by the whites, and though her son never saw her again, his devotion to her continued unabated. She was never fully reconciled to her separation from the tribe and died soon after the death of her little daughter, who had been captured with her.

Quanah became a famous war leader like his father. While fighting the whites, he remembered his white mother with whom he hoped some-day to be reunited. His love for her formed the basis for his later recon-ciliation with white society.

Parker's last great struggle with the whites was in 1874 at the cele-brated Battle of Adobe Walls. Many Indians surrendered at that time, but Parker did not. In 1875 he at last yielded, having determined to adjust himself to the new life and to urge his people to do likewise. It was only after his surrender that he learned of his mother's death.

Parker set about building a life for his people which would combine Indian and white ways. He became a prosperous farmer and rancher and lived in a large house with a separate room (and sewing machine) for each of his seven wives. He encouraged house-building and agri-culture and strongly supported education, sending three of his children to Carlisle. One of his sons became a Methodist minister.

At the same time Parker remained very much an Indian, a chief whose prestige was high among Indians and whites not only in Okla-homa, where he lived, but also in the nation. He often lobbied in Wash-ington for Indian interests and became a friend of President Theodore Roosevelt, with whom he went on hunting trips in the Indian country.

Parker's connection with the peyote religion began in 1884 when he was almost forty years of age. Previously he had been opposed to peyote, but, when he took it during a serious illness and was cured, he became a convert. Throughout his life he was one of the most effective exponents and missionaries of the peyote religion.

Parker was already a peyotist at the time of the Ghost Dance in the late eighties and the nineties. He staunchly opposed the Ghost Dance and prevented its spread among the Comanche, who "considered their own mescal [peyote] rite sufficient to all their needs." [5] It was no doubt due in part to his prestige and leadership that the peyote religion spread and flourished in Oklahoma. Parker frequently conducted peyote meetings, often lecturing the younger people on right conduct. He also composed a number of peyote songs.

Parker was active in the legal defense of his religion. In 1908 he testified before the Oklahoma State Legislature in a successful effort to repeal the state anti-peyote law which had been passed in 1899.[6] His lobbying efforts in Washington to allow peyote to come into the United States legally were not successful, however.

Quanah was friendly to Christianity and had a number of friends among the missionaries in Oklahoma. Like them, he was strongly opposed to drinking. He summed up succinctly his view of the difference between Christianity and the peyote religion in these words, "The white man goes into his church house and talks *about* Jesus, but the Indian goes into his tipi and talks *to* Jesus." [7] But the peyote religion as practiced by Parker had in fact few Christian elements.

Parker had many white friends in Oklahoma and also kept in touch with his mother's relatives. A few months before he died, he had his mother's remains brought from Texas to a Mennonite mission near his home. At the services, Parker spoke in Comanche and English. "My mother was captured by Indians when she was a little girl. She learned to be Indian, and loved them so well, she never wanted to go back to white folks. God say all same people any way. She was good woman. I love my mother. I love white folks because she was white. I want my people to learn white man's way, get education, know work. Soon the government will stop paying money. Then all Indians must make their own living. Learn white way, learn white man's God. My people die today, tomorrow, or ten years, I want them to be ready like my mother. Then we all live together again." [8]

Several months later, Parker contracted pneumonia. In his last hours he was attended first by a white doctor and then by a peyotist. He died in February, 1911. After his death, the Comanches did not choose another chief to replace him. He was "the last great chief of the Comanches." [9]

Another important figure in the early history of the peyote religion was John Wilson (Moonhead). Wilson was born about 1840 in Indian Territory (later Oklahoma). Like Quanah Parker, he was part white, being one-quarter French. He was also of intertribal ancestry, one-half Delaware and one-quarter Caddo. Wilson traveled widely in Indian country, becoming acquainted with a number of tribes and with whites as well. He had some religious instruction in Roman Catholicism, and the peyote ritual which he invented shows strong Christian influence.

Also like Quanah Parker, Wilson did not become converted to the peyote religion until he was a mature man. His conversion occurred about 1880. According to one version, he first came into contact with peyote through his travels in New Mexico and Arizona. According to another and probably more authoritative version, he was given a dry peyote plant at a Comanche dance. Then, together with his wife who was a Caddo, he withdrew for some weeks "into a clean and open place," gave himself up to religious meditation, and ate a number of peyote buttons, during which time he received many revelations. These included "a body of moral and religious teachings, and details of ceremonial procedures, minute instructions as to the construction of the Moon, or Peyote altar, the paraphernalia to be employed in the ritual; and was taught the songs." [10] Wilson believed that the peyote had shown him "the open grave of Christ and the road leading from it to the Moon. He learned that this was the road over which the founder of Christianity traveled to reach his father. He was enjoined to walk on this road, called 'Our Creator's Road' or the 'Peyote Road,' during his life time. He was told that through the use of Peyote and by honest endeavor to understand this spiritual force, his knowledge would increase until he reached the very end. Death would then bring him in the presence of Peyote and Christ, marking the end of the journey." [11]

When Wilson returned from his retreat, he began to preach the new doctrine and to conduct peyote meetings. He soon gained followers in a number of tribes for his rite using the crescent-shaped Moon altar. Wilson's Moon generally resembled the altar used by the Kiowa and Comanche but differed from it in many details, including the incorporation of a number of Christian elements.[12] In fact, by the middle eighties, Wilson was being strongly criticized by other peyotists for mixing Christianity and peyote.[13]

Like Quanah Parker, Wilson was already an influential peyotist at the time of the Ghost Dance. But where Quanah opposed the Ghost Dance, Wilson embraced it. He became a leader of the Ghost Dance among the Caddo, continuing this activity at least until 1893. He frequently went into trances, believed that he visited the spirit world, and healed the sick.[14] For a time Wilson was thus a leader in two different Pan-Indian religious movements. During the nineties, Wilson's fame and influence as a peyote leader grew through both his own exertions and the work of his followers. Wilson's teachings included the injunction to "seek knowledge by direct communion and to avoid consulting the Bible or the Gospels for the purpose of moral instruction," holding that "the Bible was intended for the white man who had been guilty of the crucifixion of Christ and that the Indian who had not been a party to the deed was exempt from guilt on this score and that therefore, the Indian was to receive his religious influences directly and in person from God through the Peyote Spirit whereas Christ was sent for this mission to the white man." [15]

"[Wilson also] worked against indulgence in alcohol and gambling, sexual license—prohibiting even the discussion of sex—matrimonial infidelity, falsehood, and was most emphatic against fighting, which was defined so as to include even a show of bad temper. Injury would be forgotten and forgiven if recourse was had to prayer and Peyote. He was opposed to witchcraft and love magic, considering these practices as social evils. The conduct prescribed for the Peyote worshipper, then, was not unlike that idealized in Christianity; an equanimity of mind, respect for one's neighbors, a peaceful disposition, forgiveness, and a reverent attitude toward the spiritual world." [16]

As Wilson's influence grew, so did the number of his detractors. He was accused of claiming that he would return to life after death, of asking his followers to pray to him, and of using the peyote religion for personal gain by charging fees and by receiving presents. Wilson's followers defended him vigorously against such charges. After he was killed in an accident in 1901, he became object of such veneration that the anthropologist Frank Speck could report only a few years later that "the man has been deified since his death." [17]

Quanah Parker and John Wilson represented two varying tendencies in the peyote religion. Both varieties stressed right conduct, abstinence from alcohol, and peyote as a cure for disease. But Parker's version was less Christianized than Wilson's. In its subsequent development the peyote cult continued to exhibit similar variations.

In the last two decades of the nineteenth century, the peyote religion was confined largely to New Mexico and Oklahoma. Although it flourished among many tribes in the latter area, the Five Civilized Tribes remained almost completely unaffected by it. During this period, opposition to the cult among white officials, missionaries, and reformers was sporadic. In 1888, the Superintendent of the Kiowa, Wichita, and Comanche Agency in Indian Territory forbade the use of "Mescal Beans" on the reservation, stating that "This order is for the good of the Indians—many of whom are being destroyed by the use of the bean." In 1890, the Indian Bureau issued an order directing agents to "seize and destroy the mescal bean, or any preparation of decoction thereof, wherever found in the reservation. The article itself, and those who use it are to be treated exactly as if it were alcohol or whiskey, or a compound thereof; in fact it may be classified for all practical purposes as an intoxicating liquor." [18]

But while peyote religionists were periodically harassed by the Indian Bureau and suffered the disapproval of some local missionaries, the religion received scant attention elsewhere either from its potential friends or its potential enemies. It was still a local development, little known outside its home grounds.

During the next decade, the peyote religion flowered. Between 1900 and 1910 it spread rapidly beyond its center in Oklahoma, gaining new adherents in Arizona, Iowa, Nebraska, Wisconsin, and Wyoming.[19] It especially engaged the interest and loyalty of educated and Christianized Indians. One of the most significant centers of conversion was among the Winnebago and Omaha of Nebraska, where some of the leading members later became involved in the Society of American Indians.

The Winnebago first acquired peyote through John Rave, a Winnebago born about 1855 into a respected clan which traditionally was in charge of punishing wrong-doers in the tribe. In spite of this Rave himself led a dissolute life, was a heavy drinker and, according to Oliver Lamere, a "bad man." Like many Indians, Rave traveled a good deal. In Oklahoma during 1893–94 he first ate peyote with the Oto and the Pawnee. The use of peyote seems to have coincided in Rave's case with a period of psychological and physical crisis. He believed that peyote had enabled him to stop drinking and had cured him of a serious illness. When he returned to Nebraska, he attempted to introduce it into the tribe, largely as a curative measure, though probably with some Christian and other religious elements also.

Rave brought the peyote to the Winnebago around 1901. At first only a few people, mostly his relatives, were attracted to its use. Soon, however, his following began to increase and with it the antagonism of the conservative elements of the tribe who viewed peyote as an alternative and threat to old Winnebago customs—an alien religion. Rave began to attack the old Winnebago ways, and bitter conflict developed in the tribe between the peyotists and the conservatives. Rave also traveled to other tribes, visiting South Dakota and Minnesota to spread the new religion during 1903 and 1904.[20]

When the hostility between the peyote adherents and the conservative Winnebago was at its height, much more specifically Christian influences were introduced into the cult by Albert Hensley, a Winnebago who later joined the Society of American Indians and attended a number of its conferences. The date of Hensley's innovations is not certain but it was probably around 1906, the date used today among both the Winnebago and the Omaha peyotists for their anniversary celebrations of the founding of the religion in their tribes.[21]

Hensley was a former Carlisle student. He had attended Carlisle at the urging of the anthropologist Alice Fletcher who was then the allotting agent among the Omaha. Hensley had had a miserable childhood. His mother died when he was an infant, and he had been placed in the care of his paternal grandmother who died when he was five years old. Thereafter Hensley was "kicked here and there in different families," as he put it, occasionally working for his father, with whom he was on very bad terms. The prospect of escaping from his unhappy situation on the reservation must have seemed almost a miracle to the sixteen-year-old boy. When his father refused to allow him to go to school despite Miss Fletcher's pleading, she helped him to run away and provided him with a railroad ticket to Carlisle. There he acquired English, Christianity, and the skills of various trades, including plumbing, carpentry, and blacksmithing. He also participated in the outing system. He remained at Carlisle from 1888 to 1895. In his senior year he became gravely ill with "consumption" and was sent home to the reservation to die. But Hensley recovered in a few months, held a number of responsible positions at the agency, and served one term as an elected county commissioner of Thurston County.

When Hensley returned from Carlisle he joined the Episcopal Church and remained a member for six years. Gradually, he reported, he fell into "wicked" ways and began drinking a good deal, gambling, and working "for the devil all the time." Then he joined the peyote cult.

For Hensley, as for Rave, conversion was a means to personal reformation. He abandoned drinking and worked as a farmer to support his wife and children.

Hensley's innovations gave the cult a much more Christian cast. He introduced the reading of the Bible into the Winnebago group, having twelve educated members read and interpret portions of it for nonreading members. The worshippers used the New Testament, especially Revelations. Hensley's ceremony included peyote songs with a strong Christian flavor which he had learned from peyotists in Oklahoma, and also the giving of testimony. The peyote was believed to reveal the meaning of the Bible to the members. Thus combined, the Rave-Hensley ceremonials were a blend of Christian and Winnebago ideas and practices, plus elements drawn from other peyote adherents, especially the Oto.[22]

The Winnebago version of the peyote religion had a good deal in common with Protestantism, especially Protestant fundamentalism, and was considered by its members to be a Christian faith. In fact, the peyotists attempted to unite with a local Protestant church but were rebuffed by its clergyman. Rave then began baptising members himself by dipping his fingers in a diluted peyote infusion, passing them over the forehead of a new member, and praying, "God, his holiness." [23] The syncretistic quality apparent in Winnebago peyote beliefs and practices fit in well with general Pan-Indian attitudes. At any rate peyote worship was attractive and spread rapidly. According to Hensley, the religion came to bring peace among the Indians so that they might love one another, and all members were enjoined to spread its message.[24]

Oliver Lamere, a former Carlisle student who was treasurer of the peyote society, was attracted to the peyote religion because of its mixture of Christianity, Winnebago customs, more general Pan-Indian attitudes, and the fact that its adherents came from the progressive wing of the tribe. Throughout his life Lamere was devoted to Pan-Indian causes, being active in the Society of American Indians in its heyday and an official of the fraternal Grand Council Fire in the twenties.[25] Lamere's peyote orientation was strongly Christian, as he described it. "We have made earnest efforts to become Christians since we began eating and drinking this peyote, but many people say sarcastically that we have drunk ourselves into Christianity, and that we are demented. I am a peyote eater, but I have never found a demented person among them," Lamere stated. Peyote enabled him "to grasp the meaning of the Bible," which had hitherto been "meaningless" to him.[26]

The Winnebago peyotists attracted a number of able younger men who had received some education. It is not surprising that by 1909 they had built a "very comfortable church," and were engaged in winning converts and spreading the religion to other Indians through services held in a cloth tepee used for traveling meetings. The church was called the Union Church, instead of "Mescal-Eaters," as it had been formerly.[27] Others referred to it as the "Sacred Peyote Society." [28]

By 1911, the number of peyotists in the Winnebago tribe had increased until it matched the conservatives, with Christians in a minority. The peyotists were "the most prosperous members of the tribe" and the best businessmen.[29] According to Henry Roe Cloud, who was a Winnebago, the religion attracted "the younger men of the tribe because it offered more leadership to them, whereas the conservative Medicine Lodge is composed largely of the old men of the tribe and does not offer much opportunity to the younger men." [30]

A similar religious development was taking place among the neighboring Omahas where a "Mescal Society" was formed in 1906 through the efforts of an Omaha who had visited the Oto in Oklahoma and upon his return consulted with the Winnebago peyote group, whose Christian orientation he shared. Among the Omahas, also, the peyotists regarded their religion as a cure for alcoholism. Although the apostles of the new religion encountered much opposition among the elders, more than half of the tribal members had joined by 1909.[31] By 1915, the Omaha group had become "The Omaha Indian Peyote Society." [32] One of the Omaha, Allen P. Dale, who attended his first peyote meeting in 1908 at the age of twelve, many years later became national president of the Native American Church, which grew out of the peyote cult.[33]

Included in the Omaha membership were some highly acculturated men like the lawyers Hiram Chase and Thomas L. Sloan. Such men thought in terms of a more formal organization which would unite the local peyote congregations. At a Winnebago peyote meeting Chase told the group, "My friends, I am glad I can be here and worship this medicine [Peyote] with you, and we must organize a new church and have it run like the Mormon Church." [34]

Thus by 1910 a decidedly Christianized version of the peyote religion was well established in Nebraska among the Winnebagos and

Omahas. These groups contributed both leaders and members to the Society of American Indians, as well as to other reform and fraternal Pan-Indian organizations.

Another Christianized branch of the peyote religion arose during the decade 1900–10 among the Oklahoma Oto, whose influence upon the Winnebago and the Omaha has already been noted. The peyote cult reached the Oto before 1896 as "the standard pre-John Wilson Plains type," in LaBarre's characterization; that is, with few if any Christian elements.[35] The use of the Bible was probably introduced around 1900.[36] By far the most influential man in the introduction of Christian elements was Jonathan Koshiway, an Oto born in 1886, whose Oto mother was enrolled in the Sauk and Fox tribe of which his father was also a member.[37] Before becoming a peyote leader, Koshiway had lived in northeastern Kansas, where he was a Bible student. His religious views were fairly eclectic. He had served as an Indian evangelist for the Church of Latter Day Saints (Mormons) and had also been attracted to the Jehovah's Witnesses. "As an individual Koshiway was considerably influenced by Middle Western Protestantism, and solved for himself the adjustmental problem of double culture-bearers by discovering that the old native religion of his childhood was the *same* as the White Christianity of his maturity, with merely differing phrasing and vocabulary," La Barre reported.[38] Koshiway's version of the peyote religion was a kind of Indianized Christianity heavily influenced also by the doctrines of Jehovah's Witnesses or Russellites.[39]

By the end of the first decade of the twentieth century the peyote religion had spread far beyond its Oklahoma heartland into the Great Plains and the Prairies and had developed a number of new local groups, many with a strong Christian orientation. The religion showed great flexibility, adapting itself to particular local and tribal conditions while retaining its Pan-Indian character. In spite of local differences, all the peyote groups exhibited certain basic patterns of belief and ritual.

"The belief is that God put some of his Holy Spirit into peyote, which he gave to the Indians. And by eating the sacramental peyote the Indian absorbs God's Spirit, in the same way that the White Christian absorbs that Spirit by means of the sacramental bread and wine. . . .

The traditional practice of many Indian tribes was to go off in isolation and fast until a supernatural vision was achieved. This is now replaced by a collective all-night vigil in which, through prayer, contemplation, and eating peyote, the Peyotist received a divine revelation. For the Peyotist, this occurs because he has put himself in a receptive spiritual mood and has absorbed enough of God's power to make him able to reach God." [40]

Peyote services were normally begun on Saturday night and ended at dawn on Sunday. In some tribes they were held every week, in others several times a month. Meetings were often called for specific purposes, such as doctoring a sick person. The congregation gathered in a tepee, in the open air, or in a permanent church house erected for the purpose. The ceremonies were in charge of a recognized peyote leader known as a "road chief," who was a man of considerable prestige in the local community and who was often known far beyond his locality. He was assisted by a "drummer" and a "fire-chief."

The peyote ceremonials, which required the use of special religious objects, included singing, drumming and rattling (with gourds), praying, and the eating of peyote buttons. Unlike most tribal religious ceremonies, dancing was not used in peyote worship. At midnight a special ceremony was held. Curing of the sick was frequently featured, as peyote was considered a panacea. After dawn the congregation ate a ritual breakfast. In the morning a lecture or sermon was often delivered. Sunday was devoted to socializing, often with a communal midday dinner.[41]

The composition of the peyote congregations varied. In most tribes both men and women participated. In a few—largely those who had been early peyote users when the religion "still had the flavor of a warrior's society about it"—women were barred. Indians of any tribe were welcome at any peyote service, and normally the congregation included visitors from other tribes. Even the presence of whites at peyote meetings was not uncommon. Negroes were normally unwelcome, but a few tribes permitted them to attend.

Extensive intertribal visitation and correspondence by mail constituted the informal channels through which established peyote groups kept in touch with each other and new groups were formed. The absence of centralized organization was consonant with Indian customs and encouraged the variation and adaptability which were one of the religion's chief sources of strength.

As peyote congregations began to appear on reservations hitherto unaffected by the religion and as increasing numbers of progressive Indians were attracted to it, opposition grew both within the Indian Bureau and among some missionary groups. Between 1900 and 1910 the most concerted attack on the peyote cult developed as part of the Bureau's anti-liquor campaign. In 1906, the Bureau assigned a special officer, William E. ("Pussyfoot") Johnson, to the suppression of the "liquor traffic" among Indians. Johnson soon extended his anti-liquor activities to include peyote. In 1909 he bought up the entire peyote stock in Laredo, Texas, the chief source of supply, and destroyed it.[42] But Johnson seems to have over-stepped himself. At least his efforts did not get the support he believed they deserved, even within the Bureau.[43]

During this decade, also, some leading missionaries became deeply concerned over the effect of the growth of the peyote religion on the spread of Christianity. Dr. Walter C. Roe, whose protégé Henry Roe Cloud played so important a role in Pan-Indian affairs, wrote in 1908 that "one of the worst results of its [peyote's] use is that it creates a very strong barrier in the way of the presentation of the Christian religion to any tribe that has adopted its use, and is an attempt on the part of the more enlightened of the Indians to establish a racial and tribal religion as against what they call the white man's religion." [44] By 1910 opposition to peyote was beginning to acquire powerful allies outside the Indian Bureau, but not until the next decade did the peyote religion engage the serious attention of the Indian defense organizations and the national missionary groups. Until this had occurred, the campaign against peyote could not assume major proportions.

Between 1910 and 1918, the religion gained in strength where it was already established and spread rapidly to new groups. One Christian missionary journal reported in 1915 that "a regular missionary propaganda, similar to that of the Mormon Church, is carried out by the more established 'peyote lodges.' Attractive young men are sent out by twos to visit other reservations and encourage their cult." [45] By 1918, some 12,000 Indians were peyote religionists, with congregations in Iowa, Kansas, Montana, Nebraska, New Mexico, North and South Dakota, Oklahoma, Utah, Wisconsin, and Wyoming.[46]

The Pan-Indian character of the growing religion and its relationship to Christianity were described by James Mooney in 1918: "The Indian, under the influence of this peyote religion, has given up the idea that he and his tribe are for themselves alone, and is recognizing the fact of the brotherhood of the Indian race particularly, and beyond that the brotherhood of mankind. It is an essential uplift, as compared with the original tribal religion." Mooney called the peyote cult "not a Christian religion" but "a very close approximation," adding that "as Indian religions and Indian psychology go, it is as close an approximation to Christianity and as efficient a leading up to Christianity as the Indian, speaking generally is now capable of. By a process of evolution the Indian has interwoven with this peyote the salient things of Christianity. . . . It comes through the channels to which he is accustomed. Its central idea is human brotherhood. Its cordial precepts are good will and sobriety." [47]

So extensive and growing a Pan-Indian religious movement with its message of universal Indian brotherhood was bound to alarm the Bureau, which had never been entirely comfortable with Indian efforts toward unity, even of the reform variety which had little impact on reservations. While some agency superintendents remained neutral and a few were even sympathetic, reports on the religion coming into Washington were frequently unsettling, expecially as the memory of the Ghost Dance had not entirely faded. Nor could Christian missionaries ignore a religion which seemed an attractive alternative to Christianity. But probably neither of these factors would have been sufficient in themselves to arouse the fears and hostilities which the peyote religion evoked and to result in a concerted campaign for its suppression. It was the use of a drug as symbol and sacrament and the linking of opposition to peyote with the increasing tempo of the prohibition movement which mobilized opinion against the peyotists.

Certainly most reform Pan-Indians would have taken a different view of religious Pan-Indians had not an anti-peyote crusade been launched. The Society of American Indians took little notice of the peyote religion for some time and welcomed peyotists to its membership. Peyote adherents became leaders and prominent members of the Society. The suspicions with which they were sometimes viewed did not seem at first to have run very deep. The opposition to peyote which eventually developed in the SAI no doubt stemmed from a genuine conviction that peyote represented a serious danger to Indian health and morals. But it seems clear that the most important factor in the Society's attack on peyote and support for legislation outlawing it was the influence of the white reformers and churchmen who were closest to the SAI and who were most exercised over "the peyote menace."

Even among these groups support for the Bureau's somewhat spasmodic anti-peyote efforts grew slowly. Before 1914 it does not seem to have amounted to much beyond a rather routine concern—with some notable exceptions. One of those who took a much more serious view of the matter was the Reverend Robert D. Hall, who was then in charge of the Indian work of the YWCA and later served as associate secretary of the Society of American Indians. By 1911, Hall had become thoroughly alarmed at the extent of the "peyote drug habit" among Indian young men. He resolved to put peyote to the test by eating it himself under scientific auspices. Accordingly, he arranged to take it at Yale under the direction of the head of the Psychology Department, Professor Roswell P. Angier. Hall's experience, together with Angier's analysis, convinced him that peyote was harmful. Hall was particularly fearful that peyote would cause him to lose his self-control.[48] Hall's and Angier's evidence was later widely quoted as a scientific statement against peyote.[49]

In 1914 the religion for the first time became a major topic of discussion at the Lake Mohonk conference. In a speech entitled "Liquor and Peyote a Menace to the Indian," Fred H. Daiker, Chief of the Law and Order Section of the Indian Bureau, reported that the BIA had "attempted to procure legislation in this subject but thus far has been unsuccessful." [50] Other speakers labeled peyote "a dangerous drug," and "a more dangerous and potent substitute for alcohol." Peyotists were referred to as "mescal fiends," and a peyote missionary was called "a second Benedict Arnold . . . betraying his people, the whole Indian people." The Reverend Dr. Edward Ashley, an Episcopal missionary from South Dakota, reported, "The authorities say they desire to put down this evil, but are up against the fact that it is a religious institution and comes within the Constitution of the United States." [51]

The discussion at Lake Mohonk of the "menace" of peyote was effective in arousing opposition to the religion. For the first time the Lake Mohonk conference platform resolved: "It is now well known that the increasing use of the mescal bean, or peyote, is demoralizing in the extreme. We recommend accordingly that the Federal prohibition of intoxicating liquors be extended to include this dangerous drug." [52]

The effort to outlaw peyote through federal legislation was in part the result of the failure to halt the spread of the peyote religion through administrative rulings and court proceedings. In 1910 the Indian Bureau attempted without success to induce the Treasury Department through its Bureau of Customs to prohibit the importation of peyote from Mexico. After the passage of the Harrison Narcotic Act in 1914, the Bureau tried to secure an interpretation of the law which would include peyote, but the Commissioner of Internal Revenue ruled that peyote did not come under its provision and that specific legislation would be necessary. The attorney general also ruled that peyote did not come under the act.[53] In 1914, also, an attack on peyote through the courts failed in a case involving a Menominee peyotist charged with introducing "an intoxicant, peyote" into an Indian reservation. He was acquitted on the grounds that "the [peyote] meeting was of a religious character and that peyote was used to celebrate religious rites." [54] In 1916 the conviction of an Indian for introducing and giving away "mescal beans" on the Pine Ridge Reservation was overruled by the judge on the grounds that the law forbidding intoxicating liquor under which the defendant had been convicted did not apply to peyote. Thomas L. Sloan was a witness for the defense in the case.[55]

The only Bureau effort which was even moderately successful came in 1915 when the Department of Agriculture issued a regulation detaining all shipments of peyote coming into the country. This procedure made it "less convenient to get peyote" but did not lessen the supply.[56] It seemed obvious that peyote could not be stopped by administrative rulings alone; federal legislation was necessary.

The first federal anti-peyote bill, the Gandy Bill, was introduced in the House in 1916 with the strong support of the Indian Bureau. A similar bill was introduced in the Senate. But neither these bills nor later measures introduced in 1917 by the same sponsors were enacted into law. In 1917 the Indian Bureau moved against peyote through the Post Office Department. At the Bureau's instigation, the Post Office Department issued an order "prohibiting the use of the mails" for the shipment of peyote.[57] While these federal efforts were meeting with only limited success in the executive branch and no success at all in Congress, three western states—Utah, Colorado, and Nevada—passed anti-peyote laws in 1917.[58]

The Indian Rights Association did not give major attention to the matter until 1916. In its *Annual Report* of that year an article entitled "The Ravages of Peyote" attacked the "baneful" effects of the religion.

"The successful farmer neglects his fields and home: his health is often affected, and interest is lost in the things which tend to better living," the article stated.

Despite its concern with the "ravages of peyote," the IRA was mindful of the criticism that interference in religious ceremonials would violate freedom of religion as guaranteed in the constitution. "If that view is accepted," the IRA declared, "any vicious practice or use of drugs which undermines the health and morals may be upheld with equal force if it is associated with so-called religious ceremonials."

The peyote religion's demoralizing effect on Christian Indians was also cited by the IRA. "Its followers seem to abandon Christian teaching, and in their frequent nightly gatherings indulge in excesses through the midnight hours in which men and women participate. It is claimed that in these nocturnal debaucheries there is often a total abandoment of virtue, especially among the women." The specific evidence adduced in the article came largely from the Uintah and Ouray Reservation in Utah where the Utes had only recently taken up the peyote religion. Included in the evidence was a statement from Gertrude and Raymond T. Bonnin, who were stationed at the agency, where Mrs. Bonnin ran the Community Center under SAI auspices. The Bonnins alleged that peyote "excited the baser passions," "created false notions in the minds of the users," caused them to "reject the teachings of the church," "to ignore the advice and aid of physicians," and "appears to be the direct cause of death of 25 persons among the Utes in the last two years." The Bonnins believed that the peyote cult was being promoted by "an unscrupulous organization" which, "under a religious guise," was operated "solely for the easy money gotten from their superstitious victims." The IRA article quoted also from the agency physician and the resident Episcopalian missionary.[59]

The publication of the extended attack on peyote in the 1916 IRA *Annual Report* signaled a determined IRA effort for the enactment of federal anti-peyote legislation. By 1918 the anti-peyote campaign had gathered considerable strength. No doubt the feverish atmosphere in a country at war made the campaign more intense. Certainly the prohibitionist crusade lent it momentum. But despite the war and despite the identification of "the peyote menace" with the "liquor evil," the fight over peyote was confined largely to persons directly involved in Indian affairs: the Bureau, the missionaries, the Indian defense organizations, anthropologists, the Bureau of American Ethnology, and of course, the Indians themselves. Outside the fact that the use of peyote was a "problem" largely confined to Indians, the delicate question of religious freedom was probably the most important factor in limiting support for the anti-peyote campaign.

In 1918 Congressman Carl M. Hayden of Arizona introduced a bill (HR 2614) relating to the revision and codification of laws relating to the liquor traffic among Indians which included peyote as an "intoxicant" and outlawed its use by any Indian over whom the Indian Bureau had jurisdiction, whether or not he was a citizen.

The hearings on the section of the bill dealing with peyote marked a turning point in the history of religious Pan-Indianism. They revealed to the peyotists the strength of the forces arrayed against them and the grim possibility that harassment might soon escalate into suppression. Some new and more adequate defense had to be devised if the peyotists were to protect their religion against the dangers which now loomed before them.

11

THE NATIVE AMERICAN CHURCH

The hearings on the Hayden Bill were held before a subcommittee of the Committee on Indian Affairs of the House of Representatives in February and March of 1918. Indians and whites testified on both sides, setting forth the major arguments for and against the use of peyote in religious observance. Supporting the prohibition of peyote were reform Pan-Indians, white reformers and missionaries, the Indian Bureau, and scientists. Opposing it were religious and reform Pan-Indians, white and Indian anthropologists from the Bureau of American Ethnology, and other scientists.

The Indian Bureau was represented by Fred H. Daiker, its chief law-enforcement officer. Daiker's major points were as follows: (1) peyote was a harmful drug whose use was increasing rapidly; (2) the religious services connected with peyote were subterfuges "held whenever they wanted to use peyote"; (3) peyote did not destroy the taste for whiskey, and Indians who used peyote also used whiskey; and (4) the majority of the superintendents of agencies where it was in current use condemned it. Under questioning, Daiker admitted that some of the superintendents stated that "it had stopped the use of whiskey." [1]

Dr. Harvey W. Wiley, former chief of the Bureau of Chemistry of the Department of Agriculture, also testified in favor of the bill. Wiley reported that James Mooney of the Bureau of American Ethnology had brought him some peyote in 1893 and had asked him to "determine, as far as possible, the physiological properties of the product." Not having a pharmacological laboratory, Wiley turned over the investigation to Drs. D. W. Prentiss and F. P. Morgan of the George Washington Medi-

259

cal School. Meanwhile one of Wiley's assistants investigated its chemical properties and also, somewhat against Wiley's judgment, took it himself, during which time he saw visions. Wiley stated that the experiments "under my initiative were only of a temporary character, they were not repeated, so that we had no opportunity to determine what the final effect would be by a repetition of this experience upon the mental and physical qualities of the individual." Wiley believed, however, that continued use of the drug would be injurious, and that an increasing quantity would be "necessary to produce the excitation." Classifying peyote with strychnine, opium, and cocaine, he believed it to have "some therapeutic value," but urged that it be used only under the advice and on the prescription of a physician. Wiley supported the prohibition of peyote as provided in the Hayden Bill.[2]

Dr. Lyman F. Kebler, chief of the Drug Division of the Bureau of Chemistry, Department of Agriculture, stated that though he had wished to do so, he had "not made any special study of peyote, and what I know about peyote has been gleaned entirely from the literature," a synopsis of which he gave in written form to the committee. Kebler testified that peyote resembled both cocaine and morphine, especially the former, though he did not know "whether or not peyote has the same demoralizing effect that cocaine has." Upon questioning, Kebler agreed emphatically that he would regard peyote "as a deleterious drug and harmful to the Indians." He did not, however, specifically endorse the Hayden Bill.

S. M. Brosius, the Washington representative of the Indian Rights Association, testified in its behalf, repeating the general case against peyote that had been set forth in the 1916 *Annual Report,* which he offered as evidence. Brosius was careful to state that as far as he was concerned, "I have never had any experience in the eating of peyote or the drinking of mescal wines or under whatever terms they may be called, but my attention was called to the evil effects of the use of peyote among the Indians during a trip to the Uintah and Ouray agency at Fort Duchesne, Utah in 1916." Sexual immorality and the involvement of the "better class" of Indians at the Ute reservation were the points that particularly brought peyote to his attention, Brosius stated. His specific knowledge of peyote was limited almost entirely to the Unintah and Ouray situation, where his informants were persons hostile to the peyote religion—the superintendent, agency doctor, missionaries, and the Bonnins. He did not observe a peyote meeting or see an Indian "under its influence" nor does he seem to have interviewed any peyotists. But it is quite possible that the situation at this agency was indeed unfortunate; at least the man who had introduced the religion had many critics among the peyotists themselves.[3]

Brosius was at pains to explain that his knowledge was "only general," that he "had never made a special study of peyote and the effect of it" but that he had been "hearing of it for the last five or six years." Such a lack of information was unusual in IRA operations, which were normally characterized by careful investigation and documentation. In such matters as "pagan" ceremonies, however, the IRA was more apt to rely on hearsay evidence. For whatever reason, Brosius was surprisingly poorly informed on the peyote religion, its diffusion, and its point of view.[4]

General Pratt also testified for the Hayden Bill and, like Brosius, displayed only a vague knowledge of the peyote religion. "My knowledge of the effects of peyote is confined almost entirely to hearsay, and you have had so much of it that is direct here that it is hardly worth while for me to speak of it," the General stated, adding that "I have relied upon Dr. Wiley for my opposition to it, because I have known the doctor for a great many years and I have great confidence in his judgment and his insight into such matters."

Pratt was especially concerned about "the very demoralizing effect [of peyote] on some very excellent products of the Carlisle School." His major example was Delos Lone Wolf, who was center rush on the Carlisle football team and who became a peyote leader in Oklahoma. Lone Wolf had recently visited Washington to lobby against the Hayden Bill.

Pratt, speaking after several ethnologists from the Bureau of American Ethnology had testified against the bill, also excoriated his old enemy, the BAE, which he said had "blocked the way of Indian education very largely; that is by keeping the country misinformed about the Indians." Pratt charged that "the Bureau of Ethnology has never been helpful to the Indians in any respect. You will be unable to find, if you go through all of the Indian tribes where they have taken an Indian by the hand and said, 'My brother, you can become a citizen of the United States; you can become civilized, and you can become thoroughly useful in the United States.' On the contrary, the ethnologists always lead the Indian's mind back to the past."

Pratt went on to attack "my friend, Mr. [Francis] LaFlesche," the Omaha Indian BAE anthropologist as a "victim" of Bureau employment and ideas. "He is not lifting up his race," Pratt averred. Warming to his subject, Pratt declared that "It was well established at the time of the ghost-dance craze among the Indians that white men were its promoters if not its originators. That this peyote craze is under the same impulse is evident from what appears in the evidence." Pratt thus clearly implied that James Mooney was a promoter of both the Ghost Dance and the peyote religion.[5]

Mooney categorically denied these accusations. He defended ethnologists against the charge that they had never helped the Indians. On the contrary, Mooney stated, ethnologists

"have always endeavored to help the Indians, as is borne out by hundreds of letters from representative Indians showing to what extent they appreciate the work of the ethnologists. We have helped them in congressional matters and have been delegated to help in matters of allotment; some of us have been sent out to make allotments for them; that is, to help choose the best land, and avoid being victimized by the white settlers. We have helped them to civilization in every way; we have helped them in the choice of schools, in the choice of education; we have helped them to raise cattle and build houses; we have gone into their tepees and shown them how to cook and live decently. All these things have been done by the ethnologists, both men and women. . . .

If you want to get at the truth of this thing [the peyote religion] have the Indians come from the tribes that are directly concerned. An Indian delegate from a sectarian body or alleged uplift organization is not a delegate for his tribe." [6]

No doubt Mooney was referring in such disparaging fashion to the Indians testifying in behalf of the Hayden Bill. The chief of these were Gertrude Bonnin, secretary of the Society of American Indians, and her colleague, Charles Eastman.

Mrs. Bonnin based her attack on peyote largely on her firsthand experience among the Utes, among whom she had lived for fourteen years. During the last two years she had seen the introduction of peyote and observed its effects. Her charges against the peyotists fell under four main categories: (1) peyote "excites the baser passions"; [7] (2) peyotists got money from Indians under false pretenses; (3) peyotists drank; (4)

at least thirty deaths among the Utes could be attributed to peyote. A central figure in all these accusations except the last was one "Peter Phelps" or "Cactus Pete," whom Mrs. Bonnin stated was a peyote agent from another (unspecified) tribe.[8]

Attacks upon peyote could "not be represented as being made because of a difference in religions," Mrs. Bonnin testified. Christians opposed it on the grounds that it was demoralizing. "Even Indians who are Christians become addicted to the habit of using peyote right along," she added.

Peyote was a danger to all men, red and white alike, Mrs. Bonnin concluded. "This habit of using peyote is not going to be limited to the red man alone. . . . And today, in the face of national prohibition, this menace is going to spread . . . like wildfire, and we need to protect all the citizens of America by quenching that little spark." [9]

Of all those appearing in opposition to peyote, Charles A. Eastman had probably considered the movement most carefully. "I have made a study and investigation of the peyote question ever since it developed, because I felt I was not in a position to know all of the features of it," Eastman stated. His resulting opposition was on social, medical, and moral grounds.

The effort to defend peyote on religious grounds was "purely a subterfuge," Eastman believed. He urged that "the two things should be separated entirely. It is not an Indian idea nor is it an Indian practice. It is more like what happened a few years ago during the ghost-dance craze, which, as we all know, was gotten up by irresponsible, reckless, and unprincipled people who thought that under the conditions that the Indians were suffering from something like that would go, and that they would get some benefit out of it. That is the way the ghost dance started, and it started in that quarter down there [Oklahoma]. It came from that direction, and this is exactly the same way."

Eastman branded peyote as "absolutely dangerous . . . among our Indian race or any other race." He had no objection to a church, he stated, but "the use of peyote and keeping up its use all night is absolutely against all common sense." Peyote appealed to educated Indians on whom it had disastrous effects, Eastman declared. "Some of the brightest boys that were ever educated at the Indian schools have become peyote eaters, and those men have been ruined in their character, and you can not depend on them," he asserted.

Among the Sioux "there are three classes who go into it," Eastman explained. One class uses it "absolutely for physical reasons or medical relief, especially for consumption and rheumatism. They try it and come back not any better off. Some of them die soon afterwards." Another group "is liable to go into any thing like that. They are of the character that do not stick anywhere." A third class was made up of those "opposed to the white man's religion, claiming there is something hypocritical in the white man's religion, and that something ought to be developed for the Indians that is superior to the white man's religion. Now, there is nothing in that, and they have simply dropped back." As a specific example of the adverse effects of peyote, Eastman cited the case of Delos Lone Wolf, who, Eastman stated, is "old in mind and body." [10]

Other Indians who spoke for the Hayden Bill included Joe Claymore, a Sioux stockman from South Dakota and "a delegate of the Sioux people," and Chester Arthur from Montana, also a Sioux, a Presbyterian, and a member of the Board of Directors of the YMCA. Arthur warned that "the effect of this drug is undermining the work of civilizing [the Indians] and educating them, and is bringing them back to their old superstitious beliefs. Whiskey plays havoc among our people, and peyote is coming in its footsteps, and we pray for legislation that will prohibit its use as well as the use of liquor." Arthur also stated that the use of peyote led to "sexual excesses." [11]

Supporting evidence offered at the hearing and later read into the Congressional Record by Congressman Hayden indicated the range of opposition to peyote and support for its prohibition. Among those opposing peyote were the Anti-Saloon League of America ("It is evidently an easy way to get a cheap drunk"), the National Women's Christian Temperance Union, the National Congress of Mothers and Parent-Teachers Associations, the Board of Indian Commissioners, the Bureau of Catholic Indian Missions, and the Home Missions Council.[12] Anti-peyote statements were also submitted by agency physicians, agency superintendents, and Indians who had used peyote with ill effects.[13]

The peyote religion was vigorously defended in the hearings by anthropologists, Indians, and scientists. The man who spoke most extensively in its defense and in opposition to the Hayden Bill was James Mooney, the first anthropologist to make a study of the peyote cult. He had initially encountered peyote during his investigations of the Ghost Dance. For some twenty-seven years thereafter, Mooney's major task for the Bureau of American Ethnology was the study of the tribes using peyote. He had attended a number of peyote meetings and had himself taken peyote.

Mooney began his testimony by recounting the history of the investigation of peyote in the United States which, he stated, he had initiated in 1891 by turning over a number of peyote buttons to Dr. Wiley at the Department of Agriculture. Mooney offered in evidence one of Prentiss' and Morgan's articles dealing with the therapeutic uses of peyote and a report by Dr. Weir Mitchell, to whom Mooney had also given some peyote buttons for analysis.

Peyote, Mooney stated, was often confused with mescal, a misunderstanding which "formerly, if not now, has been the cause of a great deal of prejudice and public sentiment against this peyote and against the religion of the Indians in that connection." Mescal, Mooney explained, was used to make a highly intoxicating distilled brandy with "no religious connection whatever" and should be sharply distinguished from peyote, which the Indians used in the crude state and never distilled. It should be noted that this confusion was often shared by the Indians who, though actually using peyote, often referred to it as "mescal."

Next Mooney sought to demonstrate that the peyote cult was a genuine religion. The religious use of peyote "dates as far back as our knowlege of the Indians in the Spanish territories," he said. Today, Mooney continued, the peyote cult had become an intertribal religion emphasizing "Indian brotherhood" and involving a large number of tribes, an Indian "approximation" of Christianity. Mooney outlined a peyote ceremony in some detail, describing the role of "curing" in the rite.

In analyzing the reasons for the spread of the peyote religion, Mooney said:

"The Indians now are largely civilized; they are becoming citizens; they are educated, and they travel about and take an interest in each other. A great many of the young men who have been sent to eastern schools, in a climate damper than the one to which they have been accustomed, come back with weakened lungs, coughs, and hemorrhages, and they are told by their Indian friends at home that if they use the peyote it will relieve the coughs and check the hemorrhages, and they have found that to be true. That is the universal testimony of the Indians, and it is corroborated by Dr. Prentiss' experiments. The result is that the young men, not the older uncivilized ones, but the younger, middle-aged and educated men, have taken up the peyote cult and organized it as a regular religion, beyond that they knew before among the various tribes. In some tribes they have their own church houses, built at their own expense."

Mooney had considerable respect for native medical practice though not for native medical theory, and was impressed by the medical properties of peyote. It might, he thought, become a valuable medicine as had quinine, which had also been used originally in an Indian religious rite. The use of quinine had been opposed by the Spaniards and missionaries also, Mooney added.

Mooney defended the peyote religion on temperance grounds, pointing out that "followers of the peyote rite say that the peyote does not like whiskey, and no real peyote user touches whiskey or continues to drink whiskey after he has taken up the peyote religion," which is the Indian's "greatest shield against intemperance." Charges of immorality on the part of peyotists were completely false, Mooney stated.[14]

Several other anthropologists from the Bureau of American Ethnology also testified. Dr. Truman Michelson reported that the effect of peyote as he had observed it differed somewhat in its effect on users in the different tribes. He urged further research to determine whether all the tribes were using the same plant and "to note its effect in various places," stating that "No one has been completely satisfied with the previous analysis." He also reported that peyote users did not drink whiskey.[15]

Francis LaFlesche (Omaha) of the BAE described the effects of the peyote religion upon his own tribe as first reported to him by his sister, a physician, who said that the Omahas had "quit drinking. They pray intelligently, they pray to God, they pray to Jesus, . . . they ask help from God." LaFlesche regarded the peyote religion as responsible for the moral regeneration of the Omaha, following a period after allotment when drunkeness and lawlessness prevailed on the reservation and when the Indian Bureau, the Indian Rights Association, and the missionaries did "absolutely nothing." The Omahas, LaFlesche explained,

"could not understand the white man's religion; it was a thing too intricate for them. . . . But the teaching of this new religion was something that they could understand. 'The peyote,' they said, helped them to think intelligently of God and of their relations to Him. At the meetings of this new religion is taught the avoidance of stealing, lying, drunkenness, adultery, assaultism, the making of false and evil reports against neighbors. People are taught to be kind and loving to one another and particularly to the little ones.

The persons who are opposed to the use of peyote by the Indians in their religion say that it makes them immoral. This has not been my observation. The Indians who have taken the new religion strive to live upright, moral lives and I think their morality can be favorably compared with any community of a like number in the country. To be sure, some of them go astray from the path of virtue, as white people do."

Many of the Omaha peyotists, LaFlesche stated, had won prizes for farm products at the tribal fair, thus attesting to their industry and ability.

LaFlesche reported that he had attended peyote meetings among the Omaha, the Osage, and the Ponca. The meetings were not prearranged and there had been no immorality. He had made an intensive study of the Osage tribe, where he found that the morals of the peyotists "compared favorably with those of the white people." [16]

Opposition to the Hayden Bill was also voiced by William E. Safford, economic botanist for the Department of Agriculture who in 1915 had published an authoritative article on peyote.[17] Safford traced briefly the history of the use of narcotics for religious purposes and then discussed the effect of peyote:

"Those who have taken peyote, in a limited amount, have had a pleasant sensation from it. If they take a greater amount, it causes certain hallucinations, and in this stage, when certain things are suggested to them, they see them. . . . But it is only the practice which has been handed down from generation to generation, from century to century, the effects of these narcotics which they attributed to something supernatural. . . .

Peyote is undoubtedly a narcotic and if taken in excess it has bad effects. In all cases I have investigated I have not found any instance where it was taken to excess. Tobacco, and even coffee, if taken to excess, is poisonous."

Safford also stated that the Indian religious ceremonies "had nothing to do with sexual appetites," "irregularities," or "debauchery." He believed that possible ill effects of peyote were outweighed by the harm that would come from banning it:

"I realize the evil which would result if they undertook to cure malignant diseases with drugs of this kind. I have not any more faith in the beneficent effects of peyote than I have in faith cures. I think harm may be done by it if used medicinally but I know this; that by taking away this ritual from the Indians it would humiliate them greatly and I would be afraid that if deprived of it they would fall back into their old bad habits. It would be a faith forced upon them if they had to adopt the ceremonies of the Christian churches, and they would feel that nothing was left to them of their ancient customs and their ancient traditions if peyote were taken away from them." [18]

A number of Indian peyotists also testified in defense of their religion. Most were former Carlisle students. Most affirmed that peyote had cured them of drinking. Arthur Bonnicastle, Osage, a former Carlisle student who had served in the American army during the Boxer Rebellion, described the effects of peyote thus:

"It trains the mind to higher ideas in worshipping God. The principles laid down in the use of this peyote as it is taught in these meetings by the leader, teaches the Indians to things that will lead to better life in worshipping the Almighty; that is to train the mind to that end. I don't see any bad effects from its use. [To outlaw peyote would be] an injustice—because they don't use it to excess and use it to good advantage—use it in religion and their prayers and in times of sickness, and they don't use it between times of religious meetings." [19]

Thomas L. Sloan described the peyote religion among the Omaha and Winnebago where, he said, "it has changed a large number of men from drunkards to decent people. It has been reported that there was some immorality connected with the ceremony. I am convinced that there is nothing of the kind. The old-time medicine men are opposed to the use of peyote. They are some of the persons who make detrimental remarks and spread rumors against it." Others opposing the use of peyote "are those who have grown rich out of the sale of liquor to Indians," Sloan asserted in a neat reversal of the anti-peyote contention that peyotists were using the religion to exploit the Indian. "There is now an active wave of Christianity among the Omaha and Winnebago Indians and it is a growth among the Indians themselves, and due in part to the religious use of peyote," Sloan declared.[20]

Paul Boynton, a Cheyenne-Arapaho, also a former Carlisle student, testified that peyote cured sin and disease. "Through the conscience of this peyote I was made well," Boynton said, "because I could think higher, I could see that there was something greater than the medicine itself. I saw God planted the herb I was using, so I say; 'I am going to use God's herb. If there is such a thing as all things are possible, because God planted this herb and blessed it, and I am going to take God's blessing.' " [21]

Cleaver Warden, Arapaho, a former Carlisle student who had worked for "the Chicago Museum and the New York City Museum," also pointed to what he believed to be the curative powers of the peyote.[22] Warden had come to the hearings after reading Mrs. Bonnin's testimony in an Oklahoma newspaper. "That Indian lady is not right but is instigated by wrong advice," Warden commented. "We only ask a fair and impartial trial by reasonable white people, not half breeds who do not know a lot of their ancestors or kindred. A true Indian is one who helps for a race and not that secretary of the Society of American Indians. Our intentions are good but obstructed by such persons." [23]

Warden summarized his view of what the peyote religion stood for in a letter offered in evidence:

"You understand we believe what we see, hear, etc. of the works of the Great Spirit, therefore we placed the tepee facing towards the sunrise. We carried out the vow or purposes of an individual who wishes and desires the presence of divine power, by offerings of prayer in Indian religious doctrine. Just consider the Indians gathered in the tepee, having a fire blazing therein for the sole object of developing the spiritual temperaments of the race as well as obtaining physical strength. This gotten by self-reliance and self-control. There is justifiable reason for being a part or a member of that Indian religious tepee." [24]

Another former Carlisle student who testified was Wilbur Piawo (Comanche) who stated that the peyote cult "is a religion that the Indians have practiced long before they have seen the white man, according to what my people say, and they are still worshipping in this form." Peyote, Piawo asserted, "makes me feel kind."

Congressman Snyder asked Piawo,

" 'What do you think would become of your religious society if the bean was taken away from you entirely? What would happen to the association?'

Piawo: 'I do not know what would happen to them, but I don't think they will exist much longer.'

Snyder: 'And you don't think there is anything else that could be brought in to take the place of the peyote to keep the society together?'
Piawo: 'No, sir.'
Snyder: 'Why could you noι take the form of the Methodist Church or the Baptist Church or the Episcopal Church or the Catholic Church and use bread and wine in place of the peyote bean?'
Piawo: 'Well, I don't know about that; but it is the way the Indians have been worshipping in the past.' "

Snyder pressed his suggestion but Piawo did not comment on it further.[25]

Several of the chiefs who testified could not speak English and spoke through an interpreter. The most extensive such statement was that of Fred Lookout, chief of the Osage:

"We use [peyote] in the right way. We have church houses, ourselves, among the Osage people. . . . Since the use of peyote amongst the tribe of Osage Indians my young people, or my young men, have developed quite a good reputation. They are living up to their words. They are living under the laws of the State [Oklahoma] where we live. They are prosperous; they are gaining; and they are living a better life and making money, settling down in their homesteads and raising their own cattle and horses and everything. By using this peyote they have lived a whole lot better life. On the other hand, before they began to use peyote, my people would use whiskey and it ruined a lot of our people."

Over half the "full-blood" members of the tribe were members of the peyote society, Lookout stated. The Osage, he said, did not use the peyote for healing the sick.[26]

Chief Little Hand of the Cheyenne also spoke through an interpreter:

"I am going to tell you about this peyote. . . . I come to tell the truth. We heard that those missionaries were going to make a complaint about this peyote. . . . There are four different tribes here to see you about this peyote [Osage, Cheyenne, Arapaho, Comanche], and you gentlemen are appointed as men to look after the facts, and we are now here to see you on behalf of these four different tribes. . . . All these stories what the missionaries tell are not so, I wish you to give consideration to this peyote matter in deciding whether it is to be taken away from us, and we want you to take our word for it. That is all." [27]

An important peyote leader, Jack Bull Bear, who was not present at the hearings, was represented by a statement inserted in the record. Bull

Bear was a former Carlisle student, an Arapaho chief, and a prosperous farmer. He called peyote the "religion of the Indian race" which keeps "alive our unwritten book." Peyotists, he said, have Christianity as their "motto through life," "try to live as prohibition people," "try to help our State wherever we live," and "help Indians to live the real civilized life." [28]

In the hearings on the Hayden Bill secular and religious Pan-Indian leaders thus took opposite views about the peyote religion. The peyotists considered their cult a genuine Indian religion of considerable antiquity. The anti-peyotists regarded it as a subterfuge invented and used to legitimize drug-taking. The peyotists believed that peyote had curative powers. The anti-peyotists denied this, contending that reliance on peyote was not only physically harmful but would deprive its practitioners of real medical care. Both peyotists and anti-peyotists were firmly against liquor. But the peyotists believed that their religion enabled them to give up drinking while the anti-peyotists regarded the cure as illusory and even more deadly than the disease. The peyotists affirmed that their religion helped them to lead a better, more upright, and civilized life; the anti-peyotist asserted that peyote was demoralizing and that the rites were in truth orgies.

Both sides of the dispute held a conception of the Indian that transcended tribal lines, but the controversy was not simply between two different brands of Pan-Indianism. Most of the English-speaking Indians who testified were, or had been, members of the Society of American Indians or had attended SAI annual conferences. And, as seemed inevitable in this period, most of the Indians involved on both sides were either former students at Carlisle or had close connections with it.

The Hayden Bill was passed by the House but was not enacted into law. The campaign against peyote, despite the efforts of its partisans, thus suffered at least a partial defeat. And in the bargain the anti-peyotists unwittingly inspired their enemies to new protective action. As a result of the hearings, the peyotists became thoroughly alarmed at the imminent legislative dangers now confronting them. If the use of the peyote so central to their religion were outlawed, the religion itself would be doomed. Protective measures beyond the kind they had already taken were clearly in order. Appropriately enough, the new defensive measures began in the heartland of the peyote religion, Oklahoma.

Throughout the summer of 1918 a number of Oklahoma peyotists debated "the matter of organizing their own native religion on a regular business basis, like any other church society, as American citizens." [29] A conference of Oto, Kiowa, and Arapaho peyotists was held at Cheyenne, Oklahoma, to discuss what action should be taken. At the conference Jonathan Koshiway, the Oto leader of the peyotist First-born Church of Christ, urged the incorporation of the religion, a defensive step his group had taken four years previously.[30] At the time, the Koshiway peyotists did not know that the Indian Shaker Church, a Pan-Indian religious group in the State of Washington, had incorporated in 1910, in order to gain "the respect and protection due them as a religious congregation." [31]

In the summer of 1918 James Mooney was in Oklahoma studying Kiowa peyotism for the Bureau of American Ethnology. At this or a subsequent peyotist conference, he used his considerable influence in persuading the group to obtain a charter. Mooney was convinced that the peyotists needed a firm legal status which would place them clearly under the protection of religious liberty guaranteed in the Constitution.

It has been suggested that the name "Native American Church" rather than the "First-born Church of Christ" was chosen because "many of the group apparently objected to the element of white religion implied in the title 'First-born Church of Christ' and rejected the name." Native American Church "emphasized the intertribal solidarity of the cult as well as its aboriginality." [32] But the fact that the Articles of Incorporation eventually agreed on characterized the church as a "Christian religion" makes this explanation somewhat inadequate insofar as it applies to Christianity. Perhaps the group did not wish to gather all the peyote groups together under the name already held by one association. The acceptance of Koshiway's name might also have implied the acceptance of his theology or his leadership. In any case, the term "Native American" frequently occurred in general literature about the Indian during this period. It was a Pan-Indian designation acceptable to peyotists from many tribes using different varieties of the peyote ceremonies. It also defined its adherents as Americans.

Thus was born the Native American Church, which was incorporated in the State of Oklahoma on October 10, 1918. The organization of the church was clearly a defensive measure. But for the well-organized campaign against them, peyotists would probably have gone on for years using the informal structure which was both culturally congenial and adequate to their religious purposes. Thus the anti-peyote drive served not to discourage the religion, but rather to force it into a more stable and permanent organizational form. As the anti-peyote campaign continued, other peyote groups in other states followed the lead of the Oklahoma peyotists and incorporated to protect themselves.

The rationale of the Oklahoma Native American Church, as outlined in the charter, referred both to its Pan-Indian and Christian character.

"The purpose for which this corporation is formed is to foster and promote the religious belief of the several tribes of Indians in the State of Oklahoma, in the Christian religion with the practice of the Peyote Sacrament as commonly understood and used among the adherents of this religion in the several tribes of Indians in the State of Oklahoma, and to teach the Christian religion with morality, sobriety, industry, kindly charity and right living and to cultivate a spirit of self-respect and brotherly union among the members of the Native Race of Indians including therein the various Indian tribes in the State of Oklahoma, with the right to own and hold property for the purposes of conducting its business or services." [33]

The charter provided for a general council, a governing body composed of two trustees elected from each affiliated local church "established in each Indian tribe in the State of Oklahoma." The officers to be elected by the council included a president, vice-president, secretary and treasurer. The first trustees representing churches in the seven tribes named in the Charter were: Mack Haag and Sidney White Crane (Cheyenne); Charles W. Dailey and George Pipestem (Oto); Frank Eagle and Louis McDonald (Ponca); Wilbur Piawo and Man Sookwat (Comanche); Kiowa Charley and Delos Lone Wolf (Kiowa); Apache Ben and Tennyson Berry (Apache); Paul Boynton and Cleaver Warden (Arapaho). Three of the trustees had testified at the Hayden Bill hearings while Delos Lone Wolf had been in Washington at the time though unable to wait to testify.

The first officers elected by the council were President Frank Eagle, Vice-President Mack Haag, Treasurer Louis McDonald, and Secretary George Pipestem. Carlisle influence was strong in the founding group. At least seven of the trustees were former Carlisle students—Eagle, McDonald, Peawa, Lone Wolf, Berry, Boynton, and Warden. President Eagle also attended Haskell. McDonald, the NAC treasurer, was sufficiently important in Carlisle affairs to be later selected as a pallbearer at

General Pratt's funeral, in company with other reform Pan-Indians like the former SAI stalwarts Dennison Wheelock and Howard Gansworth.[34]

The "seat of government and principal place of business" of the church was established at El Reno, Oklahoma, where a young men's Indian fraternal organization known as "The Wigwam" had a museum-meeting room for conclaves. The church's annual conventions were held at El Reno for many years, with English as the lingua franca.[35]

James Mooney's role in the formation of the Native American Church did not go unnoticed by the Indian Bureau. In October, 1918, shortly after the NAC had incorporated, the Bureau expelled Mooney from the Kiowa Reservation, and his study was halted as a result. "In 1919, and again in 1920, the Smithsonian Institution asked that he be permitted to return to the reservation, submitting a physician's report that he had a bad heart and could not live much longer. The Bureau of Indian Affairs refused the request, and Mooney died [in 1921] without having completed a study which probably would have been on a par with his classic monograph on the Ghost Dance." [36]

Meanwhile the campaign against peyote continued. In 1919 the Indian Rights Association again called for legislation prohibiting the use and sale of peyote. "Now that national prohibition of the liquor traffic is an assured fact, it is not surprising that persons who have been addicted to the use of intoxicants are found to be indulging in the use of stimulating drugs to a much greater degree than formerly," the IRA warned.[37] Congressman Gandy's bill introduced in 1919, however, failed of enactment, as did subsequent bills introduced in the 67th, 68th, and 69th Congresses between 1921 and 1926.

Prohibition of peyote at the state level was more successful. In 1920, Kansas outlawed peyote, followed in 1923 by Montana, North Dakota, South Dakota, and Arizona. Peyote was prohibited in Iowa in 1924. The strong peyote prohibitionist trend in the states subsided after 1924, to be renewed in the late twenties, with Wyoming and New Mexico passing similar laws in 1929.[38]

The Indian Rights Association's campaign against peyote continued to be linked with liquor. "Evidence shows that while Indians are the class most addicted to its use, other races are becoming its slaves," the IRA reported. "This condition no doubt is accelerated by the prohibition of intoxicating liquor, the habitués resorting to substitutes by which to becloud the senses and secure temporary exhilaration." [39]

The most nearly successful congressional effort to outlaw peyote occurred in 1924 in the form of a rider to the Indian Appropriation Bill which for the first time metioned peyote specifically under the standard item for the suppression of the liquor traffic among Indians. But the rider was virtually unenforceable. As E. B. Merritt of the Indian Bureau testified several years later, "The language of this appropriation was changed a few years ago to include the suppressing of the traffic in peyote, but practically nothing can be done to suppress that evil because there is no substantive law specifically prohibiting traffic in peyote and providing a penalty for violations of the law. Bills have been submitted for that purpose, but none of them has become law." [40]

Thus the high point of the anti-peyote attack was reached in 1923–24, after which the agitation began to die down. The compromise resolution of the Committee of 100 at the end of 1923, urging a thorough National Research Council investigation of peyote and the enactment of anti-peyote legislation only if peyote had thereby been found "fundamentally detrimental to the health and morals of its users," was a severe blow to the opponents of peyote. Hitherto they had maintained that the adverse effect of peyote on the health and morals of its users was beyond dispute. The fact that the anti-peyotists were willing even to consider such a compromise showed that their ardor was cooling. After 1923, the subject of peyote disappeared from the IRA *Annual Reports*.

Behind all this was the fact that new forces had entered the Indian field, and a basic policy shift was under way. The campaign against peyote had not assumed major proportions until it was able to enlist the support of the Indian Rights Association and other national white reform and religious groups. The supremacy of these older groups was now challenged. The new forces of reform—especially the American Indian Defense Association led by John Collier—were committed to the protection of all Indian religions, including the peyote religion. With interest in the suppression of peyote waning among the older meliorists, and the strength of the new reformers waxing, the anti-peyote campaign largely subsided, though the Indian Bureau continued to harass peyotists, and many Christian groups maintained their opposition to the religion. The postwar reaction was abating in the country, and there was less national interest in restrictive legislation than had existed in the years immediately following World War I. Prohibitionist fervor, which had helped to sustain the anti-peyote campaign, was melting away. Groups specifically concerned with Indian affairs turned their energies increasingly to formulating a new Indian policy.

By 1928, when the Meriam Report was published, the opposition to peyote was largely quiescent. This voluminous study mentioned the peyote religion only briefly, stating that "in some parts of the south and east of the Indian country the Peyote Church flourishes. The Indians assemble for meetings in churches, so-called, where they fall into trance-like stupor from the use of peyote. The organization is of no practical value to the community, and peyote addiction is probably harmful physically as well as socially." It added that the peyote church "is reported to be growing." [41] In spite of the reference to "addiction," the report elsewhere declared that "the habit forming character of this drug [peyote] has not been definitely determined, although many Indians were reported to use it constantly." [42] Although those references were hardly friendly, they revealed a considerable retreat from the extremes of earlier charges. The Meriam Report made many recommendations for changes in Indian policy, but the prohibition of peyote was not one of them. The peyote religion was by this time considered a nuisance rather than a menace.

From the peyotists themselves the vigorous attacks which continued until the mid-twenties evoked a strong response. During this period peyote churches continued to be incorporated in a number of states. As had been the case in Oklahoma, the peyote religion was thus strengthened rather than weakened by opposition. Both in name and in purpose the incorporated churches followed the general pattern of the Native American Church of Oklahoma (1918), but with some significant variations.

The first group to incorporate outside Oklahoma was, appropriately enough, the Winnebago peyotists of Nebraska, who received their charter on June 29, 1921. Initially they used the name "The Peyote Church of Christ" and set forth the following statement of goals:

"That the purpose for which this corporation is formed is to worship the one true and living God and to devote and consecrate our lives and works to his service.

We recognize all people who worship God and follow Christ as members of the one true church.

We believe that all earthly sects are all human organizations.

We abominate creeds as relics of the 'DARK AGES' in dividing the followers of a Risen Savior into contending factions and wee [sic] seek for union in worship and in spirit.

We do not condemn the practices of any but in so far as the same tend to spirituality believe in the same.

We believe in the sacrament and the sacramental bread and wine, but in so much as the use of the same is forbidden to Indians, we of the people who cannot obtain or use the same have adopted the use of bread as Peyote and water as wine.

We find consolation and encouragement in Romans the fourteenth chapter and second verse and the rest of the said chapter as to this practice.

THE FOLLOWING ARE TENETS OF OUR RELIGION

ONE LORD, ONE FAITH, ONE BAPTISM, ONE GOD, THE FATHER: TO THOSE WHO ARE FAITHFUL IN BOTH KING-DOM OF NATURE—HEAVEN AND EARTH. OUR HOPE IS GLORY, HONOR AND IMMORTALITY. Ephesians fourth chapter, fifth and sixth verses.

To consumate [sic] and effect those objects this church is being in-corporated." [43]

The 1921 Winnebago Articles of Incorporation showed little influence of the Native American Church of Oklahoma. However, this situation changed dramatically in 1922, when the Nebraska group altered its name to "Native American Church" and adopted the purposes of the Oklahoma NAC almost verbatim, with the specific addition of "teaching the scriptures." The purview of the group was broadened to include "the Winnebago Indians of Nebraska and Wisconsin, and all Indians within the United States." Provision was made for keeping records of births, marriages, deaths, and separations and for a burial ground.[44]

The neighboring Omaha peyotists duly incorporated under the name "The Peyote Historical Society Church," probably around this period. Both the Winnebago and Omaha groups had considerable goodwill in Nebraska from politicians, the Nebraska Historical Society, and other citizens. A number of the Bureau agents in charge of the two tribes looked either with favor or at least neutrality on the peyote practitioners.[45]

In South Dakota the Native American Church was first organized on a local basis in Allen in 1922, and in St. Charles and Rosebud in 1924.[46] In the late fall of 1924 a statewide Native American Church of South Dakota was formed with a central council and local churches and councils "to be organized in each Indian reservation in the State of

South Dakota." Its statement of purposes was almost exactly that of the amended Nebraska NAC articles of 1922 except that the phrase "among the Sioux Indians of the State of South Dakota" was substituted for the Winnebago reference. However, specific mention of peyote was omitted, probably because its use was illegal in the state.[47]

In North Dakota a group of Sioux peyotists incorporated as the Native American Church in 1923. The Articles of Incorporation referred to their previous association as the "Peyote Church of Christ." The statement of the purposes of the church was substantially that of the Nebraska (1922) NAC except that "the wine" was substituted for "peyote" for sacramental and religious use, no doubt because peyote had been outlawed in the state.[48]

While the North and South Dakota churches followed the Oklahoma pattern as modified by the Nebraska group, in Idaho the Native American Church which incorporated in 1925 went directly to the Oklahoma NAC for its statement of purpose and organization. Mention of Christianity was, however, omitted. Formed by Shoshones and Bannocks, the church was to encompass "the several tribes of Indians in the State of Idaho."[49] In 1925 the church was also incorporated in Kansas under the name "Native American Church of God," by Potawatomi peyotists who had originally gotten the religion from Oklahoma about 1910.[50] In the same year a Montana Native American Church was incorporated by Crow and Northern Cheyenne Indians. A statement of purposes generally similar to that of the Oklahoma and Nebraska churches was adopted. For "Christianity" was substituted "the worship of a heavenly father," and reference to peyote, illegal in the state, was omitted, as was any mention of Indians outside Montana.[51]

Thus by 1925 Native American Churches had been incorporated in at least seven states and possibly in a few others as well.[52] Their statements of purpose and organizational formats were broadly similar, the major differences being their varying emphases on Christianity. The period between 1918 and 1925 when the anti-peyote campaign was most vigorous marked the height of incorporation efforts.

The legal protection which the peyotists thus acquired proved reasonably effective. There can be little question that the NAC charters discouraged action against the peyote religion by placing it more firmly under the constitutional guarantee of religious freedom which had always been the shield of religious Pan-Indianism.

Other important consequences flowed from the incorporation of the Native American Churches. A sense of common crisis and the consultation involved in writing and obtaining charters further strengthened bonds among the peyotists. The adoption of Native American Church as a name in a number of states gave a more organized cast to the religion. The organizational machinery provided in the charters was used, and election of state officers and councils, annual conventions, dues payments, and other such formal arrangements became part of the accepted operating procedures of the churches. In Oklahoma, and probably in other places as well, the state organization engaged in mobilizing political power and organizing pressure to prevent encroachments on the peyotists' religious liberties.[53] Within this formal machinery, there continued to be considerable flexibility and decentralization and a wide variety of local patterns.

Both the incorporated Native American Churches and the unincorporated peyote groups continued to flourish in the period between the First World War and the New Deal. Whether incorporated or unincorporated, the similarities in ritual and doctrine continued to be sufficiently close so that a member of one could feel at home in the other's. The visitation among churches which had always characterized the religion continued, made easier by improved transportation. Differences among groups usually involved the degree and nature of Christian influences, the particular rite used, adaptation to local tribal customs and ideas, and the kinds of auxiliary activities engaged in, such as men's and women's clubs. They were not unlike the local and denominational differences to be found among Christian churches.

In a number of instances, peyotists also belonged to Christian churches. "Among peyote leaders may be found devout Catholics, Mormons, Mennonites, Baptists, and Methodists. In fact among its members are representatives of every Christian denomination within the tribe in which the cult is practiced; indeed the majority of its members are adherents also of some Christian Church," it was reported in 1930.[54] This is probably an overstatement, but the evidence strongly indicates that many Indians did not regard membership in the peyote religion and in a more orthodox Christianity as mutually exclusive.

An interesting example of this fact was a Pan-Indian wedding in Oklahoma in which Frank Cayou, an Oklahoma peyote leader, officiated, together with the Reverend Moty Tiger (Creek) at a marriage ceremony held in the First Christian Church of Sapulpa, Oklahoma, in November, 1930.

The bride was a Creek whose religious views were presumably represented by the Creek Christian minister; the groom was a Potawatomi-Sac-Fox. The inclusion in the ceremony of Cayou, who was an Omaha, with an assist from Mrs. Cayou, an Osage, no doubt meant that the ceremony was in part peyotist, representing the groom's beliefs. No mention of peyote appears in the news story reporting the happy event, but Cayou is described as "using the ancient rite." A photograph shows a tepee erected on the altar for the occasion, flanked with an American flag, the bride and groom in Indian costume, Cayou in Indian dress, and the Reverend Tiger in a clerical suit.

In this wedding, secular and religious Pan-Indianism were joined. The bride's father, Joseph Bruner, was a prominent Creek active in the reformist Society of Oklahoma Indians, while the editor of Oklahoma's Pan-Indian paper, *The American Indian,* was a member of the wedding party. To cap if off, the "Indian Love Song" was played on the organ and sung by "Princess Pakanti" while the bride and groom marched down the aisle. Both Indians and whites attended. It would be hard to imagine a more Pan-Indian occasion.[55]

The growth of the peyote religion cannot be accounted for by any single factor, but was due rather to a combination of factors. Among these, the following twelve seem most important:

First, the weakening of the old tribal religions and the influence of Christianity were major reasons for the rise of the cult. For many Indians the old tribal religion no longer seemed relevant, or was too difficult to carry on. For many, also, Christianity seemed remote and difficult to understand. A religion which combined Indian and Christian elements offered a viable compromise between the old ways and the new.

Second, the peyote cult's identity as a Pan-Indian rather than a tribal or a white man's religion enabled its adherents to express through their religious life the idea of Indian brotherhood. This process was strengthened and undergirded by extensive intermarriage among the tribes.

Third, the influence of Carlisle students was crucial in the peyote religion, as it was in other types of Pan-Indianism. Many of the leaders were from Carlisle, visited each other frequently, and retained great loyalty to their alma mater. For instance, despite General Pratt's heated opposition to the peyote cult, a number of leading peyotists—including Ned Brace, Tennyson Berry, Herman McCarthy, Frank Cayou, Albert Hensley, Amos Mitchell, and John Abbott—contributed to the "Pratt Memorial Fund." [56] Gradually, Haskell Institute in Kansas took Carlisle's place as a producer of Pan-Indian leaders, among them the Arapaho peyotist Jack Bull Bear and the Omaha Allen P. Dale.

Fourth, through the peyote religion many Indians cured themselves of alcoholism. This was one of the most potent appeals of the cult, for it deeply affected not only the lives of individuals but the social health of their local communities.

Fifth, many Indians regarded peyote as a panacea, believing that it cured such prevalent and dreaded afflictions as tuberculosis. Curing was one of the most frequent reasons for holding a peyote meeting. For people who traditionally suffered great anxiety over their health, as was especially true in the Plains, peyote as a medicine had great appeal.

Sixth, the peyote religion was a social as well as a religious force, offering its participants a chance to get together, often in situations where the opportunity for socializing was limited. This was especially apparent on the Sunday after the all-night rites, when people gathered for pleasant conversation and dinner. In this respect the peyote religion was much like religions among other rural Americans.

Seventh, Indians have an ancient tradition of travel and intertribal visitation. With the development of modern transportation facilities, they could make longer journeys in much shorter time. It was through such journeys, with the personal contacts they involved, that the peyote religion spread. Improved communication also made it possible to obtain peyote buttons quickly. Almost all of the peyote groups were located outside the areas where the plant grew, and the peyote buttons were obtained either through a journey or through the mail.

Eighth, another probable reason for the spread of the peyote religion was its transmutation of the vision quest of the Plains—a hallucinatory experience in which a spirit helper was sought—into the visions induced by the eating of the peyote. This factor helps to account for its popularity among the Plains tribes, who constituted many of its adherents.

Ninth, the role of Oklahoma in the cult's growth and dissemination was crucial. Here many Indians from many tribes lived near each other; intertribal contacts were extensive; and Indians participated in many common activities, such as county fairs and powwows. For Indians outside Oklahoma, also, the state had a special magnetism. Indians from other sections of the country often visited there, returning home bearing word of the new religion and peyote buttons as well.

Tenth, the loose organizational structure which characterized the religion was in harmony with Indian attitudes towards religious and other organizations. This flexibility also meant that the religion could be adjusted to suit local conditions.

Eleventh, the leading role of men in the peyote religion also helps to account for its strength. The impact of white civilization required more adjustment for Indian men than it did for Indian women, who were able to retain much more continuity in their roles in the household than were the men in their occupations. In the peyote rituals, the men were able to regain important and recognized social functions.

Twelfth, probably most basic of all was the fact that the peyote religion was an Indian religion—something Indians had created for themselves, something in which they could take pride, something which linked them with the Indian past but could function in the new and changed Indian present.

Due to all these factors, the peyote cult would no doubt have grown in any case. But, as we have seen, the anti-peyote campaign provided a common crisis experience which resulted in more stable organizational forms, a strengthened religion, and the wide use of a common name— the Native American Church. Eventually also, the attack on the religion brought to its defense national support from the newer reformers who wielded far more influence than had the handful of anthropologists who were its long-time friends.

It is easier to explain the spread of the peyote cult than the limitations on its acceptance. Even in Oklahoma, the Five Civilized Tribes were little affected by the peyote religion. Many had been Christianized for generations and felt no need for the type of Indian religious identity which the peyotists offered. The Rocky Mountains probably formed a barrier in the West, while in the Pacific Northwest the Indian Shakers, a Pan-Indian cult with many resemblances to the peyote religion, became established in the late nineteenth century. Among the Pueblos, with their tight religious organization, Taos alone—the only Pueblo with strong Plains influence—was affected by the religion. In the East the most important Indian group, the tribes of the Iroquois Confederacy, had already an accommodative religion in the Longhouse religion of Handsome

Lake, while many Iroquois were Christians. Most of the other tribes in the East existed only in isolated remnants. Distance from the Oklahoma heartland was no doubt a factor in most of these cases, and the anti-peyote campaign in a few or none.

The coming of the New Deal brought far-reaching changes in Indian policy, based on a consensus of most of the groups concerned with Indian affairs, but led by the newer reformers, whose most eminent spokesman, John Collier, became Indian Commissioner. Under the Collier administration, the earlier Indian Bureau opposition to peyote changed to tolerance, in line with the general policy of guarding Indian religious freedom. And as opposition had encouraged the growth of the religion, so also did the policy of toleration.

In 1934, the Native American Church of Oklahoma made a significant move toward national federation of the peyote churches by obtaining an amended charter enabling churches outside the state to affiliate with it in a Central Council of the Native American Church. At this time both the president, Ned Brace, and the vice-president, Frank Cayou, were former Carlisle students, thus exemplifying the continued role of Carlisle in Pan-Indian affairs. The statement of purposes in the amended charter was as follows:

"This corporation is formed for the purpose of jointly combining, be-cause of our relationship to our forefathers, to push forward our religious worship. Founded upon the four great Primal Laws of God— Love, Faith, Hope and Charity.

The American Indian recognizing the sacramental use of the Earthly plant known as Peyote; with its teachings of love of God and right-living, which embodies morality, sobriety, kindness and brotherly love for all mankind. Including therein the various members of the Faith in the State of Oklahoma, with the right to own and hold property for the purposes herein stated that he may conduct its business or hold services according to the rituals of the Unwritten Code, as given to him by his Maker, the creator of the Universe, God Almighty." [57]

Both the 1918 and the 1934 charters had the same incorporators, re-vealing a strong—almost incredible—continuity in leadership. But the new statement of purposes differed in several significant ways from the earlier one. First, promotion of belief in the Christian religion was omitted, probably due in part to a desire to include in the expanded church peyote groups which did not consider themselves Christian. At the same time, "God Almighty" was invoked. He had not been mentioned in the earlier document. The shift of emphasis from Christ to God probably reflected a similar shift in the theology of the group. Secondly, the statement included the conception of the sacred peyote plant as teacher—a very old conception in the cult with clear links to the aboriginal past, but one which orthodox Christians had frequently derided. The fact that the incorporators were not afraid to include it reflected the increased atmosphere of toleration for the religion, especially on the part of the Indian Bureau. Third, "the Native Race of America" was transmuted into "the American Indian," spoken of in the singular, mirroring the decline of "race" as a unifying factor among Indians and the rise of a more culturally oriented conception of the Indian. Lastly, the statement appealed to "our relationship to our forefathers," thus defining peyotism as a traditional Indian religion.

By 1934 the peyote religion had indeed become the traditional religious faith of many Indians. As the most important Pan-Indian religious movement in the United States, it continued to gain new adherents. It had taken the first crucial step towards its future existence as a Native American Church organized formally on a national basis.

Of all the varieties of Pan-Indianism, it was religious Pan-Indianism which reached the largest number of Indians and from them received the most enduring loyalty.

IV
SURVEY AND
RETROSPECT

———————— ✳ ————————

12

SINCE 1934

The Indian New Deal opened a new era in Indian affairs. Its keystone was the Indian Reorganization Act of 1934, which represented as fundamental a change in Indian policy as the General Allotment or Dawes Act of 1887. Each of these basic pieces of legislation set governmental Indian policy on the course it would follow in subsequent decades, though both were modified in practice. As modern Pan-Indian movements arose in the general context of the Dawes Act policy, so they continued to develop in the general context of New Deal policies in Indian affairs.

The chief figure in the formulation of the philosophy and program of the Indian New Deal was President Franklin D. Roosevelt's Indian Commissioner, John Collier. He was the leader of the new reformers of the twenties, a major critic of the Dawes Act, and the most important exponent of a policy which would respect and encourage Indian tribal life. Collier summarized the purpose of the Indian Reorganization Act and of the other legislation and policies which complemented it in characteristic fashion:

"[The] intention was that the grouphood of Indians, twenty thousand years old in our Hemisphere, should be acknowledged as being the human and socially dynamic essential, now and in the future as of old. It should be grouphood culturally, as rooted in the past as the group at issue—each group among the hundreds—might desire, and as modern, American-oriented and implemented as the group at issue might desire. Definitely, finally, cultural determination for Indians was not to be a function of governmental authority from this point forth. Cultural determination, by American public philosophy, has been and is the function of all our many thousand of human groups; the IRA only restored this fundamental of mental and moral health to the only group which officially or governmentally had been denied it, the Indians." [1]

The Indian Reorganization Act was the programmatic expression of this philosophy. The act reversed the process of liquidation of Indian lands. Allotment was prohibited. The new legislation authorized the voluntary consolidation of "fractionated lands," purchase of further lands by the tribes, and the institution of conservation practices.

The Indian Reorganization Act stressed tribal self-help and self-government. Tribal home-rule constitutions and charters for economic enterprise were provided for on a voluntary basis. Tribes were permitted to contract for services with state and local agencies and with unofficial groups. A revolving credit fund was set up. The act directed that yearly appropriations be submitted to organized tribes for criticisms and suggestions.

The Indian Reorganization Act also set in motion steps for greatly expanded Indian participation in the operation of the Bureau. Preference in the Service was given to Indians. Funds for advanced educational and professional training for Indians were authorized.

Other reform measures, accomplished both by legislation and by administrative order, included stronger support for public or federal Indian day schools with decreased emphasis on the boarding schools, encouragement of Indian arts and crafts through the Indian Arts and Crafts Board, freedom for Indian religious observances, federal-state cooperation in Indian affairs, and the codification of Indian law.

One of the most important aspects of the Indian New Deal was its close identification with social science and social scientists, who participated extensively in both the formulation and implementation of Indian New Deal measures. The Indian Reorganization Act, social scientists asserted, was "a landmark not only for the American Indian but for social scientists in the United States because it brought to Indian affairs and to the United States government, for the first time, an explicit use of social science principles." These included "two axioms of human behavior":

"First, the recognition of the importance of Indian group life and of the necessity to preserve and encourage native social controls and Indian values as the foundation upon which such changes and innovations as various Indian groups themselves decided were worthwhile should be made.

Second, a recognition that constructive change must not destroy psychological security and must preserve continuity in the lives of both the group and the individual so that personality integration and stability may be maintained. This is contrary to the popular American assumption that change in itself is a good thing, which stems from the confusion of 'change' with 'progress.' . . . In the IRA [Indian Reorganization Act] the objective of leading the Indians into fuller participation in American society is assumed, but at their own speed and in their own way." [2]

The Indian New Dealers were not unsympathetic to those who wished to leave the tribe or to develop an Indian identity not primarily tribal. But such persons were peripheral to their major concerns. Both Indian and white reformers poured their energies into the preservation and encouragement of Indian tribal life. Even Arthur C. Parker headed a government-sponsored Iroquois arts and crafts project based in the Rochester Museum of which he was director.

During the thirties reform Pan-Indianism was quiescent; the reformers were busy implementing the New Deal. But the Collier policies were not universally popular with the Indians. Some of this discontent crystallized around the American Indian Federation, a nonpartisan, nonsectarian Pan-Indian organization which bitterly attacked the Collier administration and all it works as "red," an un-American attempt to force Indians back to the blanket. Several of its leaders were men who had gotten their organizational training in earlier movements. They included President Joseph Bruner, long active in the Society of Oklahoma Indians; Thomas L. Sloan, former president of the Society of American Indians; and the peyote leader Delos K. Lone Wolf. In ideology and activities the Federation resembled white extremist right-wing groups, with which it developed close ties. Cordial Federation relations with the German-American Bund were thought to be legitimized through the German government's bizarre declaration that the Sioux, and presumably by extension all Indians, were in fact Aryans. [3]

Not until 1944 did there arise a national reform Pan-Indian organization sympathetic to the Indian New Deal. By this time Dr. Win-the-War had replaced Dr. New Deal, and as a result many domestic reforms, including Indian reforms, languished. The National Congress of American Indians (NCAI), like the Society of American Indians, emerged when basic Indian policy was in trouble.

There seems to have been no direct connection between the first major Pan-Indian reform organization and the second. The National Congress of American Indians differed radically from the Society of American Indians in its strong tribal emphasis. Its founders included important tribal officials. In its tribal orientation it showed clearly the impact of the Indian New Deal. Yet, striking similarities are also quite apparent.

First, the men who founded the NCAI resembled in many ways the founders of the SAI. They were Indians prominent in the professions and business, Indian anthropologists, and Indian Bureau employees. Many had attended Carlisle or Haskell, and a number were college graduates. The first president of the NCAI, Judge Napoleon B. Johnson of Oklahoma, was a college graduate and a Mason. Its first secretary, Dan M. Madrano, was educated at Carlisle as well as at the Wharton School of Commerce and the National School of Law; he too was a Mason. The NCAI's national council included the anthropologist D'Arcy McNickle, a field representative of the Indian Office; Archie Phinney, Superintendent of the Northern Idaho, an anthropologist who had attended Haskell; and none other than Arthur C. Parker himself, making a brief return appearance as an Indian elder statesman.[4]

There were other similarities. In familiar fashion, the NCAI founding conference, held in Denver in 1944, debated the question of whether Indian Bureau employees could hold elective or appointive office in the organization and decided that they could. The program adopted at the conference dealt with long-familiar subjects: legal aid, legislative action, education, special training for Indians in the Bureau, and establishing a publication. The NCAI "would confine itself to the broad problems confronting the total Indian poulation or large segments of it." Like the SAI, the new organization hoped in this way to avoid involvement in partisan or local squabbles and the consequent dilution of its broad representative character. Because Indian groups were so varied, *"great elasticity should be allowed in organization and local activities."* The organization had *"no axes to grind,* supports no political party and is for any and all individuals, groups, and organizations of good repute regardless of race, color, and creed, who are conscientiously working for, and with the American Indians for their welfare."[5]

Initially, membership in the NCAI was restricted to persons "of Indian ancestry" and was both individual and group, with appropriate safeguards reminiscent of the SAI's. Any "Indian tribe, band, community" could join. Thus the NCAI was set up as both a federated body and an individual membership organization in terms somewhat like the very early but abortive SAI conception of itself.[6] Later, the familiar pattern of nonvoting non-Indian associates emerged, with provision for both individual and organizational associate affiliation.

Today the National Congress of American Indians continues to be the most important Pan-Indian reform group. Its tribal emphasis has grown stronger. The tribes themselves have produced leaders knowledgeable in the ways of the wider society, many of whom have played a leading role in NCAI affairs. The main strength of the organization lies in the Great Plains, though it has both tribal and individual members outside that area. Indians in the East have played only a negligible role. In format and activities it resembles other reform organizations. It holds annual conventions, issues the *NCAI Sentinel* and many special publications, and lobbies on Capitol Hill. It has fought hard and on the whole successfully against the "termination policy" of the late forties and fifties, which threatened to end federal supervision of the tribes. It became deeply involved in the anti-poverty programs of the sixties. Its major problems have been factionalism, insufficient funds, and a tendency of the tribes to give only lukewarm support when not faced with a crisis situation. Such problems are not unlike those of other reform movements.

The Indian common ground of the NCAI is only occasionally described as "race." Its spokesmen are more apt to refer to "the Indian people" or "Indian people," "the American Indian," "Indian Americans" or just plain "Indian." "Indian culture" is also used. NCAI leaders tread a delicate line in proclaiming the common interests of Indians without giving offense to particular tribal sensitivities.

These terms are used by other Pan-Indians as well. The term "Pan-Indian," however, is seldom used by Pan-Indians, except by a few anthropologists and other intellectuals. It seems first to have been used in 1950 by Charles S. Brant in a study of the Native American Church.[7] The term was quickly adopted by other anthropologists and applied to secular as well as religious Pan-Indian manifestations and to early as well as contemporary movements. It provided a convenient label for a phenomenon which had been frequently described but for which there was no specific name. The term was picked up by a few historians and other students of Indian affairs, but its widespread use is still confined to anthropologists.

A new wing of reform Pan-Indianism developed in the early sixties following the American Indian Charter Convention (AICC) held in Chicago, June 13–20, 1961. The AICC was a joint effort of the National Congress of American Indians and the University of Chicago, with the white anthropologist Sol Tax as coordinator. Its purpose was to bring together a representative group of American Indians to review past policies and formulate new ones.

A number of Indian college students and recent graduates attended the meeting and in August, 1961, set up the National Indian Youth Council, an Indian version of the youth movements of the sixties. The NIYC is more militant than the NCAI, as one might expect of a youth organization, and shows more clearly the influence of the civil rights movement. It has staged several "fish-ins" in an attempt to secure Indian fishing rights. Its leaders occasionally talk of "red power" and "Uncle Tomahawks" and sometimes attack the "middle-class Indian" and "Indian Bureau Indians." Many of its members are students of the social sciences, especially anthropology and sociology. Most live off the reservation, and frequently their connection with tribal life is fairly remote. Many of these Indian young people are quite as sophisticated as their white counterparts, and also as angry and alienated. They are familiar with "the identity crisis," "alienation," and "the marginal man," terms which they apply freely to their own situation. They are deeply respectful of what they believe to be the values of Indian life, as well as of tribal institutions and tribal elders, an attitude that they do not always apply to their elders in the NCAI. They are passionate "Indian nationalists," determined to assert an Indian as well as a tribal identity.[8] Their slogan is "For a Greater Indian America."

The NIYC devotes a major part of its efforts to education, and its program in this regard is very much in line with current educational trends. A recently completed NIYC report on Indian education, conducted under a Carnegie Corporation grant, sharply differentiates Indian "material poverty" from "cultural deprivation," stating firmly that "Indian children do not suffer the deep psychological deprivations associated with the broken families of the urban poor." Terming "education for Indians to be largely a failure," the report proposes the establishment of a new but temporary federal commission to assume control of Indian education for a five-year period, during which time control would be transferred to Indian communities, Indian staff would be trained, funds for the revision of "curricula to reflect the history, culture, and values of the Indian people" would be provided, and consultant assistance given to Indian school boards.[9]

In 1964 the NIYC became a sponsor of the United Scholarship Service (USS), founded in 1960 to give guidance, counsel, and scholarship aid to Indian and Spanish (Mexican) American youth in independent schools, colleges, and universities. The original sponsors were the Board for Homeland Missions of the United Church of Christ, the Executive Council of the Episcopal Church, and the Association on American Indian Affairs. When the latter organization withdrew, the NIYC took its place. A further change in the structure and viewpoint of the USS occurred in 1969 when the service became an independent agency, shedding all its sponsors, evidently in a move to assert control by Indians and Spanish Americans.[10] Since the change, the USS has shown considerable interest in student power movements.[11] Some of the NIYC leaders were beneficiaries of USS scholarships and some are currently on the staff.

The National Indian Youth Council is a true reflection of its times. In its base in the college-educated young, its high but sometimes cloudy idealism, its search for "identity," its militancy, its ambivalence toward its elders, its distrust of the values and bona fides of American society, and its rather casual organization, it displays many of the characteristics of contemporary non-Indian youth movements.[12] In addition to the NIYC, there are numerous Indian student clubs and councils in colleges and universities having a significant number of Indians. These organizations exhibit a wide variety of viewpoints. At San Francisco State College a Department of Native American Studies in the School of Ethnic Studies is at this writing in the process of organization.[13]

While reform Pan-Indianism has produced national organizations since the New Deal, fraternal Pan-Indianism only occasionally coalesces in a national effort, as in the annual "Miss Indian America" contest, started in the fifties. It continues to flourish on a local basis in numerous Pan-Indian clubs. During the last twenty years many people have moved from the reservation to urban areas as a result both of World War II and of the Federal Relocation Program which encourages Indian migration to the city. In some cities, such as Chicago, Oakland, and Seattle, Indian centers function somewhat on the settlement house pattern, providing a place where people of many tribes gather. The patterns of Indian identification arising from Indian urbanization are exceedingly complex.

For men and women fresh from the reservation, urban life is often even more bewildering than it is for other rural in-migrants. They search for other Indians wiser in urban ways who will help them adjust to the city and with whom they can find a satisfying social life in the midst of urban impersonality. Many people in this situation embrace Pan-Indian, tribal, and American identities at the same time.[14]

Of all the basic types of Pan-Indian organization, religious Pan-Indianism has shown the most stability and continuity, as might be expected of a religious movement. In 1945, at just about the same time that the NCAI was formed, the Native American Church in Oklahoma was incorporated as "The Native American Church of the United States." Perhaps the times were particularly conducive to Pan-Indian organization. Ten years later it widened its purview to become "The Native American Church of North America." [15] By that date there were peyote congregations in Arizona, California, Colorado, Idaho, Iowa, Kansas, Minnesota, Montana, Nebraska, Nevada, New Mexico, North and South Dakota, Oklahoma, Utah, Texas, Wisconsin, and Wyoming.[16] Thus while the religion had spread beyond the Great Plains, it remained essentially a Plains movement covering an area very much like that of the National Congress of American Indians.

The Native American Church continues as a reservation-based, rural church, a loose federation of local, denominational, and state affiliates encompassing many but not all peyote groups. It holds annual national conferences as well as state meetings. It engages in many of the activities characteristic of other rural churches. In addition, it has been energetic in securing state charters for its affiliates and in fighting various anti-peyotist efforts.

Major peyotist difficulties are no longer with the Bureau of Indian Affairs or the missionaries and refomers. The Indian New Deal policy of toleration for the peyote religion has held firm with only minor infringements. Protestants have, with a few exceptions, followed a hands-off policy although the cult has met stronger opposition from Catholics.[17] Its chief opponents are in the states.

The Native American Church, with white support, has been fairly successful in overcoming such attacks. In 1964 the Supreme Court of California overthrew the conviction of three NAC members on a charge of violating the state narcotics law. The court held that under the constitutional guarantees of religious freedom, the peyotists had the right to use the plant in religious ceremonies. In another recent development, Navaho peyotists, after a bitter fight, won the right to practice their religion on the Navaho reservation, which had hitherto been forbidden by the Navaho Tribal Council. Religious freedom thus continues to be the shield of religious Pan-Indianism.

National anti-peyote campaigns in the past have seriously threatened the peyotists only when they rode on another important force, such as the prohibition movement, and when they became a major focus of groups directly influential in Indian affairs. It is possible that the current national concern with drugs might provide such a force, but it is exceedingly difficult to envisage which influential national groups in the Indian field would sustain an attack on the peyote religion.

The Native American Chuch has also suffered from factionalism both local and national. There have been indications that some of the younger, more highly acculturated people have turned to more orthodox forms of Christianity.[18] Nevertheless, it remains the most influential, most important, and largest Indian religious body, directly involving more Indians than any other Pan-Indian group.

Pan-Indian activities and organizations on a local and regional basis are much more widespread and varied today than was the case in the formative period. Powwows, intertribal federations, and groups devoted to Indian history or art, as well as the fraternal Pan-Indian groups mentioned above, flourish. News of their activities is carried in various Pan-Indian publications. One of the most influential has been the monthly *Indian Voices,* edited by the Cherokee anthropologist Robert K. Thomas and published at the University of Chicago.

The white friends of the Indian are still drawn from much the same groups as in the formative period of Pan-Indianism: churchmen, reformers, romantics, and anthropologists. The two most influential and stable organizations in the friends-of-the-Indian tradition date from the pre-New Deal period: the older Indian Rights Association and the Association on American Indian Affairs. The latter organization, while formed in the thirties, grew out of John Collier's American Indian Defense Association of the twenties. The most marked change since 1934 in white support for Pan-Indian causes lies in the greatly increased interest and activity of white anthropologists, who have befriended all the varieties of Pan-Indianism. The white anthropologist J. Sydney Slotkin, whose book *The Peyote Religion* was written essentially as a manual for the Native American Church, was actually an official of the church and edited its *Quarterly Bulletin*. Professor Sol Tax of the University of Chicago and many of his students have concerned themselves with Pan-Indian affairs. A number of universities, particularly in the Midwest and Southwest, have taken a serious interest in Pan-Indianism. The union between academia and Pan-Indianism has developed in a manner far different from that envisioned by Arthur C. Parker, and with consequences more far-reaching than he imagined.

Indians also are on the periphery of the concerns of a few other groups. They have received some attention from the hippies and from the "underground press," mostly of a highly romantic variety, in a contemporary version of the noble savage theme. Indians are attractive as an example of the small, non-urbanized, oppressed, and exotic peoples so currently appealing to those in retreat from a mass industrialized society. Some efforts, largely unsuccessful, have been made to participate in the ceremonies of the Native American Church. As in the past, non-Indians thus use Indians as symbols for their own dreams and discontents.

On a different level, Indians are regularly listed with those minorities whom American society has neglected—usually at the end of the list. The problem of Indian education, especially the question of Indian community control and the type of education appropriate for Indian students, has received a certain amount of attention. This type of interest seems clearly an outgrowth of the civil rights movement and in some cases probably represents a deflection from it, a search for a new minority to befriend. Whatever the reasons, the rather vague current interest has not yet been translated into an informed public opinion or into support for concrete programs of action on a broad basis.

Despite the continuing Pan-Indian tradition and the efforts of friends of the Indian, the Indian remains a shadowy and peripheral figure to most Americans. Most history books pay scant attention to the American Indian except for some references to Indian wars or removals of an earlier period. "The frontier" is still commonly thought of as the thin edge of white settlement bordering the trackless wilderness rather than the dividing line between different regions of human occupation involving differing uses and conceptions of the land and man's relationship to it. Even comprehensive monographs covering the history of a national administration rarely analyze its Indian programs: in the twentieth century the Indian policy of the New Deal is usually the only one mentioned. So far as Pan-Indianism is concerned, historians have ignored it, with only one or two exceptions. There are a number of reasons for this, including the political focus of most American historians, the fact that they rarely employ a cross-cultural perspective, and the nature of the sources they are accustomed to using, which tend to be written records, documents, and manuscript materials. Such Pan-Indian records exist, but they are not highly visible. The fact that Indians themselves have not produced historians is probably an important factor also: after all, much Negro history has been written by Negroes and much immigrant history by immigrants and their sons and grandsons.

If general Indian history is little known to most Americans, including many American Indians, the history of Pan-Indianism is almost completely unknown even to contemporary Pan-Indians, despite the fact that modern Pan-Indianism has existed for two-thirds of a century. This is largely due to two factors: the paucity of written accounts and the discontinuity of many Pan-Indian organizations. As a result, both Pan-Indians and their white friends continually discover problems and advocate solutions which they believe to be new but which are in reality old and persistent.

The only type of Pan-Indianism about which there is an extensive written literature is the one which has also the strongest historical continuity as an organized movement: the peyote religion–Native American Church. That such a literature exists is probably due not so much to the continuity of the religion as to the fact that it early engaged the attention of anthropologists, beginning with James Mooney, resulting in a number of studies based on direct observation. As a religion of the reservation, the peyote cult was accessible for anthropological study. The major focus of the study of the peyote religion for some time was largely on individual tribes or tribal groupings with some attention to its diffusion. When the volume of such studies became sufficiently large and had been conducted over a sufficiently long period of time, it was possible to trace historical development. Nevertheless, the anthropological character of these studies means that the peyote religion has continued to be viewed largely—though not, of course, wholly—in relative isolation as an Indian phenomenon seen from within itself. Interpretations of the role of broad forces in American society in the development of the religion—

such as education, Christianity, communications, major ideas, and organizational forms—have been offered also. But except for the role of Christianity not a great deal of consideration has been given to these factors, which tend to lie outside the areas of traditional anthropological interest.

The peyotists seem to have a stronger sense of their own past than other Pan-Indians, perhaps more because of organizational continuities than the existence of a written literature. Other Pan-Indians have not been so fortunate. It is highly doubtful whether any contemporary reform Pan-Indians have even heard of the Society of American Indians or of Indian reformist efforts antedating the National Congress of American Indians. Among reform groups, who tend to be the most highly acculturated and who therefore like their non-Indian counterparts are oriented to the written word, the absence of historical accounts and interpretations has deprived them of an historical memory. The Indian New Deal, with its emphasis on a decisive break with governmental Indian policies of the past, probably helped to make the reform Pan-Indian past seem irrelevent and its memory quickly blurred and faded. The gap between the Indian reform movements of the Dawes and the Collier eras was thus psychologically and temporally sufficiently great to render the reform past invisible to Indians, while anthropologists and historians did not consider reform Pan-Indianism an important and legitimate area of study. This has been largely true also of fraternal Pan-Indianism.

Many anthropologists have noted the phenomenon of "ethnological feedback" in which Indians consult the work of anthropologists to find out about their own tribes, which information is then frequently incorporated into current tribal practices. The creation of a written history also seems to create an "historical feedback" through which people define the present in terms of a past usuable to them. Perhaps Pan-Indians need both anthropological and historical feedback to help them develop a sense of their own history, of its relationship to broader forces in society and of the ideas, the struggles, the joys and the grief of the men and women who created the movements in the past which the present inherits.

13

HISTORICAL PERSPECTIVE

The experience of rapidly accelerating change which we sometimes view as peculiar to our own times has in fact been characteristic of the American experience. In a single lifetime men transformed the cabin in the wilderness to the thriving commercial farm and the sleepy hamlet to the bustling city. People who in their childhood saw the Western frontier close in their old age saw a new frontier open on the moon. Since the founding of the Republic most Americans have had to make marked—often drastic—changes in their ways of thinking and doing. The relative exceptions were usually people who were isolated from the American mainstream.

One of the ways Americans dealt with change is through the creation of a wide variety of voluntary organizations—national, regional and local—serving a wide variety of purposes. These were generally accommodative in character, often attempting to retain or regain something considered valuable from the past while keeping in step with the present and hoping to ensure some desirable development in the future. During periods in which change is, and is perceived to be, unusually rapid, the tendency to organize new groups becomes particularly marked.

It was in such a time of accelerating change that modern Pan-Indian movements arose. During the first third of the twentieth century, changes in the country were rapid and profound, resulting in a proliferation of organizations on the time-honored American pattern. The extent and nature of these changes also affected the tribes, whose hopes of a Pan-Indian armed resistance or supernatural deliverance now lay in ruins. It was among Indians with considerable experience in the ways of the dominant society that the new movement emerged, accommodative in character and clearly evidencing, in the nature of its ideas and organizational forms, the degree to which its participants had become acculturated to the wider society. They too were in fact responding to change in a characteristic American fashion.

Since Pan-Indians had a special relationship both to tribal life and to the dominant culture, their reaction to change differed from that of other Indians. On one end of the Indian continuum was the vanishing Indian. Throughout American history many Indian blended into American society as individuals. They made their own adjustment to change in purely personal terms. This process continued in the early years of this century and is still going on. At the other end were Indians who remained primarily tribal, some steadfastly attempting to keep alive as much of the old life as they could, others adapting themselves in some degree to the surrounding culture and to the cultures of other tribes. A third group, which formed the basis of modern Pan-Indianism, had unusually extensive contacts both with white society and with a broad spectrum of tribes from widely separated geographical areas. Pan-Indians were typically of part-white or intertribal descent, often married whites or members of other tribes, spoke English at a time when relatively few Indians did so, had at least a few years of formal education, engaged in occupations typical of white society, and often belonged to Christian churches and other non-Indian organizations. In the period in which Pan-Indianism emerged, this group was more numerous and those who comprised it were in closer contact with each other than at any previous period. Their experience as participants in multiple cultures made them particularly aware of change, afforded them the ideas and skills to respond to it, and aroused in them the need to establish an Indian identity beyond the tribe and within the American social order. Pan-Indian movements offered to their adherents a socially recognized expression of their position in and between several worlds, a projection of their own situation, formalizing and legitimizing it. These movements were channels for outward mobility, and often for upward mobility as well. For Indians who did not participate actively in Pan-Indian organizations, Pan-Indianism served to define new dimensions of Indian life, to create other ways of being Indian.

The first two types of Pan-Indianism which developed on a national scale were the religious and the reform varieties, both of which felt most strongly the impact of governmental policy and needed national organization to deal with it. Religious Pan-Indianism was an accretion of local groups, a national movement which developed formal organizational structures largely in defense against governmental harassment. Reform Pan-Indianism, on the other hand, sprang into being as a national body and remained as such for a considerable period before developing local affiliates, though there is some evidence of the prior existence of local reform groups. Both reform and religious Pan-Indians were sustained in part by their relationship or similarity to powerful forces of religion and reform in the dominant society. But religious Pan-Indianism at least partially transformed basic tribal institutions into Pan-Indian ones. Reform Pan-Indianism had no such tribal institutions with which to work and had to rely much more heavily on non-Indian sources. Not until tribal institutions themselves had been modified, strengthened, and adapted through the Indian New Deal could a reform Pan-Indianism arise more firmly based in the tribes. Fraternal Pan-Indianism, which became nationalized only in the twenties—and that in rather shaky fashion—existed in many localities long before its nationalization. As a movement neither persecuted by the government nor directed to the reformation of governmental policy, it had less need for a national existence than the other types. The impulse to fraternization which it represented could be satisfied on a local basis and indeed usually was, in diverse activities from dancing in powwows to collecting funds for the education of deserving Indian youth.

The changes which in the opening decades of the twentieth century were helping to transform America also affected the Indians but were refracted through the special circumstances of their life. Only those ideas and forces which were powerful, pervasive, or especially relevant to the Indian situation penetrated the "buckskin curtain." One of these was the transformation of the United States into an urban industrial nation. This involved, among other things, a massive migration to the cities, the rapid development of transportation and communication, and the extension of urban attitudes and amenities to rural areas. While the national direction was clear, states and localities participated in these trends in varying degrees. Most Indian reservations were located in areas least affected by urbanization and industrialization. Normal rural isolation was, in the case of Indians, further compounded by the isolation of reservations, by their special relationships to the federal government, and by cultural differences among Indian tribes and between them and their white neighbors.

Yet all the varieties of Pan-Indianism were affected by urbanization. Reform Pan-Indianism was led largely by people who had already left the reservation in search of the wider opportunities of urban life. Their feelings about the reservation mingled dislike of its constraints with nostalgia for the vanished childhood home—an attitude similar to that of other Americans who abandoned farm and village in response to the lure of the city. Pan-Indian ambivalence thus functioned in a more general American ambivalence towards country life. Fraternal Pan-Indianism found new recruits. It was essentially an urban phenomenon, the creation of individuals who in the face of the loneliness of the city attempted to create an Indian community not of residence but of sentiment. Religious Pan-Indianism was based in the rural areas and was least influenced by urbanization, but like the other movements it benefited from greatly improved transportation and communication facilities.

As urbanization grew, so did the fear that values derived from healthy contact with nature might be lost from American life. The rise of modern Pan-Indianism coincided with the rise of conservation movements, of camping, and of nature-oriented organizations like the Boy Scouts, Girl Scouts, and Camp Fire Girls. Not the farm but the forest, lakes, and mountains were the cynosure of these movements. For them the Indian, as the man of nature *par excellence,* was a natural hero and symbol.

The Pan-Indian organizations were affected by this sentiment in somewhat different ways. Reform Pan-Indianism extolled the traditional values of Indian closeness to nature but envisioned the Indian future in terms of the professions, business, and modern farming. Some of its leaders, like Charles Eastman and Arthur C. Parker, were involved in the scouting and camping movements. To reform Pan-Indians, life in the woods and on the plains was avocation rather than vocation. Most of their white supporters also asserted man's need for refreshing his spirit amid the wonders of nature. Their meeting place at Lake Mohonk, with its magnificent lake, its beautiful woodland trails, and its rustic gazebos, was thus a sympathetic setting for their annual deliberations on the Indian. The leaders of fraternal Pan-Indianism were camping and scouting enthusiasts who considered themselves ambassadors from the great outdoors to city folk. In the romantic ritual and the many titles which they gave themselves, they tried to recapture the mystique of the forest as they imagined it. Much of the white support for fraternal Pan-Indianism came from men and women who dreamed of a lost world of the wilderness. For religious Pan-Indians, nature was a living, breathing force always to be respected and reckoned with in a world in which man was not set apart from nature but was one of its elements. Religious Pan-Indians had their own version of the Indian as the symbol of man living in harmony with nature. There seems little question that the anthropologists who were the chief friends of the peyote religion were deeply attracted to this view.

The rise of modern Pan-Indianism was due, as much as it could be attributed to any single cause, to expanding educational opportunities for Indians, especially in the non-reservation boarding schools. Pan-Indianism would have been impossible without English as a lingua franca. The growth of Indian education reflected the profound national commitment to education—a commitment shared by Pan-Indians of all varieties. Carlisle, Haskell, and Hampton were the chief producers of Pan-Indian leaders, but there were important differences in the status accorded them by the various movements. All the SAI presidents except Thomas L. Sloan attended non-Indian institutions of higher learning, as did Gertrude Bonnin, the most important figure in reform Pan-Indianism during the twenties. Many other SAI leaders were the product of white colleges and universities. The eastern boarding schools furnished secondary leadership and much rank and file support. Less is known about the education of the leaders of fraternal Pan-Indianism. One or two seem to have been college educated but a number were former students at Carlisle or Haskell. Religious Pan-Indianism, also, had a solid core of leaders from the eastern boarding schools and Haskell. These varying educational patterns were appropriate to their respective groups: the professional middle-class SAI, the lower middle-class fraternal orders and clubs, and the rurally based peyote religion.

No debate developed among Pan-Indians over vocational versus academic education, as was the case among Negroes. Pan-Indians believed in the widest possible educational opportunities and welcomed both vocational and academic education as legitimate ways of meeting the needs of various sectors of the Indian population. The differences between the Indian and Negro views arose from several factors, including class, caste, and leadership. Although class differences were present and played an important role in Pan-Indian affairs, most Indians did not have as strong a sense of class as did Negroes. Probably this was because tribal societies were relatively classless, while Negro society had a highly developed class structure. Indian anxieties over the equation of a particular type of education with class do not seem to have run very deep. Unlike Negroes, Indians were not locked into a caste. Those who wanted an academic or professional education could get one in a white school without insuperable difficulties. Indians, also, did not produce a leader like Booker T. Washington, someone who would be a spokesman for "the race" and chief negotiator with the white world. The dispersion of Pan-Indian leadership helped prevent such a polarization of views as occurred in the debate over education between Washington, who advocated a vocational education, and W. E. B. DuBois, who favored an academic one.

Modern Pan-Indianism developed during the period when modern social science came of age. The relationship of anthropology and sociology to Pan-Indianism stands out as one of its most interesting aspects. Although the founder of the Society of American Indians was a white sociologist, sociologists in general took little interest in its affairs. Their main concerns lay elsewhere, particularly with immigrants and Negroes. So far as is known, there were no Negro anthropologists during this period, though there were a number of important Negro sociologists. Negroes sought to understand themselves through sociology, Indians through anthropology.

All the professional anthropologists of Indian "blood" in the United States participated in Pan-Indian organizations and sought to bring to them the insights of their science. They do not seem to have been troubled that involvement in Pan-Indianism would compromise their objectivity as scientists, though Arthur Parker was much concerned over the practical possibility that his activities might hamper his professional relationship with the Iroquois. None of the Indian anthropologists supported fraternal Pan-Indianism of the Tepee Order variety; they found its pinchbeck romanticism offensive. Indian anthropologists parted company over the peyote religion, whose most eminent anthropological adherent was Francis LaFlesche. Probably the differences over the peyote cult between Parker the Seneca and LaFlesche the Omaha were due in large part to the situation in their respective tribes. The Seneca and the rest of the Iroquois tribes were ignorant of, indifferent, or hostile to the peyote religion. The Longhouse religion of Handsome Lake had originally performed an accommodative function somewhat similar to that of the peyote cult. By Parker's time, however, the longhouse represented conservative forces in most of the Iroquois tribes while the Christians were the progressive party. Among the Omaha, on the other hand, the progressives adhered to the peyote religion. In short, both Parker and LaFlesche belonged to the progressive wings of their tribes.

Among white anthropologists the situation was quite different. Like Indian anthropologists they showed little interest in fraternal Pan-Indianism. But unlike Indian anthropologists they ignored reform Pan-Indianism. Only Mark R. Harrington and Alanson Skinner, both close friends of Parker, gave continued backing to the SAI while he was associated with it. James Mooney played an important and sympathetic role in the development of religious Pan-Indianism, which received some support also from other anthropologists from the Bureau of American Ethnology.

The central figure in American anthropology in this period, Franz Boas, remained aloof from all Pan-Indian movements. Most of his students followed suit. Probably Boas' indifference to Indian causes stemmed from several sources, among them his devotion to scientific objectivity and his passion for recording data on "primitive" cultures— including Indian tribal groups—before they disappeared. Boas' interest in Indian life thus lay in those aspects least affected by modern society. His interest in problems of race and ethnicity, and in the situation of the Negro and the immigrant to which he devoted so much fruitful attention, may also have reflected the preoccupations of a German immigrant teaching in a great metropolitan area whose own life was more touched by such questions than by the current status of the American Indian. Ironically, in 1933 Boas opposed the appointment of John Collier as Indian Commissioner, declaring that Collier's ideas were impractical and idealistic. Collier states also that, in the twenties, the only anthropologists "who helped the Indians in their struggles" were Alfred L. Kroeber, who was a board member of Collier's American Indian Defense Association, and John L. Harrington of the Bureau of American Ethnology.[1]

In a somewhat different category were Indian "informants," men and women who interpreted tribal languages and tribal life for anthropologists. They were the eyes and ears of Indian anthropology. Little is known about these people; they have not been studied as a group. It seems clear that from their association with professional anthropologists they learned something of current anthropological thought. A number of them participated in Pan-Indian movements.

Anthropology helped Pan-Indians to define their common ground. Probably the most important idea was "race." Throughout the formative period, all the Pan-Indian organizations evoked race as a basic factor uniting Indians. Dominant anthropological thought regarded all races as inherently equal in potential if not in performance, a view enthusiastically shared by Pan-Indians. The eugenics movement of the twenties, with its fears of inferior genes, seems to have affected only such highly acculturated Indians as Arthur C. Parker, though it filtered down in somewhat garbled fashion to fraternal Pan-Indians. Even in the twenties, "race" was a sufficiently positive term to continue to be freely used by Pan-Indians. It was not until the thirties that the term "Indian race" fell largely into disuse as "race" did in the larger society, probably a casualty of Hitler's "master race" ideas.

The term "culture" was used by Pan-Indian movements in two ways: to refer to the Indian past in a positive sense and somewhat vaguely in application to the Indian present. Many valuable cultural traits had been shared by Indians in earlier times, it was assumed, and were the common heritage of the race. Reform Pan-Indians on the whole did not use "culture" in referring to contemporary Indians until after World War I. Fraternal Pan-Indians used it sporadically, and some religious-reform Pan-Indians, like Oliver Lamere, employed the term, but it does not seem to have been popular among peyotists. Clearly "race" was a more powerful idea for Pan-Indians than "culture," and understandably so. "Race" emphasized a common element, "culture" a somewhat divisive one because of its tribal connotations.

Another major source of Pan-Indian ideas was the changing conception of American nationality, through which Indians defined their relationship to the country and to each other. The traditional and dominant melting pot view was that persons of varying nationalities and backgrounds did and should contribute to the American melting pot, whose product was a continually renewed and changing American. The melting pot concept was oriented to process; change was considered inevitable and desirable though sometimes slow. The major focus was on the individual as the unit of change. Undergirding this conception of American nationality was an ebullient optimism, a belief that the country had the capacity to sustain this process. In fact, the successful operation of the melting pot was seen to represent a central element in the meaning of the American experience.

The perspective of the Dawes Act had placed governmental policy directly at odds with the melting pot idea so far as Indian cultural contributions were concerned. It was held that contemporary Indians had no such contributions to make to the melting pot. Indian assimilation was thus conceived not as a mutually enriching process from which all Americans would benefit but as a one-way affair in which everything culturally Indian would be swiftly and finally extinguished. The rise of reform Pan-Indianism was in part a reaction of educated Indians against this "vanishing policy," which in any case became substantially modified as the Progressive Era developed.

The traditional melting pot view of American nationality was strongly advocated by reform Pan-Indians, who regularly proclaimed the value of continuing Indian contributions. Reform Pan-Indians believed in both the desirability and the inevitability of this process. They expected that melting would take time, they recognized that it would require an often painful process of adjustment, and they were determined to control and direct it as much as possible so that the Indian contribution would be worthy both of the Indian past and of the American future in which they would share.

Reform Pan-Indians frequently cited the immigrant experience as a desirable model for the Indian and pointed to immigrant or "nationality" organizations as examples for the Indian to follow. They were particularly impressed at the ease with which immigrants, unlike Indians, could become citizens. They stressed also how the immigrant acquired English and a knowlege of the new country through the public school. Organizations of immigrants and the descendants of immigrants along the lines of their previous nationalities seemed to Indians both natural and right and in no way in conflict with their becoming Americans. In asserting the positive value of the immigrant model they believed that they were in consonance with the beliefs of most Americans; they spoke of the immigrant not as a man who needed to be defended but as one who should be emulated.

The "new Indian" of the reformers was seen as evolving through a process similar to the operation of the national melting pot. Pan-Indians did not use the phrase "Indian melting pot," but they frequently described the process. The new Indian thus produced would partake of the best attributes of the tribes, especially of those characteristics deemed general throughout Indian life: dignity, fidelity to one's word, love and

reverence for nature, cooperation, artistic expression, respect for age
and wisdom, bravery, belief in a higher being, an aversion to crass
materialism, independence, self-respect, pride, and other such aboriginal
virtues. These virtues, happily, were held in high esteem by the dominant
society. Other widespread characteristics of aboriginal life which might
with as much justice have been cited, such as common ownership of
land or devotion to traditional ways, were quite understandably neglected. These would be left for a time later in the century when more
Americans admired them. This is not to imply that Pan-Indians were
slavishly toadying to white opinion but rather that they emphasized those
Indian qualities which they themselves admired and which they believed
could legitimately and realistically be contributed to the national life.
Thus the new Indian of the reformers was to partake of the best attributes of the tribes but would no longer be bound by tribal parochialism.
The new Indian would also adopt the best qualities of the larger society;
his Indianness and his Americanness would complement and refresh
each other. The American nationality always in the process of being
created would be strengthened and broadened by its Indian infusion.
This Pan-Indian reform conception of the melting pot came to be shared
by many, though not all, of the older white reformers. Religious Pan-
Indians did not express their relation to the melting pot so explicitly.
They believed that the Indian had a positive contribution to make to
the nation. They considered themselves Americans; they affirmed their
Pan-Indian identity in syncretistic religious terms; they were at the same
time more tribally oriented than the other types.

World War I and its aftermath brought a profound change in the
national mood, a decline of faith in the validity and practicality of the
melting pot and an increasing tendency for Americans old and new to
identify themselves by country of origin. Belief in the melting pot began
to give way to different conceptions of American nationality. These
varied widely but held in common two basic characteristics: a shift of
emphasis from the value of change to the value of preservation, and
from a focus on the individual to a focus on the group. In the 1920's,
newer reformers like John Collier were skeptical of what they believed
to be the melting pot idea. In their view, it was a way of "whitemanizing"
the Indian which resulted not in a new synthesis but rather in a man
deculturated and divided. Instead they fought for both tolerance and
encouragement for groups like the Indian tribes to pursue their tradi-

tional ways of life. Tribal societies, Collier believed, represented a priceless asset which could be a source of strength and wisdom for other Americans, a living demonstration of the rich human values of a close-knit community. Collier's position was different but not at an opposite pole from the melting pot perspective. Both conceptions welcomed Indian—and immigrant—contributions to the national life. Both valued diversity. Both interpreted the American experience in positive terms. Both were optimistic. Both recognized change as inevitable. Collier was not opposed to Indian individuals leaving the tribe, but for him, it was group contributions, group diversity, group continuity, and group solidarity that were important.

Other alternatives to the melting pot were neither as humane nor as tolerant as Collier's. Some reflected hostilities among groups, as each asserted the superior value of its own culture and believed that further change was both impossible and undesirable. One prominent example was "Anglo-Saxonism" or "Anglo-Americanization," which proclaimed its superiority over lesser breeds, fortified by a powerful boost from eugenics.

Reform Pan-Indianism responded to this rather confused mood about national identity in a rather confused fashion. Initially, the most direct influence came from the Wilsonian idea of self-determination which was applied loosely to the Indian situation. The net effect of these ideas on Pan-Indian reform was to produce a stronger tribal emphasis and a fitful hostility to immigrants. In the late twenties, reform Pan-Indianism reflected the rising influence of the Collier philosophy while still retaining some of its old melting pot ideology.

Fraternal Pan-Indianism, especially in its Tepee Order guise, attempted to identify itself with Anglo-Americanization, from which it absorbed anti-immigrant and anti-Negro biases. Other fraternal Pan-Indian groups seem to have been less affected by the virulent variety of Anglo-Americanization, though evidence on this point is extremely scanty. Religious Pan-Indianism seems to have been affected least, being preoccupied with self-defense and further removed than other types from the American mainstream.

None of the Pan-Indian movements used the term "cultural pluralism" to define their relationship to American life. Indeed, it would have been most surprising if they had, since the term was not used by its inventor, Horace Kallen, until the mid-twenties and then was employed only by a few intellectuals and had no general currency. But the idea of cultural pluralism, of America as a "nation of nations" which could and should exist indefinitely within the body politic, was certainly present in embryonic form in post-World War I Pan-Indianism. Its later emergence among Pan-Indians as an important and widespread conception of American nationality had strong roots in this earlier period.

Attitudes toward the Negro are difficult to document because Pan-Indians rarely expressed them in print. In traditional melting pot thinking, the Negro was a marginal if not completely excluded figure. But the white reformers most closely associated with reform Pan-Indianism took a much more positive view of the Negro. This probably helps to account for the fact that reform Pan-Indians seldom voiced anti-Negro prejudice publicly—which is not to say that it had no existence. Traditionally Indians have been fearful of being bracketed with the Negro. Little is known of the attitudes of religious Pan-Indians on this matter, though there are some indications of prejudice. The fraternal Pan-Indianism of the twenties was often explicitly anti-Negro.

It is worth noting that as the Society of American Indians and the National Association for the Advancement of Colored People were founded at the end of the first decade of this century, so the Tepee Order and Marcus Garvey's Universal Negro Improvement Association arose in the second decade and had their heyday in the early twenties. The parallels between the two Indian and Negro reform organizations with their educated middle-class leadership, their emphasis on race pride, their commitment to democratic procedures, and their strong white support are quite striking. Parallels between the fraternal organizations are more tenuous and cannot be pushed too far without becoming misleading. Yet both of the latter represented a response to urbanization, both relied heavily on pageantry, costume, symbols, and elaborate titles, and both were hostile to outlanders—the Tepee Order to Negroes and immigrants, the Garveyites to whites in general. The SAI and the NAACP arose during a period of national reform while the Tepee Order and the Garveyites emerged as the reform tide ebbed and intergroup hostilities began to intensify. The difference in historic positions, status, traditions, and numbers between the Indian and the Negro made the differences between their movements understandable and inevitable; their similarities were probably as much a function of the climate of opinion in the country as a whole as of the particular experiences of each group.

Christianity played a crucial role in all the Pan-Indian organizations. Christian ideas of human brotherhood and the equality of all men before God complemented anthropological ideas of inherent racial equality. Most of the reform Pan-Indians were Christians—Protestant and Catholic—and some were clergymen. The reformer-peyotists belonged to that cult's most Christianized wing. Indian Protestants and Catholics in the SAI seem to have worked together amicably with only one minor and obscure conflict around the period of World War I. But the Christian missionaries and reformers who provided the major white support for reform Pan-Indians were also deternined foes of the peyote religion and helped to commit the Indian reform movement to an anti-peyote policy.

The impact of Christianity on religious Pan-Indianism was twofold. The peyote cult borrowed heavily from both Protestantism and Catholicism, so much so that many of its adherents considered themselves Christians; indeed, some were also members of conventional Christian denominations. The Christian campaign against peyote strengthened the cult and was probably the most important factor in the formation of the Native American Church. Christianity thus spurred the development of religious Pan-Indianism both as model and as enemy.

The cloudy Christianity of the Tepee Order was exemplified by its moving spirit, the Reverend Red Fox St. James, who had about him the air of a minister conducting an earnest but not very well attended prayer meeting. The Tepee Order shared the bias of many non-Indian Protestants against Catholicism, a circumstance which got it into difficulties with Catholic Indians. Outside the order, many—probably most—fraternal Pan-Indians seem to have been Christians, though doubtless the pattern varied among local groups.

There seems to have been no anti-Semitism in Pan-Indian organizations, even in the Tepee Order where one might have expected to find it. Tepee Order attacks on immigrants were quite generalized and did not single out Jews as particular objects of hostility, while in at least one instance a Tepee Order leader cited the "Hebrews" as a model for Indians in opposing intermarriage. Reform Pan-Indians sometimes spoke admiringly of the Jewish experience in preserving an identity in spite of persecutions. Until the twenties few Jews took an interest in Indian movements. Among the new reformers of the twenties led by John Collier, however, there were a number of Jews. Since that time many of the white anthropologists most active in Pan-Indian affairs—especially in recent years—have been Jews. Perhaps like James Mooney, they bring to Pan-Indianism "a personally experienced model."

Despite other differences, Pan-Indian organizations in the formative period endorsed the ethic of work and individual responsibility for a job well done. Indians were to be industrious, educate their children, and above all, stay away from alcohol. The "liquor evil" meant personal and social disintegration, a denial of Indian ability to succeed in modern life, a terrible source of shame.

One of the most widespread influences in the lives of most leaders of reform and fraternal Pan-Indianism was their participation in various non-Indian fraternal orders, especially in Masonry. Evidently Indians were welcomed in many fraternal orders. The security of an explicit series of steps by which members rose in these orders may have been especially appealing to men whose position in white society was often ambiguous, while the elaborate rituals represented a substitute for the rituals of the tribe. Even the Improved Order of Red Men, which nominally barred real redmen, seems to have had a number of Indian members, and served the Tepee Order for a time as both a model to be emulated and an exclusivist organization to be attacked. Not enough is known of the life histories of religious Pan-Indian leaders to state whether they also belonged to non-Indian fraternal organizations. However, the Indian experience strongly suggests that fraternal orders were much more influential as acculturating agencies than is generally realized.

As Pan-Indians adapted to their own use basic ideas from the larger society, they also appropriated organizational forms suitable to their situations and purposes which were drawn from parallel organizations in the dominant society. This much is obvious. What is not as obvious is the relationship of these models to the perennial problem of Indian factionalism. It is a commonplace among Indians and their friends that "Indians can't stick together." But when Pan-Indian organizations are placed in the wider perspective of their white counterparts, and viewed comparatively, the situation looks somewhat different. Factionalism is no stranger to reform movements, fraternal orders, social clubs, and Christian denominations. If the Indian movements are compared not with the most stable but with the garden variety of white organizations, they no longer appear excessively factional. Indeed, when the many potentially and actually divisive forces among Indians are considered,

Pan-Indian movements can be justly credited with a surprising degree of stability.

In other ways, also, the Pan-Indian organizations resembled their white counterparts. The position of women in the various movements was virtually identical with their roles in similar non-Indian organizations. Reform Pan-Indianism had its devoted females who ran the office. In the Society of American Indians there were occasional women officers though never, of course, a woman president: this would have been inconsistent with the pattern of most of the non-Indian reform groups which included both men and women. Mrs. Bonnin's position as president and chief factotum of the National Council of American Indians reflected the influence of the many women's organizations in which she was active. Fraternal Pan-Indianism had its women's auxiliaries and clubs. The leadership of religious Pan-Indianism was male, with women playing subordinate roles of the type familiar in other churches, including the running of ladies' auxiliaries and women's clubs. But women did play a specific though subordinate part in conducting religious services. As one might expect, this ritual role was derived from Indian rather than white sources.

One of the most critical aspects of Pan-Indian movements lay in the members' conceptions of the reservation and their relationships to it, a question which continues to preoccupy Pan-Indians. At least three basic conceptions of the reservation are discernible: the reservation as prison, the reservation as community, and the reservation as refuge. These views have persisted into the present. In the period in which modern Pan-Indianism arose, viewpoints about the reservation operated within the context of the Dawes Act policy, with its objectives of phasing out the reservation system over a period of decades, of "getting the government out of the Indian business," of "putting the Indian in civilization and keeping him there." At the beginning of the twentieth century the memory of the free Indian was sufficiently close and vivid to make the reservation system seem ever more deadening by contrast.

In the conception of the reservation as prison, reservation existence was thought of as sapping the manhood of the Indian by forcing him to eke out a precarious existence as a virtual prisoner, sustained by handouts from a capricious government, with no control over the property that was rightfully his, cut off from the opportunities available to other

Americans, and excluded from the promise of American life. It is interesting to note that many of the attacks on the reservation as prison foreshadowed later criticisms of the welfare state and of the bitter culture of poverty.

In a free society, the argument ran, the reservation was an anomaly and the involuntary segregation of the Indian branded him as inferior. To become a free man, the Indian had to live under conditions of freedom. The reservation was believed to be at best a temporary way-station on the path from his former condition of aboriginal freedom to his future condition of freedom as a member of modern society. Therefore the reservation system should be ended as speedily as possible—to the minds of a few Pan-Indians that meant immediately. While the conditions of prison life could and should be modified for the better, this was at best a temporary expedient and only the end of the system itself would end the evils which were part of its very nature. Yet most reform Pan-Indians drew back from immediate abolition in order to protect those older Indians who could not adjust to the exigencies of a life so traumatically different from the one to which they were accustomed.

The conception of the reservation as prison was usually, though not always, coupled with an attack on "the social tyranny of the tribe." By this was meant the pressures of conservative tribal members against Indians who wished to change to more "modern" or "progressive" ways of life. The often bitter resentment against the "social tyranny of the tribe" seems much like the resentment of any people who want to escape from the confining atmosphere of any small, close-knit community. Reform Pan-Indians especially, who were frequently viewed with suspicion by conservative Indians as trying to "whitemanize" themselves, were very sensitive to these pressures. In the view of many reformers, the conservative grip of the reservation system could not be broken until the system itself was ended.

A variant of the reservation as prison conception regarded the prison-like aspects of the reservation as susceptible to modification or abolition without destroying the system itself. This seems to have been the position of many religious and fraternal Pan-Indians. On the whole, both seem to have taken the system for granted while protesting particular acts of injustice and suggesting ways in which it might be made more workable and equitable. Religious Pan-Indians, for example, fought hard against Bureau interference with their religious ideas and practices.

Neither fraternal nor religious Pan-Indians seemed to have been bothered by "the social tyranny of the tribe." Fraternal Pan-Indians were frequently so far removed from tribal life that such a question was quite outside their experience. In some instances, religious Pan-Indians *were* the tribe, or a substantial and influential part of it. In others, where religious Pan-Indianism came into conflict with traditional tribal religion, the freedom to worship as they pleased as members of the tribe was the objective. To these men and women, the peyote religion was itself a modern version of the tribal religion, retaining its viable elements and discarding those which were either too difficult and complicated to retain or which seemed too much in conflict with present-day life.

The conception of the reservation as community was held in varying ways by the different types of Pan-Indian movements. Religious Pan-Indians lived in reservation communities and simply assumed their continued existence as such. Often they were active in various kinds of community betterment activities, from holding fairs and powwows to combating the "liquor evil." Frequently peyotists were community leaders and some were chiefs. Reform Pan-Indians, of whom only a very few were resident members of reservation communities, viewed most of those communities as poverty-stricken, downtrodden, isolated, and lacking in essential services. However, some reservation communities, the reformers pointed out, prospered or at least were well on the way to prospering by dint of hard work and sacrifices, thus proving that Indians could "achieve" in spite of the vicissitudes of reservation life. Reform Pan-Indians believed that it was their duty to extend a helping hand to their less fortunate country brethren with aid in legal, educational, religious, and other social areas. Among fraternal Pan-Indians the Tepee Order partook of the helping hand viewpoint while others with stronger ties back home seem to have moved back and forth rather freely between reservation and city, conceiving of themselves as belonging to both, but probably not satisfied with either.

Thus all the Pan-Indian movements assumed the continuing existence of Indian communities. Even the reformers most bitterly opposed to the reservation system did not equate the abolition of the system with the abolition of the communities. But it was not until the Indian New Deal that the contemporary Indian community was widely cast in a heroic role. In the Collier philosophy, the Indian community had a remarkable potential for social health and satisfaction for its members, exhibited extraordinary staying power by enduring through centuries of oppression, and pointed the way for the survival and reconstruction of other small communities threatened with oblivion. Hitherto, only a few Indian communities, like the Pueblos or the Navahos, were described in such terms, and even these had their vociferous critics, both Indian and white.

The idea of the reservation as refuge is more diffuse and difficult to document than the other conceptions. Nevertheless, it seems to have been held by participants in all the varieties of Pan-Indianism. All conceived of the reservation as a refuge for older, less acculturated Indians. In some cases, the refuge was also valued as the remembered childhood home, a place recalled nostalgically where one was secure. The refuge was a refuge of memory rather than of present actuality. Sometimes, it was a place to visit or retreat to temporarily, a kind of standby home. For others, it was a place where one could escape the continual effort to get along in the white man's world. And for some Pan-Indians whose connections with the reservation were exceedingly tenuous, the reservation as refuge was even more vague, existing as a Pan-Indian country of the imagination.

The varying conceptions of the reservation help to explain the support which the Dawes Act received from so many Pan-Indians. The reservation, with its humiliations and indignities, was definitely to be abolished —but not quite yet. Meanwhile, it could function as a place of refuge— actual, psychological, or both. And its eventual end would not end the Indian communities—or at least this was sufficiently problematical and far enough in the future not to be immediately troublesome.

The conceptions of the reservation as prison, as community, and as refuge were held also by the white allies of the Pan-Indian movements. The older reformers viewed the reservation as prison, a system to be eventually abolished, but they assumed the continuing existence of Indian communities. As models of the latter, they pointed to "progressive," acculturated communities which were still recognizably Indian. The newer reformers proclaimed the reservation as community; their models were cohesive and traditional communities. At the same time, they fought the reservation as prison. But unlike the older reformers, they believed that the system itself could and should be transformed into a force which would encourage the continued life of tribal groups rather than fragment it. Such friends of the peyotists as James Mooney also emphasized the reservation as community while attacking unfair restrictions in reservation governance. Mooney's position seems to have been somewhere between that of the older and newer reformers, though much closer to the latter. The white supporters of fraternal Pan-Indianism were town-dwellers and displayed only a mild interest in the reservation.

Whatever their other conceptions, however, all the white friends of Pan-Indianism thought of the reservation as refuge—that is, as refuge for themselves. Even to the most crusty investigator from the Indian Rights Association, Indian country had great appeal. However much the older reformers might proclaim the necessity of "putting the Indian into civilization and keeping him there," and however much they attacked the system, still the attraction of Indian life was undeniable. Perhaps it was a taste for the exotic, perhaps a missionary impulse, perhaps a retreat from the hurly-burly of modern life. Some newer reformers also seem to have experienced a healing contact with another culture, a reverence for the old rituals, a delight in another variety of human experience, an affirmation of the enveloping warmth of a small community. The friends of fraternalism had their own version of the reservation as refuge: a long ago and faraway country which could be recreated through ritual; full of chiefs and princesses, of brave men and stalwart women; where the grimy workaday world could for the moment be left behind. It is not questioning the validity or sincerity of these views to point out that for whites to visit the reservation, whether in actuality or in imagination, was a little like traveling in a foreign land; it was easier to savor its color and romance when one was not permanently caught up in its less happy aspects.

Each of the Pan-Indian movements also held conceptions of white society, which they regarded with some ambivalence, and with which they had varying degrees of contact. On the whole, there is little evidence of much hostility to whites as whites, though the available record on this matter cannot be fully revealing. Members of each of the Pan-Indian movements conceived of themselves as related to the social strata represented by their white friends or models, whether that of middle-class reform, of lower middle-class fraternalism, or of rural Christianity. Each tended to share with their white counterparts similar views of the deficiencies of white society while at the same time sharing considerable optimism as to its ability to offer them a respected place in it. The various movements also had differing relationships with their allies. All were to some extent fearful of white control. Reform Pan-Indians explicitly organized to avoid such control. They gave whites a recognized but subordinate role. As factions developed, however, these arrangements were sometimes relaxed in order to bring white influence to bear against an opposing faction. Nevertheless, the ideal remained that of a movement run by Indians. Religious Pan-Indianism, the most "Indian" of the movements, welcomed whites as occasional participants in or observers of the ceremonies but in only a very few instances did whites play an important internal role. The attitude of adherents of fraternal Pan-Indianism was much more diffuse. At some points whites were an integral part of the fraternal organizations, at others they were explicitly excluded. But all the Pan-Indian organizations needed and used white help; indeed, it is difficult to see how any of them could have survived without it, though this very dependence did sometimes create resentments on both sides.

One of the aspects of white society as a whole with which all Pan-Indians were deeply, often passionately, concerned was the white image of the Indian. To most Americans, Indians belonged to a colorful and rapidly receding past, interesting to recall but largely irrelevant to modern life. Sometimes, the "vanishing Indian" was referred to in a now-forgotten phrase as "Poor Lo," a designation contracted from "Lo, the poor Indian!"—a line from Alexander Pope's poem "Essay on Man." While "Poor Lo" has vanished, other images of the Indian held in the early decades of this century have remained remarkably persistent. Indians were variously—and vaguely—thought of as noble savages, romantic redmen, drunken degenerates, oil-rich primitives, pathetic victims of the white man's greed, "the vanishing Americans," bloodthirsty savages, at once strong, silent, war-whooping, enduring, and nonexistent. An Indian spoke in a deep gutteral and said "How," "Heap Big," "Ugh," added "um" to most of his words, and never used the definite article. Sometimes Indians stood with arms impassively folded. In greeting, an Indian raised his arm in solemn salute. Indians also appeared on horseback on a promontory silhouetted against the sky before swooping down on a wagon train. Indians smoked peacepipes, referred to money as "wampum," and wore magnificent feather war bonnets. Indian women were "squaws"—hard-working and oppressed drudges who did the heavy labor while the men danced around the campfire. All the "squaws" wore a beaded band across their foreheads and sported braids. Indian warriors delighted in taking scalps but were otherwise lazy. However, a few Indians went to an eastern college called Carlisle where their main activity was playing on winning football teams. Most Indian men were chiefs and women princesses. Everyone knew that Indians worshipped "the Great Spirit" and went to a place called "the Happy Hunting Ground" when they died. Occasionally, actual Indians turned up at important public ceremonies, like presidential inaugurations, mounted on horseback and wearing spectacular Plains warbonnets. The Indian, when he was thought of at all, thus lived in a never-never land, detached from space and time, unconnected with the familiar everyday world.

Outside of those comparatively few whites well acquainted with the realities of Indian life, this image of the Indian was so pervasive that it affected how most whites reacted to the Indians they met and how Indians thought about themselves. It is exasperating and dehumanizing constantly to be treated as an image rather than as a person, "to have to play Indian in order to be Indian," in Arthur Parker's poignant phrase. All the Pan-Indian movements reacted strongly to this Indian image. Reform Pan-Indians bitterly attacked the cigar-store, wild west image and attempted to substitute for it an image of a sober, industrious, up-to-date middle-class citizen. Religious Pan-Indians attempted to project an image remarkably similar to the reform one, but with more Indian or Pan-Indian elements added, and with a more rural orientation. Fraternal Pan-Indians, while exercised over the unfavorable aspects of the Indian image, often conformed to the positive ones, especially the romantic redman syndrome.

The image of the Indian prevalent in the formative period of Pan-Indianism has survived virtually intact to the present, making it one of the hardiest stereotypes in American history. The growth of mass media has done little to dispel and much to strengthen it. It is a conception of the Indian still held by otherwise highly educated and sophisticated people who use it with a lack of self-consciousness which attests to their naivete in this regard.

Only a few decades ago most students of Indian affairs, together with many Indians, assumed that the Indian would eventually disappear as a distinct element in the American population. The assumption was shared by both those who regretted and those who welcomed its inevitability. This view has changed dramatically: it is now widely assumed that Indians will continue indefinitely as subgroups of the American people. If this latterday analysis is correct—and the evidence supporting it is formidable—Pan-Indianism seems likely not only to continue but to increase in importance.

Pan-Indian movements in their modern accommodative form have represented a characteristic aspect of Indian relationships to the larger society and among each other throughout this century. Despite fluctuations in the significance and impact of particular types at particular periods, Pan-Indianism has shown itself to be remarkably durable, deeply rooted in Indian historical experience, and capable of considerable flexibility.

The forces which have helped to produce modern Pan-Indian movements are neither transient nor ephemeral. Some, like mass communications, urbanization, and education, are fundamentals of American life which will become more rather than less important in the future. Ideas travel fast. The "mocassin telegraph," the Indian version of the grapevine, still operates, and no doubt will continue to do so. But today Indians can and do get news and views directly from television and popular magazines, now found in many an Indian home which even a decade ago was largely insulated from such immediate contact with the outside world. Automobiles and airplanes increase Indian mobility, enabling people with a long tradition of traveling to do so more rapidly, more frequently, and over longer distances. The national commitment to education is resulting in increasing numbers of young Indians going to colleges, including community colleges, where they imbibe new ideas not only in the classroom but probably more importantly from their peers, Indian and non-Indian.

Other factors are more closely restricted in their impact to Indians. The special relationship of the government to Indians seems to be a permanent one, and it is difficult to foresee a situation in which it could be ended. Indians will continue to be defined through governmental policies as a distinct group in the population with a collective identity beyond that of individual tribes. The image of the Indian, a necessarily Pan-Indian conception, will persist as a factor deeply influencing how Indians define themselves. Although the specific content may change, it is unlikely that Americans can or will abandon a generalized Indian image whose symbolic uses reflect as much about themselves as about Indians. Both governmental policy and the image of the Indian help to sustain a socially recognized Pan-Indian identity.

Pan-Indian movements will continue to receive the white support which has played so important a role in their development. The groups which historically have befriended Pan-Indianism show no signs of withdrawing while new sources of support will no doubt emerge as other variations of Pan-Indianism appear.

The sector of the Indian population from which Pan-Indian movements have historically risen will probably grow in size and importance. There can be little question that Indians will continue to leave the reservation, either permanently or temporarily, in significant numbers. Despite efforts to create viable reservation communities, the reservation base is unlikely to be sufficient to support its growing population. Some of these men and women will be lost in the general population but others will seek to retain or create an Indian identity. The immigrant experience is instructive in this regard. Even Americans separated by decades or centuries from their previous countries of origin are apt to refer to their previous "nationality"—or "nationalities," since by this time they have often acquired several. Even those whose forebears came from places where there was little or no consciousness of an identity beyond locality or region have found it necessary and natural to create a "national" identity, the latest example being the renewed discovery of Africa by American blacks. Some form of "national" or ethnic identification, however vague, is thus so characteristic of the way Americans think about themselves that it seems highly likely that people whose homeland was reservation or tribe will continue to call themselves Indians, though they may not be readily identifiable either in appearance or life style as such. The Pan-Indian base will probably encompass not only Indians fresh from the reservation but also many who have lived in the larger society for generations.

Pan-Indianism will grow in local communities on or near reservations and in towns and cities as a result of increasing contacts among Indians and with whites. It will take a variety of forms from powwows to local and regional intertribal bodies. While these groups will have different degrees of tribal emphasis, they will of necessity assert a common Pan-Indian bond distinct from or complementary to tribal loyalties. This network of Pan-Indian ideas and activities will help to provide the kind of local base which national Pan-Indian movements have often lacked, and from which they may in the future arise.

The development of a Pan-Indian subculture, already noted by students of Indian affairs, may well satisfy the needs of Indians whose concerns are primarily local or fraternal. But today even fraternal Pan-Indianism engages in some national activities, as witness the annual "Miss Indian America" beauty contest which is supported by local Pan-Indian and local tribal groups. When Indians believe that they need to organize nationally, for whatever purposes, they will do so, supporting those national Pan-Indian organizations which exist or creating new ones to fulfill new functions.

The problem of who is an Indian will continue to be a central concern of Pan-Indians. This definition, which may seem self-evident to non-Indians, is by no means an easy one. Many Americans who are of partial Indian ancestry, or "blood"—the term is still used—are indistinguishable in appearance from other Americans. Does one-quarter or one-sixteenth or some much smaller fraction of Indian ancestry qualify one as an Indian? Many Indians living on reservations do not look "Indian," but residence or former residence in Indian communities is normally accepted as evidence of being an Indian. Persons who appear on the tribal rolls are also considered Indians whether or not they reside with the tribe. The most difficult problems arise in the case of people who are Indian neither in appearance nor residence. Some contemporary Pan-Indians attempt to solve the problem by asserting that anyone who is "culturally" an Indian should be considered Indian, or even that if a person chooses to identify himself as an Indian, he should be so considered. But how is this to be interpreted—in tribal or in Pan-Indian terms? And if a person claims to be an Indian, on what basis are such claims to be substantiated? These questions have risen in the past when Indians sought to define membership qualifications in Pan-Indian organizations. In the future they will no doubt continue to be a source of controversy, especially in Pan-Indian groups far removed from the reservation.

Pan-Indian movements will involve to some extent the reemergence of once-vanished Indians, or of persons whose Indian ancestry is exceedingly remote or even nonexistent. The more Pan-Indian the emphasis, the easier is such an occurrence, which is likely to be viewed with some skepticism by "real" Indians. Such skepticism will almost certainly be more pronounced in the case of Negroes who wish to participate in Pan-Indian movements. Some tribes have an admixture of Negro "blood," a circumstance which frequently causes considerable perturbation among other Indians. In some localities Negroes, whether or not they have or claim any Indian ancestry, participate in powwows and other fraternal activities. No doubt there is, and will be, a wide range of reactions among Indians; very little systematic study has yet been given to Indian views of Negroes. But it seems probable that Negro claims to be Indian will get a much cooler reception than similar white ones. People who view themselves as both different from the rest of society and as unfairly dealt with by it are usually notably unenthusiastic about confusion or fusion with groups whose social status is generally lower than their own. This is not of course to say that Pan-Indian movements will not advocate civil rights for all, or will not cooperate with black movements, or will not appropriate black tactics, but that they will do so in terms which make clear distinctions between the situation of Indians and the situation of Negroes.

In the future as in the past, Pan-Indian organizations will often serve as a decompression chamber for individual Indians from which they vanish into the larger society. But movements are quite capable of surviving such a process if the forces underlying them are sufficiently strong and persistent. Like the now-discarded idea of the vanishing American, the concept of the vanishing Pan-Indian should be revised in the light of historical evidence and of discernible future trends. The vanishing-American hypothesis was discarded not because no Indians vanished, but because so many Indians remained. Similarly, individual Pan-Indians will vanish, but Pan-Indianism itself gives every evidence of being a permanent rather than a temporary phenomenon.

What specific varieties of Pan-Indian movements will arise in the future will depend to a very large extent on the climate of opinion, ideas, and styles of organization in American society as a whole. As in the past, Pan-Indian organizations will constitute not carbon copies but freehand versions of parallel organizations in the wider society, combining and adapting ideas, organizational forms, activities and definitions of the Indian drawn from both Indian and non-Indian sources. This process has been so fundamental in the development of Pan-Indianism as to make its continuation highly predictable.

But whatever Pan-Indian movements may arise in the future and whatever directions they make take, the nature of their historical antecedents is clear. In the formative period Pan-Indianism was a movement of accommodation. It was not just a reaction to cultural deprivation; nor was it only a shield against white domination or simply a rejection of the old Indian ways or solely an expression of marginality, though it contained all of these aspects. It was also an endeavor by men and women who through their own experience had found much of value in both Indian and white worlds, to create an identity which drew from both. As people in transition they defined themselves in the terms currently available to them.

It would be easy to cast their experience in today's language: genocide practiced against men whose only crime was self-defense; the imprisonment of helpless people in ghettoes and their manipulation by a far-off Washington bureaucracy unsympathetic and venal; the systematic destruction of basic cultural institutions, including the family and religion; the dreary subsistence on governmental handouts voted by a capricious Congress; the inertia and hopelessness punctuated by sporadic outbreaks of violence; the appalling conditions of health and the prevalence of the diseases of poverty; the alcoholism, the drugs; the education of children in inferior and segregated schools manned by poorly trained middle-class teachers ignorant of the values of the community and conducted in a foreign tongue; the drop-out rate; the treatment of the Indian in history books, ranging from utter neglect to unfair stereotype thus denying him a usable past; the refusal to see the Indian as an ordinary human; the cupidity of foes; the uncomprehending idealism of friends; the constantly disappointed expectations of quick and spectacular results from particular programs or policies; the massive indifference of the establishment—all these immediately invoke contemporary parallels. Every item in this indictment has truth in it and each was expressed in some form by Pan-Indians in the years in which their movements arose.

Yet as a summary of their viewpoint it is false. They preferred not to dwell too long on historic grievances, for they had seen too many of their kinsmen paralyzed by so doing, recounting over and over the old injustices. Despite past brutality and present injury they looked to the future with hope for they, and other Americans, had confidence in the essential promise of American life. When and if Americans lose that confidence, and when and if American life does not deserve it, then Pan-Indians, like the rest of us, will cling to an identity narrower, more parochial, and more hostile to those outside our own groups.

NOTES TO THE CHAPTERS

1—THE ROOTS OF MODERN PAN-INDIANISM

1. See Harold E. Driver, *Indians of North America* (Chicago and London: University of Chicago Press, 1961), pp. 15–18, for the eight "culture areas" in what is now the United States. According to Driver's classification, which is a somewhat simplified version of that of A. L. Kroeber, the areas cover the following states: Northwest Coast—parts of Washington, Oregon, and California; Plateau—parts of Washington, Idaho, Oregon, and Montana; Plains—parts of Montana, Wyoming, Colorado, and the Dakotas, Nebraska, Kansas, Oklahoma, and Texas; Prairies—all of Wisconsin, Michigan, Illinois, Iowa, and Missouri, and parts of the Dakotas, Minnesota, Nebraska, Kansas, Oklahoma, Texas, Arkansas, Tennessee, Kentucky, and Indiana; East—all of New York and the Middle Atlantic states, southern New England, and most of the southern states as far west as Louisiana; California—about two-thirds of the state; Great Basin—all of Nevada and Utah, parts of California, Oregon, Idaho, Wyoming, and Colorado; Oasis— most of Arizona and New Mexico. The Northwest Coast, Plateau, Plains, and East include parts of Canada, while Oasis includes parts of Mexico.

2. Carl F. Klinck, ed., *Tecumseh* (Englewood Cliffs, N.J.: Prentice-Hall, 1961), p. 105.

3. *Annual Report of the Commissioner of Indian Affairs, 1887*, pp. 117–18.

4. *Annual Report of the Commissioner of Indian Affairs, 1888*, pp. 126–28.

5. So far as is known, there was no connection between the Indian Shakers and the Shakers led by Mother Lee.

6. James Mooney, *The Ghost-Dance Religion and the Sioux Outbreak of 1890*, originally published as Part 2 of the *14th Annual Report of the Bureau of American Ethnology*. The edition cited here is abridged and edited by Anthony F. C. Wallace (Chicago: University of Chicago Press, 1965), p. 14.

7. Biographical details from Paul Bailey, *Wovoka The Indian Messiah* (Los Angeles: Westernlore Press, 1957).

8. "The Indian Ghost Dance and War," by W. H. Prather, I, 9th Cavalry, quoted in Mooney, *Ghost Dance Religion*, p. 137.

9. *Ibid.*, p. 1.

10. *Ibid.*, p. vi.

11. Pratt's biography, *Pratt, the Red Man's Moses* (Norman, Oklahoma: University of Oklahoma Press, 1935), was written by a former teacher at Hampton,

Elaine Goodale Eastman, who married Charles Eastman, one of the major Pan-Indian figures.

12. *Annual Report of the United States Indian School at Carlisle, Pennsylvania, 1897*, p. 14.

13. *Annual Report, Commissioner of Indian Affairs, 1905*, p. 12.

14. *Annual Report, Carlisle, 1908*, pp. 19–20.

15. "Returned students" was a term used normally for dropouts, but occasionally to mean students who returned to the tribe after graduation.

16. *Annual Report, Carlisle, 1912*, pp. 84–85.

2—THE RED PROGRESSIVES

1. Charles A. Eastman, *The Indian Today* (Garden City, N.Y.: Doubleday, Page, 1915), p. 131.

2. Fayette A. McKenzie, *The American Indian in Relation to the White Population of the United States* (Columbus, Ohio: Fayette McKenzie, 1908), p. 93. Subsequent references to this book will be made in the text.

3. Manuscript in Arthur C. Parker Papers, New York State Museum, Albany. Cited hereafter as Parker Papers, NYSM.

4. In this period, Indians and their friends occasionally referred to the possibility of the emergence of a "race leader"; no doubt Booker T. Washington was the model.

5. An account of the organization of the temporary American Indian Association is given in *Report of the Executive Council on the Proceedings of the First Annual Conference of the Society of American Indians, 1912* (Washington, D.C.), p. 9–11. Cited hereafter as *First Proceedings*. This is the only *Proceedings* published separately. The call is in Parker Papers, NYSM.

6. Manuscript, Parker Papers, NYSM.

7. Ohiyesa—Charles A. Eastman, M.D., "First Impressions of Civilization," *Harper's Monthly Magazine* (November, 1904), 588.

8. Eastman, *The Indian Today*, pp. 109–10.

9. Several of Eastman's books are autobiographies or contain extensive autobiographical accounts. They include *Indian Boyhood* (New York: McClure, Philips & Co., 1902); *From the Deep Woods to Civilization* (Boston: Little, Brown & Co., 1916); *The Soul of the Indian* (Boston: Houghton Mifflin Co., 1911); *Indian Scout Talks* (Boston: Little, Brown & Co., 1914); *Indian Heroes and Great Chieftains* (Boston: Little Brown & Co., 1918).

10. Biographical information on Daganett in Records of the Bureau of Indian Affairs, Carlisle Indian Industrial School, Files 1324–33.

11. *First Proceedings*, p. 51.

12. Edward H. Spicer, *Cycles of Conquest: The Impact of Spain, Mexico, and the United States on the Indians of the Southwest, 1533–1960* (Tucson: The University of Arizona Press, 1962), p. 531.

13. Biographical information on Montezuma is contained in the *Quarterly Journal of the Society of American Indians*, I, 1 (1913), 50–53. Cited hereafter as *Quarterly Journal*. Eastman, *The Indian Today* and in *Who Was Who in America, 1897–1942*.

14. Coolidge's biography appears in *Who's Who in America, 1924–25; Quarterly*

Journal, III, 3 (1915), 220–23; Louise Seymour Houghton, *Our Debt to the Red Man* (Boston: Stratford, 1918), pp. 154–55. See also Sherman Coolidge to Arthur C. Parker, March 7, 1913, Parkers Papers, NYSM.

15. *Quarterly Journal,* I, 2 (1913), 130.

16. A biography of Sloan appears in the *American Indian Magazine,* VII (1919), 143. The article also includes information on Chase. Sloan's activities with the American Indian Federation are described in a letter with enclosure, John Collier to Oliver LaFarge, May 19, 1939, Office Files of Commissioner John Collier, Bund, German, Record Group No. 75. Further information on Sloan in a letter from Jane F. Smith, Acting Director, Social and Economic Records Division, General Services Administration, National Archives and Records Service, to Hazel W. Hertzberg, January 31, 1967. In the author's possession.

17. Biographical information on the Roe Clouds is contained in *The Indian Leader,* Haskell Institute, Lawrence, Kansas, September 8, 1933, p. 6, and February 24, 1950, p. 1; *The Indian Outlook,* Official Organ of the American Indian Institute (September, October, November, 1931), 7; Marion E. Gridley, ed., *Indians of Today* (Chicago: Towerton Press, 1960), p. 63.

18. Interview with William N. Fenton, Iroquois scholar and then Assistant Commissioner of the New York State Department of Education, January, 1966.

19. Arthur C. Parker to W. P. Campbell, Custodian of Oklahoma Historical Society, August 13, 1913, Parker Papers, NYSM.

20. Interview, William N. Fenton.

21. Arthur C. Parker, "Where Questions Are Answered," *Museum Service* (December, 1953), 163, quoted in W. Stephen Thomas, "Arthur Caswell Parker: 1881–1955, Anthropologist, Historian and Museum Pioneer," *Rochester History,* XVII, 3 (quarterly publication of the Rochester Public Library, July, 1955).

22. For a brief period prior to entering Dickinson, Parker was a "special student" at Centenary Collegiate Institute in Hackettstown, New Jersey, which he entered in the fall of 1899. The alumni records do not indicate how long he stayed. Some students left the Institute after the main building was destroyed by fire in October, 1899, and Parker may have been among them. Perhaps he transferred immediately to Dickinson, whose records indicate that he entered in 1899. At the time Parker was at Centenary, it was a coeducational institution. Information on this matter in a letter from Ernest H. Dalton, Dean of Instruction, Centenary College for Women, to William N. Fenton, June 6, 1969.

23. William N. Fenton, ed., *Parker on the Iroquois: Iroquois Uses of Maize and Other Food Plants; The Code of Handsome Lake, the Seneca Prophet; The Constitution of the Five Nations* (Syracuse: Syracuse University Press, 1968), p. 10.

24. Arthur C. Parker to Joseph Keppler, October 6, 1906, Keppler Papers, Museum of the American Indian Library, New York, cited hereafter as Keppler Papers, MAIL; and Arthur C. Parker to Joseph Keppler, October 27, 1906, Parker Papers, NYSM.

25. Fenton places this incident in the mid-thirties.

26. William N. Fenton, "The Present Status of Anthropology in Northeastern North America: A Review Article," *American Anthropologist,* 50 (1948), 507–10.

27. Arthur C. Parker to Rosa B. LaFlesche, November 27, 1911, Parker Papers, NYSM.

28. Besides the sources already referred to, other useful materials on Parker

include William A. Ritchie, "Arthur Caswell Parker—1881–1955," *American Antiquity*, XXI, 3 (1956), 293–95; W. Stephen Thomas, "Arthur Caswell Parker—Leader and Prophet of the Museum World," *Museum Service* (Bulletin of the Rochester Museum of Arts and Sciences), XXVIII, 2 (1955), 18–25; Preface by "F.H.S." to Parker, *The Life of General Ely S. Parker, Last Grand Sachem of the Iroquois*, XXIII (Buffalo: Historical Society Publications, 1919), vi–xi; *Who's Who in New York, 1938; Who's Who in America, 1948–49*. Information on Parker's career at Dickinson is contained in a letter from Patricia Miller, Registrar, to Hazel Hertzberg, October 5, 1967, in the author's possession.

3—A NEW BEGINNING

1. Arthur C. Parker to Joseph Keppler, November 5, 1911, Keppler Papers, MAIL.
2. *First Proceedings*, pp. 27–28.
3. *Ibid.*, p. 55.
4. McKenzie's report appeared in the *Red Man*, the Carlisle paper, and was carried in *First Proceedings*, pp. 171–77.
5. See *First Proceedings*, pp. 68–76, for Parker's paper.
6. *Ibid.*, pp. 76–80, contains the discussions of Parker's paper.
7. *Ibid.*, pp. 82–93, contain Mrs. Deitz's paper and the ensuing discussion.
8. Oskison's paper and the comments on it are in *ibid.*, pp. 100–110.
9. *Ibid.*, pp. 112–13.
10. *Ibid.*, p. 117.
11. *Ibid.*, p. 161.
12. Henry Standing Bear, a Sioux, was a Carlisle graduate who participated in a number of Pan-Indian movements throughout his life.
13. Arthur C. Parker to Joseph Keppler, November 5, 1911, Keppler Papers, MAIL.
14. *First Proceedings*, pp. 128–29.
15. Arthur C. Parker to Charles Daganett, December 22, 1911, Parker Papers, NYSM.
16. Matthew Sniffen to Arthur C. Parker, December 5, 1911, Parker Papers, NYSM.
17. Arthur C. Parker to Rosa B. LaFlesche, November 23, 1911, Parker Papers, NYSM.
18. Emma Johnson to Arthur C. Parker, November 20, 1911, Parker Papers, NYSM.
19. Arthur C. Parker to Emma Johnson, December 5, 1911, Parker Papers, NYSM.
20. *First Proceedings*, pp. 3–5.

4—RACE AND COUNTRY

1. An account of this meeting is carried in the *Quarterly Journal*, I, 2 (1913), 230–32.

2. The text of the provisional constitution is not available. The amended constitution as adopted by the 1912 conference, together with the debate on its adoption, is included in the 1912 conference proceedings, *Quarterly Journal,* I, 2 (1913). The text of the constitution is on pp. 223–29, and the debate on pp. 211–12, 146–49. I have assumed that the executive committee's constitution and the constitution as adopted by the next conference are the same except for the minor changes noted in the 1912 proceedings.

3. For membership lists, see *First Proceedings,* pp. 180–82.

4. Arthur C. Parker to Albert Hensley, April 2, 1912, Parker Papers, NYSM.

5. Arthur C. Parker to Joseph Keppler, June 4, 1912, Keppler Papers, MAIL.

6. The text of Gladden's speech is carried in the *Quarterly Journal,* I, 1 (1913), 13–19.

7. *Ibid.,* 18.

8. See *ibid.,* I, 2 (1913), 110–25, for Hill's speech.

9. *Ibid.,* 125.

10. *Ibid.,* 127.

11. *Ibid.,* 134–35.

12. *Ibid.,* 135.

13. *Ibid.,* 136.

14. *Ibid.,* 138.

15. *Ibid.,* 139.

16. The text of Roe Cloud's speech is in *ibid.,* 149–55.

17. *Ibid.,* 140–44.

18. *Ibid.,* 126.

19. *Ibid.,* 171.

20. *Ibid.,* 135–36.

21. *Ibid.,* 197–204.

22. This was probably a reference to the work of Charles Daganett of the Indian Bureau in getting off-reservation jobs for Indians.

23. *Quarterly Journal,* I, 2 (1913), 204–208.

24. *Ibid.,* 177–81, contains Abbott's remarks and the discussion that followed.

25. *Ibid.,* 183–85.

26. *Ibid.,* 218.

27. See *ibid.,* 220–21, for the debate over Daganett. It is difficult to evaluate Parker's estimate of "over 150" presumably active members present. The list of active members at the conference (45) given in the *Journal* is obviously incomplete, since more than this number voted on the question. The debate on this issue is not fully reported in the *Journal.*

28. In addition, an advisory board to perform "purely advisory" functions was elected with Henry Roe Cloud as chairman. A number of its members were graduates of Carlisle or Hampton or were at that time associated with these schools. The members, in addition to Roe Cloud, were: John M. Oskison, Mrs. Emma D. Goulette, Mrs. Marie L. Baldwin, Howard E. Gansworth, Mrs. Rosa B. LaFlesche, Dr. Roland Nichols, Mrs. Angela-Decora Dietz, Horton G. Elm, the Reverend Joseph K. Griffis, the Reverend Asa R. Hill, Charles D. Doxon, Oliver Lamere, Michael Wolfe, and the Honorable Charles D. Carter. See *Quarterly Journal,* I, 2 (1913), 222. Although its functions were honorary, the composition of the advisory board's membership throughout SAI's history indicates the elements in Indian life associated with the organization.

29. Arthur C. Parker to Carlos Montezuma, November 6, 1912, Parker Papers, NYSM.

30. The platform and resolutions of the conference appear in the *Quarterly Journal*, I, 1 (1913), pp. 71–74.

31. The question of continuing the board, an unpaid official body set up originally as part of President Grant's "peace policy" and functioning somewhat like a board of visitors, was then in controversy.

32. Arthur C. Parker to Joseph Keppler, June 12, 1912, Keppler Papers, MAIL. See also Marie Baldwin to Arthur C. Parker, November 18, 1913, Parker Papers, NYSM.

33. *Quarterly Journal*, I, 2 (1913), 214–15, gives Sloan's resolution and the discussion on it.

34. *Ibid.*, I, 3 (1913), 304–305.

35. J. N. B. Hewitt to Arthur C. Parker, September 11, 1912, Parker Papers, NYSM.

36. *Quarterly Journal*, I, 2 (1913), 204.

37. Arthur C. Parker to S. J. Nori, Carlisle Indian School, November 8, 1912, Parker Papers, NYSM.

38. Arthur C. Parker to William DuBois, September 1913, Parker Papers, NYSM.

39. *Quarterly Journal*, I, 1 (1913), 2–3.

40. *Ibid.*, 40, 3, 7.

41. These organizations are mentioned in a typed copy of an excerpt from *The Tomahawk* of April 10, 1913, published in White Earth, Minnesota, edited by Gus H. Beaulieu, a Chippewa. The copy is in the Parker Papers, NYSM.

42. *Quarterly Journal*, I, 1 (1913), 74.

43. See *ibid.*, 30–35, for Hewitt's article.

44. *Ibid.*, 47–49, contains Ignatius' speech.

45. Fayette McKenzie, "The American Indian of Today and Tomorrow," *The Journal of Race Development*, III, 2 (1912), reprinted in the *Quarterly Journal*, I, 4 (1913), 383–400.

46. "Report of the Legal Aid Committee," October 15, 1913, Parker Papers, NYSM.

5—THE CAMPAIGN FOR REFORMS

1. For a list of active members, see the *Quarterly Journal*, I, 2 (1913), 247–49.

2. Among the associates were Lyman Abbott of the *Outlook;* the writer Natalie Curtis; Edith Dabb of the YWCA; Superintendent Moses Friedman of Carlisle; Caroline Andrus and H. B. Frissell of Hampton; General Pratt; George Bird Grinnell; Frederick W. Hodge of the Smithsonian; Thomas Jesse Jones of the U.S. Bureau of Education; Secretary Carl Kelsey of the American Academy of Science; G. E. E. Lindquist of Haskell; Warren K. Morehead of the Board of Indian Commissioners; Thomas C. Moffett of the Home Missions Council; Edgar B. Merritt of the Indian Bureau; Robert Valentine and Francis F. E. Leupp, former Indian Commissioners; Professor Frederick W. Putnam of Harvard; Supervisor H. B. Peairs of Haskell; E. M. Wistor of the Indian Rights Association; Professor Frank Thilly of Cornell; and the Reverend G. W. Watermulder of the

Winnebago Indian Mission. A number of the associates were also active in the Lake Mohonk conferences. For a list of the associate members, see *ibid.*, 250–55.

3. The *Quarterly Journal* printed a number of speeches made at this conference and a summary of what transpired, but it no longer carried a partially verbatim account as in the case of the first two conferences.

4. For the roster of those attending the Denver conference, see *ibid.*, I, 4 (1913), 413–14.

5. *Ibid.*, 329.

6. *Ibid.*, 361–63, gives Lamere's speech.

7. *Ibid.*, II, 1 (1914), 23–32, contains McKenzie's speech.

8. See *ibid.*, 78, for Roman Nose's remarks.

9. This platform is in *ibid.*, I, 4 (1913), 411–12.

10. *Ibid.*, 405

11. *Ibid.*, II, 1 (1914), 58–59.

12. For Montezuma's speech, see *ibid.*, 69–74.

13. Frank G. Speck to Arthur C. Parker, February 19, 1914, Parker Papers, NYSM.

14. Arthur C. Parker to Frank G. Speck, February 25, 1914, Parker Papers, NYSM.

15. *Quarterly Journal*, II, 1 (1914), 64–68, carries Speck's undelivered speech.

16. *Ibid.*, II, 2 (1914), 97–99.

17. *Ibid.*, 99–101, contains the peyote article.

18. *Ibid.*, II, 3 (1914), 165–66.

19. For the roster of the Madison conference, see *ibid.*, II, 4 (1914), 319. It is almost certainly incomplete.

20. Quoted in *ibid.*, II, 3 (1914), 234, from a report by Caroline W. Andrus in *The Southern Workman*, the Hampton paper.

21. The Madison platform is given in the *Quarterly Journal*, II, 3 (1914), 229–30.

22. Arthur C. Parker to Chauncey Yellow Robe, October 26, 1914, Parker Papers, NYSM.

23. *Proceedings of the 32nd Annual Meeting of the Lake Mohonk Conference of Friends of the Indian and Other Dependent Peoples, 1914*, p. 7, cited hereafter as *Lake Mohonk Proceedings*. The platform consisted of "only those principles on which the members unanimously agreed," presumably including the Indian SAI members attending.

24. *Quarterly Journal*, II, 3 (1914), 174.

25. *Ibid.*, II, 4 (1914), 270–71, carries the text of the memorial to President Wilson.

26. James Mooney, who had been invited, did not attend because of ill health. He gave a rather lukewarm endorsement to the SAI: "Your organization seems to hold the promise of good for the Indian, if it can secure the cooperation of the intelligent fullblood leadership." James Mooney to Marie Baldwin, December 8, 1914, Parker Papers, NYSM.

27. *Quarterly Journal*, II, 4 (1914), 269–79.

28. *Ibid.*, 305–308, gives an account of James's ride and quotes endorsements from prominent citizens.

29. See *ibid.*, III, 1 (1915), 11–15, for Hunter's article.

30. *Ibid.*, III, 2 (1915), 86–97, gives Parker's article.

31. *Ibid.*, III, 3 (1915), 217.

32. J. N. B. Hewitt to Arthur C. Parker, September 27, 1915, Parker Papers, NYSM.

6—THE GROWTH OF FACTIONALISM

1. For a list of delegates, see the *Quarterly Journal*, III, 4 (1915), 313–15.

2. *Ibid.*, 281–82.

3. An extract appears in *ibid.*, IV, 1 (1916), 32–33.

4. Mrs. Baldwin was of Chippewa-French ancestry. Her father, J. B. Bottineau, was a lawyer—described as "the devoted champion of the Turtle Mountain Band of Chippewas"—a strong advocate of Indian education, and a Carlisle supporter. Mrs. Baldwin followed in her father's footsteps. She graduated from the Washington College of Law and was admitted to the Bar of the District of Columbia in 1914. For many years she was an expert accountant in the Education Division of the Indian Bureau. She was an ardent suffragist. For biographical details, see Houghton, *Our Debt to the Red Man*, pp. 170–73.

5. For the full platform see the *Quarterly Journal*, III, 4 (1915), 285–87.

6. *Ibid.*, 281–83.

7. Biographical details in Houghton, *Our Debt to the Red Man*, pp. 205–206, and Marion E. Gridley, ed., *Indians of Today* (Crawfordsville, Ind.: Lakeside Press, 1936), p. 19.

8. *Quarterly Journal*, III, 4 (1915), 322–25.

9. *American Indian Magazine*, IV, 2 (1916), 113.

10. Arthur C. Parker to General Pratt, April 25, 1916, Parker Papers, NYSM.

11. *American Indian Magazine*, IV, 1 (1916), 8–14, contains Parker's article.

12. *Ibid.*, 57.

13. See *ibid.* 2 (1916), 60–65, 118 for Parker's discussion of American Indian Day.

14. *Wassaja*, I, 1 (April, 1916).

15. *Ibid.*

16. *American Indian Magazine*, IV, 2 (1916), 171.

17. *Ibid.*, 112.

18. *Ibid.*, 114–15.

19. Seymour's article appears in *ibid.*, 160–63.

20. Gertrude Seymour to Arthur C. Parker, April 12, 1916, and Arthur C. Parker to Gertrude Seymour, April 22, 1916, Parker Papers, NYSM.

21. William A. Ritchie remarked to the author that Parker had told him that he himself had tried peyote, apparently to see what its effects would be. When Parker did so is unknown.

22. *American Indian Magazine*, IV, 3 (1916), 228.

23. *Ibid.*, 262.

24. *Ibid.*, 259–60.

25. A verbatim record of this debate is carried in *ibid.*, 252–56. The fact that the editor chose to present the debate verbatim attests to the importance of this question in the SAI.

26. *Ibid.*, 266.

27. *Ibid.*, 236.

28. *Ibid.*, 237.

29. *Ibid.*, 257–59, contains Lone Wolf's statements.
30. *Ibid.*, 238–44, carries Peairs' speech.
31. *Ibid.*, IV, 4 (1916), 310, gives Mrs. Bonnin's report.
32. Full text of the platform may be found in *ibid.*, IV, 3 (1916), 223–24.

7—THE EFFECTS OF WORLD WAR I

1. Parker's article appears on pp. 285–304 of the *American Indian Magazine,* IV, 4 (1916).
2. Mrs. Brown, who was a friend of the Coolidges, made an impassioned and highly romantic speech at the SAI's Lawrence conference, in which she pronounced civilization a failure and called for the United States to return to the "Golden Age" of aboriginal America.
3. Arthur C. Parker to Sherman Coolidge, March 7, 1917, Parker Papers, NYSM.
4. Arthur C. Parker to Gertrude Bonnin, March 12, 1917, Parker Papers, NYSM.
5. *American Indian Magazine,* V, 1 (1917), 13.
6. *Ibid.*, 5–11.
7. Gertrude Bonnin to Arthur C. Parker, November 29, 1917, Parker Papers, NYSM.
8. *American Indian Magazine,* V, 1 (1917), 152.
9. Gertrude Bonnin to Arthur C. Parker, June 28, 1916, Parker Papers, NYSM.
10. *American Indian Magazine,* V, 2 (1917), 129.
11. *Ibid.*, V, 3 (1917), 137–38.
12. Arthur C. Parker to Sherman Coolidge, October 2, 1917, Parker Papers, NYSM.
13. *American Indian Magazine,* VI, 1 (1918), 28–29.
14. Arthur C. Parker to Gertrude Bonnin, February 12, 1918, Parker Papers, NYSM.
15. Arthur C. Parker to Walter Kennedy, August 5, 1918, Parker Papers, NYSM.
16. *Wassaja,* III, 4 (1918) and III, 5 (1918).
17. See *American Indian Magazine,* VI, 3 (1918), 138–40, for the platform and resolutions of the Pierre conference.
18. Thomas Moffett and Matthew Sniffen to Arthur C. Parker, September 28, 1918, Parker Papers, NYSM.
19. *Ibid.; American Indian Magazine,* VI, 3 (1918), 125.
20. Gertrude Bonnin to Arthur C. Parker, October 3, 1918, Parker Papers, NYSM.
21. Gertrude Bonnin to Arthur C. Parker, October 25, 1918, Parker Papers, NYSM.

8—TRANSITION IN THE TWENTIES

1. *American Indian Magazine,* VI, 4 (1919), 161–62.
2. *Ibid.*, 181–83.

3. *Ibid.*, 196–97.

4. Ben Brave, whose father was a cousin of Sitting Bull, attended Hampton, becoming a teacher and finally a missionary. Margaret Frazier was a nurse. I have been unable to find further information about Tinker.

5. *American Indian Magazine*, VII, 2 (1919), 62–63.

6. *Wassaja*, IV, 2 (1919) and IV, 1 (1919).

7. The article is carried in the *American Indian Magazine*, VII, 2 (1919), 82–87.

8. *Ibid.*, 98.

9. A copy of the call to the conference, dated August 21, 1919, is in Parker Papers, NYSM.

10. Arthur C. Parker to Thomas Moffett, July, 1919, Parker Papers, NYSM.

11. *American Indian Magazine*, VII, 3 (1919), 145–52, carries Eastman's address.

12. *Ibid.*, 152–53.

13. *Ibid.*, 161.

14. *Ibid.*, 162. A bill conferring citizenship on all Indians serving in the armed forces who desired it became law on November 6, 1919.

15. Carl's tribe is not specified in the account of the proceedings.

16. A list of advisory board members appears on the SAI stationery. See Thomas L. Bishop to Arthur C. Parker, March 13, 1920, Parker Papers, NYSM.

17. James Irving to Arthur C. Parker, January 14, 1920, Parker Papers, NYSM.

18. Arthur C. Parker to James Irving, January 22, 1920, Parker Papers, NYSM. Senator Curtis had been a member of the SAI, according to Houghton, *Our Debt to the Red Man*, p. 172.

19. Arthur C. Parker to James Irving, February 20, 1920, Parker Papers, NYSM.

20. Thomas G. Bishop to Arthur C. Parker, March 13, 1920, Parker Papers, NYSM.

21. For Mrs. Rinehart's article, see *American Indian Magazine*, VII, 4 (1920), 3–5.

22. *Ibid.*, inside front cover.

23. *Ibid.*, 30.

24. *American Indian Tepee*, II, 2 (1921), 13–16, and II, 3 (1921), 12–16, carry accounts of the conference.

25. *Ibid.*, II, 3 (1921), 1.

26. Arthur C. Parker to Charles Daganett, October 13, 1921, Parker Papers, NYSM.

27. *American Indian Tepee*, II, 4 (1921–22), 4–5; also, Captain R. D. Parker to Arthur C. Parker, n.d., Parker Papers, NYSM.

28. "America the Melting Pot of Nationalities," typescript, Parker Papers, NYSM. The paper was given on January 18, 1922.

29. *American Indian Magazine*, IV, 4 (1916), 304.

30. M. Austine Stanley to Arthur C. Parker, June 13, 1923, Parker Papers, NYSM.

31. *American Indian Tepee*, V, 1 (1923), 21.

32. Arthur C. Parker to M. Austine Stanley, August 6, 1923, Parker Papers, NYSM.

33. Madison was president of a local Pan-Indian group, the Indians of Greater

Kansas City, organized in 1921. It was a nonpolitical, nonreligious organization composed of about 250 Indians living in the city. The group encouraged Indians to leave the reservation and migrate to the city. In 1921 and 1922, Madison was also associate editor of the *American Indian Tepee* and its successor. *American Indian Tepee*, II, 4 (1921–22), and *American Indian Advocate*, III, 1 (1922).

34. Accounts of the conference are carried in the September 23, 25, and 27–30 issues of the *Chicago Tribune*, 1923. The stationery of convention lists sponsors and committees. See Anne Fitzgerald to Arthur C. Parker, August 25, 1923, Parker Papers, NYSM.

35. See *Indian Rights Association 39th Annual Report*, pp. 41–44, and *40th Annual Report*, pp. 15–19, for an account of the Fall controversy.

36. *IRA 41st Annual Report*, pp. 26–27.

37. This number includes archaeologists. It also includes men like George Heye, the founder of the Museum of the American Indian. Franz Boas was not invited, though he was one of the most important anthropologists in America. The membership of the committee is given in Herbert W. Work, *Indian Policies* (Washington, D.C.: Government Printing Office, 1924), which contains an account of the meeting.

38. See Parker's explanatory letter in IRA *41st Annual Report*, pp. 45–46.

39. *Southern Workman*, LIII, 3 (1924), 96b–99.

40. Lewis Meriam, *The Problem of Indian Administration* (Baltimore: Johns Hopkins, 1928).

41. The debate between Mrs. Seymour and Miss Austin is carried in *Forum*, LXXI, 3 (1924), 273–88, while letters commenting on it are in LXXI, 4, 551–58; LXXI, 9, 420; and LXXI, 10, 711–14.

42. M. K. Sniffen to Arthur C. Parker, March 10, 1925, Parker Papers, NYSM.

43. Jennings C. Wise, *The Red Man in the New World Drama* (Washington, D.C.: W. F. Roberts, 1931), p. 574.

44. I am indebted for this information to the anthropologist Donald Collier, John Collier's son. The American Indian Defense Committee *Bulletin* also occasionally carried news of the National Council.

45. *Indian Newsletter*, No. 5, July 10, 1930.

9—INDIANS IN THE CITIES

1. *Tepee, teepee,* and *tipi* were used interchangeably as spellings. To avoid confusion, *tepee* is used in this chapter.

2. The purpose and rules of the Order are set forth in a mimeographed document entitled "Tepee Order of America founded by Red Fox James—Blackfoot Indian" (n.d. but probably 1915), Parker Papers, NYSM.

3. Besides the names mentioned here, he also called himself the Reverend Barnabas Skiuhushu and the Reverend Dr. Barnabas, Ph.D., Arch-Herio-Monk. See, for example, a letter using the latter signature in the *American Indian Magazine* (Oklahoma), V, 3 (1931), 4. According to St. James, "Barnabas" was the name by which he was "known by the members" of "The Holy Orthodox Eastern Church under the Seven Ecumenical Council," in flyer, "Dr. Skiuhushu—Ethnologist" (n.d. but post-1930), Museum of the American Indian Library. To minimize confusion, he will be referred to hereafter as St. James.

4. Francis Fox James to the Honorable Commissioner Sells, July 24, 1913, National Archives, Record Group No. 75, File No. 90513-13-120, General Services.

5. *Quarterly Journal*, II, 2 (1914), 163–64.

6. *Ibid.*, II, 4 (1914), 305–308.

7. *American Indian Tipi*, V, 1 (1923), 23.

8. Biographical data on St. James comes from several sources, the most important of which is the Tepee Order–American Indian Association publication whose name was often altered. See *American Indian Teepee*, III, 2 (1925), 15; and *American Indian Tipi*, V, 1(1923), 23. A letter to Arthur C. Parker on January 20, 1923, Parker Papers, NYSM, from Little Bear Holt, Jr., an associate of St. James, gives further details. Several letters in the files of the Indian Bureau give biographical information: Francis James to the Honorable James B. Adams, June 23, 1911; Francis Fox James to Commissioner Cato Sells, July 24, 1913. The reliability of the sources is somewhat open to question.

9. The name of the publication, characteristically, was changed or modified frequently, while its volume numbers were sometimes confused, irregular, or nonexistent. Names include: *American Indian Tipi; American Indian Tepee; American Indian Teepee; American Indian Advocate; Indian Tepee.*

10. For a description of the IORM, see Arthur Preuss, *A Dictionary of Secret and Other Societies* (St. Louis, Mo.: B. Herder Book Co., 1924), pp. 180–82, and C. W. Ferguson, *Fifty Million Brothers* (New York: Farrar & Rinehart, 1937), pp. 356–57. In the early twenties, the IORM had over half a million members.

11. *Quarterly Journal*, III, 1 (1915), 16.

12. *American Indian Magazine* (Oklahoma), V, 3 (1929), 4.

13. See, for instance, the *American Indian Tepee*, I, 3 (1920), 31, which reports a State of Washington Council Meeting of the Tepee Order in which forty-nine candidates, "mostly members of the I.O.R.M." were installed, with a Head Chief who was also Great Sachem of the Red Men of Washington.

14. *American Indian Tepee*, II, 1 (1921), 6.

15. *American Indian Tipi*, V, 2 (1923), 3.

16. *Ibid.*, 3.

17. *Ibid.*, 2.

18. Little Bear Holt, Jr., to Arthur C. Parker (n.d. but probably 1923), Parker Papers, NYSM.

19. *American Indian Advocate*, III, 1 (1922), 13.

20. Charles Merz, *The Great American Band Wagon* (New York: Literary Guild of America, 1928), p. 36. Merz's chapter on secret fraternal orders, called "Sweet Land of Secrecy," is informative, amusing, and affectionate.

21. *American Indian Tepee*, I, 3 (1920), and *American Indian Advocate*, III, 1 (1922), 4.

22. *American Indian Tepee* (no volume number), Autumn, 1920.

23. *American Indian Advocate*, IV, 4 (1922), 4.

24. *American Indian Tepee*, V, 2 (1923), 3.

25. *American Indian Advocate*, IV, 4 (1922), 3–4, and V, 2 (1923), 2–6.

26. *American Indian Teepee*, VII, 2 (1925), 16.

27. *American Indian Tipi*, V, 3 (1923).

28. *American Indian Tepee*, II, 2 (1921), 4.

29. *Ibid.*, VI, 2 (1924), 6.

30. *Ibid.*, 5.

31. *Ibid.*, VIII, 5 (1926), 16.

32. *Ibid.*, VII, 2 (1925), 8.

33. *Ibid.*, 6–7. The term "Atlantean race" was at one time used to describe both the inhabitants of the Western Highlands of Scotland and more generally a variety of Western European man. See J. W. Jackson, "The Atlantean Race of Western Europe," *Anthropological Institute Journal* (London), II, 3 (June, 1873), 397–402.

34. *American Indian Tepee*, VIII, 1 (1926), 4.

35. *A Little Information on Short History American Indians and Indian Nature Free-Masonry*, second edition (n.p., 1925). Parker's articles on Indian Free-masonry were widely reprinted in Indian publications in this period.

36. *American Indian Tepee*, V, 3 (1923), 2.

37. At this time, Strong Wolf was chief editor of the magaine. He later became Executive Head Chief of the order and was active in its affairs for most of its existence. Strong Wolf was a "full-blood" Chippewa who claimed that he had attended Carlisle. However, his name does not appear in the school archives. He was a World War I veteran and had been "a student in anthropology at the University of Pennsylvania." He frequently urged his readers to study anthropology so that discussion of the Indian past could be founded on fact rather than fancy. Strong Wolf was also a member of the Boy Scouts and a lecturer and speaker. He thus combined many of the characteristics familiar in earlier SAI members. Biographical details in *ibid.*, VIII, 4 (1926), 16. For Strong Wolf's views on anthropology see, for example, *ibid.*, VI, 1 (1924), 4–5.

38. *Ibid.*, VI, 2 (1924), 4.

39. A. W. Cash to Arthur C. Parker, October 27, 1923, Parker Papers, NYSM.

40. New York *Times*, February 6, 1927; *American Indian Tepee*, IX, 1 (1927).

41. *American Indian Tepee*, IX, 1 (1927), 2.

42. *Ibid.*, IX–X, 5, 1 (1927–28 [combined issue]), 3.

43. U.S. Department of the Interior, *Biographical and Historical Index of American Indians and Persons Involved in Indian Affairs*, VI (Boston: G. K. Hall, 1966), 233. Cited hereafter as *Biographical Index*.

44. Manifesto of Indian Association of America, "In the Great Spirit We Trust" (n.d. but probably early 1930's), Parker Papers, NYSM.

45. *American Indian Tipi*, V, 1 (1923), 23.

46. The life of the Princess was strikingly similar to many other Pan-Indians. She had somehow become separated from her family as a child and knew only that she was a Cheyenne. She claimed to have attended Carlisle, but her name does not appear in the records. She later became a teacher in New York City. Although referred to as a "full-blood," she was, of course, quite unsure as to whether this claim was based on fact. Her title of "Princess" was unknown either among the Cheyenne or any other Indian tribe but was a favorite among Indian women who had become separated from their tribal origins. When she was past sixty, the Princess undertook an unsuccessful pilgrimage to the Cheyenne Tongue River Reservation to attempt to learn more about her origins. Princess Chinquilla spent many years teaching Indian art and was active in numerous Indian causes. At the time that the American Indian Association decided to bar whites as national officers, she was a national officer of the group. Biographical details in *The American Red Man*, I, 1 (1929), 18–19.

47. *American Indian Tepee*, IX, 1 (1927), 2–3.

48. *Biographical Index*, VI, 235.

49. Miller later became Sachem of the Confederation. Program of the Indian Confederation of America, September 30, 1934, Museum of American Indian Library.

50. Indian Confederation of America, Program of Annual Pow-Wow, 1938, Museum of American Indian Library.

51. Souvenir programs of annual powwows, 1937, 1938, Museum of American Indian Library.

52. For a description of the work of the Confederation, see Fairfax Downey, "The Redskin's Return to Manhattan," *This Week* (Sunday Magazine section, New York *Herald Tribune*), June 11, 1939.

53. New York *Times*, September 9, 1936.

54. *Ibid.*, September 26, 1937. Emerson was probably white. *American Indian Tepee*, IX, 2 (1927), 4, in reporting that Emerson took the "Brave" degree of the Order, does not identify him as Indian, though others are so identified.

55. A. W. Cash to Arthur C. Parker, two letters (n.d. but probably 1923), Parker Papers, NYSM.

56. *American Indian Magazine* (Oklahoma), I, 5 (1927), 7.

57. Around 1925, Cayou went to Homing, Oklahoma, where he was active in the affairs of the Native American Church. He served as treasurer of the Indian Protective Association of America in the early thirties. See *Biographical Index*, VI, 234. The president of the latter organization was also a Pan-Indian: Joshua Wetsit (Assiniboine) who had been vice-president of Gertrude Bonnin's National Council of American Indians. In the thirties, Cayou was also vice-president of the Native American Church in Oklahoma, and attempted unsuccessfully to obtain a national charter from Congress for the church. Weston La Barre, *The Peyote Cult* (Hamden, Conn.: Shoestring Press, 1964), p. 171.

58. Marion E. Gridley, *Indians of Today* (1936), p. 98.

59. *American Indian Magazine* (Oklahoma), III, 7 (1929), 4.

60. "Memorial of the Grand Council Fire of American Indians," U.S. *Congressional Record*, 70th Cong., 1st Sess., May 11, 1928.

61. "Report of work of the Indian Council Fire 1934–1935," mimeographed, Museum of the American Indian Library.

62. Meriam, *Problem of Indian Administration*, pp. 720–22.

63. *Ibid.*, pp. 722–23.

64. *Ibid.*, p. 723.

65. *Indian Truth*, IV, 1 (1927), 467.

66. *Indian Tepee*, IV, 11 (1922), 4.

10—THE PEYOTE CULT

1. "(From the Aztec Peyotl) a small, spineless, carrot-shaped cactus, *Lophophora williamsii* Lemaire, which grows wild in the Rio Grande Valley and southward. It is mostly subterranean, and only the grayish-green pincushion-like top appears above ground, with spiral radial grooves dividing the puffy prominences which bear lineally spaced tufts of fine gray-white flocculence, somewhat like artists' camels-hair point brushes. Cut off horizontally about ground level, and dried into a hard woody disc, this top becomes the so-called 'peyote button'—often

called 'mescal button,' confusingly since it does not come from the non-cactus succulent, the mescal proper, from whose fermented sap, pulque, the brandy mescal is distilled; also, erroneously, called 'mescal bean' which is the Red Bean, *Sophora secundiflora* (ortega) Lag. ex DC; and further, once quite mistakenly identified with Aztec narcotic mushroom *teonanacatl*, a Basidiomycete, a true member of the Fungi. Nine psychotropic alkaloids, an unusual number even for a cactus, are contained in natural pan-peyotl: some of these are strychnine-like pharmacodynamically, others (notably mescaline) hallucinogenic." La Barre, *Peyote Cult*, p. 195.

2. M. E. Opler, "The Influence of Aboriginal Patterns and White Contact on a Recently Introduced Ceremony, The Mescalero Peyote Rite," *Journal of American Folklore*, XLIX (1938), 166.

3. Charles S. Brant, "Peyotism Among the Kiowa-Apache and Neighboring Tribes," *Southwest Journal of Anthropology*, VI, 2 (1960), 212; and La Barre, *Peyote Cult*, p. 113.

The sources on the nature of the Christian influence in the peyote religion are largely anthropological. Those anthropologists who have discussed this question tend to be more interested in Christian influence on rituals and ceremonial objects than in the specifically Christian aspects of peyote doctrine. There are bits and pieces of references to Jesus, recognizably Christian phrases in peyote songs, and some rather sketchy accounts of how specific tribes incorporated Christian doctrine into peyote doctrine. The specific incidents or evidence cited are quite varied, reflecting the influence of varying Protestant denominations plus Roman Catholicism in a few instances. Since the sources are frequently vague as to time, it is often difficult to tell just when a peyotist or a Christian belief was held by a particular tribe or by a particular tendency in the religion. See LaBarre, *Peyote Cult*, Appendix B.

4. Ruth Shonle, "Peyote, The Giver of Visions," *American Anthropologist*, XXVII (1925), 57.

5. James Mooney, *Ghost-Dance Religion*, p. 159.

6. Subsequent attempts to reenact it in 1909 and in 1927 also failed.

7. C. S. Simmons, "The Peyote Road" (manuscript), quoted in La Barre, *Peyote Cult*, p. 166.

8. Zoe A. Tilghman, *Quanah The Eagle of the Comanches* (Oklahoma City: Harlow, 1938), p. 189. Quanah's biography was writtten by the wife of a white friend, William Tilghman, who had been hunting near Adobe Walls at the time of the battle and later became a friend of Parker's.

9. Biographical details on Parker are drawn from the following sources in addition to those already cited: La Barre, *Peyote Cult;* short biography by James Mooney (a friend of Parker's) in Frederick W. Hodge, ed., *Handbook of American Indians*, Vol. II, Bureau of American Ethnology Bulletin 30 (Washington, D.C.: Government Printing Office, 1912), p. 204; Angie Debo, "Quanah Parker," *American Heritage*, IV, 4 (Summer, 1953), 30–31; *Indian Leader*, XXXIII, 37 (1930), 5–6; Francis Leupp "A Great Comanche Chief," obituary in New York *Evening Post*, February 25, 1911. Leupp states that Parker "even joined a Christian Church in his later years," but Tilghman denies this, and it is unlikely.

10. Vincent Petrullo, *The Diabolic Root* (Philadelphia: University of Pennsylvania Press, 1934), p. 82.

11. *Ibid.*, p. 82.

12. *Ibid.*, p. 83.

13. Elk Hair, a prominent Delaware peyotist leader, believed, "The Christian way of worshipping is good and Peyote is good, but the two should not be mixed. Mixing the ways of worship is bad, and Elk Hair told Wilson that. They were mixing the white man's way with the Indian way. Elk Hair preferred the Comanche way because it was the pure Indian way: it was the true Peyote way." Petrullo quoted a statement by Joe Washington, Elk Hair's nephew, in *ibid.*, p. 43.

14. Mooney, *Ghost-Dance Religion*, p. 161.

15. Frank Speck, "Notes on the Life of John Wilson, the Revealer of Peyote, as recalled by his nephew, George Anderson," *General Magazine and Historical Chronicle*, XXXV (1933), 539–56, quoted in La Barre, *Peyote Cult*, p. 160.

16. Petrullo, *Diabolic Root*, p. 85.

17. Speck, "Notes on the Life of John Wilson," quoted in La Barre, *Peyote Cult*, p. 160.

18. James Sydney Slotkin, *The Peyote Religion* (Glencoe, Ill.: Free Press, 1956), pp. 127–28.

19. *Ibid.*, pp. 36–40.

20. For biographical details, see *ibid.*, p. 80; Paul Radin, *The Winnebago Tribe*, *37th Annual Report, Bureau of American Ethnology* (1915–1916) (Washington, D.C.: Government Printing Office, 1923), pp. 389–91, 394, 419, 423, 425–26; La Barre, *Peyote Cult*, p. 121. See also a statement by Rave's brother Harry Rave, October 11, 1911, U.S. Congress, Senate Subcommittee on Indian Affairs, *Hearings, Survey of Conditions of the Indians in the United States*, 1937, Part 34, p. 18264. Cited hereafter as U.S. Congress, *Survey*, 1937.

21. Wesley R. Hurt, Jr., "Factors in the Persistence of Peyote in the Northern Plains," *Plains Anthropologist*, V, 9 (May, 1960), 17.

22. For biographical details on Hensley, see his autobiography written in his own hand to Miss Mollie V. Garther, superintendent of the Springfield Indian School in South Dakota where Hensley sent his daughter. Mollie V. Garther to Superintendent O. H. Lipps, February 25, 1916, in Records of the Bureau of Indian Affairs, File No. 44674-32-820. See also, Radin, *Winnebago Tribe*, pp. 397–98, 394–95, 421–22.

23. Radin, *Winnebago Tribe*, p. 389.

24. *Ibid.*, pp. 395–96.

25. For biographical details, see Chapter 5.

26. Radin, *Winnebago Tribe*, pp. 395–396.

27. Emma H. Blair, ed., *Indian Tribes of the Upper Mississippi Valley*, II (Cleveland: Arthur H. Clark, 1911), 282.

28. John Semans, Affidavit, October 11, 1911, U.S. Congress, *Survey*, 1937, 18262.

29. Thomas E. Roddy of Winnebago, Nebraska, to E. H. Blair, April 15, 1909, Blair, *Indian Tribes*, II, 282–83.

30. Superintendent Albert K. Kneale to Robert W. Hall, November 28, 1911, U.S. Congress, *Survey*, 1937, pp. 18272–74.

31. Melvin Gilmore, "Ethnobotany of Omaha Indians," *Collections of the Nebraska State Historical Society*, XVII (1913), 318–19.

32. A petition using this name was sent to Commissioner Cato Sells in 1915. Records of the Bureau of Indian Affairs, File No. 2989-08-126.

33. Slotkin, *Peyote Religion*, p. 79.

34. John Semans, Affidavit, October 11, 1911, U.S. Congress, *Survey*, 1937, 18263.

35. La Barre, *Peyote Cult*, p. 167.

36. Slotkin, *Peyote Religion*, p. 119.

37. *Ibid.*, p. 79. The date of Koshiway's innovations is not known but it can hardly have been much before the end of the first decade of the twentieth century, since Koshiway was born in 1886 and was therefore twenty-four years old in 1910.

38. La Barre, *Peyote Cult*, p. 167.

39. *Ibid.*, p. 168.

40. Weston La Barre, David P. McAllester, J. S. Slotkin, Omer Stewart, and Sol Tax, "Statement on Peyote," *Science*, CXIV (1951), 582–83. The anthropologists add, "A scientific interpretation might be that the chemicals in peyote diminish extraneous internal and external sensations, thus permitting the individual to concentrate his attention on his ideas of God and, at the same time, affecting vision and hearing so that these ideas are easily projected into visions."

41. For a full description see, La Barre, *Peyote Cult*, pp. 57–92.

42. *Annual Report, Commissioner of Indian Affairs*, 1909, p. 14.

43. Johnson later worked for the Anti-Saloon League.

44. Slotkin, *Peyote Religion*, p. 126.

45. Mrs. Delavan L. Pierson, "American Indian Peyote Worship," *Missionary Review of the World*, XXXVIII (1915), 201–206.

46. The estimate of 12,000 adherents was made by James Mooney. U.S. Congress, House Subcommittee on Indian Affairs, *Hearings, Peyote*, 1918, Part 1, p. 111. Cited hereafter as U.S. Congress, *Peyote*, 1918. The states covered are given in a 1919 Bureau of Indian Affairs survey in Robert E. L. Newberne, *Peyote an Abridged Compilation from the Files of the Bureau of Indian Affairs* (Washington, D.C.: Government Printing Office, 1922), pp. 35–36.

47. U.S. Congress, *Peyote*, 1918, pp. 88–89.

48. For Hall's and Angier's statements, see *ibid.*, pp. 28–31.

49. The Hall-Angier experiment raises a question which has recurred frequently in the argument over the effects of peyote: Is it a harmful and habit-forming drug? Evidence pro and con has been presented frequently. The evidence was summarized in 1961 in a special issue of *Indian Affairs*, the bulletin of the Association on American Indian Affairs, No. 41A: "In summary, a review of the medical properties of peyote and their effects leads mainly to negative evidence. Peyote is not a cure-all. It is not a narcotic under the usual definitions of being a soporific or habit forming. Peyote does, through the element of mescaline, significantly, although only temporarily, alter human perceptions and mental processes.

"Here we must make a reservation; any drug having such powerful psychic effects may effect the long-term habitual user, or one who takes it to excess, in some manner, possibly harmfully. On this as yet we lack adequate information, and we must await medical and anthropological studies over extended periods of time to make clear what, if any, dangers of this kind may exist under ceremonial control and the current social conditions of Indians." The statement was adopted by the Board of Directors of the Association on American Indian Affairs, Inc., April 18, 1961.

50. *Lake Mohonk Proceedings*, pp. 68–76.

51. *Ibid.*, pp. 68–76.
52. *Ibid.*, p. 8.
53. Slotkin, *Peyote Religion*, p. 53.
54. Newberne, *Peyote*, p. 18.
55. *American Indian Magazine*, IV, 4 (1916), 345–46.
56. Newberne, *Peyote*, p. 24.
57. U.S. Congress, *Peyote*, 1918, p. 22.
58. Slotkin, *Peyote Religion*, p. 56.
59. Newberne, *Peyote*, pp. 20–23.

11—THE NATIVE AMERICAN CHURCH

1. U.S. Congress, *Peyote*, 1918, pp. 22–25.
2. *Ibid.*, pp. 51–55.
3. It should be noted that the man who introduced peyote on this reservation had many critics among the peyotists themselves. See Omer Stewart, *Washo-Northern Paiute Peyotism: A Study in Acculturation* (University of California Publications in American Archaeology and Ethnology, XL, 3. Berkeley: University of California Press, 1944), pp. 4–5.
4. U.S. Congress, *Peyote*, 1918, pp. 15–20.
5. *Ibid.*, pp. 141–45.
6. *Ibid.*, p. 146.
7. Mrs. Bonnin offered in evidence an instance of sexual intercourse taking place just outside a peyote meeting which was sworn to in an affidavit by a peyotist witness.
8. "Cactus Pete" was a "full-blood" Sioux from Pine Ridge Agency. He was listed on the tribal roll as Sam Lone Bear and had a number of other names as well. Probably this is the same man referred to in Brosius' testimony. David F. Aberle and Omer Stewart, *Navaho and Ute Peyotism* (University of Colorado Studies, Series in Anthropology, No. 6. Boulder: University of Colorado Press, 1957), p. 13.
9. U.S. Congress, *Peyote*, 1918, pp. 123–31.
10. *Ibid.*, pp. 139–41.
11. *Ibid.*, pp. 136–37, 120–23.
12. U.S. Congress, *Survey*, 1937, pp. 18281, 18282, 18284, 18278.
13. U.S. Congress, *Peyote*, 1918, pp. 26–28, 48–51, 126–31, 189.
14. *Ibid.*, pp. 60–74, 77–79, 88–94, 107–13, 145–47.
15. *Ibid.*, pp. 74–77.
16. *Ibid.*, pp. 113–20, 137–38.
17. William E. Safford, "An Aztec Narcotic," *Journal of Heredity*, VI (1915), 291–311.
18. U.S. Congress, *Peyote*, 1918, pp. 186–89.
19. *Ibid.*, pp. 79–80.
20. *Ibid.*, pp. 82–84.
21. *Ibid.*, pp. 182–88.
22. *Ibid.*, pp. 191–92.
23. Cleaver Warden to James Mooney, February 25, 1918, in *ibid.*, pp. 106–107.
24. *Ibid.*

25. *Ibid.*, pp. 172–81. Piawo's name was also spelled Wilber **Peawa**.

26. *Ibid.*, pp. 149–59.

27. *Ibid.*, pp. 170–71.

28. *Ibid.*, pp. 104–106, 111.

29. James Mooney to Mrs. Julia Brent Prentiss, July 29, 1918, quoted in Slotkin, *Peyote Religion*, p. 136.

30. Jonathan Koshiway and a few other leaders had gone to a white lawyer for advice on how to defend their religion. The lawyer had helped them write up articles of incorporation, and the group was chartered in Oklahoma as "The First Born Church of Christ" in December, 1914. Slotkin, *Peyote Religion*, pp. 135–36.

31. H. G. Barnett, *Indian Shakers* (Carbondale, Ill.: Southern Illinois University Press, 1957), pp. 110–12.

32. La Barre, *Peyote Cult*, p. 169.

33. Articles of Incorporation, Native American Church (Oklahoma). Filed October 10, 1918.

34. *American Indian Magazine* (Oklahoma), I, 12 (1926), 13. Pratt died in 1924. It should be noted that Pipestem and Dailey, "had been away to school and were considerably influenced by white Protestantism," in La Barre, *Peyote Cult*, p. 167. The names of the schools attended are not given. McDonald also sent his two daughters to Carlisle.

35. La Barre, *Peyote Cult*, p. 171.

36. Slotkin, *Peyote Religion*, p. 55.

37. *Annual Report, Indian Rights Association*, 1919, p. 54.

38. Slotkin, *Peyote Religion*, p. 56; La Barre, *Peyote Cult*, p. 224.

39. *Annual Report, Indian Rights Association*, 1922, p. 38.

40. E. B. Merritt in U.S. Congress, House Committee on Appropriations, 1928, quoted in Slotkin, *Peyote Religion*, p. 131.

41. Meriam, *The Problem of Indian Administration*, p. 628.

42. *Ibid.*, p. 272.

43. Articles of Incorporation, The Peyote Church of Christ (Nebraska). Filed June 29, 1921. Perhaps the statement that wine was forbidden to Indians referred to the prohibition against alcohol on the reservation.

44. Amended Articles of Incorporation, Native American Church (Nebraska). Filed June 29, 1922.

45. A letter from Fred Grant, secretary of the "Omaha Peyote Historical Society Church," to the Commissioner of Indian Affairs, September 1, 1932, lists the anthropologist Francis LaFlesche as treasurer of the group. Records of the Bureau of Indian Affairs, File No. 44674-32-820.

46. Articles of Incorporation: Native Americans' of Allen, South Dakota. Filed September 30, 1922; Native American Church of St. Charles, South Dakota. Filed February 18, 1924; Native American Church of Rosebud, South Dakota. Filed June 28, 1924.

47. Amended Articles of Incorporation, Native American Church of South Dakota. Filed November 10, 1924. Another Native American Church of Washabaugh County was chartered in 1928, quoted in Slotkin, *Peyote Religion*, p. 61.

48. Articles of Incorporation, Native American Church (North Dakota). Filed September 20, 1923.

49. Articles of Incorporation, Native American Church (Idaho). Filed March 24, 1925.

50. Robert L. Bee, "Potawatomi Peyotism: The Influence of Traditional

Patterns," *Southwest Journal of Anthropology*, XXII, 2 (Summer, 1966), 195–96.

51. Articles of Incorporation, Native American Church (Montana). Filed March 24, 1925.

52. Slotkin lists the names and incorporation dates of the Native American Church in *Peyote Religion*, pp. 60–61. The Articles of Incorporation were obtained for all of these with the exception of the NAC of Washabaugh County, South Dakota, 1928. A further exception is the Kansas Church, not listed in Slotkin, but cited by Bee. One other organization, the "Native American Lodge" of Colorado, incorporated June 21, 1926, is also cited by Slotkin. However, the Articles of Incorporation identify it as a secret social and fraternal organization, providing sick and death benefits for its members. Indians are nowhere mentioned. Its incorporators all have "Spanish" names which may or may not mean that they were Indians. Neither its purposes nor organizational format reveal similarities to the peyote churches. For these reasons, it is omitted.

53. La Barre, *Peyote Cult*, p. 171.

54. Edward Curtis, *The North American Indian*, XIX (published by the author; Norwood, Mass.: Plimpton Press, 1930), p. 202.

55. *The American Indian* (Oklahoma), V, 1 (November, 1930), 13. Bruner was later a leader of the Pan-Indian "American Indian Federation," the only national Indian group to oppose the Collier policy in the thirties.

56. *Ibid.*, I, 8 (1926), and III, 7 (1928).

57. Amended Articles of Incorporation, Native American Church (Oklahoma). Filed April 24, 1934.

12—SINCE 1934

1. John Collier, "The Genesis and Philosophy of the Indian Reorganization Act," *Indian Affairs and the Indian Reorganization Act, the Twenty Year Record*, ed. William H. Kelly (Tucson: University of Arizona Press, 1954), p. 7.

2. Clyde Kluckhohn and Robert Hackenberg, "Social Science Principles and the Indian Reorganization Act," in *ibid.*, p. 29.

3. A dittoed letter from Joseph L. Bruner to the Members of the Indian Affairs Committee and an issue of the federation organ, *The American Indian*, IV, 4 (1934), Parker Papers, NYSM. The magazine is inscribed, "Compliments of Alice Lee Jemison," an Iroquois active in its affairs. Information on the federation's ties with right-wing groups and the German government's Aryanization of the American Indian is contained in John Collier to Oliver LaFarge, May 10, 1939, with enclosures, National Archives, Record Group No. 75 Office Files of Commissioner John Collier, Bund, German.

4. For biographical information on NCAI leaders see Gridley, *Indians of Today* (1947). Although Parker was a member of the National Council, he seems to have played only a minor role in NCAI affairs.

5. *NCAI*, dittoed newsletter of the National Congress of American Indians, I, 2 (July, 1945), Museum of American Indian Library, New York. This issue contains the names of the officers and a report of the Denver convention.

6. *Constitution and By-Laws of the National Congress of American Indians*, printed leaflet, no date or place of publication, Museum of the American Indian Library.

7. Charles S. Brant, "Peyotism Among the Kiowa-Apache and Neighboring Tribes," *Southwest Journal of Anthropology*, VI, 2 (1950), 222. See also Charles S. Brant to Hazel W. Hertzberg, January 17, 1967, in author's possession.

8. One NIYC anthropologist defines nationalism as "the devotion to, or advocacy of, group interests or group unity and independence." Shirley H. Witt, "Nationalistic Trends Among American Indians," *Midcontinent American Studies Journal*, VI, 2 (Fall, 1965), 53. Both Witt and Robert K. Thomas, the latter in an article entitled "Pan-Indianism" in the same issue, refer to Indians as an "ethnic group."

9. For a summary of the NIYC report, see *Carnegie Quarterly*, XVII, 2 (Spring 1969), 1–5.

10. See *United Scholarship Service News*, 1, 3 (February, 1969).

11. For example, the lead article in the *United Scholarship Service News*, I, 5 (May, 1969), is entitled "Chicano [Mexican-American] Students Struggle for Rights in Denver Schools."

12. The NIYC intermittently publishes two periodicals, *ABC—Americans Before Columbus* and *The American Aborigine*.

13. See "Native American Studies Proposal" (submitted by the United Native Americans), Department of Native American Studies, *The Daily Californian*, March 4, 1969, and flyer "Position Available" seeking an American Indian to teach certain courses in the new department, in author's possession. For information about the San Francisco State situation, I am indebted to Dr. Stuart Miller, an American studies scholar on the San Francisco State faculty.

14. For a discussion of Indian urbanization, see Wesley R. Hurt, Jr., "The Urbanization of the Yankton Indians," *Human Organization*, XX, 4 (Winter, 1961–62), 226–31, and Joan Ablon, "Relocated Americans in the San Francisco Bay Area: Social Interaction and Indian Identity," *ibid.*, XXIII, 4 (1964), 296–304. I am also indebted to Wesley Huss, director of Inter-tribal Friendship House in Oakland, California, and Robert Reitz, director of the American Indian Center in Chicago, for informative interviews shedding light on the relationship of Pan-Indianism and urbanization.

15. Slotkin, *Peyote Religion*, p. 62.

16. *Quarterly Bulletin of the Native American Church of the United States*, I, 1 (January–March, 1955), in author's possession.

17. See, for example, the sympathetic treatment of the NAC in Ernest L. Shusky, *The Right To Be Indian* (published by the Institute of Indian Studies, State University of South Dakota, and the Board of National Missions of the United Presbyterian Church, 1965), pp. 84–86. The volume is part of an Indian Goals Study initiated by the National Council of Churches.

18. Ruth Underhill, "Religion Among American Indians," *Annals of the American Academy of Political and Social Science*, CCCXI, May, 1957, 136.

13—HISTORICAL PERSPECTIVE

1. John Collier, *From Every Zenith* (Denver: Sage Books, 1963), pp. 161, 216–17.

BIBLIOGRAPHICAL ESSAY

Pan-Indian movements, especially those since the turn of the century, have received relatively little attention from scholars. Some of the reasons for and results of the varying perspectives—or lack of them—on the part of historians and anthropologists on this subject are set forth in Chapters 12 and 13.

The notable exception to the neglect of modern Pan-Indian movements is the continued anthropological interest in religious Pan-Indianism. Systematic study of the latter began in the last decade of the nineteenth century with James Mooney's classic work on the Ghost Dance, which also dealt briefly with the peyote cult. Although Mooney conducted an intensive investigation of the peyote religion, he died before the full results could be published.

Mooney respected the people whose movements he studied and felt at ease both with them and with his material. While his general stance was sympathetic, he was by no means romantic and he infused his work with a sinewy common sense. He set a high standard in careful reporting, in delineating the circumstances under which he made his observations, in acquainting the reader with his own point of view, and in literary excellence. He attempted also to set the Pan-Indian movements he investigated in broad perspective by suggesting a general thoretical framework which he did not attempt fully to develop. All subsequent students of the subject are heavily in his debt.

Today the interest in Pan-Indianism among scholars is growing and encompasses a few historians and a number of anthropologists. Anthropologists are now concerned with Indians in urban as well as rural settings and in the development of a Pan-Indian subculture in both. American Pan-Indian religious movements are seen today as a local example of a much wider response of small societies faced with the impact of a technologically complex society—the "religions of the oppressed." Among historians like William T. Hagan and Stuart Levine, specific interest in Pan-Indianism is due in part to a more general approach to history which emphasizes cultural factors. Underlying both anthropological and historical interest is the present

347

deep concern with minorities, with their relationships to an urban culture, and with their situation in American life.

A major problem in this study has been the fact that reform Pan-Indians have been much more articulate and self-conscious about their Pan-Indian ideas than either fraternal or religious Pan-Indians. This circumstance, of course, tells us much about the nature of the different movements and indicates where their primary interests lie. Nevertheless, it is quite possible that if we could elicit from fraternal or religious Pan-Indians fuller responses on some of the major questions considered in this study—such as definitions of nationality or race, attitudes toward the reservation, and views of education—a much more complex picture would emerge.

In this essay I shall not attempt to identify all the sources consulted but only those which have proven most useful for my purposes. Included also are some suggestions for further research.

When a historian ventures into hitherto unexplored territory he is bound to make mistakes. On the most basic level, that of his sources, he is to a large extent dependent on the record available to him. The present study is biased by that record, necessarily the product of literate people and/or people whose actions and thoughts were committed to writing by themselves or by observers. This circumstance presents particularly difficult problems when one is dealing with a group where the number of literate people was relatively small and where people often had to struggle with the intricacies of an unfamiliar language in which they sought to express ideas drawn from divergent cultures. The fact that modern Pan-Indian movements were led by literate people partially mitigates this difficulty but does not wholly dispel it. I have attempted to compensate somewhat by interviewing both Indians and whites involved in Pan-Indian affairs and by observing a number of Pan-Indian events.

It should be noted that the present study covers only movements national in scope, supplementing the sources with local ones when appropriate. Hopefully there are other sources on national Pan-Indian organizations which will be unearthed when there is sufficient interest in the subject. It is highly possible that there exist more records of Pan-Indian organizations and papers of Pan-Indian leaders which will in the future shed new light on the development of Pan-Indianism. In addition there is a wealth of data as yet unmined on local and regional movements.

The major focus of this study is on the first thirty-five years of this century. The sources available for this period were checked as thoroughly as possible. The discussion of the period since the mid-thirties was included in order to trace the development of Pan-Indian movements since the advent of the Indian New Deal. A much more thorough study of the past thirty years is needed, and the sources available for such a study are quite voluminous.

The general reader seeking a good one-volume history of the American Indian will find that there are suprisingly few. The best over-all historical account is William T. Hagan's *American Indians* (1961), which contains also a handy chronology. Ruth Underhill's *Red Man's America* (1953), written from an anthropological viewpoint, is informative and includes a summary section on Indian history in various periods. Clark Wissler's older *Indians of the United States* (1940) and Harold E. Fey's and D'Arcy McNickle's *They Came Here First: The Epic of the American Indian* (1949) are also useful. On a more technical level, see Harold E. Driver's comprehensive *Indians of North America* (1961).

The present study is based largely on primary sources. They fall into seven major categories and are discussed below together with some secondary works.

I. The first group of sources consists of publications of Pan-Indian organizations, periodicals, pamphlets, articles of incorporation of the peyote churches, and some manuscript material. For reform Pan-Indianism before 1934, these basic sources were employed:

The preliminary steps in the organization of the SAI are detailed in its *First Proceedings* (1912), which Arthur C. Parker edited and which is a separate publication. This is a rare and important source. While large sections of it are probably verbatim, I suspect that some of the speeches were edited by Parker, who was much concerned over the public image of the Indian. This is likely to have been the case also in subsequent proceedings of the annual SAI conferences as long as Parker was active in the organization.

The Arthur C. Parker Papers in the New York State Museum in Albany are the single most important manuscript source on the SAI and were used extensively in this study. They are a rich source and deserve further study and use. They consist of extensive correspondence between Parker and other Society leaders, many letters to and from reservation Indians, some SAI records of finances and membership, newspaper clippings and leaflets from other organizations, and correspondence with white supporters. Covering the time from just before the founding of the Society to the early thirties, they are, as one might expect, more complete for the period before World War I than subsequently. They show that SAI leaders had an excellent command of English.

The Joseph Keppler Papers at the Museum of the American Indian Library in New York contain a number of letters to and from Arthur Parker, including a few from his student days. Some deal with the SAI.

Together with the Parker Papers, the most important source on the SAI is the society's journal (*Quarterly Journal*, 1913–15, *American Indian Magazine*, 1915–20), which contains not only conference proceedings and organizational news, but a wide variety of articles by Indians on a wide variety of subjects. The biases of the editors must, of course, be taken into account. Some large universities have fairly complete runs. The nature of the sources used in analyzing the SAI inevitably biases the interpretation somewhat toward Arthur C. Parker's viewpoint, a circumstance which I have attempted to take account of but could not fully overcome without a broader range of primary material than was available to me.

For the abolitionist view, Carlos Montezuma's personal journal *Wassaja* is extremely valuable. Frankly polemial, it is written in a lively and informal style, obviously intended for a more popuar Indian audience than the SAI's *Quarterly Journal*. The articles are short, and many small items are included. Unfortunately it is difficult to find: the only copies which I was able to locate are in the Newberry Library in Chicago.

For the SAI in the twenties, the periodical of the Tepee Order–American Indian Association under the various names mentioned below is the best source, although it is poorly edited and probably less reliable than the other publications mentioned.

A few copies of the National Council of American Indians bulletin, *Indian Newsletter*, are to be found in the Museum of the American Indian Library in New York.

One of the best sources for twenties Pan-Indian news of all varieties, but especially of reform and fraternal activities, is the excellent Oklahoma publication, *The American Indian*, also called *The American Indian Magazine*, 1926–31. The magazine deals largely with Oklahoma but includes a broader coverage as well. For fraternal Pan-Indianism, the major source is the *American Indian Tepee*, published by the Tepee Order–American Indian Association, 1920–28, with varying titles, including *American Indian Tipi*, *American Indian Teepee*, *Indian Tepee*, *Indian Tipi*, *American Indian Advocate*. Volume and issue numbers are sometimes incorrect or nonexistent. It is difficult to locate. The most complete run that I was able to find is in the University of Chicago Library. The New York Public Library also has a few copies.

For the Indian Council Fire, see "Memorial of the Grand Council Fire of American Indians," U.S. Congressional Record, 70th Congress, 1st Session, May 11, 1928, and "Report of the Indian Council Fire, 1934–1935," a mimeographed document in the Museum of the American Indian Library in New York.

The only sources of the type discussed in this section on the peyote religion which I was able to find are the articles of incorporation of the peyote churches. They are valuable for the viewpoints expressed, for their lists of officers, for organizational structure, and for tracing diffusion, but must be used with the knowledge that they formed part of a defensive strategy which tended to emphasize those elements most acceptable to the dominant society.

Since 1934, some of the sources on reform Pan-Indianism used are the following:

The bulletin of the National Congress of American Indians, called variously the *NCAI Sentinel, NCAI, NCAI Bulletin*, is an excellent source, as are the various other special publications of the organization.

The Robert Marshall Fund papers, which I was able to consult, are a rich source on the NCAI. The fund contributed to the NCAI for a number of years, and the papers contain reports, correspondence, publications, and other valuable data. The papers are housed in New York City in the office of Marshall's brother, James Marshall.

The best sources for the National Indian Youth Council are its periodicals, *The American Aborigine* and *ABC-Americans before Columbus*. They contain extended discussions of ideological as well as organizational matters. For the related United Scholarship Service, see the bulletin, *United Scholarship Service News*.

For the sixties, see Robert K. Thomas' *Indian Voices,* a highly useful Pan-Indian publication covering a wide variety of Pan-Indian activities, viewpoints, and readers' comments. It frequently lists the titles and addresses of bulletins of local Indian groups, both tribal and Pan-Indian.

For fraternal Pan-Indianism, see *Indian Voices* mentioned above and *Amerindian,* edited by Marion Gridley. Most of the Indian urban centers also issue bulletins. Unfortunately much of the fraternal Pan-Indian material is highly transient in nature.

As is evident from the above listing, the primary sources emanating from Pan-Indian organizations and other Pan-Indian periodicals, pamphlets, and flyers are often rare and hard to find. Many have no doubt disapeared, but many are scattered in libraries and museums, having usually been acquired through the particular interest of a staff member. A great deal of the transient material is no doubt in private collections. If the full range of Pan-Indian movements and activities is to become a field of serious scholarly interest, as I believe it should, then it would be most useful to have a central repository for Pan-Indian materials. Both historical and contemporary items should be collected systematically. Such a collection might attract manuscript materials as well, including the archives of Pan-Indian organizations and the papers of Pan-Indian leaders. Oral history tapes of participants in Pan-Indian movements would be especially valuable. I have made a very modest attempt in this direction by giving the Museum of the American Indian Library in New York Xeroxed copies of everything that I collected that they wanted, to add to their already fairly good collection. But the Library is small and under-staffed. Preferably a Pan-Indian collection should be housed in a great university which has a special interest in Indian affairs.

II. The second type of source used consists of official records. Published records include the annual reports of the Commissioners of Indian Affairs, congressional hearings and debates, annual reports of the Bureau of American Ethnology, and various special reports by government agencies. There is a wealth of manuscript material in the BIA records in the National Archives. A useful but incomplete reference is the Department of the Interior's *Biographical and Historical Index of American Indians and Persons Involved in Indian Affairs* (1966).

Official records tend, of course, to reflect official viewpoints. But there is considerable diversity in the official records. The annual commissioner's reports frequently include reports from local reservation agents which express differing viewpoints and interests. Congressional hearings are one of the best sources for getting a range of opinions and attitudes, often from persons who have not expressed themselves in print, as can be seen in the hearings on peyote.

III. The third type of source is the material published by non-Indian organizations concerned with Indian affairs. The annual reports of the Indian Rights Association, beginning in 1882, are an indispensable source, which should be supplemented by the IRA bulletin, *Indian Truth*, which began publication in the mid-twenties. Much valuable material may be found in the annual proceedings of the Lake Mohonk Conference of Friends of the Indian, 1883–1916, 1929. Both are older reformist in viewpoint. *American Indian Life*, 1925–34, the bulletin of the American Indian Defense Association, is an important source for the twenties and early thirties and indispensable for the viewpoints of the newer reformers. For the later period, see especially *Indian Affairs*, the bulletin of the Association on American Indian Affairs. All of the non-Indian reform publications contain scattered information about Pan-Indian organizations.

One of the most valuable sources for twenties Pan-Indianism is the weighty Meriam Report, *The Problem of Indian Administration* (1928), which was based on extensive staff research in the field. In viewpoint it is strongly influenced by the older reformers but with considerable modification.

IV. The fourth group of sources used comprise anthropological studies, mostly dealing with the peyote religion but recently including descriptions of fraternal Pan-Indianism. Specific titles will be found in the notes to appropriate chapters. For broad discussions of religious Pan-Indianism, including historical materials, two books are essential: Weston La Barre's *Peyote Cult* (first published in 1938, with an enlarged edition in 1964), and J. Sydney Slotkin's *Peyote Religion* (1956). Fortunately, the bibliographies in each are complementary rather than repetitive. La Barre's book is based on his own field studies, in which he haa the cooperation of a number of the religous Pan-Indian leaders mentioned in this book, as well as on a thorough study of the existing literature. It includes many statements by peyotists and descriptions of the various types of peyote ceremonies and their diffusion. The enlarged edition brings the discussion of peyote literature to date and analyzes many of the conflicting or varying interpretations therein. Slotkin's book has a somewhat different viewpoint, being more partisan than La Barre's. Slotkin was a white anthropologist who became an official of the Native American Church and who conceived of his study as a manual for NAC members. It is especially valuable for the NAC documents which it contains, its summary of the history of the legal status of peyote, and its extensive documentation. Its partisanship is both a strength and a weakness. On the one hand it offers the view of a man whose commitment to and participation in the religion is sympathetic and deep, while tempered by his social science training. In this it resembles other analyses of religious sects made by scholars loyal both to their religion and their scholarship. However, Slotkin's partisanship is sometimes narrow, not towards differences within the cult but towards the outside world. It is not always easy to differentiate Slotkin's general interpretation from that of other peyotists. The book is unfortunately out of print and should be reissued.

Two collecions of studies on the American Indian by anthropologists, sociologists, and others are especially valuable. "American Indians and American Life," *Annals of the American Academy of Political and Social Science,* May 1957, contains a wide range of articles, including some dealing with the NCAI, the peyote religion, acculturation, integration and education. A special issue of the *Mid-Continent American Studies Journal,* "The Indian Today," VI, 2 (1965), is highly useful. See especially Robert K. Thomas' informative article *"Pan-Indianism";* Nancy O. Lurie's important survey and analysis of the results of extensive questionnaires dealing with such topics as Pan-Indianism, Indian identity, and attitudes towards whites and Negroes, sent to "persons familiar with Indian affairs, including anthropologists, government personnel, church workers and individual Indians"; and Stuart Levine's interesting and suggestive historical comparison between Indians and other American minorities, including immigrants, Negroes, and members of small religious sects. The collection has since been issued, with some changes, as a book, *The American Indian Today* (1968), edited by Stuart Levine and Nancy O. Lurie.

V. Indian school publications—federal and private—constitute the fifth group of sources used. These include the annual reports of the Carlisle Indian Industrial School, 1897–1912; *The Red Man,* the student publication at Carlisle; the *Southern Workman and Hampton School Record; The Indian Leader,* published at Haskell; and *The Indian Outlook,* 1928–31, the bulletin of Henry Roe Cloud's American Indian Institute. All are useful and tend to reflect the viewpoints of the older reformers. The various school publications often contain news of alumni. The unpublished records of Carlisle are in the National Archives and contain much valuable material, including correspondence and biographical data.

"The Carlisle Indian Industrial School," by Carmelita S. Ryan (unpublished Ph.D. thesis, Georgetown University, 1962), is highly useful as institutional history, but it does not deal with the impact of Carlisle on the subsequent careers of Carlisle students. Such a study, which should include Hampton, Haskell, and other boardng schools as well, is badly needed if we are to have a more informed view of the strengths and weaknesses of the boarding school system as an acculturating agency.

VI. A sixth category of sources used comprises books by Pan-Indians and by white friends of the Pan-Indian movements. Some are autobiographical. Among those which I found most helpful are the works of Charles A. Eastman, including *Indian Boyhood* (1902), *The Soul of the Indian* (1911),

Indian Scout Talks (1914), *The Indian Today* (1915), *From the Deep Woods to Civilization* (1916), and *Indian Heroes and Great Chieftains* (1918). *Tahan: Out of Savagery into Civilization* (1915), by the Pan-Indian Joseph K. Griffis is a fascinating account of his adventures, while a classic peyotist autobiography is *Crashing Thunder: The Autobiography of an American Indian* (1926), collected by Paul Radin. Zitkala-sa's (Gertrude Bonnin's) *American Indian Stories* (1921), gives insights into her approach, while John Oskison's *Tecumsah and his Times* (1938) reveals how a Pan-Indian looked at Tecumsah. *The Middle Five* (1900), by Francis LaFlesche, is a classic account of his school days. For the older white reform viewpoints see Richard H. Pratt's, *Battlefield and Classroom: Four Decades with the American Indian, 1867–1904* (1964), edited by Robert M. Utley; G.E.E. Lindquist, ed., *Red Man in the United States* (1923); *The American Indian on the New Trail* (1914), by Thomas C. Moffett; and *The American Indian in the United States* (1923), by Warren Morehead. Fayette A. McKenzie's *American Indian in Relation to the White Population of the United States* (1908) is indispensable as is John Collier's autobiographical *From Every Zenith: A Memoir* (1963). Especially interesting in the latter work is Collier's discussion of the major influences in the development of his thought about Indians, including his concern with rebuilding a sense of community in an urban environment as exemplified by his work with the Peoples Institute in New York City, and his deep interest in the British colonial system of indirect rule.

Two important sources for brief Indian biographies are Marion E. Gridley, ed., *Indians of Today* (1936, 1947, 1960), which is the nearest equivalent of an Indian Who's Who, and the much less comprehensive *Our Debt to the Red Man* (1918), by Louise Seymour Houghton. Both are somewhat limited by the biases of their authors. See also *Biographical and Historical Index* cited above.

VII. The seventh category of sources consists of personal interviews with Pan-Indian leaders and persons interested in Pan-Indian affairs and observation of a number of Pan-Indian events. Some of the persons interviewed are listed in the acknowledgments. In addition, I attended numerous meetings of reform and fraternal Pan-Indian organizations—but not, regrettably, the Native American Church—as well as Indian powwows and fairs. I also visited the Indian Centers in Chicago and San Francisco. I found this personal contact invaluable, not only for the specific information gathered, but also in helping to acquire some sense of the living reality of the movements whose history I was investigating.

INDEX